This Ayr United Thing

The Ayrgonauts

Carmichael, Andrew (5 x great grandfather)
Carmichael, Archie (great grandfather)
Carmichael, Carol (wife)
Carmichael, Claire (niece)
Carmichael, David (son)
Carmichael, Douglas (brother)
Carmichael, Duncan
Carmichael, Jill (daughter)
Carmichael, Margaret (5 x great grandmother)
Carmichael, Margaret (mother)
Carmichael, Margaret (sister-in-law)
Carmichael, Peter (brother)
Carmichael, Peter (father)
Carmichael, Peter (grandfather)

This Ayr United Thing — More Iliad than Illyria

Duncan Carmichael

Kennedy & Boyd

Kennedy & Boyd,
an imprint of
Zeticula Ltd,
Unit 13,
44-46 Morningside Road,
Edinburgh, EH10 4BF

http://www.kennedyandboyd.co.uk
admin@kennedyandboyd.co.uk

First published in 2025
Copyright © Duncan Carmichael 2025
Cover design © Zeticula Ltd 2025

Photographs copyright © as credited 2025

Every effort has been made to trace copyright holders of images. Any omissions will be corrected in future editions.

Hardback ISBN 978-1-84921-261-8
Paperback ISBN 978-1-84921-262-5

All rights reserved. No part of this publication may be reproduced, stored in a retrieval system, or transmitted in any form or by any means, electronic, mechanical, photocopying, recording or otherwise, without the prior permission of the publishers.

Acknowledgements

I am very grateful to the people who have kindly allowed their photographs to be reproduced.

The McDiarmid Park image is most pertinent to the subject matter of this book and I really must thank David Sargent.

In 1966 photographs were taken of the England squad at Somerset Park. These are hitherto unpublished and I am glad to thank John McCall for granting permission for them to be used. I must also thank Andy McInnes for the tip-off that these photographs existed.

Back in 2002 Kenneth Ferguson allowed me to use his photograph of the Ayr United scarf draped round the Rabbie Burns Statue. Kenneth's legacy lives on in this wonderfully evocative image.

The screenshot from BBC Sportscene is reproduced by the joint permission of the BBC who hold the broadcast rights and the Scottish Football Association who hold the match rights. Kenny Millar at the SFA was especially co-operative.

My son David is due thanks too for taking some of the photographs contained within.

Many of the photographs in my vast Ayr United collection were inherited.

The late Hugh Nelson gifted me piles of original old photographs and his relatives gifted me the remainder of his collection after he passed away. These were gratefully received. They came to a home where they have been well cared for.

The same may be said of the photographs I received from the *Ayrshire Post* following the transformation to digital.

I also thank Jane Round for some of the illustrations used. Jane kindly gifted me a mass of material which had belonged to her father Len, a former Ayr United goalkeeper.

For many years my focus fell predominantly on amassing information and pictorial material was a blind spot. That oversight has long since been corrected largely through the generosity of some kind people.

The co-operation of Gordon 'Call me Syd' Sydney is worthy of acknowledgement. Anything he does not know about Clyde is not worth knowing and he was most helpful in confirming some details I required.

Within these pages is an illustration of an old Swedish newspaper clipping about Ayr United. Orjan Hansson, please consider yourself a hero for unearthing this gem.

It would be remiss not to thank the people who have given me a lift to matches over the years. On the occasions when I have reciprocated it has not always been a smooth run. While rushing to a midweek game at East Stirling the accelerator pedal jammed and the car was doing 70 mph towards Sandyford despite my feet being off the pedals. It unjammed when I luckily managed to stall the engine. Phew!

Without the guys out there in the white shirts and black shorts there would be no story to tell. They are the catalyst for tales of adventure and misadventure. Success, failure and the middle ground between the two would define our lot down through the decades. It is a proud achievement to pull on an Ayr United shirt and it is worth acknowledging the efforts of everyone who has done so.

Contents

Acknowledgements	v
Contents	vii
List of Illustrations	ix
Introduction	xiii
1. Creamery Park to Somerset Park	1
2. Pencaitland Amateurs	36
3. And now, The Few	45
Snapshot of attendances three-year cycle 1961/62 to 2024/25	56
4. The Ally MacLeod Revolution	57
5. The Yoyo Years	63
6. The Dawn of a New Decade and New Hope	72
7. The Awakening	117
8. The Fightback	147
9. Life Beyond Ally	164
10. Happy Days Are Here Again	200
11. New Century New Hope	228
12. The Descent	246
13. The Seaside League	259
Post war Scottish Cup crowds at home	288
14. The Centenary and Beyond	289
15. The Revival	324
16. Championship Consolidation	344
Index to the Iliad: places visited	393
Index to Illyria: the football	394

List of Illustrations

Fog stops game at Coatbridge.	2
This is an extract from The Brockville Bairns.	5
When Falkirk departed from Brockville in 2003 the club produced a commemorative shirt.	6
Pencaitland Amateurs with the Logan Cup in 1951.	7
Peter Carmichael in discussion with a colliery official.	8
Erected in memory of the forty men who lost their lives.	9
Peter Carmichael with his family in 1913.	11
Pencaitland 1955. The brothers Carmichael (left to right).	15
Glasgow 2025. The Carmichael brothers.	16
Bathgate Thistle revisited in 2021.	19
Bob Hepburn.	21
Peter Price clinching a hat-trick in a 6-2 win.	27
Ayr United FC on 12th September, 1959.	28
Peter Price scoring on 12th September, 1959.	29
Evening Times on 19th September, 1959.	30
5th December, 1959. Willie Paton (behind Sam McMillan).	31
Peter Price has just equalised against Hearts	32
Ayr United FC 1961/62.	34
Two off after collision	37
The Pencaitland football field in its picturesque setting.	38
The Tranent coat-of-arms bearing the legend Lie Forrit.	42
Fans on the North terrace.	44
Hugh Rodie	45
Neil McBain on 15th January, 1963.	48
A future visit in April 1966.	55
Alf Ramsey and his squad tread the hallowed turf.	55
Eddie Moore completing a hat-trick in a 6-0 win.	58
Billy Kerr is beaten by Partick Thistle goalkeeper.	59
Ian Crawford stalled our promotion drive in 1969.	71
Ayr United FC 1969/70.	73
Hibernian programme cover, 13th December, 1969	75

Douglas Symington (left) and myself planning a revamp of the match programme.	80
John Doyle.	81
Ayr United versus Kilmarnock on 12th September, 1970.	83
21st November, 1970. Ayr United 2 Rangers 1.	84
I was seated next to Ross Mathie in 2024.	85
20th February, 1971. Tommy Reynolds has just clinched it.	86
20th March, 1971. The Aberdeen trip was aborted.	87
The Black and White Shop just after completion.	89
Ayr United FC 1972/73.	92
Brian Bell.	100
Dumbarton programme cover for visit of Ayr United.	102
The state of play on 22nd October, 1973.	104
Nottingham Forest programme cover.	110
Ayr United's last Premier League fixture, so far.	116
Wallacefield Amateurs. June 1982.	118
Ally MacLeod on his return. 27th September, 1978.	120
Celtic programme for visit of Ayr United.	125
17th October, 1981, versus East Stirling.	129
The abandoned match on 4th January, 1982.	131
Versus Dunfermline Athletic on 9th April, 1983.	135
Stevie Evans in action against Alloa Athletic.	139
Ayr United versus Kilmarnock on 31st August, 1985.	142
Easter Road on 16th February, 1986.	146
Promotion celebrations at Stirling on 26th March, 1988.	152
The Ayrshire Cup final at Kilmarnock on 10th May, 1988.	155
Ned Fullarton is second from the right in the back row.	165
23rd October, 1990. Ian McAllister gets a shot away.	167
Tommy Walker in action at Kilmarnock, 1990.	168
Henry Templeton in the 1990 Centenary Cup final.	170
Glad to be in the illustrious company of Ally MacLeod and Peter Weir.	172
25th January, 1992. Duncan George's shot hits the net.	176
David Kennedy as an emergency goalkeeper, March, 1993.	183
Ayr United Boys' Club under 16s with the Gothia Cup.	185
A champagne celebration for finishing seventh.	190
John Sharples scoring against Kilmarnock.	194

Ayrshire Cup winners 1994/95.	196
Vinnie Moore heading the winner against Dundee.	198
George Watson makes a save from Owen Coyle at Clydebank's Kilbowie Park.	199
3rd October, 2024, at the same spot.	199
The title is won at Berwick on 10th May, 1997	210
Paul Bonar in action against Coventry City, 1997	212
Jim Dick maintaining possession against Partick Thistle.	216
Ayr United played in Sweden for the first time since 1928.	220
Hibs at Ayr on 27th February, 1999	223
The 'Two Clubs' flag at Accrington Stanley.	253
When Ally MacLeod passed away it was front page news.	258
Privileged to be in the company of Peter Price and Robert Connor at a book launch.	271
Brian Reid	278
The Somerset Park boardroom, 7th September, 2008	281
Centenary 1910-2010 Logo	289
Centenary Dinner Ticket	291
Jill Carmichael presenting her cross stitch to Alex Ingram.	295
Hibs versus Ayr United. The Carmichaels from the east meet the Carmichaels from the west.	306
An unlikely result	336
Lawrence Shankland leads the 124-goal table	343
Burns in Ayr United Colours	347
Islay House in Pencaitland.	349
Caught on the BBC on 18th January, 2020.	354
The Ally MacLeod Memorial Plaque.	368
The Our Wullie Chippy was a convenient food stop.	374
Fraser Bryden – sponsored by the Ayr United Strollers.	375
After watching Bristol Rovers 0 Barnsley 0	376
Bristol Rovers versus Barnsley on 4th March, 2023.	377
15th July, 2023, at Forthbank Stadium, Stirling	380
25th July, 2023, at McDiarmid Park, Perth.	380
Somerset Park on 24th October, 2023.	382
Somerset Park on 13th February, 2024	383
The Somerset Road End showing my favoured spot behind the crush barrier at the front.	392

Introduction

There can be a natural inclination to skip the preamble to a book in order to head straight to the story.

However, on this occasion please accept a respectful request to persevere with an introduction to what you are about to read. It may be helpful for you to understand the premise of the book before embarking on the first chapter.

The title - *This Ayr United Thing – More Iliad than Illyria* might merit something in the way of an explanation. The first part is easy to comprehend. This Ayr United thing is a common affliction which manifests itself as an addiction to pitch up at Somerset Park.

The *Iliad* is an epic poem rooted in Greek mythology, credited to a chap called Homer. Couching it in succinct terms, it is a tale of years of struggle against hostile forces. Do you see the parallels starting to appear?

Illyria was a land inhabited by ancient Greeks and other displaced tribes. Shakespeare imagined it as a magical place where happiness could be found.

This book relives the years of the author's suffering and occasional joy watching Ayr United on their search for Illyria, the happy place which could be a metaphor for the Scottish Premier League.

You will be relieved to know that the book has not been written in Homer's Greek!

In broad terms I have tracked my journey in football from my earliest recollections of attending matches in 1957. Predominantly, but not exclusively, the topic is Ayr United. There is a lesser emphasis on, for example, Bathgate Thistle, Pencaitland Amateurs and Bristol Rovers. It is hoped that these passages of the book will be just as engaging.

Family history has been woven into the narrative in order to add context. There really is a strong relationship between family matters and football matters. Nonetheless this project has not been an entirely autobiographical work. It would have been an interesting exercise to make it quasi-autobiographical i.e. a true account laced with fiction. Such fun could have been had by inventing great glories.

Anyway that notion will hereby be dismissed by letting you know that factual accuracy has remained paramount, notwithstanding that opinions have been put into the mix.

Learned scholars believe that Homer wrote the *Iliad* around 750 BC. It is extraordinary therefore that his name is still heard in public places in the modern day.

If a referee makes controversial decisions against Ayr United at, typically, Firhill or Cappielow, you can be assured that Homer's name will ring out!

The theme of ancient Greece might be sustained by reference to another icon from that culture. Homer's *Odyssey* might be defined as the long and complicated return journey from a fixture which didn't go quite as intended.

By now you should get the picture.

Duncan Carmichael.
July 2025

1. Creamery Park to Somerset Park

Long term devotees of football are routinely labelled as lifelong fans. In suggesting that this definition is open to question there is no intention to be disparaging about such a level of devotion. It is simply that lifelong means from birth. In truth our love of the game is fostered from infancy. Baby-sized Ayr United tops or bibs bearing the legend 'Best dribbler at Somerset Park' are no more than an indication of where the newborn's football allegiances will likely be. Yet it is likely that for most people the earliest recollection of being taken to the football will date to a time when they were aged about four or five. Anyway let us move on from such pedantry. It is now time to start exploring how, when, where and why a personal devotion to Ayr United evolved. Devotion is hardly the word. Some would call it fanaticism. They wouldn't be far wrong. It has to be admitted that there are more important things than football. Sometimes though it doesn't seem like it.

Saturday, 29th November, 1952, was a day of meteorological misery. Baltic would be an apt description in the vernacular of today. Scotland had its lowest temperatures since 1921. The *Evening Times* had a front page headline of **COLDEST WEATHER SPELL FOR ABOUT 30 YEARS**. In shivering detail it was described in these terms: "Scotland was today in the grip of the most bitter November weather experienced for about thirty years. Soccer fans faced the prospect of viewing this afternoon's games in Arctic-like conditions. Supporters were travelling to the various grounds over icebound and treacherous roads and in some areas visibility was made poor by drifting patches of fog." Thereafter the story lapsed into a series of sporting and travel mayhem.

FOG STOPS GAME AT COATBRIDGE

(By W. H.)

Cliftonhill was frost-bound. It was also fog-bound until two o'clock, when the sun broke through, and it was decided to carry on with the match. The United were at full strength, but Albion had two trialists—in goal and at centre forward. R. M'Kirdy, transferred from Hamilton Acads., made his first appearance at inside left.

Albion Rov., 0 Ayr United, 1

ALBION ROVERS—Newman; Muir and Clark; Dickson, Quigley, and Robb; Lang and Kiernan; Junior; M'Kirdy (Hamilton Acads.) and Hodge.

AYR UNITED—Round; Thomson and Leckie; W Fraser, M'Neil, and Nesbit; Japp and Robertson; J. Fraser; Hutton and M'Kenna.

Referee—J. Barclay (Kirkcaldy).

Down came the fog for a bit, and Robertson was seen to shoot over Newman's goal. When it lifted Kiernan led a likely Rovers assault, which was turned by Thomson.

However, Albion kept at it, and Junior eluded M'Neil—but was dispossessed by Leckie, whose speed was proving useful.

The first goal went to Ayr in 12 minutes. W. Fraser led up to it with a dribble, and scorer M'KENNA accepted the final pass to shoot hard and score via the upright.

After 21 minutes' play, however, heavy fog again blocked out the proceedings, and at this stage the referee declared the game abandoned.

Some of the mayhem just referred to was clearly in evidence at Cliftonhill Park, the home of Albion Rovers. Clearly in evidence? Not much was clear. With Ayr United winning 1-0 the proceedings were abandoned after twenty-one minutes due to the fog. On an iron-hard pitch it had not been much of a spectacle. In fact for many it had not been a spectacle at all. At one stage Mike McKenna was the only player visible from the press bench. The seemingly lonesome McKenna had the joy of scoring in the 12th minute only to have his goal voided amidst a termination that caused a hostile crowd to assemble outside demanding their money back in a most unconciliatory tone.

If you like football trivia you may delight in the knowledge that McKenna was an uncle of Fish who achieved fame as the lead singer of Marillion before embarking on a career as a solo artist. This fleeting reference to family history links seamlessly to an event that occurred later on that grim afternoon.

Situated fifty-five miles east of Coatbridge and roughly on the same latitude, (apologies for yet more pedantry!) is the small East Lothian town of Haddington (coincidentally the afore mentioned Fish is a former resident). At 5.25 pm on that day I was born in Haddington's Vert Hospital. The abandonment of Ayr United's match two hours before was wholly attributable to fog and had nothing whatsoever to do with a mark of respect for my pending birth. These events occurring on the same afternoon amounted to a coincidence rather than any pretence at messianic connotations.

Haddington! Ayr United! How did this cosmic collision occur?

The earliest traceable ancestor in the Carmichael lineage was born in Ancrum in the sixteenth century. By the 1700s there was no further trace of Roxburghshire in our ancestry. The shift was overwhelmingly to Stirlingshire in which county the family roots were to become deeply entrenched as can be illustrated by reference to an experience on 14th September, 2013. On that date three Carmichaels travelled to support Ayr United in an away fixture against Stenhousemuir. They were myself, son David and daughter Jill. David was driving and, on the way there, I asked him if he would mind taking a detour into Kilsyth so that I could browse the graveyard at the old parish church. Buried there is my great great great great great grandfather Andrew Carmichael and his wife Margaret. There is documentary proof that their gravestone is there but, in the limited time we had, we failed to find it (didn't want to miss the kick-off!). They got married on 26th November, 1775. Succeeding generations of the family remained settled in Stirlingshire and, on 13th May, 1880, my grandfather, Peter Carmichael, was born at Polmont. At a very tender age he was a miner at Redding Colliery. Just how young can be gauged from the fact that in 1893 the school leaving age was raised from ten to eleven.

My grandfather was a boyhood friend of Alex Raisbeck who was raised in Wallacestone, a district adjoining Polmont. Raisbeck was a great centre-half who captained Liverpool when they won their first two Football League championships in 1900/01 and 1905/06. At international level he made eight appearances for Scotland including five as captain. At a humbler level Peter Carmichael turned out at centre-forward for Redding Athletic. He must have been conspicuously good because Falkirk asked him to sign. On Friday, 20th February, 1903, he duly obliged. The terms were a signing-on fee of £5 and a wage of £1 a week when playing and ten shillings per week when not selected. Training took place on Tuesday and Thursday evenings between 6.30 pm and 9.30 pm. The contract was signed on the eve of a Second Division fixture at home to Raith Rovers. This was Falkirk's first ever league season and the match comprised eighth versus eleventh in the twelve-club league. The decision to pitch him straight in was vindicated. With ten minutes played he scored with a twenty-five yard drive. He also scored the final goal in their 4-2 victory. Two goals on his debut was most satisfactory. It was a little disappointing that it was played "in the presence of a moderate attendance". Moderate or not he would have been known to many of the spectators.

One week later he led the Falkirk attack in a league fixture against local rivals East Stirling, again at Brockville. This was a fortnight after East Stirling had won 3-1 there in the Stirlingshire Cup. Peter Carmichael opened the scoring in an eventual 2-2 draw. Three goals in two games! Falkirk's next fixture was at Ayr. On 7th March, 1903, my grandfather became the first Falkirk centre-forward to play at Somerset Park. Ayr FC won 2-0. He did not play in the first team again and he was released at the end of the season with an average of a goal per game in the three league matches played.

THE FIRST LIST OF FALKIRK LEAGUE PLAYERS

The first Falkirk players, who were registered as League players in 1902/03 were the following:-

Robert Leishman
William Scott
John Kellock
James Hill
William Kemp
James Reid
Charles Pringle
Andrew Burt
William Allan
George Drummond
William Goudie
Donald Cameron
James Russell
Thomas Miller
Eben Taylor
George Campbell
Hugh Dale
Patrick Malloy
Isaac Begbie
Patrick McLaughlin
Peter Carmichael
William Scott

Falkirk F.C. 1902
W. Lawson, P. Rae, J. Hill, W. Allan, W.B. Goudie, J. Reid, M. M'Intyre,
W. Nicol, T. Waugh, G. Chapman;
W. Scott, J. Russell, J. Kellock, A. Burt, R. Leishman, W. Kemp, R. Nimmo.

This is an extract from The Brockville Bairns. Peter Carmichael is on the list of those who played for Falkirk in their first ever league season but he was still with Redding Athletic when the photograph was taken.

About 5 am on Tuesday, 25th September, 1923, Redding Colliery was flooded by water from old workings. Sixty-six men were left trapped in the pit. A huge rescue operation was mounted and, after five hours, twenty-one men had been rescued via an old shaft. On 4th October five more men were rescued. Over a period of weeks the bodies of the other men were recovered. The fortieth body was recovered on the fortieth day of the rescue operation. My grandfather was in the rescue team. The disaster gripped the nation. At an Ayr United versus Motherwell fixture a collection for the disaster fund topped £40.

When Falkirk departed from Brockville in 2003 the club produced a commemorative shirt containing the name of every player who had appeared in their first team. Note too the name of Ayr United legend Alec Beattie.

Throughout the Carmichael ancestry the neighbouring Stirlingshire locations of Redding and Polmont are dominant. Grandpa Carmichael was Polmont-born. Similarly his father Archie was Polmont-born on 31st March, 1858, and his grandfather Peter was born on 10th March, 1817, at Larbert, about six and a half miles from Polmont. Siblings of successive generations raised their families in and around the Polmont/Redding area to the extent that the Carmichaels had very deep roots there. So what possessed Grandpa Carmichael to uproot his family from that locality when he was aged forty-three? It cannot have been a mere coincidence that the flitting took place in the almost immediate aftermath of his experiences in the disaster at Redding Colliery, albeit that he was going to work in another pit. Herein the catalyst for the move can be identified.

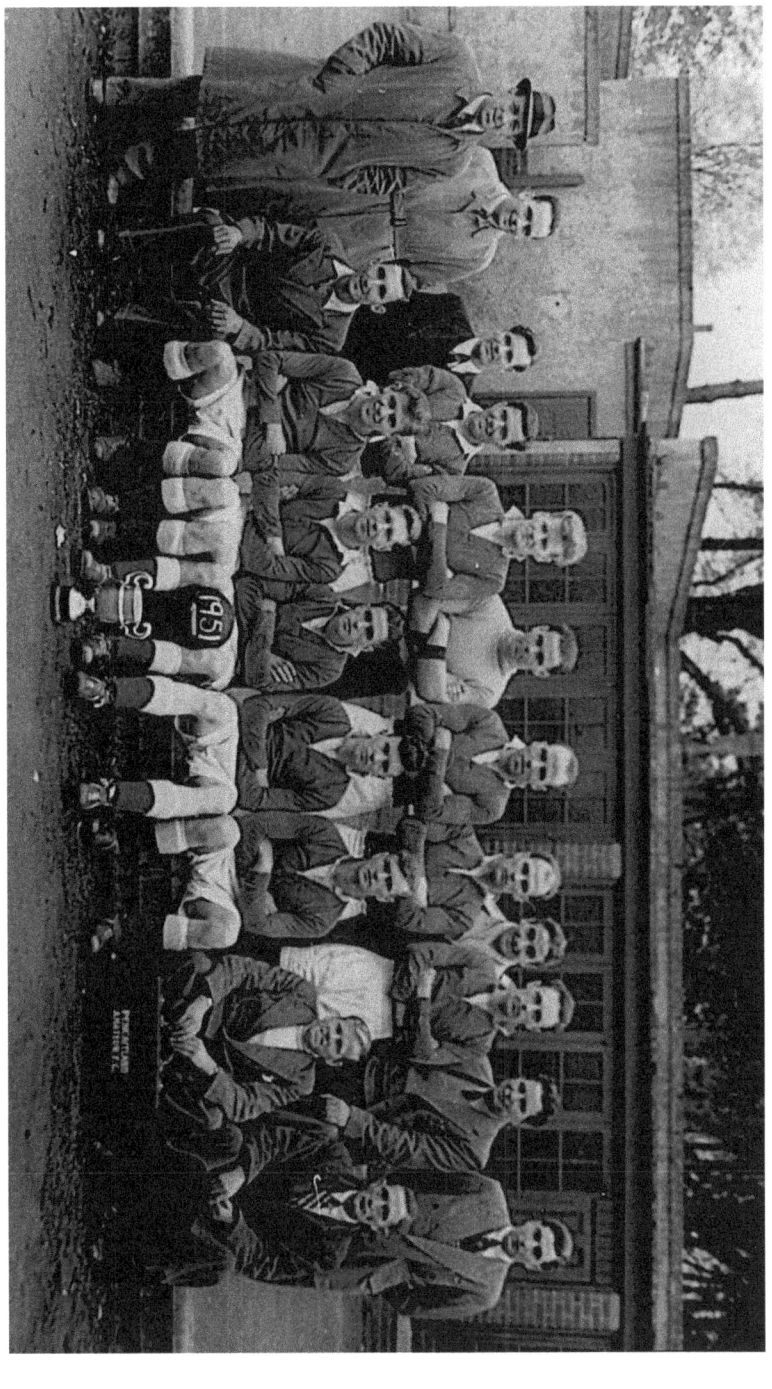

Pencaitland Amateurs with the Logan Cup in 1951. My father is standing second from the left. Next to him is Rob Robison. The trainer is Tester Anderson whose box was made by my Uncle Alex. James Strang is fifth from the right standing. Jock McGovern is the first player on the right of the front row. Also in there are John Drysdale, Jock Anderson, Wullie Purves, Ecky Pryde and Jacky Taylor who was the father of Jock Taylor who became world champion motorcycle sidecar racer then got killed in a race aged 28.

Peter Carmichael in discussion with a colliery official in the aftermath of the pit disaster.

Erected in memory of the forty men who lost their lives in the disaster at Redding Colliery, Tuesday 25th September, 1923.

The flitting took place in the latter part of 1923 and it was a big undertaking to move forty miles eastward with nine children including my then infant father. The family settled in the East Lothian village of Pencaitland. It is sadly ironic that he was destined to suffer a fatal accident on the return from a flower show rather than at a pitface. The show was at Haddington, six miles away, on Saturday, 14th September, 1935. After missing the 10 pm bus he and a friend decided to walk back to Pencaitland rather than wait for the next bus at 11.45 pm. The tragic chain of events was spelled out in the fatal accident report. On the way back they encountered a car approaching towards them in the inky darkness so he moved behind his companion and closer to the verge. That car passed safely just as another car was approaching from behind. This one struck them both. He died three days later in Edinburgh Royal Infirmary without regaining consciousness. His colleague survived with facial injuries and shock. He left a footballing legacy having not long before tipped-off Newcastle United about Archie Livingstone who was born in Pencaitland on 15th November, 1915. Livingstone, an inside-forward, was at Newcastle United in seasons 1935/36, 1936/37 and 1937/38. After being transferred from Bury he was with Everton in season 1946/47, scoring two goals in his four first team appearances. His next transfer was to Southport.

My father became a grocer in the Co-operative in Pencaitland and my mother was a cashier in the Co-operative based in the nearby village of Ormiston. In East Lothian it was never referred to as the Co-operative. The Store was the terminology used. Cutting butter and slicing bacon was hardly a reserved occupation and the inevitable brown envelope came through the door a couple of months after the declaration of war. He served in the 15th Scottish Reconnaissance Regiment, less formally known as "The Recce". Active service eventually followed in France, Belgium, Holland and Germany. Normandy was especially hazardous. On night patrols he drove a bren gun carrier behind enemy lines. His map reading colleague could not afford even the slightest of errors. It could have been fatal and there was always the fear of mines and booby traps. At all times they were primed to leap from the vehicle in the event of getting hit by enemy fire. For operational reasons the accuracy of their reports was vital. Aged twenty-four at the time, his will was written in the back of his Army paybook. In 1943 he had married my mother in Ormiston Parish Church.

Sergeant Peter Carmichael was demobbed having been awarded the Commander-In-Chief's Certificate for good service. This was in March 1946. Thereafter he settled in Pencaitland with wife Margaret and two-year-old son Peter. Douglas, my other brother, came into the world in 1948. The purpose of this book is to explore a life immersed in football. It may therefore seem that this emphasis on family history is a deviation from the main subject matter. That would be a wrong impression. Family life and football are intertwined. In the overall context it has been necessary to give some background to the Carmichael migration from Stirlingshire to East Lothian.

Around the time that dad blended back into Civvy Street Pencaitland Amateurs got formed and he became a committee member. By this time he was working for the Co-operative Insurance in Edinburgh. The nature of his work took him into many households with the consequence that he would occasionally hear about good amateur players in the city.

Peter Carmichael with his family in 1913 which was six years before my father was born. Three of the children became centenarians. Jean (the baby) reached 104 years 111 days, Eleanor, who is standing beside her, reached 102 years 54 days and Jenny, next along, reached 101 years 268 days.

Dad was persuasive. He would tell players that they were anonymous playing on public playing fields in Edinburgh and that they would be local heroes if signing for Pencaitland. He wasn't bluffing. Youngsters in the village had a respect for amateur players on a scale bordering on what might be expected for professionals. On a match day it was common for a player to step off the bus from Edinburgh then get besieged by youngsters with the request: "Can ah cairry yer bag?" Dad spoke about a fifteen-year-old Wallyford boy who played in a trial. This would have been in the summer of 1951. He was a goalkeeper who was simply brilliant. The committee came to the conclusion that if they signed him they would soon be looking for another goalkeeper because he was clearly destined to play at a higher level. On that basis they declined to sign him. It was Jock Wallace.

Pencaitland Amateurs played in the same colours as Hearts, i.e. maroon shirts and white shorts. In later decades dad loved to talk about some of the great characters amongst the players. In particular he singled out Ecky Pryde, Wullie Purves (pronounced Purris) and Jimmy Swinton. He mentioned too that Ecky Pryde was skilled in the art of conning referees by feigning injury. There was also a recollection of a game at Burntisland when they had to go over by the ferry. My dad missed this game owing to work commitments and in The Smiddy Inn that evening he asked a fellow committee man how it had gone. With no mention of the game the reply was: "Ah hud a couple o' haufs on the sail across and a couple o' haufs" on the sail back." Another reflection dad had was of showing the players cine film of the great Hungarian national team of that era. In 1951 Pencaitland won the Logan Cup. After the cup was won it stayed in our house overnight. (Our? It was the year before I was born!). The family home was in Institute Place and youngsters in the area knocked on the door to ask if they could see the trophy. A worry for dad around this time was the possibility of being called up for Z training which would have been the preliminary to fighting in Korea.

The nearest senior team to the village was Hibs and although the term Hibby had not yet been coined dad would have fitted the description, albeit a part time one. Pencaitland Amateurs always took precedence. These were great times for Hibs and I grew up being regaled on tales of the Famous Five. Hibs were league champions in 1947/48, 1950/51 and 1951/52. The tribal nature of local footballing rivalries can and do breed hatred but my father had no ill-feeling towards Hearts. He was actually happy to see them win. To many this will seem like an alien concept, albeit a commendable one. In Pencaitland's Smiddy Inn there was a proliferation of football talk on a Saturday evening.

Dad got a promotion in the Co-operative Insurance in 1956. This meant the family decanting westward to Bathgate. In suggesting that our house in Glasgow Road was a stone's throw from Bathgate Thistle's ground this is barely an exaggeration. Not that we ever did throw stones at it! Creamery Park was located just across the back. Bathgate Thistle got founded in 1936 and the club was located right next to the Co-operative Creamery. I have a distinct childhood memory of rows of vast milk urns sitting outside the creamery. At least they seemed vast. In infancy there is a constant sense of wonderment. Nowadays the creamery is long gone, thereby creating potential for confusion about the origin of the name Creamery Park. Bathgate had formerly had a league club which folded under the weight of financial pressure in 1929. Their Mill Park ground had been located close to the centre of the town whereas Creamery Park lay more towards the western fringe. Ayr United thrice played at Mill Park, each time in a Second Division fixture. The results there were depressing; Bathgate 2 Ayr United 1 on 21st November, 1925, Bathgate 4 Ayr United 2 on 14th August, 1926, and Bathgate 1 Ayr United 1 on 17th September, 1927. When Livingston FC got formed in 1995 there were reports that this would be the first ever league club in West Lothian. This was incorrect. In addition to playing at Bathgate, Ayr United had already played league football at Armadale, Bo'ness and Broxburn, all located in West Lothian.

On the evening of 18th April, 1956, my father went from Bathgate to watch Hibs versus Reims in the semi-finals of the European Cup. This was the inaugural European Cup competition and in Britain it was treated with indifference. Aberdeen were league champions in 1955 but Scotland were represented by fifth-placed Hibs. English champions Chelsea did not compete either and nor did any other English club. Hibs were 2-0 down from the first leg which was played a fortnight earlier. Clawing back the deficit must have been a realistic prospect when it is considered that Easter Road was packed with a crowd of 44,941. It was too bad that the prospect was not realised and there was a 1-0 defeat on the night. Even the final did not attract a crowd as large as that. Reims had the advantage of playing it in relative proximity to their own town, Paris being ninety miles away. In the Parc des Princes 38,239 watched Real Madrid win 4-3.

Three days after Hibs versus Reims, Hearts beat Celtic 3-1 in the Scottish Cup final. That evening my dad got the family into the car and drove over to Harthill so that we could see the Hearts bus passing through with the trophy. The M8 did not exist then. Being aged three I have no recollection of this but I was glad to be appraised of it in later years. It was a shining example of the manner in which my dad bore no ill will towards a club rival. In the year of writing there is only one survivor from the twenty-two players who contested that final. That man is Billy Craig, now resident in Prestwick. He played for Celtic. On a personal level I am proud to count Billy as a friend. The friendship was fostered through his active membership of a walking group aptly entitled the Ayr United Strollers.

My earliest memory of watching football relates to Creamery Park in 1957. In August of that year, aged four, I started school and this phase of time coincided with my first experience of being taken to the football. From our house we literally walked round the corner to the ground.

Pencaitland 1955. The brothers Douglas, Duncan and Peter Carmichael (left to right).

Glasgow 2025. The Carmichael brothers replicating the photograph from seventy years before (on the previous page).

Yes literally! In Scotland the expression 'round the corner' sometimes means several streets away. This is just one of the odd quirks about the Scottish vernacular. By the same token 'hunnerz' can mean five. As a prequel to entering the ground the turnstile attendant would be assailed with the request "Can ah lift the laddie ower?" There was never any objection. Parents may know the potential perils of taking an infant to the football. Perils? Let us revise this viewpoint and invoke the singular rather than the plural. The potential peril of taking an infant to the football is the child's disinterest. It is a moot point though. Even in that long ago 1957/58 season watching Bathgate Thistle was an absorbing experience for me. We stood under the enclosure roof which ran the length of the touchline. The dressing rooms were located at the back of the enclosure and the teams would make their way downward through the middle of it to emerge onto the field. Half-oranges were given to the players as half-time sustenance. I know this because on one occasion a lady emerged from the dressing room carrying a tray bearing the already-quaffed half-oranges. Amidst the remnants one remained intact and she offered it to me. It was gratefully received. This was at a time when an orange was one of the contents of a Christmas stocking. Post war austerity was slackening and our family was not impoverished but this did not diminish the fact that an orange, even half of one, was a treat. As an infant, football presented me with some problems which I struggled to work out. It was beyond my comprehension why, at the end of a cup game, there was never any sign of a cup. The concept of first and second round ties had not entered my young brain. I was aware that Scotland had an international team and I struggled to understand why Scotland only played occasionally rather than every week. Football teams are supposed to play every week, aren't they?

In 1958 we flitted from Glasgow Road to Falside Terrace. No longer did we live in immediate proximity to Creamery Park. This was no impediment to attending in season 1958/59. A ten-minute walk was nothing. On average, of course, home games are played fortnightly. Quite often my dad would fill the in-between Saturdays by going to watch the next nearest club, Armadale Thistle. Armadale was a short drive along the A89. The history of football in Armadale had strong parallels with the history of football in Bathgate. Armadale Football Club stepped up from the Central League to become a Second Division club in season 1921/22. After completing seventeen league fixtures in 1932/33 the club got expelled from the league in November for non payment of debts to other clubs. Their results got expunged and the club went defunct. In 1935 Armadale Thistle got founded and the club was accepted into the Junior ranks. Note the parallels between Armadale and Bathgate. Both were represented at league level by clubs bearing just the town name, both lost their league status on account of debts and football was resumed in each community by a Junior club bearing the name Thistle. One marked difference was that Armadale Thistle did not change location. The club remained at Volunteer Park, the ground inhabited by their senior predecessors.

Joe Baker was a fabulous centre-forward who had the unique distinction of playing for England despite having a strong Scottish accent. He was born in Liverpool to Scottish parents and was raised in Wishaw. Hibs farmed him out to Armadale Thistle in season 1956/57 and my father could recall watching him there at that time. I was not taken to the football until the following season so I narrowly miss out on being able to boast that I was there when the fabulous Baker played for Armadale. He wasted no time in realising his potential, soon becoming a star striker at Hibs. My father and oldest brother were in the crowd to see Baker playing in the 1958 Scottish Cup final. Clyde won that match 1-0. There was a contrast when both of my brothers were at Hampden to witness Hibs beating Rangers 3-2 in the 2016 final. In 1962 Arsenal paid Torino what was then a club record fee for Baker. While at Torino he was a team mate of Denis Law.

Bathgate Thistle revisited in 2021.

In resuming the topic of similarities between the histories of football in Bathgate and Armadale there is another common factor. Ayr United had a poor record in both towns. The two defeats and a draw at Bathgate is eclipsed by the three defeats and a draw at Armadale. These results at Volunteer Park were Armadale 1 Ayr United 1 on 21st February, 1920, Armadale 1 Ayr United 0 on 13th March, 1926, Armadale 4 Ayr United 1 on 20th November, 1926, and Armadale 3 Ayr United 1 on 31st March, 1928. Compounding the statistical misery is the fact that the sole draw in 1920 was a Scottish Cup third round tie and Armadale, then non league, won 1-0 at Somerset Park in the replay. The other matches were Second Division fixtures. While the 1928 match was in progress Scotland's legendary Wembley Wizards were destroying England 5-1 so it was something of a chequered day for Ayr United supporters. In the 1926 match Ayr goalkeeper Bob Hepburn and the Armadale centre-forward got sent off for fighting each other. Hepburn got suspended for fourteen days. Cochran was promoted from the reserves to replace Hepburn for the period of his absence. The results were Ayr United 2 Raith Rovers 1 (11th December) and Dumbarton 3 Ayr United 5 (18th December). Cochran's replacement in the reserves on the respective Saturdays was a seventeen-year-old on loan from Celtic. This was John Thomson, who would go on to become immortal in Scottish football history. Thomson's appearances in the Alliance League resulted Queen's Park Strollers 4 Ayr United 'A' 0 at Hampden and Solway Star 4 Ayr United 'A' 3 at Kimmetton Park, Annan. There was a dramatic sequel to the Bob Hepburn/John Thomson connection. On 5th September, 1931, John Thomson died of injuries suffered while playing for Celtic against Rangers at Ibrox on that day. A fortnight later, also at Ibrox, Bob Hepburn filled the void left by Thomson when he appeared for Scotland in a 3-1 win over Ireland. The next Ayr United player to be capped for Scotland was John Doyle who played against Romania on 17th December, 1975.

My father was in the crowd at Armadale when Whitletts Vics won 2-1 there in a 6th round Scottish Junior Cup tie in March 1956. Many years later this match cropped up in conversation in our household and my dad raved about the fantastic performance from the Whitletts goalkeeper. It was George Anton who was to break into the senior game with Kilmarnock, Stranraer and Ayr United.

Bob Hepburn

A resident of Bathgate in our time there was Willie Cringan. Although raised in Ponfeigh, a Lanarkshire mining village, he was born in Muirkirk. The local football club in Ponfeigh was Douglas Water Thistle and Cringan played at centre-half for them. His next club was Sunderland. During the Great War he returned to Scotland, initially playing for Wishaw Thistle before making his Ayr United debut in a 3-1 win at home to Hearts on 8th January, 1916. It was a great result since Hearts sat second in the league at the time. At the start of the 1916/17 season he was joined in the Ayr United team by his brother Robert, formerly of Parkhead Juniors. In May 1917 he was temporarily loaned to Celtic and in September that year the loan arrangement was resumed on an intermittent basis, ultimately becoming permanent. While there he won league titles in 1919 and 1922 and the Scottish Cup in 1923. He also made six Scotland appearances if we include one victory international. The reason for mentioning Cringan is to convey the point that my father knew him and he attended his funeral in Bathgate in May 1958.

My Bathgate Thistle experience lasted only for seasons 1957/58 and 1958/59. In May 2021 I paid a nostalgic visit to Creamery Park on a non-match day. I was browsing outside the ground, together with the family, when Ben the groundsman appeared. He was exiting the ground in his car but he was curious enough to stop for a chat. After regaling him with a tale of bygone days watching football there he kindly offered to unlock the gates in order that we could look round the place. Quite frankly it was surreal. It had been modernised but the layout was the same. Beyond the far side of the ground was an area that I remembered as a field but was now a housing estate. Prior to this visit I had the equally surreal experience of standing outside the nearby house I had lived in. I have already used a 'just round the corner' description of the distance between the house and the ground. Ever the pedantic I did a Google search of the actual distance. It came up as 0.1 of a mile. You can be sure that even this small measurement was rounded up.

The Proclaimers had a song lyric 'Bathgate no more'. In 1959 the Carmichaels had a 'Bathgate no more' experience of our own. The difference was that our experience had no negative connotations. My father, by now, was an assistant manager with the Co-operative Insurance. Driven by ambition and a strong work ethic, he applied for a managerial vacancy in Perth. The interview was in Manchester and after it he was told something along the following lines: "I'm sorry, Peter. We are offering the Perth job to someone else but we would like to offer you the manager's job in Ayr." This was unbelievable. Admittedly the word 'unbelievable' is often used in the context of situations that are eminently believable. This though was a dream outcome and here is why. At this time we had been living in Bathgate's Falside scheme since the previous year. During our time there some enterprising residents of the scheme organised a day out to Ayr. On the big day veritable convoys of buses lined the streets. Ayr had an invasion coming its way. The excitement was huge. On arrival the buses parked in what I later knew to be Seafield Drive. Being next to a large expanse of grass and in immediate proximity to the seafront, this was ideal (although maybe not ideal for the people who lived there and had their area besieged!). It was a great day, so much so that Ayr was considered to be like paradise. When it later emerged that we were going there to live it was like the fulfilment of a dream. In the Falside area Ayr had so much kudos that my friends thought that I was fibbing when I said that I was going there to live. The scenario could have been the inspiration for the film Sliding Doors. It involved a character who misses a train. The film then alternates between two storylines, one where the train is caught and one where the train is missed. It illustrates how life can pan out so differently through a seemingly inconsequential occurrence. By the same principle it is possible to contemplate that if my father's interview responses had been even slightly different he may have landed the Perth job he applied for. He had a philosophy that you should support the team who play where you live. With this mindset his teams were Pencaitland Amateurs/Hibs,

Bathgate Thistle then Ayr United. However the last named was close to being St.Johnstone. There is no doubt whatsoever that I would have been a Muirton Park regular had the Perth move materialised. An alternative title for this book could have been Nearly a Saintee. It is not a typo for Nearly a Saint! Sometimes in a raffle the second prize is better than the first prize. Based on the experience of a glorious outing Ayr just had to be better than Perth. During the Bathgate years our annual holidays were at the Red Lion Caravan Park at Arbroath. We would have passed through Perth on the way but to myself as an infant it was no more than a town name, unlike Ayr which had a magical quality about it.

The bliss of it all was tainted a little by the fact that there was an elephant in the room (metaphorically speaking of course!). We would need to find a house in Ayr before we could move. Initially my father commuted to Ayr, returning to Bathgate at the weekends. He stayed in digs at Fisherton. During this phase he had his first taste of Somerset Park when attending a League Cup tie against Falkirk on the Wednesday evening of 12th August, 1959. Decades later he would still recall that night. Chief amongst those recollections was the crowd size. The *Ayr Advertiser* estimated it at 11,000. Before the match there was a bit of pomp and ceremony when the new broadcasting studio was opened at the south-west corner of the ground. My father would have had no difficulty in recognising the Falkirk goalkeeper. It was Tommy Younger who was player-manager. He had been a goalkeeper at Hibs for eight years, winning two league titles in the process. In 1956 he was transferred to Liverpool from whom he joined Falkirk in 1959. He made twenty-four Scotland appearances and had played in the 1958 World Cup finals in Sweden. On this night at Ayr he was beaten by John Telfer in the tenth minute. It was a wonder strike from a 25-yard free-kick. In Scottish football there is a traditional taunt which goes "Get in the hoose." It would come from a terracing barracker and would be directed at a player who, for a variety of reasons, may have incurred disfavour. Had John Telfer been a victim it would have been easy to comply if taken literally. He lived in one of the tenements in Tryfield Place. It is said that a team is vulnerable when they have just scored. By way of credence it could be argued that they are still mentally celebrating (after celebrating mentally!). Rather than deliberate any further you will now be appraised of what you have already guessed. Falkirk equalised within a minute of the recentre. The scorer was John White who was close to being transferred to Spurs. Eight minutes later Peter Price scored and it remained Ayr United 2 Falkirk 1. The favourable impression my father took from this match, in turn, had a favourable impression on me.

In September 1959 the process of house hunting had a result. There was a Mactaggart and Mickel Estate just off Hunter's Avenue. We were the first occupants of 48 Tweed Street which was situated on a corner site. By a quirk of the layout of the estate the other half of the semi-detached was 57 East Park Road. Across the back, houses in Teviot Street were still under construction. Still aged six, I was about to start my third school. Primary One was spent at a school officially known as Bathgate West but colloquially known to the locals as The Wee Mair. A new school was opened in Bathgate in the summer of 1958 therefore primary two and a small part of primary three was spent at Boghall Primary. Now it was time to join Heathfield Primary where I was immediately smitten by the red blazers. By now I had experienced a very tenuous connection with Ayr United. Prior to the flitting we had made several trips to the new house, presumably for the purpose of transferring over some knick knacks or to fulfil some odd jobs. Each time we stopped at a baker's in Galston to pick up pies. On a wall behind the counter was what I would claim to be the first team group photo I consciously saw. It was an Ayr United photo. Between this and my dad's story of the Falkirk game it was probably the start of Ayr United drip feeding into the psyche.

The Carmichaels' move to Ayr coincided with great times for Ayr United. On a personal level this had an adverse effect. In an act of responsible parenting my father took the view that the crowds were too big and I was too wee. The crowds at Creamery Park had not been on anything like the same scale. At half-time at Bathgate I was even allowed to do a 360° circumnavigation of the terracing because the crowds were such that an eye could be kept on me at all times. The attraction to Somerset Park was obvious. In the previous season the club had won the Second Division title in a frenzy of goal scoring abandon. The total of 139 goals between cup and league remains a club record. Between 13th August, 1958 and 9th March, 1960, the team scored in forty consecutive home matches.

On 12th September the much trumped Ancell Babes were at Ayr. There was a hat-trick that afternoon but it was not for Motherwell striker Ian St.John who had been earning rave reviews. It landed for Peter Price in a 5-2 win. One week later the result was Rangers 0 Ayr United 3. Seven weeks after that came a 3-2 win at Celtic Park. This was ostensibly a shock result but in reality Celtic finished the season below Ayr United. Luckily I did get to Somerset Park that season because sometimes my father would relent but the Rangers and Celtic fixtures were strictly out of the question.

Not only being at the football at this time was a thrill, so too was the ostensibly normal act of walking there. After walking the length of Tweed Street we would join Hunter's Avenue and this would afford the first glimpse of other people heading for the match. Before reaching the junction with Northfield Avenue the numbers would swell with the addition of those who had crossed Newton Park from the Annpit Road area which was still under development. We usually opted to proceed via West Sanquhar Road rather than St.George's Road. The little corner shop at the junction of Northfield Avenue and West Sanquhar Road tended to be a port of call although a personal favourite in the ensuing years was Lucy's Stores, further along West Sanquhar Road right next to Newton Park School. The ever thickening numbers would gather more momentum as we progressed over the bridge into Somerset Road which was choked with people near kick-off time. Anyone who had brought their car this close to Somerset Park was foolhardy.

Peter Price clinching a hat-trick in a 6-2 win over Alloa Athletic on 25th October, 1958. Look at the crowd for a Second Division fixture.

The pavements could not cope with such a mass of humanity therefore spillage onto the road was necessary. From other directions the numbers descending on the ground were just as impressive. After reaching the head of the turnstile queue the request was the same as it had been at Bathgate and Armadale. "Can ah lift the laddie ower?"

My earliest recollection of Somerset Park is watching the match from the north terrace. There was clearly no scope for wandering off on a half-time walk round the terracing here. The whiff of cigarette and pipe smoke was everywhere. It was noisy on a much greater scale than Creamery Park. Even at that age it was possible to sense something captivating about the place. This was the Peter Price era. It is satisfying to be able to claim that I have seen Ayr United's greatest ever player yet this boast must be tempered by having to admit that I was not conscious of the fact that he and other club legends were out there on the field. On reminiscing it is easy to fall into the trap of exaggeration. It is a natural process to remember things as being better than they actually were. Viewing the past through rose tinted glasses is a common accusation. However this is not the case. There is ample photographic evidence showing a densely packed stand and terraces at Somerset Park even when the visiting club has been a relatively modest one.

Ayr United FC on 12th September, 1959. Rear left to right: Ramsay Burn, John Paterson, Ian Hamilton, Jim McLean, Willie McIntyre and Billy Elliot. Front left to right: Billy Fulton, Sam McMillan, Peter Price, Willie Paton and Jim McGhee.

When a football club goes through successful times it is not always fully appreciated at the time. The good days seem to assume a greater poignancy when looked back upon from a future decade. This is precisely what is happening here yet it does not diminish the inescapable fact that Ayr United achieved some conspicuously good results under the managership of Jacky Cox. It is relevant too that the public backed the team. There are few things more dispiriting in football than a team not getting the backing it deserves.

Peter Price scoring versus Motherwell on 12th September, 1959. He hit a hat-trick in a 5-2 win.

Ayr United were robbed of qualifying for Europe at this time. There was an Anglo Scottish French tournament in operation. It comprised eight clubs from France and four each from Scotland and England. Qualification was based on league positions, excepting of course those clubs who would be playing in other European competitions in 1960/61. Those were champions Hearts (European Cup), Rangers (European Cup Winners' Cup) and Hibs (Inter-Cities Fairs Cup). The case of Hibs was curious. They had played in the inaugural European Cup competition through an invitation and for season 1960/61 they would be playing in the Inter-Cities Fairs Cup by invitation also. This was despite higher placed clubs being overlooked. They had finished seventh which was just one place and one point above Ayr United. League runners-up Kilmarnock exempted themselves from the Anglo Scottish French tournament because the dates clashed with the New York tournament which they competed in annually. To put it succinctly Ayr United made the cut only to be disqualified because Somerset Park had no floodlights and this allowed ninth-placed Celtic in. It was somewhat galling that Celtic got a trip to Sedan. Still, if being petty about it, this could have been dismissed as an obscure tournament that was barely remembered.

Evening Times on 19th September, 1959. Rangers 0 Ayr United 3.

In 1959/60 the average crowd at Somerset Park was 10,500. The prospects for the season ahead were good. On a personal level the prospects were the same. What is meant by this is that I would still get taken there but certain matches would be ruled out. Rangers and Celtic – no chance! League champions Hearts - no chance! Ayr United had no fear of big-named opposition. In 1960/61 both Rangers and Hearts were beaten in the league at Ayr. Yet the inconsistency was stark. The team got relegated. It is said that every cloud has a silver lining. The silver lining was that life in the Second Division would eradicate the need to be left at home some of the time. In the autumn of 1959 the argument was that the crowds were too big and I was too wee. Now the crowd sizes would be depreciating, besides which I was no longer quite as wee.

5th December, 1959. Willie Paton (behind Sam McMillan) scoring versus Partick Thistle. Note the locomotive at the far corner of the ground. Drivers stopping for a peek at the football was a regular occurrence.

By the summer of 1961 I was starting to grow a greater awareness of what was happening on the field rather than being simply awe-struck by the surroundings. I was no longer desensitised to what was happening on the field. In some ways this was not an advantage. When things were going wrong I was starting to feel the pain of defeat. Regretfully it has to be recorded that defeat was soon to become an all too regular occurrence. The fall from grace was not gradual. In metaphorical terms the fortunes of the club fell off the edge of a cliff. It took so little time for the heaving masses in Somerset Road to fade into a memory.

23rd January, 1960. Peter Price has just equalised against Hearts with the last kick. The ball was not even recentred.

It is not being too indulgent in clichés to suggest that Peter Price's departure was the end of an era. He was freed on 4th January, 1962, a Thursday, then made his debut for Raith Rovers on the Saturday. In the immediate aftermath of his release the results were a 3-1 defeat at home to Albion Rovers and a 7-2 defeat at Alloa despite the home team playing with ten men for most of the second half. Price's last game had been in a Scottish Cup tie at home to Clyde on 9th December, 1961. Jacky Cox had resigned on 28th November. For his last match, three days earlier at Arbroath, he had not selected his ace striker. The man himself once told your writer that he sometimes had a strained relationship with Cox. However the seeds of his discontent were sown after he had been asked to take a £2 cut in wages to bring his pay packet into line with the other players. After signing in 1955 he failed to score in his first six matches for the club. He was then dropped for the next two. It took until his seventh match to get his first goal which came at Alloa. Patience is a rare commodity in football and, to a degree, the supporters are justified in wanting to see success sooner rather than later. You can just imagine the terracing grumblings in 1955. Football is fickle though. Peter Price became the club's greatest player of all time with 213 goals in 251 appearances. His goal count in the consecutive seasons 1957/58 and 1958/59 totalled 105. All these decades ago when I first met him he said that he did not know how many goals he had scored. Neither did I. It was the prompt to sit in the library painstakingly going through years of newspaper files in order to accurately access and calculate the statistics. Nowadays people access information by a few taps on a mobile phone but it is far from guaranteed that it is accurate.

In the early part of 1962 Peter Price was gone, the big crowds were gone and, based on results, hope was gone. However that season's malaise had long since set in. In September a 4-1 defeat at Stranraer was the type of result that could not have been contemplated in the preceding seasons. One month later a 2-1 defeat at East Stirling was described as "a pitiable effort" by Bill Hannah in the *Ayr Advertiser*. The same report did not leave the criticism at that. By way of emphasis he wrote: "The majority of this Ayr side are living on faded reputations." Intermittently he found it necessary to revisit this criticism throughout the season. Reporting on a 5-3 defeat at home to Arbroath in March he was not restrained by diplomacy and neither should he have been: "There were no queues to get into Somerset Park on Saturday. There were as many drafts blowing through the stand as paying customers." These words were written by the same man who, after winning at Celtic Park in November 1959, wrote: "A statistician delving into the records with a number nine shovel won't be able to dig up an occasion when Ayr United beat Rangers and Celtic away from home in the same season. The greatest danger to Ayr's continued progress is not the opposition but the self satisfaction which comes with success."

Ayr United FC 1961/62. Rear left to right: Willie McIntyre, Jim McLean, Dave Curlett, John Gallacher, Ramsay Burn and George McIntyre. Front left to right: Alastair McIntyre, Sam McMillan, Billy Fulton, Willie Bradley and Jim McGhee.

A ninth-placed finish in the Second Division in 1962 brought no further reference to expressions such as 'success' or 'self satisfaction'. The columns of the *Ayr Advertiser* could not have been criticised for sycophancy. A 0-0 draw at home to East Stirling in February prompted a brutal summary: "This fantastic pantomime of errors belonged on the stage – not the football field." It was on the verge of getting worse, much worse. The crowds, if they could be described as that, were reminiscent of Creamery Park. This is not intended as an insult to West Lothian Junior football. It is merely meant to illustrate the drastic downturn in the numbers attending

Somerset Park. "United's support rocks precariously on the 1,500 mark", a journalist noted at a time when the club sat fifth and still had further to fall. No longer did I live in fear of being left at home because of the crowd size. One fear did persist though. Would my father lose interest? That fear was allayed because in season 1962/63 I was allowed to go to the games with some of my friends from Tweed Street, besides which he did continue to pitch up at Somerset Park.

2. Pencaitland Amateurs

By 1962 I was immersed in Ayr United for better or worse, quickly having experienced times of success and mediocrity. Several times a year the family would spend the weekend at my maternal granny's house in Ormiston. If we were lucky Ormiston Primrose would have a home game to coincide with our stay. They played in black and white stripes. I have a recollection of teams changing in the Hopetoun Arms then walking through the village in full playing kit to the football field. Even by the rudimentary facilities of some Junior clubs of this age it was a primitive arrangement. It must have been close to a ten-minute walk. Ormiston Primrose – what a wonderful name! In the east of Scotland it was not uncommon for Junior clubs to have a flower in their name. Across the East Lothian border in Midlothian there were some fine examples at this time; Easthouses Lily, Bonnyrigg Rose and Loanhead Mayflower. Over in Fife you had Dundonald Bluebell and Crossgates Primrose. However Ormiston Primrose aroused no excitement in our family. If, during our stay, Pencaitland Amateurs were at home then this would take precedence. The two villages are only 2½ miles apart. Despite operating at amateur level it is a reasonable assumption that the Pencaitland team of this period would have beaten Ormiston Primrose.

In season 1961/62 Pencaitland had an outstanding run in the Scottish Amateur Cup. On reaching the semi-final the big match was scheduled for Tynecastle on the evening of 18th April, 1962. Conveniently this was during the Easter holidays and the Carmichaels took the car through from Ayr to Edinburgh. The opposing team was the Royal College of Science and Technology (later the University of Strathclyde). Pencaitland won 2-1.

> # Two off after collision
> ### By ALEC BAXTER
> AFTER yesterday's dispute over players Bearsden had a number of changes for the Scottish Amateur Cup final at Hampden. Pencaitland, from East Lothian, played as selected.
> BEARSDEN—F. Crampsey; J. Gray and A. Whitlock; W. Kerr, J. Russell, and H. Mailer; R. Stark and D. Miller; J. Scarlett; K. Campbell and J. McGonigle.
> PENCAITLAND—J. Brown; P. Kilday and J. Wood; W. Leckie, R. Turnbull, and J. Gray; A. Henderson and G. McFarlane; J. McGhee; G. Leith and J. Wright.
> Referee—T. Reynolds (Aberdeen).

On Saturday, 5th May, 1962, the final took place against Bearsden at Hampden. The team had the support not only of the village but also of the surrounding area. There was no inter-village bitterness. The opposite was true. Buses ran to Hampden from those surrounding villages. This final was my first visit to Hampden and I was awestruck by the sheer scale of this vast bowl. As at Tynecastle all five Carmichaels were there. For my parents it was a nice catch-up with old friends and former neighbours. The outcome of the final was a travesty.

In the 25th minute goalkeeper Jimmy Brown (a near neighbour of my granny in Ormiston) went for a free-kick from Kerr of Bearsden. In the process he clashed with team mate Leckie. Brown got stretchered off and Leckie walked off after treatment. The incident happened at the Mount Florida end of Hampden. Neither resumed and centre-forward McGhee deputised in goal. Two players short, an outfield player in goal and sixty-five minutes left! No substitutes back then! In the last minute of the first half Scarlett scored for Bearsden. The *Evening Times* report lavishly praised the second half performance: "Pencaitland were going for every ball like tigers." It ended 1-0. If nothing else it was a moral victory. That evening an Ormiston neighbour knocked on my granny's door to tell her that Pencaitland had lost. She literally did not believe it and had to be convinced. It was previously unknown for an amateur final to have the highlights broadcast on Scotsport on a Saturday night but this match was shown. There was a vested interest though. Presenter Bob Crampsey's brother Frank was the Bearsden goalkeeper.

The Pencaitland football field in its picturesque setting at the edge of the village.

The Scottish Cup run of 1961/62 was replicated in 1962/63. That run involved a couple of away ties within a reasonable distance of our Ayr home. Dad's Hillman Minx (VCS 529) was used to set out for Strathaven where the local team Glenavon were beaten. It is worth mentioning that this car was a beauty. Dad bought it from new and it had those iconic tail fins. Every Hillman Minx on the road had the same colour scheme. The top half of the car was white and the bottom half was blue. We also went to Kilmacolm where victory was cheered on by a very sober Pencaitland support. The discovery that it was a dry village did not sit well. We also saw a tie in Edinburgh which we went to from Ormiston on a weekend when we were staying there. That was against Lorwood who played on a pitch near Murrayfield. The home team played in Hibs colours so it had the illusion of a Hibs versus Hearts derby. It was a hard match ending in a draw. Pencaitland won the replay the following Saturday. Dad phoned someone to find out that particular result.

The winter weather of 1962/63 was awful with the consequence that regular postponements caused an extension of the season. It was Saturday 18th May by the time the semi-final was played. That was against Dundee NCR at Dunfermline's East End Park. Again the Carmichaels travelled from Ayr and we sat in a stand that had only been built the summer before. Pencaitland won 2-0. At this time dad was manager of the Co-operative Insurance in Ayr. His Dunfermline counterpart lived in the same street as East End Park. Both he and his son joined us at the match. After the final whistle we decamped to a bungalow in Halbeath Road for our tea. It must have been quite an undertaking for the lady of the house. There were five Carmichaels as guests. All in all it was a perfect day.

The other semi-final was contested in midweek and it was conveniently played at Ardeer so dad took us. Queen's Park Hampden X1 drew 1-1 with PO Phones. The replay was hastily rearranged for the following evening at Albert Park, Cathcart. Queen's Park Hampden X1 won 6-0. The dramatic turnaround from the original tie was considered to be attributable to Queen's Park drafting in players who had been turning out at Second Division level that season. Owing to work being carried out in the Hampden dressing rooms Queen's Park Hampden X1 were denied home advantage in the final. The venue was Powderhall in Edinburgh and the date was Saturday,

1st June, 1963. Dad went into the Pencaitland dressing room to give the players a pep talk. On the way through to Edinburgh we were talking about that 6-0 win in the other semi-final. Dad said that they would not beat Pencaitland 6-0. His prophecy was wayward. They did beat Pencaitland 6-0. It was an unfair contest. The opposition turned up with Eddie Turnbull as their coach and the assertion that league players were in their team was undoubtedly true. Future Scotland manager Andy Roxburgh was in their line-up. A village team did not stand a chance.

Finalists in 1961/62 and 1962/63 – so what happened in 1963/64? On 7th December, 1963, Pencaitland played Crosshill Thistle (1959 Scottish Amateur Cup winners). The village of Crosshill was suitably located near to our Ayr home and, of course, the Carmichaels went. A personal recollection is of side bets taking place before the game and someone considered to be an honest man held the stake money. Hearts had beaten Rangers 3-0 at Ibrox the Saturday before and one of the travelling Pencaitland fans took great delight in reminding some of the Crosshill locals. In their traditional Hearts colours Pencaitland failed to replicate their professional counterparts. Crosshill Thistle won 5-2. The home goalkeeper was a tall lad from Girvan who had only attained the age of seventeen three weeks earlier. He was Peter McCloy, who was destined for a great career with Motherwell, Rangers and Scotland.

In future years Pencaitland succeeded in winning the East of Scotland Amateur Cup in three consecutive seasons (1976/77 to 1978/79 inclusive). Of course the big one was the Scottish Amateur Cup. On 5th May, 1984, the club contested a Hampden final against Cleland Miners Welfare. They won 2-1. For the Carmichaels it did not carry the elation that would have occurred two decades earlier. Having been away from the village since 1956 the bond was not as strong and for a variety of reasons none of us attended the final. On a personal level the reason was the counter attraction of Ayr United playing at Kilmarnock.

Yet although the bond was weaker it was not yet broken. On 29th March, 1986, Pencaitland played a Scottish Amateur Cup tie at Drongan. Drongan United versus Pencaitland was a clash between the last two winners of the trophy. The tie was very conveniently located and I attended with my dad and eldest brother. While standing on the touchline in the rain we suddenly heard a shout from behind us: "Hey Peter!" A chap in a house overlooking the pitch recognised dad and invited us in. Seats were arranged in a bay window and since the house was slightly elevated from the pitch we had a perfect view. Whisky got poured (tea for me, the driver) and the lady of the house laid on sandwiches. It was just like being in a corporate hospitality box. On the eve of the game a reporter on West Sound said that Drongan United would be too strong for Pencaitland. He was wrong. Drongan were beaten 4-1. Alas the team did not go the distance and 1984 remains the only year in which the club has won the trophy. This was the last time dad ever saw Pencaitland play. It was a fantastic result and he watched it in style.

On 29th February, 2020, the Pencaitland AFC Twitter posted this message: "Unfortunately we have taken the decision to fold the team. We only had eight committed players and it's been a very long hard season so far. Apologies to all the Premier League teams but we had no choice with the lack of commitment, desire and work rate and with the general poor attitude of young players."

> 5th May, 1962: "Pencaitland were going for every ball like tigers."

> 29th February, 2020: "Lack of commitment, desire, work rate and general poor attitude of young players."

Another club in the district was Tranent Juniors. Pencaitland, Ormiston and Tranent sit in a triangle. My mother was born in Tranent but the bond to the place was never so strong as to induce our family to go and watch Tranent Juniors when staying at my granny's house. It was less than three miles from Ormiston. Yet my dad used to wax lyrical about the great Tranent Juniors teams of the 1930s. The facts are there to prove that he was not exaggerating. In 1933 they reached the

Scottish Junior Cup final. It was played at Tynecastle where the regulars would have been sympathetic to the Tranent cause not only because the place is near Edinburgh but also because their colours were identical to those of Hearts. After a scoreless draw against Yoker Athletic they lost 4-2 in the Hampden replay. They reached the final again in 1935 and crushed Petershill 6-1 at Ibrox. This was a record win for a Scottish Junior Cup final but it was identically matched by Bonnyrigg Rose against Whitburn in the 1966 final. My father once mentioned that, during those halcyon years, the club had a supporter who used to urge the team into attack by shouting "Lie forrit Turnent" (note the local pronunciation). He then said that, because of this, "Lie Forrit" eventually appeared on the town's coat-of-arms.

The Tranent coat-of-arms bearing the legend Lie Forrit.

It was an interesting tale from the past but it seemingly had to be tainted by having the clear stamp of an urban myth. With the tale long since confined to the recesses of the memory there was a fortuitous development on 18th April, 2015. At work on that day a colleague offered to go out and place bets on that afternoon's Scottish Grand National. He sent out an e-mail with a list of the runners so I thought that I would have a go on the grounds that all of the others were going to have a flutter. Listed amongst the runners was the name 'Lie Forrit'. It immediately evoked memories of the old Tranent tale so I backed it (with a small stake!). The horse did not win but the experience prompted me to do some research that enabled me to find out that the expression 'Lie Forrit' really is on the burgh's coat-of-arms. It was a delight to find out that the 'coat-of-arms' story was not a mere myth. In the year of writing Tranent Juniors are playing in Scottish football's fifth tier (Lowland League).

Fans on the North terrace on 8th August, 1953, when big crowds were regular. A decade later such crowds were occasional. The lower image shows Joe Hutton scoring the equaliser in the 2-1 win over Stenhousemuir.

3. And now, The Few

Hugh Rodie

It is a natural instinct to enter a new season imbibed with fresh hope. Judging by the positivity of the local media this was definitely the default mindset in and around Somerset Park in the summer of 1962. In the *Ayr Advertiser* Bill Hannah, writing under the pen name Carrick Hill, reported: "The Ayr United players are approaching peak fitness under new trainer Jim Florence who has as his deputy former Annbank United trainer Hugh Rodie."

With hindsight there is a limit to what could have been read into this. For decades to come it was commonplace for struggling Ayr United managers to trot out lavish praise about how well things were going in training. The fans have always been right in placing first team results as a priority. In bad times there is no consoling effect in being told: "The boys were flying in training." Yet Gerry Mays succeeded in making some good signings that summer. The cream of the crop were Des Herron, formerly of Aberdeen, Johnny Kilgannon, formerly of Stirling Albion and Johnny Hubbard, formerly of Bury but more popularly associated with his career at Rangers. Further good news was that the club would be entering a team in the Combined Reserve League. To my boyhood self this opened up an opportunity to go to Somerset Park weekly rather than fortnightly. Failure to qualify from a League Cup section brought the predictable response that the league was more important. The league start was met with trepidation – St.Johnstone away! St.Johnstone had been relegated by losing at home to Dundee in the final match of 1961/62, this result crowning Dundee as league champions. St.Johnstone 1 Ayr United 2 – what a start. Maybe, just maybe, the pre-season hype was justified.

In November it was announced that the team would be getting a new strip comprising vertical black and white stripes, white shorts and white stockings with two black hoops at the top. To a child such things are important. Through my eyes this new kit gave the players an aura of being supermen. If only! In December a 3-1 defeat at Dumbarton preceded the resignation of Gerry Mays by three days. His replacement was Neil McBain, a man about whom an entire book could be written. In November 1921 Ayr United sold him to Manchester United for what was then a record fee for the Old Trafford club. The

£4,600 transfer fee was enough to fund the new Somerset Park stand, the plans for which had already been drawn up. In his time he had also played for Everton, Liverpool and Scotland. His stock was high locally. In 1956 he managed Ayr United back to the First Division for the first time since before the war. In childhood of course I had no conception of who this man was but I do recall that the grown-ups referred to him as Auld Neilly. There was an occasion later on that season when two friends and I went to Somerset Park on a training night. We hoped that we would be allowed in to watch the players train. When we arrived in Tryfield Place the main entrance door was ajar. Cautiously we entered. Our entry had been overheard by a man who emerged from the manager's office. It was Neil McBain, of course. We asked if we could come in to watch the training and he told us that the players were training at the Old Racecourse. Then he asked if we would mind coming in to pick up litter from the terracing. We obliged and afterwards we were paid from the loose change in his pocket. The players arrived back from the Old Racecourse and did two laps of the ground. Johnny Hubbard's speed was conspicuous even though he was in the dawn of his playing career. A personal regret is that the only time I met Neil McBain was when I was aged ten rather than in later years when I had grown an obsession with the club's history. It is frustrating not to have heard his personal testimony.

The first game of Neil McBain's second managerial spell at Ayr was a 2-0 defeat at home to Stranraer. In the aftermath there was a headline of 'Promotion hopes killed'. It was mystifying that promotion was even mentioned in relation to a club sitting in eleventh place. George Anton performed heroics that day including a double-save from a Rab Stewart penalty. In 1990 I visited George to interview him for a 'Where are they now?' article for the match programme. He was destined to play for Ayr United in season 1966/67 but I asked him whether, since he lived in Ayr, he would rather have played for Ayr United in the mid to late sixties rather than Stranraer. With no hesitation his answer was no. He explained that Stranraer were actually better than Ayr United during most of his time there. He was right. The completed Second Division tables from 1961/62 until 1964/65 all showed Stranraer to be better placed. By that latter season the gap had grown to twelve places. At the time of this 2-0 win at Ayr in December 1962 Stranraer were in second place in the Second Division. The return match at Stair Park coincided with Easter weekend in 1963. We always visited my granny at Easter but she did not have a television. Still not knowing the Ayr United result I went to the local newspaper shop in Ormiston that evening. In the west people converged on such shops eager to buy the *Evening Times* and/or the *Evening Citizen*, both great football papers. The equivalent in East Lothian was the *Edinburgh Evening Dispatch*. Through that organ I was appraised of a result that read Stranraer 7 Ayr United 2. In other years the thought may have occurred that it was a misprint. It was 1963 and I just knew it to be true.

Neil McBain on 15th January, 1963.

The theme of negativity will now be maintained to mention a new frustration introduced to me in that season. Postponements! The temptation has been resisted to punctuate the word with an entire line of exclamation marks in order to emphasise the irritability. At the age of ten this was an unknown experience to me until the winter of 1962/63 tightened its grip. 'You wait half an hour for a bus then three come along at the same time' is an old British gripe. In this case it would be an understated analogy. The previously mentioned Stranraer game took place at Somerset Park on 8th December, 1962. The club's next home league match took place on 2nd March, 1963. Match days, or rather scheduled match days, started to conform to a new pattern. Communications were a lot more rudimentary back then therefore people would head for the ground without even thinking about the possibility that the game would be off. Even the whitened pavements and roads were not a clue because games would proceed on pitches that would fail an inspection at the first glance nowadays. On approaching Somerset Park there was a sense of foreboding when no music was belching out of the public address system. Then the initial fear would materialise on encountering people walking away from the ground. "Game off", they would say but by then we had guessed. This ritual continued throughout what seemed like an eternal winter. On 15th December a 2-0 defeat away to Stenhousemuir solicited a press comment that it was: "A performance almost as pathetic as the weather." Anyone with memories of this winter will know this to be a rather severe condemnation. One week later we had a 6-2 win at Forfar. There was no opportunity to build any momentum since the club's next league fixture took place on 23rd February away to East Fife. In the midst of all those postponements one game did survive. It was a second round Scottish Cup tie at home to Dundee United on 2nd February. No other ties survived so it got sole billing. The origin of Dundee United's nickname of The Arabs dates to this winter. It is on account of the Tannadice pitch having copious amounts of sand applied in an attempt to get a match played. The nickname might justifiably have been applied to Ayr

United. For Dundee United's visit the pitch was very heavily sanded. Maybe the visitors were more acclimatised to playing on such a surface. They won 2-1. This was the day when I stood at the Somerset Road end for the first time and it became a habit. It was a short migration from the north terrace. Neither stance afforded any protection from the elements anyway.

One of that winter's postponements created a quite telling comment on the situation. Bob Blane of the *Ayr Advertiser* contacted Neil McBain to ask about the state of the pitch prior to a scheduled match against Albion Rovers. The answer was: "Play football? You could skate on it." Cynically it could be observed that it was a reprieve to have so many blank Saturdays. The extended season finished with the club in thirteenth position in the Second Division. Fourteen players got freed. Regardless, I would definitely be back to take up residence in the Somerset Road end.

Through the eyes of a boy the players were heroes despite some awful results. Up front the form of Sandy Jones and Johnny Kilgannon was inconsistent with the general drudgery. Johnny Hubbard was a speed merchant on the left wing. Goalkeeper John Gallacher was so revered that he could count on a round of applause when taking up his position in goal at the Somerset Road end. Yet the presence of some quality was only tantamount to papering over the cracks. The crowds, or rather the lack of them, indicated that the public of Ayr and district had fallen out of love with the team. Rather than turn up and barrack they stayed away. The few who continued to pitch up had a tendency to display apathy rather than resentment. There was a mood of stoic acceptance. Matches lacked atmosphere and the numbers were too few for any dissent to be expressed on a loud scale. From the start of April 1963 until the end of the season the Somerset Park crowds, if they could thus be described, were: 458 (versus Dumbarton), 836 (versus St.Johnstone who were on the brink of winning the league), 797 (versus Stenhousemuir), 642 (versus Albion Rovers), 689 (versus Forfar Athletic), 654 (versus Alloa Athletic) and 616 (versus Berwick Rangers). This was at a time when, in relative terms, it was inexpensive to get in.

The close season mood of optimism manifested itself once more via the medium of press statements. I believed what I read because I wanted to believe it. As expected recruitment was from the Juniors and the free transfer market. John Murphy from Darvel Juniors – this did not seem like an inspired signing. The reality was at total odds with how it seemed. Spud gave sterling service as a left-back for fifteen years. No player in the history of the club has surpassed him for appearances or career span. His debut was in the opening match of season 1963/64, a League Cup sectional tie at home to Morton. A 1-0 defeat was witnessed by a crowd of 4,985 which, quite honestly, looked like more. Was this the return of the lost hordes? Not really. The visiting support was vast. Morton were on the brink of an all-conquering season and the people of Greenock knew it. In the following month we had 752 in the ground for a league visit from Montrose. Curiously that match was played on a Monday night, the consequence of which was that I skipped going to the Lifeboys (Junior Boys' Brigade) in order to witness a 5-2 defeat. This was the fifth of six consecutive league defeats. Someone who has no interest in football may wonder why anyone would put themselves through this. It could be interpreted as a form of masochism to keep going back to support an ailing team playing in front of sparse crowds. Most people who know me will have heard my explanation. Supporting Ayr United is a disease for which there is no cure.

At this time it was common practice for people to watch Ayr United and Kilmarnock in alternate weeks. It was mainly people from the Ayr area who did this. Not unreasonably the people of Kilmarnock were not very good at reciprocating. I often went with my father to Rugby Park in the early to mid-sixties. The picture there was vastly different. They had a great team together with the crowds that accompany success. Kilmarnock's placings in the top tier at this time were: 1960/61 second, 1961/62 fifth, 1962/63 second, 1963/64 second, 1964/65 champions and 1965/66 third. I was there for some of their European nights most notably against Eintracht, Everton and Real Madrid. Being there had no impact on me whatsoever. I was desensitised to it. On the basis of logic it made no sense. These were halcyon years at Kilmarnock but my heart was not there. On one occasion I was standing at a Kilmarnock versus Rangers game in what must have been 1964. A Rangers supporter standing next to me said: "Who do you support, son?" He laughed when I replied "Ayr United". I do not believe that he was laughing by way of a putdown. It was more likely that he expected the answer to be one of the teams out there on the field. A feature of Rugby Park was the Johnnie Walker half-time scoreboard at the Rugby Road end. By now I was a programme collector so I did not fail to buy one. The back of the Kilmarnock programme contained the alphabetical key for the half-time scores. My eyes would be cast towards the scoreboard in the hope that Ayr United were winning at Montrose or wherever else the team was playing that day. A week later I would be back at Somerset Park where my heart lay. I loved the feeling of elation when Ayr United scored notwithstanding the fact that defeats were all too frequent.

In November 1963 the crowd for a 2-1 win at home to Forfar Athletic was 582. Two Junior trialists were in the line-up. This was a desperate state of affairs at Second Division level at this point of the season. Not that this match would have made headlines anyway. John F. Kennedy was assassinated the evening before. A week earlier there had been a crushing 6-0 defeat against Clyde at Shawfield. One crumb of good news at this time was that there would no longer be an additional charge to access the railway end. Previously, if it started raining during a game, there would be a rush to pay the supplementary charge at an internal turnstile in the north-west corner. The options were to either stump up or stay where you are and get soaked. I used to stay put at the Somerset Road end and take a drenching rather than pay the concessionary sixpence for the transfer. That was enough to buy two packets of fruit gums!

All too often the BBC results service was a source of misery. Berwick Rangers 6 Ayr United 1 did not sound any better just because it was couched in a posh tone. Okay it was the last Saturday of 1963. Maybe the New Year would bring new hope. Or more likely it wouldn't, especially with a New Year's Day visit from Morton who still had a 100% league record for the season. The crowd of 6,351 was predominantly from Greenock. A 3-1 defeat was a virtual victory. One day later a 5-1 defeat at Alloa was a virtual annihilation. Cowdenbeath were at Ayr on Saturday 4th January. Three league defeats in three days. Surely that could not happen. It did – Ayr United 0 Cowdenbeath 1. The attendance, resisting the temptation to call it a crowd, was 482. It was such a marked contrast in three days. On the same afternoon 2,621 attended the nearby National Hunt racing and 1,200 pitched up at Voluntary Park for a third round Scottish Junior Cup tie which ended Whitletts Victoria 3 Johnstone Burgh 4. According to second hand accounts (I was at the Ayr game) Whitletts had shown a lot of attacking abandon and were unlucky to lose to a team on course to win the cup. A product of that Johnstone Burgh side was Charlie Oliphant who would afterwards join Ayr United.

In the Scottish Cup there was some mild progress with wins against Inverness Thistle at home and Buckie Thistle away. This set up an away tie against Aberdeen on 15th February, 1964. It was viewed with trepidation. We were in sixteenth place in the Second Division. On that afternoon I played football with my friends in Newton Park. It was one of those jackets-for-goalposts type of games. With our game still in progress I said that I was heading home to get the Ayr United score. The consensus, understandably, was that there was no point. In my heart of hearts I agreed. Results used to rattle through randomly on the BBC teleprinter with some intermittent statistical narration from David Coleman. Eventually it splurted out 'Aberdeen 1'. Momentarily there was relief that it was not an annihilation and for a second or two there was an unlikely hope that it was a draw. The teleprinter then rapidly spelled out 'Ayr United 2'. Since first watching football at Creamery Park in 1957 I had never felt such elation. It was simply sensational. As rapidly as I could I then sprinted the length of Tweed Street and back to Newton Park where my friends were still playing. Breathlessly I blurted out the result and the game stopped in an instant. The celebrations were wild. That evening we were all back in the park to recreate what we thought the goals were probably like. This was accompanied by our best efforts at adding Arthur Montford-style commentary to the proceedings. One week earlier, when Ayr United were at Brechin, I was at a game where the result was Kilmarnock 9 Falkirk 2. That evening Kilmarnock were the top-placed club in Scotland but I felt nothing more than indifference. The passage to the quarter-finals of the Scottish Cup proved to be a chastening experience. A return to the default 1964 form brought about a 7-0 hammering at Dunfermline.

The season wound on to a merciful conclusion when 592 turned up for a 1-0 win at home to Dumbarton. Fourteenth place precipitated drastic action. Only seven players were retained. Nine days after the Dumbarton game the Western League Cup final brought the curtain down at Somerset Park. The result was Craigmark Burntonians 4 Irvine Meadow 3. Your writer was one of the 1,569. This was close to one thousand more than the attendance for the recent Ayr United game. Three players on display shone well enough to get signed by Ayr United. They were Arthur Paterson and Eddie Monan of Irvine Meadow and Alex McAnespie of Craigmark who was better known as Sanny. Each would become fondly remembered for their time at Ayr United. However my personal favourite in 1964 was Eddie Moore, a rugged centre-forward who had been signed from Beith Juniors in March. Even in troublesome times it was clear to see that he was lethal in the air. His fearsome expression added to the sense of danger.

On the Wednesday night prior to the Scotland versus England game in April, a rumour swept our area that the England squad was at Somerset Park. This was the cue for a hasty scramble to get to the ground. It was more than a rumour. For once the bush telegraph had called it right. Entry was forbidden but it was later reported that they played Ayr United in a practice match. The result was not published although by implication the score was heavy. Their team bus was parked next to the officials' entrance in Tryfield Place. When the players emerged there was a scramble for autographs. I had come prepared with a pen and a diary. In the limited time I got just one autograph. Alf Ramsey no less.

A future visit in April 1966. The England squad would soon be viewing more prestigious silverware than the Ayrshire Cup. (Left to right): Bobby Moore, Derek Ibbotson (fitness coach), Geoff Hurst, Jacky Charlton, Bobby Tambling, Roger Hunt, player obscured, and Bobby Charlton.

Alf Ramsey and his squad tread the hallowed turf.

Snapshot of attendances on a three-year cycle 1961/62 to 2024/25

	First home league match		First home match in New Year	
1961/62	Ayr United 1 Hamilton Accies 0	4648	Ayr United 4 Morton 1	3351
1964/65	Ayr United 1 Queen's Park 2	1312	Ayr United 3 Queen of the South 1	1752
1967/68	Ayr United 3 Clydebank 1	3573	Ayr United 0 St.Mirren 3	6630
1970/71	Ayr United 4 Dunfermline Athletic 1	5620	Ayr United 2 Morton 1	6902
1973/74	Ayr United 2 Morton 1	5379	Ayr United 0 Dumbarton 1	4488
1976/77	Ayr United 0 Aberdeen 5	4800	Ayr United 3 Kilmarnock 1	7938
1979/80	Ayr United 1 Dumbarton 2	2647	Ayr United 4 Hamilton Accies 1	3122
1982/83	Ayr United 2 Alloa Athletic 1	1228	Ayr United 2 Clyde 0	1704
1985/86	Ayr United 0 Falkirk 3	1639	Ayr United 1 Clyde 0	1398
1988/89	Ayr United 3 Clydebank 2	3151	Ayr United 4 Kilmarnock 1	8585
1991/92	Ayr United 3 Clydebank 0	2685	Ayr United 1 Stirling Albion 2	2217
1994/95	Ayr United 1 Hamilton Accies 1	2095	Ayr United 2 St.Mirren 0	2237
1997/98	Ayr United 1 Morton 2	3481	Ayr United 2 Dundee 5	2068
2000/01	Ayr United 1 Ross County 0	2740	Ayr United 2 Clyde 0	2481
2003/04	Ayr United 1 Falkirk 1	2519	Ayr United 1 Queen of the South 1	2303
2006/07	Ayr United 0 Cowdenbeath 4	1283	Ayr United 1 Stranraer 0	1068
2009/10	Ayr United 1 Partick Thistle 1	3078	Ayr United 1 Brechin City 0	1139
2012/13	Ayr United 1 Stenhousemuir 1	1248	Ayr United 1 Queen of the South 5	1216
2015/16	Ayr United 2 Brechin City 1	1074	Ayr United 1 Peterhead 2	1155
2018/19	Ayr United 2 Partick Thistle 0	3249	Ayr United 0 Falkirk 1	2729
2021/22	Ayr United 2 Arbroath 2	1244	Ayr United 1 Arbroath 0	500 (Covid limit)
2024/25	Ayr United 5 Airdrie 0	2857	Ayr United 3 Raith Rovers 0	2733

4. The Ally MacLeod Revolution

The annual wave of close season optimism recurred. However the optimism proved to be a hoax. We were on the threshold of what remains the worst season in the club's history. I bought into the hype only to end up with egg on my face (metaphorically of course!). This may smack of blind optimism on my part but it was not like that. Including the players involved in the May signing coup, a total of sixteen were brought in. Amongst them were Charlie Oliphant, Adam Thomson, Drew Nelson, Dick Malone and Ally MacLeod, who was installed as team captain.

Progression from the League Cup section did not happen but we had a 6-0 win at home to Berwick Rangers in which Eddie Moore and Drew Nelson each scored a hat-trick. Bring on the league – or rather don't! The first five games were all lost. Supporters will tell you that they will follow their team in good times as well as bad. Your writer can testify to being a Somerset Park regular when the club suffered the ignominy of occupying the basement position in the Scottish League. Kilmarnock won their first six league fixtures to go to the top of the pile. I was still being taken to Rugby Park on a week about basis. Kilmarnock were the leading club in Scotland and were separated from Ayr United by every other league club in the country. Surely now it was time to change allegiance. This will hereby be dismissed as a preposterous suggestion. Let us suppose that the fortunes of the clubs had been reversed. What then? It was always going to be Ayr United for me regardless and it was never simply an attempt to align with the underdog. Besides, our day would come.

Eddie Moore completing a hat-trick in a 6-0 win over Berwick Rangers on 22nd August, 1964.

In November 1964 the directors sought advice on the financial viability of the club. The option of winding the club up and selling the ground to clear debts was a consideration. Boardroom changes and cash injections succeeded in pulling Ayr United back from the brink. I was at an age where I would not normally have been interested in what was happening in the boardroom. However the situation was so serious that I followed developments closely regardless of being so young. Matters had been so bleak for so long that Partick Thistle coming to Ayr for a first round Scottish Cup tie had the resonance of being a huge event. The tie was played on 6th February, 1965. Interest in the area was so great that the crowd was 7,058 excluding the stand. Some friends and I made a banner with a white sheet. The writing on it was too feint and people told us that, from a distance, it looked like nothing more than precisely that, a white sheet. After a 1-1 draw the replay was lost 7-1. Had we been at Firhill it might have been useful as a white flag of surrender.

Billy Kerr is beaten by Partick Thistle goalkeeper Jim Gray on 6th February, 1965. Eddie Moore is in close attendance.

In the second half of that season I became a programme seller. On the face of it this was a mundane job but it made me feel part of the club quite apart from the advantages of commission and free entry. The last home game of the season was a 2-0 victory against Stranraer. An incident that occurred at half-time that day would be inconceivable in the present. This was the day when Kilmarnock had to beat Hearts 2-0 at Tynecastle to win the league. The vagaries of goal average meant that 3-1 would not have done. In 1965 it was not the practice to announce half-time scores at Somerset Park. This was to encourage programme sales. The programme contained the alphabetical key for the half-time scoreboard. Yet on this day, in a departure from the usual practice, one half-time score was announced over the tannoy. It was Hearts 0 Kilmarnock 2. Believe it or not the Ayr crowd cheered.

Kilmarnock won the league by maintaining that scoreline. Two days later it was Kilmarnock versus Ayr United in the Ayrshire Cup final. It was the champions of Scotland versus an Ayr team which, with one game left, was on course for finishing second bottom of the Second Division. The embarrassment was compounded by having to apply for re-election. Sportingly the Ayr team applauded Kilmarnock onto the field. The trepidation was extreme. My Ayr United scarf attracted a comment that Kilmarnock would win by a cricket score. Kilmarnock 0 Ayr United 1 was the result. Were we on our way back? Yes we were.

Sometimes supporters can be guilty of what is known as a knee-jerk reaction. Two or three defeats can be all it takes to solicit the utterance 'worst ever'. With certainty it can be stated that 'worst ever' can only apply to season 1964/65.

The worst season in the club's history did not prompt a clearout. By way of strengthening the squad just two players were added in the close season, Johnny Grant and Ian Hawkshaw. Manager Tom McCreath said: "We have one ambition and that is to get into the First Division." With minimal changes to a struggling squad this seemed like insanity. Ally MacLeod had now retired from playing and he was solely a coach. Beyond all shadow of a doubt he was the source of the optimism even although it did sound irrational. Mr McCreath's stated ambition was on the brink of materialising. The club's progression in the League Cup was halted by a 4-2 aggregate defeat against Kilmarnock in the quarter-finals. This did not dispel the air of confidence around Somerset Park. The onfield progression from the year before was vast even although the bulk of the team was unchanged.

When two of the first three league fixtures were lost there was an element of 'here we go again'. The campaign started with a 3-2 win at Montrose which slipped under the radar in terms of it being played in a corner of Angus in midweek. Losing 3-1 at home to Queen of the South then 3-1 at Cowdenbeath should have been concerning but to a lot of us it wasn't. Ally MacLeod continued to make optimistic but plausible quotes. He was the manager in all except name and it was soon proven that he was not guilty of unsubstantiated rhetoric. Significantly 5,085 attended the Queen of the South match. The points piled up and the crowds drifted back. A league visit from Raith Rovers in October attracted yet another crowd touching 5,000. There was just a sense that something significant was happening.

In November we had a crunch game at Airdrie. That Saturday, around lunchtime, my father decided that he would drive through to this game. Arbroath (19 points from 13 games), Airdrie (17 points from 12 games) and Ayr United (16 points from 11 games) were the top three. The biggest impression made upon me that day was the size and volume of the Ayr support at Broomfield. It was passionate too, sometimes too passionate. When the diminutive Johnny Grant got felled by a hefty tackle it was the prompt for a whisky tumbler to be thrown onto the field from the covered enclosure. We lost 1-0 to a late goal from Davy Marshall but it was a great feeling just to be part of the travelling support. On the way home on that winter's night there just seemed to be a massive convoy of Ayr bound traffic snaking through the Irvine Valley.

On 3rd January, 1966, a 2-2 draw away to Queen of the South attracted 7,180. The upshot of this was that we were five points behind top-placed Arbroath with three games in hand and two points behind second-placed Queen of the South also with three games in hand. Even at two points for a win it was looking good for one of the two automatic promotion spots. Home crowds were up tenfold on the year before. Promotion was now the ambition rather than the mere survival of the club. The football was great to watch. Malone and Murphy was a great full-back partnership. Eddie Monan was dominant at centre-half. Arthur Paterson was a footballing artist. Sam McMillan was an inspirational captain. Press reports were glowing although the national media had not yet fully shrugged off the highly irritating 'Wee Ayr' label. Such was the positivity that a cup draw at home to First Division St.Johnstone was viewed as an indication as to how we might fare the following season. In a 1-1 draw most of the game was played with ten men due to an early injury to John Murphy. A 1-0 defeat in the replay suggested that the challenge would not be too formidable. The assumptiveness was refreshing.

On 23rd April, 1966, the Scottish media basked in a Celtic versus Rangers Scottish Cup final. My personal feeling was one of indifference. Ayr United required at least a draw at Arbroath to guarantee promotion. 1-1 – This was magic! A win away to Stenhousemuir on the Monday night was needed to clinch the title. Communications were such that I did not know about the 4-0 win until seeing the story in the *Daily Express* on the Tuesday morning. This was one very distracted schoolday at Ayr Academy. Conveniently there was one game left. This was at home to East Fife on the Wednesday night. Prior to the kick-off the teams were introduced to Provost O'Halloran. After a 2-0 win a human tide took to the field and I took great pleasure in being part of it. It may seem repetitive to make continual reference to crowd figures but this is after all a gauge on a club's success. For the visit of East Fife 4,865 came through the turnstiles. Many of them could vividly recall a promotion night in 1956 when the crowd was massively higher. The difference in 1966 was that the club had not long since been flirting with Armageddon.

Tom McCreath praised Ally MacLeod's contribution as coach then stepped aside to allow him to take over as manager. The season's end coincided with the Carmichaels flitting from Ayr but we were still within walking distance of the ground. We only moved as far as Prestwick!

5. The Yoyo Years

By the summer of 1966 I had been collecting football programmes for several years — and not just Ayr United programmes. Pocket money was used to buy from dealers' lists advertised in *Football Monthly*. My best friend at the time was Douglas Symington, who was also a collector as well as being, of course, a big Ayr United supporter. One day we agreed to amalgamate the two collections into one quite fabulous collection which we continued to expand. Eventually this worked to the benefit of Ayr United, more of which later. Programme collecting was popular too amongst a lot of our fellow pupils at Ayr Academy. It was so popular that a thriving programme market evolved in the playground. Issues were swapped and bought with a vigour that belied the school's status for rugby. Several years later, in the course of research, I took smug satisfaction in discovering that Ayr Academy belonged on the Ayr United family tree.

Reverting to the topic, readers will not require to be told how a yoyo works. It was the object of a recurring craze in the sixties in a similar manner to the hula-hoop. Another recurring sixties craze was labelling Ayr United as a yoyo club because of a perception that we were too good for the Second Division but not good enough for the First Division. There is a cross section of pessimists in any society but here in 1966 they seemed to breed. Rather than bask in the glory of winning the Second Division title, many preferred to take great delight in proffering the view: "They'll go straight back doon." The annoyance of hearing this was bad enough but it was even worse when the predictions of doom proved to be pinpoint accurate. Then the grim retort was: "Ah telt ye".

Another source of annoyance was that I got an occasional game for the 8th Ayr Boys' Brigade. You see the issue was that they played in blue and white stripes and white shorts. Killie colours! It may have been a blessing that my football ability meant that any passers-by would not have spotted me anyway. Technically they weren't Killie strips. The officer who acquired them was a Rangers supporter and these were the colours of the Rangers change strip. When I tell you that the name of the officer was Billy Mason I swear that I am not joking. It is the honest truth.

To go from second bottom in the Second Division to the First Division in a year maybe was too quick a step. In retrospect there is no maybe about it. It happened with minimal changes in personnel. Hopes of survival hinged on nothing more substantial than belief.

Ally MacLeod's first signing was striker Alex Ingram from Queen's Park. His debut was alongside Eddie Moore against Blackburn Rovers, whom Ally had played for in the 1960 FA Cup final. It was a pre-season friendly with a carnival atmosphere.. The championship flag was unfurled and at half-time Tommy Truesdale performed his song The United Men of Ayr. There was a 3-1 defeat against a formidable team.

In the opening league engagement a 0-0 draw at home to Dunfermline Athletic was considered to be a great result. The performance was most encouraging against a team considered to be amongst the elite of Scottish football. A fortnight later Dundee United were at Ayr. Seven minutes into the second half the scoring was opened with an Eddie Monan own goal. By the 79th minute it was 7-0 for Dundee United. I bailed out at 5-0. Near Tam's Brig I encountered some supporters who had called it a day at 4-0. This remains the biggest home defeat in our history, albeit shared with the 7-0 slaughter administered by Inverness Caledonian Thistle in 2010. The difference is that when it happened in 2010 I did stay to the end. It is sometimes piously suggested that true supporters 1. Always stay to the end 2. Never boo the team. I agree that booing the team is a bad idea but not for the reason readers may think. In 2017, in a relegation six-pointer, we were 4-0 down away to St.Mirren at half-time. When the half-time whistle blew it seemed to me that the team's lack of application was deserving of a good booing so I joined in with the others who were similarly minded. It was then that I discovered that I was not very good at it because the end product was little better than a high pierced shrill. It was maybe to Ayr United's credit that I had not had enough practice.

The Dundee United debacle was the second of six consecutive league defeats. It was soon to get worse. The worst run of consecutive defeats in the club's history is eleven. These matches dated from 17th December, 1966, until 11th February, 1967. They comprised ten in the league and one in the Scottish Cup. The cup defeat at Elgin was horrible. A First Division club losing 2-0 to a Highland League club was the stuff of unfortunate headlines. A postponement on the Saturday had caused the Elgin tie to proceed on a Wednesday night. The embarrassment of facing up to it at school the next day was too much. Throughout the Thursday and Friday I said that I was no longer an Ayr United supporter and that I would not be at Somerset Park that Saturday. My willpower was not strong enough and I did go on the Saturday. Not that the team redeemed itself. We lost 5-2 to Aberdeen.

"Ayr United still without a league victory". Every Saturday David Coleman trotted this out whenever the results were coming through on the BBC teleprinter. We were in serious danger of getting through the season with no league wins at all. I admit to knowing very little about horse racing. I could not tell you the winner of last year's Grand National for example. Yet by a strange quirk I can immediately tell you that Foinavon won it in 1967. My recollection of Grand National Day in 1967 is attributable to the fact that this was the day when Ayr United recorded the club's only league victory of the 1966/67 season. Ayr United 1 St.Johnstone 0 – it had taken until fixture twenty-nine of thirty-four. It was won by an Eddie Monan penalty inside the first ten minutes. At the end there was a pitch invasion of fans chanting "Easy, Easy". Although delighted to hear the final whistle I took no part in that pitch invasion. Even as a juvenile it just seemed cringeworthy.

The season's points haul was nine, comprising a win and seven draws. Promotion had been too quick and the First Division had proven to be more of a correction centre than anything else. At least I managed to survive my post Elgin wobble.

Ally MacLeod had a very persuasive nature. When competing with other clubs to sign sought after players he had the advantage of being able to exude positivity. Financial restraint meant that the club habitually scouted the cream of the Juniors. One such was the fabulous Davy Stewart who was fresh from winning the Scottish Junior Cup with Kilsyth Rangers. Throughout his life he was quiet and unassuming. This was one goalkeeper who did not have it in him to give his fellow defenders an earbashing but he had exceptional agility. His playing kit earned him the nickname of The Man in Black. His performances were so inspiring to me that I wanted to become a goalkeeper, having so far shown no great aptitude in any outfield position. This venture was not entirely unsuccessful. Indoor football was entirely suitable for me. On the basis that I had long limbs there existed the possibility that I could save the ball with something. This glorious (?) career peaked one Sunday in 1982 at the Bell's Sports Centre in Perth. I worked for the Halifax Building Society and they held an annual five-a-side tournament for their Scottish branches. Although working for the Irvine branch I was the goalkeeper for the Paisley branch. We won the cup, beating Kilmarnock in the final. Yes I played in a team that beat Kilmarnock in a Scottish Cup final. You may call it tenuous but I am claiming it anyway! All these years after he had played for Ayr United I still felt inspired by Davy Stewart and I was still wearing an all-black goalkeeping kit right down to my footwear. I even had an Ayr United badge sewn onto the jersey. The trophy was never defended. Aggressive flare-ups during matches was the reason for scrapping it.

Would Ayr United make an immediate return to the First Division? After what had just been experienced there was a fear that it might just happen. We had been relegated with St.Mirren who were now clear favourites to win the Second

Division. However in our League Cup section we beat them home and away. In the quarter-finals we had an 8-2 aggregate defeat against Celtic. This caused no particular angst since little else was expected against the European champions. The *Daily Record*, reporting on the 2-0 second leg at Ayr, had this to say: "In the 17th minute of the second half Jim Brogan scored. Until that goal the tall Ayr keeper David Stewart had been almost contemptuous of Celtic's efforts."

St.Mirren and Arbroath set the pace for the two promotion places. With Ayr United third there was still a chance, especially with Arbroath losing a four-pointer at Ayr two days before Christmas. Around this time I had a supreme piece of luck. The Saturday Sports edition of the *Evening Citizen* used to have what was known as the Boys' Gate competition (as if they'd get away with that now). It worked on a simple premise whereby you had to send in the answers to a couple of football questions and your name would go into a draw. This was not very testing. It was virtually impossible not to know the correct answers. The five names drawn would win the complete replica strip of their choice. Replica strips were a rarity at this time. Terracing crowds still typically wore a jacket, shirt and tie while youngsters, myself included, turned up in a school blazer. I had friends who had experienced numerous failed attempts to win this great prize. The one time I entered I won. A letter was duly received for presentation at Greaves Sports in Glasgow. My father phoned up to ask if they had the Ayr United kit in stock and the answer was no. Dad then said that he had seen it in the window of Allan Stevenson's in Ayr. It transpired that the chap in Glasgow knew Allan Stevenson and he said that he would phone him and sort it out with no problem. It was a wonderful prize comprising a black and white-hooped shirt, white shorts and black and white hooped socks.

There was a common public perception that Ayr United performed poorly over the New Year holiday period because the players were imbibing too freely.

30th December, 1967 – Berwick Rangers 1 Ayr United 0,
1st January, 1968 – Ayr United 0 St.Mirren 3,
2nd January, 1968 – Queen of the South 4 Ayr United 0.

The argument was given credence but it just had to be nonsense. Although not always reflected in the results Ally MacLeod was a strict disciplinarian. In the year of writing Ayr United supporters have bad memories of Palmerston Park. I was at that game in 1968 and it does not even count as the biggest trouncing I have witnessed there.

There was a bit of a ritual surrounding travel to away games. On Thursday nights prior to away games on the Saturday, supporters had to turn up at the Somerset Park gymnasium in order to book a seat on a Supporters' Association bus. If the numbers were insufficient there would be no bus. I can remember waiting there in the fervent hope that a few more would appear in order to reach the threshold number. These buses always left from John Street.

> "Promotion chances are now slim" – *Ayr Advertiser*, January 1968.

> "Promotion chances shattered" – *Ayr Advertiser*, March 1968.

For some of us the promotion chances still existed. It had to be do-able. Then the reality bit with run-in defeats away to Forfar Athletic, Stranraer, Brechin City and East Stirling. Finishing fifth gave lie to the misguided belief that is so often the default emotion of the rabid supporter.

Somerset Park had a shabby look. At the railway end the terracing was comprised of railway sleepers that used to shift if there was any appreciable crowd movement. Crush barriers throughout the ground were flimsy and a lot of weeds were visible. Visiting supporters used to mock what they thought were the floodlights. The mirth would increase when it was explained that they weren't floodlights at all, just training lights. Outside of the stand the only cover was at the railway end. Even the music played over the tannoy was dated. Had the place really depreciated since 1959 or had I fallen into the trap of remembering it as being better than it actually was? What did it matter? This was 1968. All that mattered was the first team result.

New signings were Jacky Ferguson and Bobby Rough. Davy McCulloch had been signed on the last day of March, at which point the season was a lost cause. Now we would see him in games that mattered. The club had brushed aside offers for Alex Ingram. He was a hero to the fans for his 'run through a brick wall' style. I was blind to any shortcomings. Would this be the season for promotion? Admittedly the heart ruled the head in believing it would.

For the fourth consecutive season the League Cup quarter-finals were reached. Alas for the fourth consecutive season we lost at that stage, this time against Clyde. In the first leg a 1-0 home defeat was watched by 7,942. This was fantastic on what was for me a school night literally and metaphorically. The second leg was lost 2-0 and I can recall overhearing a Clyde supporter mention to somebody in the car park that their striker, Harry Hood, was earmarked for Celtic. In the Second Division an obstacle to our progress was Motherwell, a club that had been considered too big to get relegated.

Ayr United 7 Stenhousemuir 1. This was the match in which Dick Malone became the only Ayr United player to score a hat-trick while playing as a full-back. The Stenhousemuir left winger who was in direct opposition to him was Iain Ritchie. My cousin from Grangemouth was a friend of his and he was permitted to come to the game in the Stenhousemuir team bus. The plan was that the two of them would stop off at our house in Prestwick for the rest of the weekend. This was a long time before John Cleese said: "Don't mention the war." Well, to paraphrase John Cleese, it was a matter of: "Don't mention the game." We tried our best to be diplomatic but it was just a little bit subdued at the tea table.

1968/69 was a season when I started to get to more away games, sometimes by the Supporters' Club bus and sometimes by train. Sometimes too by getting a lift from my good friends the Nelsons. A particularly magic trip was to Dumbarton in November. I have singled out this one because we had a 3-0 win and it was a good day overall. One highlight occurred in Central Station on the way home. That day's football results were being displayed in neon lights on a loop. There was a crowd of us and we greeted the Ayr United result with a cheer. Good times were on their way and people could sense it. A week before that match at Boghead we had beaten Forfar Athletic 4-1 at Ayr. In the home team that day was a Junior trialist called Rikki Fleming. The future was starting to build.

From 23rd November, 1968, until 1st March, 1969, we had eleven consecutive league wins. This was one short of the club record set in 1936/37. The fans neither knew nor cared about the impact on club records. How it affected the league table was all that mattered. At the start of the run we were ninth and at the end of it we were third. Motherwell were rampant at the top. We were six points behind second-placed Stirling Albion with three games in hand.

During the weeks covered by that league run there was a sobering Scottish Cup experience at Tannadice in February. The Dundee United versus Ayr United tie was played with the same kick-off time as the Dundee versus Arbroath fixture in the First Division. Two matches on either side of the road at the same time! I crossed the road to get a programme from the Dundee game. I was wearing a black and white scarf which was mistaken for a Dundee United scarf because they too had black and white as their club colours then. A request to "Get aff oor street" sounded jocular. Less jocular was a 6-2 defeat.

A 2-1 defeat away to East Stirling ended a long unbeaten league run. The home team even had the temerity to field two trialists, one of whom scored. An elderly Ayr United supporter on our bus mentioned that he had been speaking to East Stirling manager Ian Crawford after the match. The conversation must have aroused some great memories. Ian Crawford was Ayr United's top scorer in seasons 1950/51 and 1951/52. He also holds the club record for scoring the most League Cup goals in a single season, thirteen in 1950/51.

With four games left we needed two points to guarantee the second promotion spot. Those stakes encouraged a crowd of 7,694 to turn up for a midweek home match against Motherwell. We took the lead with an own goal in 71 minutes but four minutes later it was 1-1 and that was how it ended. Not to worry. A point at Dumfries on the Saturday would do. Four minutes into the second half we went 2-0 up. Promotion was being celebrated. Prematurely! We lost 3-2. I was travelling with Hugh and Helen Nelson and Helen's brother Douglas Symington. We had the car radio on but the airwaves were clogged up with news about the Celtic versus Rangers Scottish Cup final. Then came the classified check. Forfar Athletic 3 East Fife 2 : Motherwell 3 Stirling Albion 0. This meant that East Fife and Stirling Albion had both finished their fixtures on forty-eight points. With two games left we were in second place on forty-nine and could not be caught. Promotion was won and we were appraised of this somewhere near Thornhill.

Ian Crawford stalled our promotion drive in 1969. Here he is in action for Ayr United versus Motherwell in the 1950 League Cup semi-finals at Ibrox. His face is hidden by an elbow. The team mates to the right are Willie Gallagher then Alec Beattie.

6. The Dawn of a New Decade and New Hope

It was a great feeling to know that the club was back in the First Division even although the bitter memory of 1966/67 was still fresh. We were better equipped (easy to say with the substantial benefit of hindsight!). Another nice feeling was the anticipation about which English club we would see in a pre-season friendly. This was much better than the outdated and boring tradition of the public trial match which clubs had now scrapped. On the Saturday prior to the start of the League Cup campaign clubs would allow free admission to their ground (free except for a charity donation). The match on view would typically be labelled as Possibles versus Probables or Stripes versus Hoops. In reality we were watching Ayr United versus Ayr United. The pre-season friendly was much better. In 1966 we had Blackburn Rovers at Ayr (1-3) then Halifax Town in 1968 (2-2). Well, the Halifax game was supposed to be a friendly but it was a bruiser of a match. In 1969 we played Bolton Wanderers at Ayr (1-2). Cutty Young, a new signing from Kello Rovers, had a scintillating debut on the right wing against Bolton. Judging by the encouraging shouts from the crowd it was apparent that he was known by a lot of people. With due allowance for it being a friendly, it was an historic day because, for the first time, the starting line-up was the one which trips off the tongue even today. As if you need a reminder it was Stewart, Malone, Murphy, Fleming, Quinn, Mitchell, Young, Ferguson, Ingram, McCulloch and Rough.

Ayr United FC 1969/70.

Habitually Ayr United could be relied upon to negotiate the League Cup sectional stage then lose in the quarter-finals. Habits can be broken and in 1969 the semi-finals were reached for the first time since 1950 and only the second time in our history. The opposition was Celtic. Who present will ever forget the 3-3 draw after extra time at Hampden? The 2-1 defeat in the replay was a travesty but you will be spared the list of injustices.

Hibs at home was a tough league opener. At least it was supposed to be. Cutty Young got sent off for retaliation in the first half and we still won 3-0. On the morning of the match there was so much talk about this game in our house that my mother went to see what all the fuss was about. It was the one and only time she entered Somerset Park but she did enjoy the experience. She used to knit me black and white bob hats. It always fascinated me how she used a cardboard disc to make a pom pom. My oldest brother Peter had departed the family nest to attend Heriot-Watt University so this gave him the opportunity to get along to Easter Road yet he has now been a Somerset Road end regular for a lot of years. My middle brother Douglas was a Somerset Park regular, even through the horrors of 1964, but he had Hibs leanings and eventually settled in Edinburgh and became a season ticket holder. My father had seen some of the great Hibs teams of the post war years and now had an Ayr United season ticket but above all else he only ever wanted to see a good game. Admittedly I had a two-team allegiance – Ayr United and Ayr United reserves!

A fortnight after the Hibs game Rangers were here on what has to be the most memorable day at Somerset Park ever. I was stood at the turnstiles just inside the main gate busily engaged in selling half-time draw tickets along with Ian McPherson and Douglas Symington. Long before kick-off time we made a decision to get away from there. It was a heaving mass of populace. People were squeezing under turnstiles and clambering over walls to gain entry to the ground by any means possible. No one had thought to make the match all-ticket. The official crowd figure of 25,225 takes no cognisance of the true number in the ground. What was the true number?

OFFICIAL PROGRAMME

HIBERNIAN

No. 15 Kick-Off 3.00 p.m.
AYR UNITED

Nº 4473

We will never know. I watched the game while sat on stairs in the stand and still wearing the white coat issued to half-time draw sellers. Periodically press men would rush past to phone in reports from the telephones in the concourse area. So many spectators were sat on the track that there was an illusion of there being no boundary wall. The Rangers support was huge although it was impossible to discern the number accurately in those pre-segregation days. Goals from Cutty Young and Jacky Ferguson meant that we were 2-0 up inside the first quarter of an hour. Colin Stein's goal came too late to save Rangers from a 2-1 defeat. There was further drama post match. In order that the vast crowd could be got out as easily as possible, fans were shepherded along the track in front of the stand so that they could exit via the main gate. The spectacle of this was too good an opportunity for the Ayr support in the stand and an 'Easy Easy' chant was started. This went down very badly with the Rangers support and suddenly bottles were being lobbed into the stand. I have experienced so many memorable days at Somerset Park but 13th September, 1969, remains the most unforgettable.

Emotions were liable to run high not only behind the goal but in other areas of the ground too. Stand patrons were, in general, deemed to be sedate. This sweeping generalisation did not apply at Ayr because there was a lot of partisanship within the stand support. When Hearts were here in October 1969 the volatility of the crowd was expressed on all four sides. The attendance was 10,061. In the first half Jim Cruickshank saved a penalty from Dick Malone and, in the late stages, it remained scoreless. In the 84th minute Peter Oliver, the Hearts left-back, fouled Cutty Young yet again! Referee Harry Dempsey's continued leniency towards Oliver was mystifying. It stretched credulity that Oliver's name did not find its way into the black book this time. Cutty attempted to push Oliver off and he was sent off for this. What happened next was closer to a riot than anything I have ever witnessed at Somerset Park. The crowd was rightly enraged at the injustice. Bottles and an assortment of other missiles rained onto the pitch. The vocal abuse aimed at the Hearts man and the referee was deafening. It finished 0-0 but thousands stayed back to let the referee know what they thought of him. He got a police escort off the pitch. That was not the end of it. The police escorted him back to his car and stuck with him until he was clear of Whitletts.

A week after that furore a 1-0 win away to Clyde meant that the club had now beaten the First Division points total for the entire 1966/67 season. Yet I still managed to harbour a bitter memory of that day at Shawfield. Before entering the ground it was necessary to endure the sight of Celtic buses passing by on their way to Hampden for the League Cup final. If there had been any justice in the world then it would have been us.

In November Alex Ingram played for the Scottish League in a 5-2 win against the Irish League at Ibrox. I was one of the paltry crowd of 4,400. A fortnight later I absented myself from Hampden when 5,004 watched Scotland beat France 4-0 in an under-23 international in which Dick Malone played. It was so pleasing to see the club get international recognition considering that we were part time and our ground still had no floodlights.

On the second Saturday of December I had a feeling of trepidation while standing on the vast Easter Road terracing. After losing their opening league game at Ayr, Hibs had lost just one other fixture and they were now top of the First Division. The first half was crazy. It was 4-3 for Hibs at half-time and the score stayed that way. To this point of the season Hibs had the best defensive record in the Scottish League with fifteen conceded, six of which were scored by Ayr United. Alex Ingram was missing through an injury suffered at Perth. Then, on the Saturday before Christmas, came the news that he had been sold to Nottingham Forest. The sense of loss was tempered by the fact that Neil Hood had scored twice at Easter Road. Over the New Year holiday period it was gratifying to have a 3-2 win at home to Kilmarnock. Our injury situation was so bad that the worst had been feared. Ronnie McColl, deputising for Bobby Rough, hit the winner in the 88th minute. His name remained synonymous with that goal.

The opinion that you cannot blame referees has always been a commonly held belief. An opinion is never wrong but that does not mean that others cannot be otherwise minded. On 17th January, 1970, I was stood in the stand enclosure at Ibrox. My stance was near the tunnel and therefore a good vantage point. Ten minutes into the second half, with the game still at 0-0, Colin Stein attempted a diving header but it was outwith the reach of headed contact. Instinctively, or mischievously, he fisted the ball into the net. The goal stood! Nearly as irritating was the manner in which the Old Firm-centric press reported it. That night's *Evening Times* described the incident thus: "There was an appeal for hands by Ayr, but for my money, from where I was sitting, it was a good goal scored by a player who acts on the spur of the moment." On the Monday the *Glasgow Herald* report backed the referee's decision on the grounds that "he was ideally placed to judge." Journalistic standards had plumbed the same depths as refereeing standards. By now I was studying for my Highers and such horrible distractions were unhelpful. At times I really had to put Ayr United out of my mind but it was impossibly difficult. Hypnotherapy would not even have worked!

On the first Saturday of March we conceded two penalties in a match at Tynecastle. Both were converted then a goal in the last minute put the seal on a 3-0 defeat. I was standing at the Gorgie Road end when the first penalty was awarded at the opposite end. The Hearts supporters were in a state of disbelief not because they thought it soft (Rikki Fleming handled it) but because it was a month short of two years since they had been given a penalty. Six minutes later their penalty drought was well and truly put to bed when they got another one. Even from a distant vantage point it could be seen that Stan Quinn had indeed brought down Rene Moller. Stan, though, was adamant that the offence had taken place outside the box. It was just unfortunate that Ayr United had to be the team to reacquaint Hearts supporters with the penalty kick experience.

A perk of being a half-time draw seller was being allowed to travel to two games in the team bus that season. My chosen games were Clyde in October and Raith Rovers in April. This provided a nice insight. The most common adjective in description of Ally MacLeod was ebullient. Not that any of us needed a description. We all knew what he was like. The morale on the team bus was sky high. On the way to Kirkcaldy he was handed a letter that had arrived at Somerset Park that morning. After opening it and perusing it he declared that it was a letter asking Ayr United to lie down to the relegation threatened Partick Thistle a fortnight later. Our 1-1 draw against Raith Rovers was enough to confirm relegation for the home club. Partick Thistle were confirmed for relegation even before they came to Ayr, not that there was a chance of the plea for mercy being anything other than laughed at. We won 2-1 anyway. In finishing comfortably above the relegation places it was like a different world compared to three years earlier.

The programme market was still operating briskly at Ayr Academy and the joint collection belonging to Douglas Symington and I had grown to 3,000 at a very rough estimate. Both in Scotland and England the standard of match programmes was mediocre but at Ayr it was positively grim. The programme was produced by the Supporters' Association and we planned a coup at that year's annual general meeting. There was a tacit acceptance that when an office bearer's post came up for re-election they would be re-elected as a matter of routine. The status quo was disturbed when the programme convener sought re-election. Douglas Symington's name was put forward and the motion was carried because we had made sure that he would have enough support to win a show of hands. The chairman made a remark about this being a "new name". Part one of the grand plan had succeeded. Then came part two. Douglas and I sat in his house and designed a dummy programme by means of paper, cellotape, sticky paper, pens and crayons. We wanted colour on the cover. This immediately railed against the club colours of black and white so we opted for blue and yellow. As far as we were aware we were not possessed of any particular artistic temperament but, whether by luck or good judgement, we were delighted by the cover design which we produced. We pencilled in dummy articles and glued in some photographs. The end product was rudimentary but nonetheless impressive in view of the tools at our disposal. It was 1970 after all. At a Supporters' Association committee meeting this prototype made a favourable impression. Ayr United would now have a new-style programme which was ahead of its time. It had an editor aged eighteen (Douglas) and an assistant editor aged seventeen (myself). I was still at school.

Douglas Symington (left) and myself planning a revamp of the match programme.

As a means of researching programme articles I started to comb through old newspapers in Carnegie Library. It truly amazed me that a vast amount of Ayr United history had remained untapped. There was an absolute wealth of material that was crying out to be in the public domain. This was the birth of my passion for researching, writing about and recording the club's history. There was no shortcut to doing this type of research accurately. It required spending an inestimable amount of time in libraries but it was a pleasurable experience. Anyone relying on AI for accurate information does so at their peril.

John Doyle

I recall a school colleague telling me that Ayr United had signed John Doyle. The feeling was one of disappointment. He was an unknown who had been playing for Viewpark Boys' Guild. What could he contribute in the First Division? I was certainly glad to have called this one wrong. His pace, skill and sheer determination turned him into one of the finest players to have ever graced an Ayr United shirt.

That summer the installation of floodlights took place. It would be November before they were officially hanselled in a 2-0 win against Newcastle United. It stands to reason that even if they had been constructed sooner it would have been impractical to use them in the summer anyway. The sight of the four giant pylons was magnificent. They were so imposing that they could be viewed from miles around, even as far away as the Hansel Village.

The League Cup heroics of a year earlier would not be repeated in 1970 but the league programme got off to a flyer with a 4-1 win at home to Dunfermline Athletic. Ian Whitehead, signed from Queen's Park in the summer, was reminiscent of the departed Alex Ingram. He scored a first half hat-trick. With Cutty Young on one wing and John Doyle on the other he got good service. Ally MacLeod was obsessive about attacking football. Hopes were high. A fortnight later there was an extraordinary incident during a 1-1 draw at home to Kilmarnock. Near the end of the match Killie's Ross Mathie went to take a throw-in on the farside, roughly in line with the eighteen-yard line at the railway end. He stepped back as if to imply that he was going to launch the ball into the penalty box. I was watching from the distant vantage point of the Somerset Road end. From there it looked as if he had taken a step back too many whereupon he had fallen backwards over the wall. I left the match in the belief that he had fallen over the wall through his own momentum. In actual fact he had been pulled over the wall by an Ayr United supporter. If you talk to Ross today he will tell you that Stan Quinn was the first person on the scene to extricate him from the situation. Somewhat unjustly he is more remembered for this episode than he is for the goals he scored.

Ayr United versus Kilmarnock on 12th September, 1970. Kilmarnock's Ross Mathie was pulled over the wall while trying to take a throw-in. Our own Stan Quinn was first in line to extricate him from his predicament.

In the same month I left school to work in a surveying practice in Irvine. My boss was a Kilmarnock supporter who was quite gracious where Ayr United were concerned, even attending a lot of our matches. I was not gracious enough to reciprocate. The visit of Rangers in November evoked memories of their previous game at Ayr when the ground was packed beyond bursting point. This time the crowd was more manageable at 17,634. The result was the same though – Ayr United 2 Rangers 1.

21st November, 1970. Ayr United 2 Rangers 1.

Christmas Day 1970 was no doubt a wonderful day although I have no recollection of it. Unfortunately I do have a recollection of being at Dunfermline for a 5-0 defeat on Boxing Day. The fickle nature of football intervened to ensure that Ayr United supporters everywhere were lifted from despair to elation just several days later. Dixie was back. Alex Ingram was purchased back from Nottingham Forest. The elation went into overdrive when he scored a sixth minute goal at home to Morton on New Year's Day. After winning 2-1 we had a match at Kilmarnock the next day. Ten minutes from the end Phil McGovern equalised to make it level at 1-1. It was the one and only time in my life that I have been in a crowd that swayed in a manner consistent with the Kop at Liverpool. When the goal celebration started to settle down I found myself much further down the terracing. At the time it seemed amusing but that evening's news changed that perspective. This was the same day as the Ibrox disaster.

Knocked out of the Scottish Cup at Cappielow! Sucked into a relegation battle!

I was seated next to Ross Mathie at the Festive Friends Lunch in 2024. Mindful of the 1970 incident I tried my best to perfect a look that said "It wisnae me."

Oh well at least there was 20th March to look forward to. I had never been to Aberdeen before far less Pittodrie. Aberdeen were top of the league and serious title contenders. There was talk of a postponement due to ground conditions. Surely not at this time of the season! I set out very early on the Saturday morning with my friend Douglas. The first leg of the journey was the train to Glasgow and we draped our Ayr United scarves over the compartment windows. At Irvine we noticed the Ayr United squad on the southbound platform amidst the team hamper. Tommy Reynolds had noticed the scarves and he frantically made signals to confirm what we had already deduced. Game off! The pitch was waterlogged. It was the only postponement in the entire British leagues that day. It was rescheduled to the immediate midweek which was out of the question by rail but we lost 4-1 anyway.

20th February, 1971. Tommy Reynolds has just clinched it at 2-0 versus Hibs.

Bottom club Cowdenbeath were correctly assumed to be goners. The dreaded second relegation place had to be avoided and it was. The gap with Kilmarnock had closed substantially since the extremes of 1965. If, as expected, we had beaten Cowdenbeath at home in the penultimate league fixture we would have finished above Kilmarnock. The sorry result was a 2-1 defeat. Yet 1970/71 concluded with winning the Ayrshire Cup for the third consecutive season. It happened after a penalty shootout at Rugby Park (technically these are not penalties because no offence has been committed). This was the second ever penalty shootout in Scotland so it was novel to witness it.

20th March, 1971. The Aberdeen trip was aborted so the alternative was the Reserve League match between the clubs at Ayr. Ian Hume is on the point of scoring.

With the season over I was able to reflect on my first Wembley trip. The train ticket was from Kilmarnock to Wembley Central and it cost £6 return. As for the match ticket it cost 80p. It was a modest outlay for a 3-1 defeat. Some of you may remember Nancy Martin who was a stalwart of the Supporters' Association. She asked me how much I had paid for my ticket and she was shocked at how expensive it was. For her last Wembley trip the price was 1/6d. That's inflation for you.

The summer of 1970 had seen transformative change with the construction of floodlight pylons at Somerset Park. A further transformation took place in the summer of 1971 with a roof being constructed at the Somerset Road end. The Supporters' Association ran the catering and the match programme as well as organising buses for away games. As a committee member I could see the industrious efforts being made by like-minded volunteers. We also started selling Ayr United souvenirs such as badges, photographs and pennants. Initially this was done from a tiny outlet close to the hospital broadcasting studio. The committee decided to exploit the potential of this humble enterprise. A garage was purchased from Fleming's of Crosshouse then deposited sideways at the back of the north terrace. The directors were appalled and its removal was ordered. There was a cautious change of mood when it was explained that extensive alterations to the structure would transform it into a programme and souvenir shop. In an act of entrepreneurial brilliance it was decided to ask the makers of Black & White whisky to commission and pay for the sign. The deal was simple. Perched on the roof the sign bore the legend Black & White Shop as well as an illustration of the black and white dogs from the whisky label. It was a form of free advertising to them. They even honoured an agreement to replace the sign whenever it became weather beaten. The end product was so good that we advertised it as Scotland's Premier Programme and Souvenir Shop. It could be argued that it was a team effort but one man in particular is deserving of special praise. That man was Hugh Nelson who worked tirelessly to maintain the shop's superb stock. Somewhat poignantly his funeral tea in 2019 was held in the Ally MacLeod Suite which covered the former site of the shop. Being one of the volunteers in the shop was a pleasurable experience. It was open on match days up until kick-off time then re-opened at half-time and again after the match. So many interesting characters used to introduce themselves.

The Black and White Shop just after completion but prior to the sign being mounted on the roof. Left to right: Myself, Douglas Symington and his sister Helen Nelson.

People could purchase the away programme from the previous week. This once had comical consequences for a match at Falkirk. The home club would not allow a discount for a bulk purchase. This, allied to postage costs, would have meant selling the programme at a loss. It was decided to just purchase them at the match. Hugh's wife Helen approached the smallest and youngest looking programme seller and asked for sixty. This exhausted her stock and a couple of colleagues had to pitch in.

The first match played before a covered Somerset Road end was a very unfriendly 'friendly' against Sunderland. It had been arranged as part of the deal for the sale of Dick Malone the previous October. The roof was a handsome addition yet it still felt unnatural to be standing under cover at that end. Various drenchings down through the years were now a memory. In victory it had hardly mattered. In defeat it compounded the misery.

The draw for the League Cup sections was tough in the extreme. We had Rangers, Celtic and Morton. You need hardly guess who the two contenders were in that group. Losing against the Old Firm was always a horrible experience but it was hardly the fault of the big two clubs that they were written about sycophantically by the fawning media. Even our recent successes against Rangers had caused them to replenish their stock of patronising adjectives. In writing about these supposed "shocks" it was a certainty that we would be described as "Plucky Ayr" or, even worse, "Wee Ayr."

An early season league win at Kilmarnock gave rise to hope that at last we would finish above them in the league. Alas it was destined not to happen in 1971/72 but the gap was goal difference only. Regular away days continued to be a joy or, rather, some of them did. Airdrie in October would be remembered for decades. We were 3-1 down with twenty-five minutes to go. Johnny Graham scored all four in our 4-3 comeback win. With no segregation in force some of our supporters had hostile verbal exchanges with the notorious Section B fans in the home support. Mercifully the lid was kept on the tension.

East Fife was a great trip in this season and the next. It involved changing trains in Glasgow for Edinburgh then changing at Edinburgh for Kirkcaldy then completing the final leg by bus. Allowing enough time for stopovers in Edinburgh before and after really did turn it into the complete day. I have often argued against the 'great day out' philosophy on the grounds that nothing matters other than the result. However I am willing to stand accused of hypocrisy by admitting to some great overall days when travelling to Ayr United away games The day can be topped off by something as simple as an ice cream or fish supper at Largs on the way back from Cappielow.

After the day of the Airdrie comeback we did not win another game until Christmas Day. Ayr United's last game on

Christmas Day was this one in 1971. Fortunately my mother agreed to having the Christmas dinner in the evening. Very fortunately! Our 1-0 win had not been expected. In their previous home match Partick Thistle had scored eight against Motherwell. The programme for the Ayr game had a photograph of the Partick Thistle players at a Civic Reception hosted for their League Cup win. On the day they had won it we had a match at Perth. At half-time the scores were slotted into the scoreboard and the alphabetical key in the St.Johnstone programme showed Celtic to be the designated 'home' team at Hampden. When 0-4 got slotted in there was the reasonable assumption that the numbers had been put in back to front. This was not so and Partick Thistle went on to win 4-1. Morale was restored with our Christmas win at Firhill. Then we had a 3-0 win away to Morton on New Year's Day 1972. The journey home was made all the more pleasant by the anticipation of the traditional steak pie awaiting.

Ayr United 4 East Fife 0 was the team's first home league win since beating Morton in the opening fixture. The date was 11th March. Ten days earlier we had lost at Motherwell in a Scottish Cup replay played on a Wednesday afternoon due to the frequency of power cuts potentially impacting on the floodlights. An understanding boss gave me the time off. It was an afternoon of frustration. Motherwell scored from a penalty awarded after Kirkie Lawson had fouled Davy Stewart who had to get treatment before facing the spot kick. That was their equaliser in a 2-1 home win.

The aborted Pittodrie trip of 1971 was now on for 8th April, 1972. From memory the train fare was more than £4 which was a hefty outlay for the time. This was partially offset by being able to get complimentary tickets for the game. Distant games with a lesser travelling support invariably created the offer of such tickets provided you were there on the arrival of the team bus. The result was a 7-0 defeat. On the return journey I was in a compartment with some other Ayr United supporters when a woman entered in search of a seat. She said: "I'm sorry to disturb you". The retort from one of our number was: "It's okay. We've had rather a disturbing afternoon."

Ayr United FC 1972/73: Rear left to right: Bobby Tait, Davy Wells, Jim Jackson, Alex McAnespie, Davy Stewart, Jim McFadzean, Rikki Fleming, George McLean and Jim Flynn. Middle left to right: Willie Wallace, Brian Lannon, Stan Quinn, Ian Campbell, Joe Filippi, Ally McLean, Alex McGregor, Jim Grier, John Murphy, Phil McGovern and Willie McCulloch. Front left to right: Davy Robertson, Bobby Rough, John Doyle, Dougie Mitchell, Sam McMillan, Alex Ingram, Ally MacLeod, Johnny Graham, Hugh Thompson, Tommy Reynolds and Davy McCulloch.

At Pittodrie George McLean had a tendency to get caught offside repeatedly. One week later he scored four in a 4-2 win at home to Dundee United. A fortnight later Johnny Graham scored four for the second time that season. This was in a comprehensive 4-0 win against Partick Thistle. It was a season of wild inconsistency. We turned up not knowing what to expect.

On the Monday evening of 1st May, 1972, an intriguing choice presented itself. The final league game of the season was at Ibrox and we required a draw to qualify for the Texaco Cup. At the same time there was a Reserve League fixture at Celtic Park in which our reserves required a win to clinch the Reserve League title. I opted for Ibrox where a 2-1 half-time lead turned into a 4-2 defeat. Fortuitously we qualified for the Texaco Cup anyway because the uneasy situation in Northern Ireland caused their four clubs to withdraw. Ibrox was ghostly on the night of that match. Media sources estimated the attendance as 3,000. The official figure was 5,869. From personal testimony the estimated figure looked more accurate. Later that month Rangers took a vast support to Barcelona for the final of the European Cup Winners Cup. Over at Celtic Park our reserves won 3-2 to become the reserve champions of Scotland.

A returfing operation meant that we were to be denied a home friendly against English opposition. The squad headed south for matches at Cambridge and Stevenage. The work at Somerset Park availed itself of a novel opportunity. League Cup sectional ties against St.Mirren and Clydebank were played and won at Dam Park. Our 'home' match against Rangers was played at Rugby Park. The away game against Rangers was mired in controversy reminiscent of the Colin Stein incident in 1970. Again my stance was the terracing area near the tunnel. With the game balanced at 1-1 Davy Stewart grabbed a bouncing ball high up. Derek Parlane then rushed in and barged him. They both landed on the ground. Parlane then knocked the ball from Davy Stewart's grasp and squeezed it over the line. In expectation of a free-kick to Ayr even the

Rangers support was muted. Diabolically the goal stood. Stan Quinn got booked for his protests and so did Johnny Graham. With justification Graham did not leave it at that and he got sent off for his remonstrations. On the touchline Ally MacLeod voiced his protests and the referee booked him too. Ten minutes remained and it finished 2-1. We also lost 2-1 in the Rugby Park rematch but glorious revenge was about to unfold just days later. Our return to Somerset Park coincided with the start of the league programme. Ayr United 2 Rangers 1 was the pleasing outcome. Less pleasing was the *Evening Times* report that referred to "Little Ayr". Rangers had been beaten at Ayr in 1969, 1970 and now again in 1972. What more was required to become accepted? A week later we had a 1-0 win at Kilmarnock. Maybe, just maybe, it was the dawn of a great season. The penalty, of course, would be to get persistently patronised by the national media.

Newcastle United was another exciting trip in prospect. The first leg of our Texaco Cup tie was drawn 0-0 at Ayr. The threat of Malcolm MacDonald, nicknamed Supermac, had been nullified. A fortnight later he was absent through injury. Before the return match he could be seen walking across the car park on crutches. At 1-0 down and having hit the underside of the bar, the tie was alive until Newcastle concluded the scoring at 2-0 with three minutes left. Yet the experience of watching Ayr United at a top flight English ground was surreal. On the Saturday prior the then mighty Leeds United had lost 3-2 at Newcastle.

It was hard to believe that Ayr United were still part time. Schoolteacher Jim McFadzean did not travel to Newcastle because he could not get time off. His replacement was Drew Rogerson who was making his debut. The logic behind the club's strategy may have been sound. A day job wage plus a football wage combined to make the players comparatively well paid.

Supporting Ayr United is a pursuit requiring an ability to accept the rough with the smooth. Yet mere acceptance is difficult when things do not go well. In December 1972

I was there to witness Hibs 8 Ayr United 1. This may be categorised with the other horror matches I have witnessed through the gaps between my fingers. It was reminiscent of the 7-0 at Aberdeen earlier in 1972 and the 7-0 at home to Dundee United in 1966. The 7-0 debacle at home to Inverness Caledonian Thistle in 2010 was yet a long way off. 1972/73 was a good season for Ayr United so what went wrong at Easter Road? It would be more appropriate to ask what went right for Hibs. I was at the 1972 Scottish Cup final in which Celtic had destroyed Hibs 6-1. In December the clubs met at Hampden in the League Cup final. Hibs won. This was the week before the Ayr game. To tumultuous applause the Hibs players did a lap of honour with the League Cup shortly before the kick-off. Then Alex Cropley scored a goal timed at eleven seconds from the start. The place was in an absolute frenzy. It was 7-0 by the 56th minute. There was a genuine fear of conceding ten. It went to 8-1 with nearly twenty minutes to go. Normal service was resumed by beating Airdrie at Ayr in the next match.

With due allowance for the Easter Road aberration these were good times to be supporting Ayr United. This perception is not formed by seeing the past through those metaphorical rose-tinted spectacles. The results and performances were there to prove it.

There is a saying that you should be careful what you wish for. This is a direct reference to my earliest Pittodrie experiences. A yearning to see Ayr United play there was rewarded with an aborted trip in 1971, a 7-0 trouncing in 1972 and a 1-0 defeat in 1973. The 1973 defeat was agonising. Drew Jarvie won the match with a header in stoppage time. The referee than had time only to signal the goal, book John Doyle and restart the game before blowing the final whistle. It was a long and reflective rail journey home. Ally MacLeod remained optimistic. We believed him. It was immaterial whether we believed him only because we wanted to. We won the next six games thereby justifying the faith. One match stood out from that run. Ayr United had never reached a Scottish Cup semi-final in the club's history. This miserable record stood to be put right if the team could win at Firhill. Would this be the year? Partick Thistle took an early lead and fighting soon broke out between the respective sets of fans. Innocent people got caught up in the crossfire. Archie Scott, bus convenor of the Ayr United Supporters' Association, was led away with blood streaming from his head. I used to love getting involved in conversation with Archie. He could clearly recall watching Ayr United in the 1920s. Archie once mentioned that he went on a special train to watch the team at Forfar on New Year's Day 1937. Surely this was an odd place to be playing on a traditional derby day? Regardless it did happen and Ayr United won 5-0. With a mild apology for going off on a tangent you may now be told that the result at Firhill was Partick Thistle 1 Ayr United 5. By the closing stages I felt absolutely intoxicated despite coffee being the strongest drink I had that weekend.

The semi-final was against Rangers at Hampden. It got underway with surface water still on the pitch. Little did we care about the pitch when Alex Ingram headed a Davy Wells free-kick past Peter McCloy in the first minute. Then came a chastening reminder that we were playing an Old Firm team in Glasgow. Disallowed for offside! This was highly dubious. A media-appeasing 2-0 Rangers win was the result. You may sense a hint of petulance in these words. There was due cause for feeling bitter.

On taking stock of 1972/73 it was the best season that most of our supporters could remember. A sixth-placed First Division finish had been bettered by finishing fourth in 1915/16. Yet memories of 1916 would hardly have invoked football as the main recollection. By factoring in the Scottish Cup run it became a fair claim that 1972/73 was the best season ever.

The last game of the season was a 1-0 win at foot-of-the-table Airdrie. It looked as if Airdrie would be joined in relegation by Dumbarton. On that afternoon Kilmarnock blew a 2-0 lead to draw 2-2 at home to Falkirk while Dumbarton were beating Dundee United 4-1 at Boghead. Ayr United supporters at Airdrie did not glory in Kilmarnock's demise. This was not through empathy to the Kilmarnock cause but rather through not being aware of it. Even a transistor radio would have been of little avail because the airwaves were probably choked with sycophantic soundbites about Celtic clinching eight-in-a row. I did not know that Kilmarnock had been relegated until I got home from Airdrie. Eight years earlier it would have been insane even to think about Ayr United being a league above Kilmarnock.

It was a mark of the club's progress that John Doyle was in the Scotland squad for the Wembley international. He was still part time. In future years a recollection of Wembley 1973 was rather rewarding. In 2021 my employer (Tesco Bank) staged a writing competition to commemorate the Euros. The competition worked on the simple premise of writing about a footballing memory. In keeping with the international theme I decided to compile a Scotland memory rather than an Ayr United one. Writing for fun can have its rewards and this was most emphatically the case. The reward was not so much a prize as a prize haul. I was grateful to receive fifteen bottles of beer, a bottle of champagne, family packs of crisps, Doritos, Pringles and savoury biscuits, a wall mounted bottle opener, an ice bucket, Euro 2020 bunting and a £50 voucher for Tesco. I had to clear the fridge of non essentials such as milk and butter in order to accommodate the beer! You may now read the winning story.

The scene is a tube train heading from the city centre in London out to Wembley Central. It is a lunchtime Saturday in 1973 and with Scotland playing England that afternoon the train is understandably packed. I was one of the Tartan Army populating that particular train but there were civilians on board as well. Civilians? Yes, these were Londoners heading home from their shopping expeditions and a few impeccably dressed gents returning from a morning's work. The Tartan Army quickly saw to it that the civilians had priority in the matter of seating. This was not the only hospitality bestowed upon the soon-to-be bemused commuters who were suddenly assailed with the request 'ye'll hae a drink'. Okay, it wasn't so much a request. It sounded like a demand. These

Londoners were mainly women who favoured drinks like port and lemon, sherry and wine. The Tartan Army had it all. Not once was it necessary to say "Sorry we don't have any of that". It was all retrieved from carrier bags and dispensed in tumblers. A little girl was even given a glass of lemonade. Then a voice boomed along the carriage. "Wullie, gonnae dae yer tap dance?" Tap dance! There was barely room to stand. Where there's a will there's a way. Space was duly cleared and the not-so-nimble Wullie did his tap dance to the accompaniment of Scots fans singing 'I'm singing in the train' (to the tune of 'I'm singing in the rain'). I am sure that Lionel Blair would have had no sleepless nights worrying about the opposition even although this impromptu cabaret was well received by the Londoners who were now indulging in a top-up. There was a further gesture. Do you remember the little girl who got the glass of lemonade? The Tartan Army had a lift for her and there were some very generous donations when loose silver got extricated from pockets and sporrans (but mainly sporrans!). What happened at the match that afternoon? Unfortunately you will not be told. I suffer from a rare condition known as selective amnesia. This condition manifests itself when either Scotland or Ayr United lose.

1972/73 was most satisfactory. It was considered that more of the same would do very nicely. A boyhood friend of mine was John Taylor and he was a Kilmarnock supporter. He was also an exceptional footballer as I could see at first hand because we played in the same Boys' Brigade team. He went on to play for Ayr Albion then he got signed by Leeds United. In the summer of 1973 he signed for Ayr United as a sweeper. Although highly skilled he would have tackled a brick wall.

There was no progression from the League Cup sectional stage but the start of the league programme was awaited with a certain relish. In consecutive seasons it got underway against Rangers, this time at Ibrox. At this time Rangers played in a very physical manner. The main hard men in their team were John Greig, Alex MacDonald and Tom Forsyth. This was a classic case of getting your retaliation in first! Four Ayr fouls were committed in the first three minutes. I was standing at my normal Ibrox spot in close proximity to the tunnel. In the second half I had a perfect view of John Doyle running alongside John Greig while raining punches on the beleaguered Rangers captain. At last we got a refereeing break at Ibrox. Neither the referee nor the standside linesman noticed this. An ill-tempered match finished 0-0. After the final whistle I turned to walk away then noticed a Rangers supporter walking towards me. He had obviously noticed the black and white scarf. It had been a hostile ninety minutes and I feared the worse. Then he said: "Who's your left-back?" When I told him it was John Murphy he went on to talk about how impressed he had been with his performance. I had totally misread the situation. There had been no warring intent.

Two days later Alex Ferguson was signed. He stepped into the team to replace the injured Alex Ingram. His debut was in a 2-1 win over Morton in which he did not score. One week later, while playing alongside Dixie, he scored both goals in a 2-0 win at Dumbarton. No one in their wildest dreams could have foreseen the sensational career ahead of him.

As a Tartan Army foot soldier at Wembley in 1973 I agreed with the point of view that Peter Shilton was the best goalkeeper in the world. His save from Kenny Dalglish, as viewed from behind that goal, was nothing short of miraculous. Four months later, to the day, the mighty Shilton was beaten at Ayr when the teenaged Brian Bell fired the ball past him. This was a Texaco Cup tie against Leicester City. Alas we conceded an own goal which brought it level at 1-1. A fortnight later the away leg was lost 2-0 and of all the Texaco Cup/Anglo Scottish Cup ties played by Ayr United in England this was the only one I ever missed. Newcastle United 1972√ Birmingham City 1974√ Mansfield Town 1975√ Nottingham Forest 1976√. So why was Leicester City 1973 not added to these trips? Well I got a notion that I could be a referee so I travelled to Kilmarnock weekly to do the course. I travelled with Louis Thow and Kenny McAlpine who had passed the entrance exam two years earlier but were now required to come on the course as a refresher.

Brian Bell

With the course completed the date was set for the refereeing exam. The date coincided with Ayr United's match at Leicester. Of those who were sitting the entrance exam only two passed and I was one of them. I now had an SFA referee's badge and I went out and bought a resplendent uniform to attach it to. From personal testimony you may be told that refereeing amateur football in the Ayrshire schemes and villages is a tough gig. My refereeing career was not curtailed for that reason. The lure of watching Ayr United home and away was too strong. After refereeing I would rush back to the car with all haste in order to get the radio on to find out the Ayr United result. I realised where I would rather be and it wasn't Dundonald, Hurlford, Kilwinning or Kilbirnie. If taking up refereeing it really is beneficial to make sure that your Saturday afternoons are free. Watching Ayr United was too much of a sentimental bond to break, especially since the team was flying. By the third week in October we were second in the First Division, just one point off the top. In the whole of 1973 only Celtic and Rangers had league wins at Somerset Park and Rangers only managed it with an 88th minute winner on the last Saturday of the year. A 1-1 draw at home to Hibs on the third Saturday of 1974 left Ayr United fourth in the First Division. A win on that afternoon would have meant sitting on the same points total as third-placed Rangers.

The next match had the novelty of being on a Sunday. So far in the club's history the only Sunday matches had been in Norway (1928) and France (1973). Here in 1974 it was a Scottish Cup tie in the Kingdom of Fife. Cowdenbeath 0 Ayr United 5 – It was exhilarating being on the road with Ayr United and in the next round it was to get even better with a 7-1 win at Stranraer.

Excitement was high when drawn away to Hearts in the Scottish Cup. A 1-1 draw was watched by a Tynecastle crowd of 17,219 and I was not one of them. Instead I was back in Ayr at Craigie Park refereeing an under-18s schools match between Ayrshire and Cumberland. Also in 1974 the title Cumberland ceased to exist but this was purely coincidental!

OFFICIAL PROGRAMME

Price 5p

Scottish League Division 1

DUMBARTON
v
AYR UNITED

Saturday,
15th September
1973.
Kick-off 3-00 p.m.

NEXT HOME GAME
Scottish League Division 1

v

Partick Thistle

on Saturday 29th Sept. 1973

Kick-off 3.00 p.m.

Your lucky programme number is on Centre page

Tom McAdam and Ross Mathie in a scene from Saturday's match against Falkirk at Brockville.

The Hearts replay was watched by 16,185 and it was a dramatic night marred by crowd trouble which was even reported in the *Liverpool Echo*. Hearts won 2-1 with a goal scored five minutes from the end of extra time. Nonetheless Ayr United's stock was high and we came very close to finishing sixth in consecutive seasons. We were beaten into seventh place by Hearts who had the same points but a better goal difference. This was the first season for the Programme of The Year awards which was organised by the publication *Programme Monthly*. The Ayr United programme was the inaugural winner. To paraphrase an ungrammatical colloquialism, "The boys done great."

It emerged that from 1975/76 the leagues were to be designated Premier, First and Second rather than just First and Second. In consequence the top ten First Division clubs at the end of 1974/75 would qualify for the new Premier League. All summer the hot topic of local conversation was whether Ayr United would make the cut for the top ten.

The season's opener was a 3-1 League Cup defeat away to Dundee United. Expectation levels were now so high that it was described as a debacle. One of the headlines referred to a "Tannadice Tragedy". The other teams in the group were Celtic and Motherwell. Collectively the results were shambolic but one match did stand out – Ayr United 3 Celtic 2. For the first time I had witnessed Ayr United beating Celtic but it would prove to be far from the only time.

For the third season in a row the league opener was against Rangers and we drew 1-1 at home. This particular mini series now amounted to an Ayr win and two draws. Rangers were not held in awe when playing at Ayr. A trip to play Birmingham City in September was an adventure. The occasion was a Texaco Cup tie. My friend Brian Johnstone and I travelled by National Express and, on arrival in Birmingham, I implemented a harebrained scheme to find accommodation for that night. The plan involved walking into a police station to ask if they could recommend anything (other than the cells of course!). A most helpful officer phoned up a nearby YMCA and that was it arranged. It was cheap too! The match was lost

SCOTTISH RESULTS AND TABLES

The state of play on 22nd October, 1973.

DIVISION 1

Aberdeen 0. Dunfermline Athletic 0.
Arbroath 2 (Sellars 2). Dundee 4 (Wallace, J. Scott, R. Wilson, Robinson).
Ayr United 1 (Ferguson). Motherwell 0.
Celtic 1 (McCluskey). Hibernian 1 (Gordon).
Dundee United 1 (Johnstone o.g.). Rangers 3 (Conn 2, O.Hara).
East Fife 0. Morton 1 (McIlmoyle)
Falkirk 1 (Thomas). St Johnstone 1 (Kennedy o.g.).
Hearts 0. Dumbarton 0.
Partick Thistle 1 (Coulston). Clyde 3 (Gillespie 2, Anderson).

	P	W	L	D	Goals F	A	Pt
Hearts	8	5	0	3	19	7	13
Ayr	8	5	1	2	16	9	12
Celtic	7	5	1	1	14	5	11
Aberdeen	7	3	0	4	7	3	10
Dundee Utd.	7	5	2	0	12	8	10
Hibernian	7	4	1	2	13	10	10
Clyde	8	3	3	2	11	17	8
Motherwell	8	2	3	3	10	8	7
Dumbarton	8	3	4	1	8	9	7
Rangers	7	3	3	1	6	7	7
Dunfermline	8	2	3	3	9	12	7
Dundee	8	2	4	2	10	8	6
Partick	8	2	4	2	6	10	6
St Johnstone	8	2	4	2	8	12	6
Morton	7	1	3	3	6	9	5
Arbroath	8	1	4	3	9	14	5
East Fife	8	2	6	0	4	9	4
Falkirk	8	0	4	4	5	16	4

3-0 with Kenny Burns scoring twice. We were standing next to a home supporter (no segregation) who appraised us of some details about their other scorer who was described as "a young lad from Glasgow". It was Jimmy Calderwood. The second leg ended 0-0.

A certain amount of fan apathy started to creep in. Sub 4,000 crowds became normal. There was a staleness. Kilmarnock's visit on New Year's Day 1975 at last stirred the passions. In front of a 9,968 crowd Gerry Phillips struck the winner in a 3-2 victory. A study of the league table indicated that we then sat tenth, just the right side of the top ten cut-off but with no margin for error. Frustration was soon upon us on losing at home to Queen's Park in the Scottish Cup. Football being football the next home match brought a 2-0 win against Aberdeen. Fans love to have heroes. We had one. His name was John Doyle. After this match Ally MacLeod set the safety target for the cut-off at thirty points. That equated to seven points from the eleven remaining matches (at two points for a win). Ultimately that would not have been enough. We finished in seventh place on thirty-six points. Ayr United would be the only part time team in the inaugural Premier League.

It had long since been thought that we had no need to fear relegation. It was just a matter of avoiding the bottom two in a league of eighteen, an obstacle which had been getting cleared with ease. Now we had to avoid the bottom two in a league of ten. It was a sobering thought that even a ninth-placed finish would mean automatic relegation. These metaphorical goalposts had been well and truly shifted.

We had pre-season friendlies at home to Hull City and JC Roda. Seeing a continental team at Ayr was a novelty although the visit from Polish club Gwardia in 1972 was still fresh in the memory not least because it fell under the category of unfriendly friendlies. In a 3-3 draw the Dutch club got a last minute equaliser scored by Dick Advocaat who was destined to have a future in Scottish football. Their first goal was scored by Dick Nanninga whose name meant nothing at the time but he had the honour of scoring for Holland against Argentina in the 1978 World Cup final. He was the first of two World Cup final scorers to play at Somerset Park. Paul Pogba played here for Manchester United in 2011 and he scored for France against Croatia in the 2018 World Cup final.

The League Cup form was too erratic to progress from the group stages. Yet this had not been the subject of the pre-season anticipation. The true eagerness was for the Premier League to get underway. 30th August, 1975, was the big day and the fixture was Motherwell away. The kick-off took place marginally before 3 pm thereby making it a certainty that Alex Ingram was the first player of any club to kick a ball in the Scottish Premier League. Ayr United's first Premier League goal was a penalty converted by Johnny Graham. I attended this game in the company of a visitor from New Guinea. This is not a joke. There is no punchline. Back home in the Carmichael abode she sounded incredulous when explaining the concept of a penalty kick to her husband who was my cousin. She was honestly of the opinion that it was impossible not to score. It ended 1-1.

As in 1975 I travelled to England with my friend Brian to watch Ayr United in what was now rebranded the Anglo Scottish Cup. Again the mode of transport was a service bus from Glasgow. This time the accommodation was pre-booked rather than winging it as at Birmingham the year before. On arrival at Mansfield Bus Station there was a poster advertising buses which would be running to the Baseball Ground for Derby County versus Real Madrid in the European Cup. Derby won that match 4-1 but lost 5-1 in the second leg. Reverting to topic the score at Field Mill was Mansfield Town 2 Ayr United 0. We had already lost 1-0 in the first leg. Our first home game after the Mansfield demise was a Premier League fixture against Rangers. Ayr United 3 Rangers 0 was the happy result. The chances of winning had been considered favourable (at least in this area) and the margin of victory was a bonus. To put it into context Rangers went on to win a domestic treble in season 1975/76. I was standing at the back of the north terrace when, in the closing minutes, there was a furore at the front. Frustratingly I could not see what all the fuss was about but there was a lot of angry shouting. Later I found out that John Doyle had displayed his crucifix in the direction of the terracing.

In the ensuing weeks rumours emerged that Ally MacLeod would be quitting to take up the managerial vacancy at Aberdeen. On 1st November there was a crowd of 7,483 for a 2-0 home win against Motherwell. With justification the team had the backing of the Ayr public but still the annoying speculation persisted. It was corroborated by local gossip. The fear was that it was not speculation or gossip. Ominously there was an Ayr United board meeting on the afternoon of 4th November. The directors agreed to release Ally in order that he could become the new manager of Aberdeen. That evening we had an Ayrshire Cup tie at Rugby Park and he was allowed the opportunity to say his farewells by taking charge of the team for the last time pending his departure. Kilmarnock 0 Ayr United 3 should have appeased the support but even in victory there was a void that would be very difficult to fill. In a manner of speaking the notion that he was taking a step up was a misconception because we were above Aberdeen in the league, a situation that would still be intact at the end of the season. People joked that if we were in danger of relegation Ally would see us okay but it was an idea that could have been turned on its head.

The next Ayr United manager was Alex Stuart and there was consensus that it was a great appointment. He came here having recently taken Montrose to the semi-finals of the League Cup. His first game in charge was at home to Aberdeen. It could not have been scripted. The sight of Ally MacLeod in the away dugout was bizarre. We won 1-0 with a speculative lob from John Murphy. From the nearby vantage point of behind the Somerset Road goal we could see that Alex Ingram played his part in the goal by providing a major distraction for goalkeeper Andy Geoghegan. Alex Stuart soon put his mark on the team with the purchase of Malky Robertson from Raith Rovers.

On 17th December, 1975, John Doyle was in Scotland's starting line-up for a match against Romania at Hampden.

He was still part time. He had been in the Scotland squad for Wembley in 1973 and it had since been thought that it was only a matter of time before he got a full international cap. The result was 1-1.

By New Year 1976 St.Johnstone were cut adrift and doomed to relegation even this early. The prospect of avoiding the other relegation spot was rendered problematical by the number of clubs in the mix. The Scottish Cup was removed as a hindrance. If you ask a veteran Queen of the South supporter about their favourite game of all time they will tell you that it was the 5-4 extra time win in a Scottish Cup replay against Ayr United in 1976. On the same evening the Ayr Battalion of the Boys' Brigade had a five-a-side football competition. I was too old to play but I was required to be the officer in charge of the 8th Ayr team. It should have been out of the question. I said that I could not help because I was going to Dumfries. Then I had to relent on being told that the team would have to be withdrawn if I did not attend. With due allowance for it being an exciting night at Palmerston at least I was spared the frustration of defeat. Unwittingly I had also missed John Doyle's last game for Ayr United. This cup match was his last prior to a 21-day suspension at the end of which he was sold to Celtic.

By the middle of April the contenders to go down with St.Johnstone were Hearts, Aberdeen, Ayr United, Dundee United and Dundee. Only the top four were safe. Despite having considerable experience of relegation haunted football I have never become conditioned to it. People will glibly tell you that it does not matter what other clubs do. Yet in these situations it is only natural to have a vested interest in rival clubs losing. Celtic 1 Ayr United 2. This result meant that Rangers won the title on this day by virtue of a 1-0 win away to Dundee United. This was not in the media's script. The Celtic versus Rangers fixture on the Monday was expected to be a title showdown but as a result of our win it was relegated to a match with nothing resting on it.

To support Ayr United is to undergo just about every conceivable emotion known to man. The climax to season

1975/76 saw a night of unbearable tension. We were at home to Motherwell and to obtain safety we thought that we required a draw but this was based on the assumption that Dundee United would lose at Ibrox the next evening. That match ended 0-0 therefore anything less than a win against Motherwell would have meant relegation. It looked bleak. We were a goal down at half-time and Malky Robertson missed a penalty with half an hour to go. The place was in a frenzy when Davy McCulloch equalised. Five minutes later it was fever pitch when Gerry Phillips scored. At least we thought he had scored. Referee McKenzie signalled a corner-kick in the belief that the ball had been cut back from behind the byeline. Then he went over to consult the farside linesman. During their conversation the tension escalated to something approaching sheer terror. Goal! Phew! It stayed 2-1. Defeat for Dundee United at Ibrox would have put them down but Dundee got relegated instead. Despite an all too close flirtation with relegation we finished sixth. From that you can gauge just how tight the league was.

Ayr United's ongoing part time status was perplexing to outsiders. Ally MacLeod had been full time as a manager despite the players only being in for training two nights a week. Alex Stuart differed in his approach. While managing Ayr United he had a day job as head teacher at Symington Primary.

I have never seen Ayr United playing abroad. The opportunities in the 1970s were unaffordable. These were Canada and France in 1973 then Canada again in 1975 and Nigeria in 1976. If you ever get into conversation with Jim McSherry please ask him about Nigeria. It was squalid. He said that they kept their hotel room doors locked in case painters and decorators broke in!

In the League Cup we were in a section which Aberdeen won. They then went on to lift the trophy which was a conspicuous success for Ally MacLeod. After dismissing Clydebank in the Anglo Scottish Cup there was eager anticipation about which English team we would be playing. Newcastle United – superb! It would not even require an overnight stay. In the first leg we won 3-0 so we would be going there with much higher prospects than in 1972. Then came this bombshell: "The board of the International Football League has dismissed Newcastle United from the Anglo Scottish Cup for fielding a weak team at Ayr. Ayr United will receive £4,000 in compensation which will be met by the fine imposed on Newcastle United. Manager Gordon Lee has been severely censured."

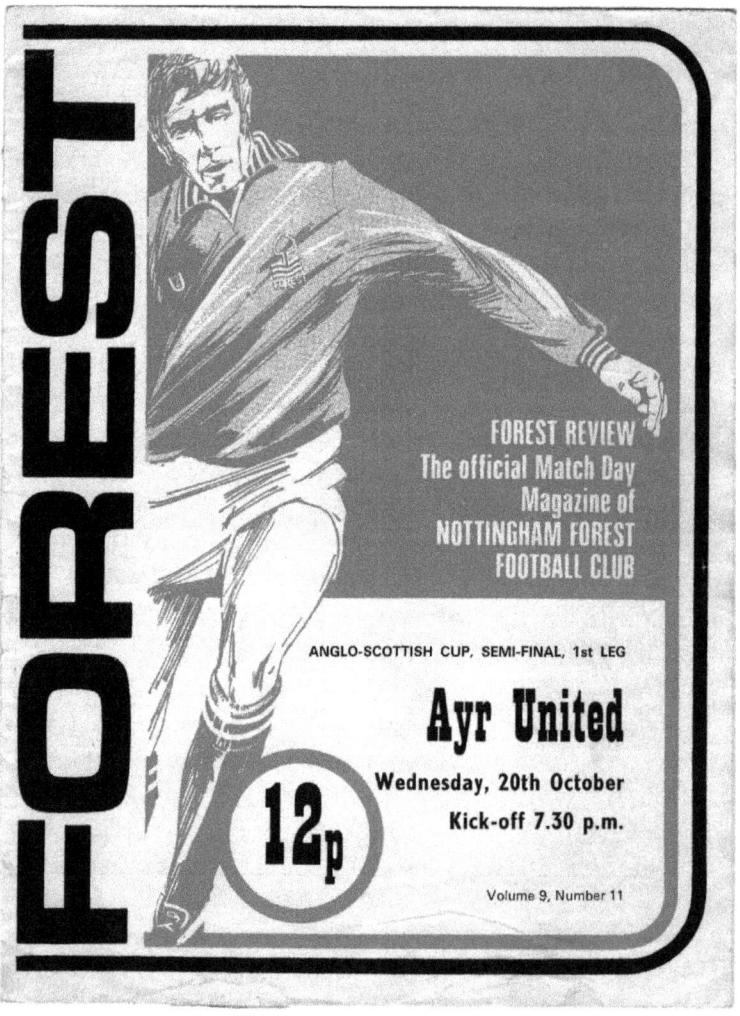

Missing out on the Newcastle trip had one considerable consolation. We were now in the semi-finals where we were drawn against Nottingham Forest with the first leg away from home. I went there by train with Ian McPherson for company. We met *Ayrshire Post* journalist Bob Shields on the train. With the homeward journey due to depart Nottingham five minutes before midnight it was possible to get a day return. In a bar close to the City Ground I tasted the worst pint I have ever had. The barman must have seen my face because he said that my pint was dredged out of the Trent. In a 2-1 defeat Johnny Graham scored with a late penalty. Surely this could be overcome in the second leg. It wasn't and we went down 4-1 on aggregate. Although managed by Brian Clough, Nottingham Forest were a Second Division club here in 1976. Not for long though. They scraped promotion with a third place finish in 1976/77. In 1977/78 they rose to become champions of England and in each of the next two seasons they won the European Cup. This would make a nice quiz question. Which club has been European champions oftener than domestic champions?

Kilmarnock had not made the cut for the inaugural Premier League but promotion brought them into this hallowed sphere for 1976/77. They went straight back down but this is not being mentioned braggingly. In October the Ayrshire derby finished Kilmarnock 6 Ayr United 1. It remains the only time I have ever been home from an away game while the match was still in progress. After winning 2-0 at Firhill on the opening day we were now nine matches in with no further victories. Kilmarnock had only won one game in nine too – against Ayr!

Gossip has a tendency to be unreliable but occasionally it can be true. It transpired that Malky Robertson really did appear for a pub team in Edinburgh. This was the guy who had scored twice in our 2-1 win at Celtic Park earlier in the same year. Fans always like to have a hero but this was one player whose stock had rapidly deteriorated in the eyes of the fans. Not to worry. We now had a pair of heroes. The twin strikers Walker McCall and Danny Masterton posed a major threat. They were perceived to be the players who would get the club out of the relegation doldrums.

New Year's Day 1977 was awaited with relish. Kilmarnock at Ayr was the perfect opportunity to avenge the horror of that 6-1 rout. In winning 3-1 there was repayment, not that full repayment had been expected. Late in the match I and others noticed some frantic gesturing from a man near the touchline on the standside of the pitch. It was Kilmarnock boss Willie Fernie who later admitted that he was trying to get the game stopped for fear that the ground conditions were unsafe. The fact that time was closing in on his team's defeat was entirely coincidental! In the cold light of day the bottom two were Ayr United and Kilmarnock in that order.

Paranoia is the default emotion of the aggrieved football supporter. Please judge for yourself whether the following situation portrays me as paranoid. The Scottish League ordered Ayr United to play Hearts at Tynecastle on the Tuesday evening of 1st March despite us having a Scottish Cup tie at Celtic Park on the Sunday. Quite apart from the proximity of the games (Hearts beat Clydebank in the cup on the Saturday) there was an assumption that Celtic were going to beat Ayr United because any replay would be staged in the immediate midweek which would rule out the possibility of playing Hearts on the appointed date. At Celtic Park, despite there being no segregation, I stood wearing my Ayr United scarf with no fear. This was on the assumption that it was safe to do so unless anything contentious happened. The game drew to a close with Celtic winning 1-0 and many of their fans were walking past having just vacated The Jungle. Then Gordon Cramond equalised with two minutes to go. In 1977 copious amounts of stoppage time did not exist and time was soon called on a 1-1 draw. The Scottish League had made no contingency for anything other than a Celtic win despite Ayr United having won there less than a year before. In the replay Celtic won 3-1. When the Tynecastle fixture did get played there were huge ramifications.

Kilmarnock were foot of the table and virtually doomed to relegation. A fortnight after the cup tie at Celtic Park an Ayr win at Rugby Park compounded their plight. Avoiding going down with them was rendered frighteningly difficult when surveying a run of fixtures containing a virtual dearth of home matches. It comprised Rangers (away), Aberdeen (away), Dundee United (away), Hearts (away) then Motherwell (home). Even allowing for it being in midweek the crowd at Ibrox was poor for a club boasting a vast support. It was 9,212. In the closing minutes I was one of the many who started to drift towards the exits. It was 1-0 for Rangers at the time. Joy of joys. Joe Filippi scored with a header. Four minutes later it ended at 1-1. On the Saturday we won at Tannadice and on the next again Saturday we won at Pittodrie. These were fantastic results in the battle for safety. Yet the next match in the glut of away games carried a certain amount of trepidation. Hearts away was a four-pointer. Hearts had never been relegated in their 103-year history but now they were second bottom of the Premier League with seven games left. We were third bottom and four points better off. An Ayr win would mean stretching our lead over them to six points with six games left. At two points for a win this would leave Hearts close to dead and buried. So much rested on this game that I did not have the bottle to travel to it. Hearts 1 Ayr United 2 was the result. The errant Malky Robertson was now a Hearts player and he got sent off. On the Saturday a Gordon Cramond hat-trick was instrumental in defeating Motherwell 3-2 at Ayr. Five matches, four away from home, four wins and a draw! The season was played out safely and Hearts went down with Kilmarnock. It was a bit of a shock to the system when Alex Ingram was on the list of released players. His status as an Ayr United legend remained intact.

For season 1977/78 we were no longer the only part time club in the Premier League. Promoted Clydebank shared that status. Our first home league game of the new season was a 2-1 win against Celtic but the national media did not run with the Ayr victory as the main story. Two minutes from the end referee Bob Cuthill pulled up John Doyle for a handling offence. Doyle then took an impetuous shot which hit the referee in the face, a transgression that got him sent off. The headlines were about the perceived injustice of the sending off and the result was of secondary importance. Yet when John Doyle had been sent off playing for Ayr United against Celtic there had been no such outrage.

Getting knocked out of the League Cup over two legs against Forfar Athletic was a depressing experience. In football not much can be taken for granted but it was an echo of Alloa Athletic five years earlier. Predictably the refrain was: "Ah well, we can concentrate on the league." This tends to be the go-to expression when teams get eliminated from cup competitions. With the Premier League effectively consisting of four rounds of nine matches, it was interesting to take stock after the first round of matches in this season. Interesting but a little worrying. We were eighth out of ten so if this could be maintained we would be only just safe from the drop. Clydebank were at the foot. Two points above them in second bottom place were Celtic. Yes, Celtic. The worrying aspect was the near certain knowledge that they would not stay in what was a relegation position. On the last Saturday in October we had a 2-1 half-time lead at Celtic Park, eventually losing 3-2 to a goal conceded five minutes from the end. The *Glasgow Herald* report commended Celtic for their "spirit and character". Compliments of this nature are ordinarily reserved for smaller clubs.

The Celtic Park defeat was avenged on the last day of the year. Ayr United 2 Celtic 1 – we had now beaten them twice to this point of the season. I slipped away at 1-1 just before the end and I had only just reached Somerset Road when an almighty roar went up. It was loud enough to be consistent with a Celtic goal and my heart sank. I turned back by which time people were emerging after full time. It was a Brian McLaughlin goal. I went from despondency to elation. Two days later, on 2nd January, Walker McCall scored a hat-trick in a 3-2 win away to St.Mirren. There was no scoring in the last half hour but this time I stayed to the end just in case.

On the first Saturday of January 1978, Steve Archibald made his Aberdeen debut in a 1-1 draw at Ayr. Ayr United had tried to sign him from Clyde before Aberdeen did. The deal with Clyde was to involve Jim McSherry going to Shawfield. It was scuppered because McSherry said that he "did not want to play at a dug track."

Weeks later we were eliminated from the Scottish Cup at Aberdeen. This brought forth the predictable response about being able to concentrate on the league. We had a reputation for relegation escapes. Alas the power of escapology deserted the club. Seven consecutive league defeats were broken by a 1-1 draw at Ibrox. The attendance that night was 12,282 despite Rangers being on course for a domestic treble. It became inevitable that we were going down with Clydebank. Ninth was a relegation position. Alex Stuart condemned fan pessimism and he spoke out against the *Ayrshire Post* too: "I'm very upset by what has appeared in your paper. From now on you can scratch around to fill your pages but I won't be helping." His comments were aimed at Bob McKenzie, the Sports Editor. Further criticism was in respect of critical letters sent in by the paper's readers. He also claimed that supporters had been shouting abuse from outside his house.

Much as I hate to see Ayr United lose, I was not too angst ridden when relegation was confirmed and not just because we could all see it coming. I derived great comfort from the certainty that we would return as First Division champions the following year. There was not the slightest doubt in my mind that we would be back in the Premier League in 1979.

Ayr United's last Premier League fixture, so far

7. The Awakening

As mentioned on a previous page, blind devotion to Ayr United debars alternative Saturday afternoon pursuits. This was mentioned in reference to my brief refereeing career. In view of the brevity the word 'career' is ill-chosen. Since 1977 I had been on the committee of an amateur club on the understanding that I was free to attend Ayr United matches. This arrangement was a complete reversal of my father's attitude when he was on the committee of Pencaitland Amateurs. He said that committee men missing matches to go and watch the seniors was a practice that was scorned upon. In his case it was Pencaitland first and Hibs second. He would only go to Easter Road when there was no clash. At Wallacefield Amateurs I was the treasurer and I was regular at training nights but irregular on match days. In 1975 some of my friends from the Northfield area used to play weekly football matches against other friends from the Wallacetown area. These matches were played in Newton Park on Sunday afternoons with jackets for goalposts. Although living in Prestwick I was the goalkeeper for the Northfield guys. When defending the tennis court end I dreaded high shots that cleared the fence. Being the last line of defence it was incumbent on me to retrieve the ball. The agility required to save shots was nothing in comparison to the agility required to scale that fence twice. Twice? Of course I had to climb back out! It was eventually decided to form a team from the best players in the two sides. That was when my goalkeeping ambitions were thwarted. The name Wallacefield was a reflection of Wallacetown and Northfield. Some of you may recall the crack amateur team Heathside. The name represented Heathfield and Lochside.

Wallacefield Amateurs. June 1982. Rear left to right: John Sykes, Johnny Telfer, Archie Dunlop, (?), Ian Jamieson, Ian Hendrie, (?), Gordon Alexander and John Hendry. Front left to right: Jim Shields, Sam Hendrie, Mervyn Dingwall, Johnny Wilson, Alastair Dunlop, Brian Graham and Duncan Carmichael. Sincere apologies to the two players I have been unable to name. I was working from memory.

The free transfer list in 1978 included Alex McAnespie (signed in 1964) and John Murphy (signed in 1963). Players who had played under Ally MacLeod for a long time shared the common view that it was not the same without Ally. Dougie Mitchell once told me that the players were so fired up that they would turn up for training early, so eager were they to start.

Alex Stuart went to Argentina to watch the World Cup finals. On his return he said: "I studied the Germans very closely." The positivity engendered by this remark did not take long to crumble to dust. After seven games of the First Division programme he resigned. It was commonly perceived that he had been sacked but chairman Myles Callaghan said: "The board did not pressurise him into resigning." In truth the board did not need to exert pressure on him to resign. That task had already been undertaken by the fans. The verbal hostility had been induced by a league record comprising one win, two draws and four defeats. During one of those defeats (at home to Hamilton Accies) there were loud renditions of "What a load of rubbish." We were joint bottom of the league. The ignominy would have been even more acute had it not been for Queen of the South and Arbroath having an inferior goal difference.

Alex Stuart's "resignation" occurred on a Saturday morning, hours before a 1-0 win against Clyde at Shawfield. Media speculation soon started to suggest that Ally MacLeod was going to quit his job as Scotland manager in order to return to his old job at Ayr. It seemed too good to be true. Less than a year earlier I was at Anfield on the frenzied night when Scotland beat Wales 2-0 to qualify for the World Cup in Argentina. Ally's stock at that time was huge. Was he really going to walk out on the national job to manage part time Ayr United? There was a sentimental bond but it seemed doubtful that it would be strong enough. The board had discussions with him just four days after Alex Stuart quit. He accepted the job and we had a home match against Arbroath that night.

Ally MacLeod on his return. 27th September, 1978.

It was won 3-0 and this was the first of a run of eight league games which yielded seven wins and a draw. We were all ecstatic at the transformation. These were great times, especially away from home. Ayr United fans have regularly had a tendency to be more celebratory at away matches. It cannot be denied that alcohol has been a factor but a greater factor has been natural exuberance. The extreme joy of a last minute winner was experienced twice during that run. This was done by courtesy of Gerry Phillips at Stirling and Walker McCall at Kilmarnock. We entered December in second place in the First Division table, just two points behind Dundee at the top. In shooting right up the table Ally had performed a miracle. During that phase we had drawn 3-3 at home to Aberdeen in the first leg of the League Cup quarter-finals, ultimately losing 6-4 on aggregate, but that first match had been highly exciting. Weeks earlier there was a 6-4 win at Montrose which amply illustrated Ally MacLeod's lust for attacking football.

TUESDAY, 12TH DECEMBER – ALLY QUITS TO BECOME THE MOTHERWELL MANAGER.

This became public via the teatime news bulletins. It was an utter bombshell. At present it is the third shortest managerial tenure in the history of the club. Bobby Flavell's seventeen-day spell in 1961 tops the list, followed by Jim Duffy's run from October to December 2021. There are only seven instances of the Ayr United manager's job being held for a period of less than one year. However in December 1978 none of us were engaged in statistical reflection. It was a massive blow. It was futile to ponder the reasons behind it.

That Saturday, under the interim managership of George Caldwell, Montrose were slain 5-0 at Ayr. The search for a new manager spilled over into January. Clyde boss Craig Brown was offered the job but he declined. The new incumbent was a friend of his. It was Willie McLean, who was now quitting Raith Rovers. In January 1979 we had six postponements so there was no particular urgency until the snow thawed.

On a February night at Shawfield the snow returned. The flakes got gradually thicker as the match progressed and the drive home over Fenwick Moor was rendered hazardous by blizzards. 927 of us were there on a night when staying indoors would have been a more sensible option. The saving grace was a 5-0 win over Clyde. On the prior Saturday we had also won 5-0 with Montrose falling victim to that scoreline at Ayr for the second time in the season.

Promotion was still a realistic possibility. Precisely one week after that Clyde match Davy Wells headed an 87th minute winner at home to Kilmarnock. This meant that we were then level on points with top-placed Kilmarnock but we had a game in hand. Despite this Kilmarnock went on to get promotion along with champions Dundee. We were left to contemplate a fourth-placed finish. In the final fixture of the season we had the power to hand Kilmarnock the title. The match was at Dens Park. Dundee needed to win or draw to win the league while an Ayr win would have made Kilmarnock the champions. There was no hint of the team lying down. In a 2-2 draw Dundee drew level with eight minutes to go. Although it had its moments 1978/79 was an overall disappointment in the context of my certain belief that our return to the Premier League would be immediate. A 6-2 Scottish Cup defeat at Aberdeen will be quickly glossed over!

In the new campaign there was no repeat of the year before when four points were taken from the first seven games. This time the haul was three points from the first seven games! Ally MacLeod's Motherwell had been relegated and were now bottom of the First Division with the same record and the same goal difference but Ayr United had scored one goal more. It was dreadful for two clubs who were thought to have been promotion aspirants. On the terracing the spirits were low then, quite unpredictably, we had a run of sixteen league games without defeat. One more would have equalled the club record set in 1958/59. The run began after a defeat at Clydebank and ended with a defeat at Clydebank. Kilbowie was a ground entered with dread.

There was an extraordinary incident when Hearts visited for a League Cup tie early in the season. When leading 1-0 the floodlights started to fade. This was the preliminary to them cutting out altogether. It was a strange spectacle. There was some natural light but not nearly enough for the tie to progress. It was abandoned with fifty-seven minutes played. The second leg was scheduled for the Saturday at Tynecastle. That day became the date of the replayed first leg. It ended 2-2 but we won 1-0 in the away leg on the Monday. In the next round we lost 3-1 to Dundee on aggregate.

The unbeaten league run included a 5-1 win at home to Alex Stuart's St.Johnstone. His "resignation" from the Ayr job was on the corresponding weekend one year earlier. Three weeks later the shift in personnel was in even sharper focus in a 2-0 win at Motherwell. It seemed odd that Ally MacLeod was in the home dugout while Willie McLean, who had done well as a Motherwell manager, was in the away dugout. The same principle applied to the goalkeepers with Hugh Sproat playing for Motherwell and Stuart Rennie playing for Ayr. Motherwell's Brian McLaughlin had also been one of our own.

Relegation from the Premier League had one redeeming feature. Trips to such destinations as Stirling and Berwick were more enjoyable and less tortuous than many of the away days in the top tier. Berwick in particular was a favoured trip since the journey there was via my native East Lothian. Arbroath away, just three days before Christmas, was an ordeal though. Cold weather at Arbroath is far from a rarity but on this particular day it was extreme. The home team had been leading 1-0 since the first half and the unbeaten run looked to be in jeopardy. Jim Fleeting squared it with four minutes left and the final whistle was a welcome relief in view of the intense weather. By the first week in January we were third in the table, just two points behind the top two who were Dumbarton and Hearts in that order. It was expected that Motherwell would rise up the table but for now they were eighth.

On 26th January, 1980, I attended a match that I barely saw. It was a third round Scottish Cup tie at Dumbarton. The *Ayr*

Advertiser report said: "The tie was far from a classic and will be remembered best for the fog which lent an unreal atmosphere to the proceedings." Far from a classic? Who could tell? In a 2-1 win Davy Armour and Robert Connor (penalty) scored. The names of the scorers are not given to you from personal testimony even although I was there. Visibility was so bad that we were lucky that it did not get abandoned for fog. At this time I went to a lot of away games in the company of my friend Hugh Cole and his brother Graham. With the fog refusing to lift it was a hazardous journey home and at times I was glad that Hugh was driving rather than myself.

In the next round we had sunshine and clear skies. I also had a weekend staying at my brother's in Edinburgh but on the Sunday we entered Easter Road at different ends. Right at the start of George Best's autobiography he mentioned his non appearance for Hibs in this tie. On the Saturday night he had been drinking in the North British Hotel along with the French national rugby team. The difference was that the rugby players had already played their match. Hibs won 2-0 anyway but there was a controversy about a Robert Connor shot which cannoned off the underside of the crossbar then down onto the line (referee's opinion) or over the line (my opinion). Unfortunately the referee paid no attention to the goal appeals from the large Ayr support amassed behind that goal.

By now I had acquired my first car. It was a Fiat 127. At 903 cc it wasn't terribly powerful but it could just about be relied upon to reach away games. One of its earlier away trips was to Tynecastle on a Tuesday night. The reason for selecting this match for special mention is wholly attributable to the result. It was Hearts 0 Ayr United 1. We were too far behind leaders Hearts to catch them. There was a possibility of catching second-placed Airdrie. A possibility yes but the probability was no. At two points for a win we were five behind them with five to play. The run-in brought three points with one draw, one win and three defeats. Had full points been taken from these five games we would have been pipped for the second promotion place on goal difference. Our final placing was third. The situation truly was an awakening. We were starting to become consolidated as a First Division club rather than a Premier League club.

Season 1980/81 began with the Drybrough Cup. The eligible clubs were the four highest scoring Premier League teams in 1979/80, the two highest scoring First Division teams and the two highest scoring Second Division teams. To weigh the prospects in favour of the bigger clubs there was a ruling that all of the Premier League clubs would have home advantage in the first round. It was all geared towards getting the lower league clubs eliminated in order to generate more revenue. There is a Scottish colloquialism to describe this sort of practice. The word is 'pochle'. We were drawn away to Celtic and on the Sunday of the tie my little Fiat was packed with friends (it didn't take much to pack it!) and we headed to the east end of Glasgow. This is being mentioned in order to highlight a traditional practice which occurs when you take your car to Celtic Park. When availing yourself of the street parking near the ground you can be sure of being accosted by a juvenile who will assail you with a request in these terms: "Can ah look efter yer car Mister?" The correct answer is yes. It's a form of protection racket. Whatever the financial arrangement it is prudent to pay the assailant on a 'half now and half later basis'. This was 1980 but I had first experienced this in 1970 when I went to an Ayr United game at Celtic Park with the Nelsons. Anyway the game got underway and Derek Frye put the ball in the Celtic net in the third minute. Offside! I subscribe to a school of thought that when you are playing Celtic or Rangers in Glasgow you need to put three in the net to get one to count. So it came to pass. A second goal was disallowed then this happened. Ian Cashmore fought hard to dispossess Mike Conroy then crossed to the far post where Eric Morris scored with a header. Just three minutes were left after which the whistle was blown on Celtic 0 Ayr United 1. That was one result. The other result was that the car still had four wheels. We lost 2-1 away to St.Mirren in the semi-final. This made way for a St.Mirren versus Aberdeen final at Hampden. The match coincided with the Paisley Fair and the attendance was 6,994. Celtic being absent from the final was financially disastrous for the tournament and it was never played again.

I was at the 1972 final in which Hibs beat Celtic 5-3 after extra time. The crowd that day was 49,462. Eric Morris's goal in 1980 effectively killed the tournament and it served them right.

Eight days later West Ham United were at Ayr. In a 1-1 draw a goal was conceded a minute from time. We were that close to a boast of beating the Scottish Cup holders and the FA Cup holders in little more than a week.

The opening league fixture was at home to Motherwell who, on their previous visit in February, had won 5-0. This time the result was 5-0 again but not for Motherwell. It remains a club record winning margin in an opening league fixture, albeit shared with Queen's Park 1 Ayr United 6 in 1921. Ally MacLeod and Hugh Sproat were both being subjected to wildly differing experiences over the two visits back at the ground they knew so well. Optimism was now high. It was not misplaced optimism. In the League Cup we knocked out Premier League Morton then Queen of the South then Premier League Hearts. This was not an easy feat since these ties were over two legs. On revising that last sentence a correction will now be made. The Hearts tie was an easy feat. It was 7-2 on aggregate. The 4-0 win in the second leg was a complete rout in which the Hearts goalkeeper made a complete series of magnificent saves to minimise the damage.

In the quarter-finals Hibs were at Somerset Park for the first leg, a 2-2 draw. This was the night when George Best played at Ayr. The *Ayr Advertiser* report made no mention of Best. In the *Glasgow Herald* it was mentioned that: "He looked unhappy in the conditions." I can offer no personal testimony on how he performed because I was on holiday in Paris that week. In the second leg Eric Morris and Derek Frye both scored with headers in extra time so we won 2-0 on the night and 4-2 on aggregate. Thus far in the club's history the semi-finals of the League Cup had been reached twice only. I had not been there in 1950 due to the flimsy excuse that I had not yet been born. Yet I once interviewed Norrie McNeil who had captained Ayr United on that occasion, a 4-3 defeat against Motherwell at Ibrox. The epic semi-final and replay against Celtic in 1969 remains clear in the memory today. In 1980 the semi-final draw was the best we could have hoped for. It was to be Dundee over two legs, the first at home. At this time the top clubs in the First Division, in order, were Raith Rovers, Hibs, Ayr United and Dundee. They had to be beatable. In the first leg it took an 88th minute goal from Robert Connor to salvage a 1-1 draw. The headlines, however, were about the crowd disorder at half-time when the respective sets of fans were changing ends. In fact some Dundee supporters changed ends by the shortest route, right down the middle of the pitch. The fallout from this prompted decisive action from the Ayr United board. Somerset Park would have segregation fences and they would be in place by the end of the season. In the second leg we had a 2-1 lead on the night only to concede twice in the last fifteen minutes. I have seldom felt more disappointed at a match. The club's first major final had been within touching distance. This was in November. In December Dundee were beaten 1-0 at Ayr in the league and in January the league fixture between the clubs ended Dundee 2 Ayr United 4.

Since its pioneering days football has had a propensity for humour and on New Year's Day 1981 it was experienced in abundance. Stirling Albion at their old Annfield ground was not what you would call a New Year derby but here we were. Arriving too early in Stirling was a mistake. On this day of all days it was, as expected, a ghost town. The mood was soon cheered. When the announcer was reading out the teams it was evident that he was drunk. He was not just a little the worse for wear but actually drunk. The team listings were heavily slurred. At half-time he was back on the microphone despite there being no improvement to his condition. He even announced a forthcoming reserve game for July instead of January. During the second half he made random announcements while play was still raging. In one of them he named a Stirling Albion supporter who wanted to wish his team the best of luck. By this time even the police were laughing. There was no other source of mirth that afternoon. In a disappointing 1-1 draw Eric Morris failed with a penalty.

17th October, 1981, versus East Stirling. Left to right, for Ayr: Gerry Christie, Stevie Nicol, (last game before going to Liverpool), Billy Hendry, (head only) and Derek Frye.

A Scottish Cup third round tie at Kilmarnock brought realistic hope of a derby win. Kilmarnock were rooted at the foot of the Premier League and we were third in the First Division. The result was a 2-1 defeat in which Gerry Christie had a penalty saved. On the day after the match Ayr United chairman Myles Callaghan was approached for permission for Kilmarnock to speak to Willie McLean about their managerial vacancy. McLean said on the Monday that he preferred to stay. On the Tuesday Kilmarnock appointed Jim Clunie.

In April McLean said: "To finish fifth or sixth in Division One is a disgrace to a club of our calibre". By that definition the season was a disgrace. We finished sixth. The decline since the start of the season was vast.

Any hope expressed now was cautious. Experience had taught us all to become a bit more guarded. Returning to the Premier League was a gradually diminishing contingency. For season 1981/82 the League Cup sections were revived. We were grouped with holders Dundee United, Partick Thistle and Motherwell with one qualifying per section. The opening match pitched the brothers Willie and Jim McLean against each other. It was Ayr United 3 Dundee United 1 at half-time. Although it transformed into a 4-3 defeat it was an exciting match. We beat Motherwell home and away and Partick Thistle home and away. The win at Firhill was 5-1. This was quite phenomenal because Partick Thistle were in the Premier League and their goalkeeper, Alan Rough, was the current Scotland goalkeeper. Derek Frye scored four. Dundee United won the group and went on to retain the trophy. Yet we had shown enough promise to light the flame of these promotion hopes again. Or would the season follow the same pattern as its predecessor?

Unbeaten in the first twelve league games, the run foundered at a place not unknown for Ayr United to end such runs. Kilbowie Park! Even in defeat we sat in second place, two points behind top club Motherwell and three in front of third-placed Kilmarnock. Hearts were fourth, on the same points as Kilmarnock. All of the top four had a recent Premier League history. It was going to be tough, more especially since the fabulous Stevie Nicol was sold to Liverpool.

The abandoned match on 4th January, 1982

When people of a certain age start to reminisce about severe winters, the winter of 1962 leading into 1963 is certain to warrant a mention. Some may recall 1947, claiming that to be even worse. It was certainly more intense in 1947 but not nearly so drawn out. Ayr United suffered one postponement only in that long ago post war winter. Winters such as 1981/82 seem to get lost in the public consciousness yet from 12th December, 1981, until 23rd January, 1982, Ayr United had to contend with seven postponements and an abandonment. That abandonment was during a home match against Kilmarnock on 4th January. The crowd of 3,878 was low for an Ayrshire derby yet it was hardly to be wondered at. Kenny Hope allowed the match to proceed in an unrelenting snowstorm. At half-time, with the score at 1-1, he called a halt with the lines obliterated and the underfoot conditions treacherous. People with either no interest or a minimal interest in football will fail to comprehend why anyone would pay money to watch football from a blizzard-strewn terracing. No explanation will suffice so it is better not to try. The same principle might be applied to televised football. It's better to watch football in the warm comfort of your home, they will tell you. These people are unreservedly wrong. Nothing beats the experience of being at the match.

On the last Saturday of January came a Scottish Cup defeat at Alloa. Willie McLean and his assistant George Caldwell were both ex-Alloa Athletic players. McLean said: "This is the biggest disappointment I have ever suffered in football." Even with experience it is difficult for supporters to become conditioned to disappointment on this scale. It is simply morale crushing and dispiriting. Yet one week later a 2-1 win at home to Clydebank was enough to rekindle promotion hopes. Motherwell, eight points ahead at two points for a win, looked to be uncatchable at the top but we occupied the second promotion place, two points ahead of Clydebank who had played three games more. In the following midweek a trip to play East Stirling was a miserable experience, ending in a 2-1 defeat. It was the first of ten matches without a win. Even after breaking the sequence the team lapsed into a stuttering run of form. In April my employer, the Halifax Building Society, sent me to work in Kirkcaldy for a fortnight. I was put up in a hotel rather than having to commute. By a stroke of luck my stay there coincided with an Ayr United midweek match at Tynecastle. Or was it a stroke of luck? Hearts won 2-1.

In the final analysis we finished sixth. Motherwell and Kilmarnock were the promoted clubs. A worrying trend had emerged. The final home match of the season, versus Queen of the South, had only attracted 863. Three days later we had an Ayrshire Cup tie at Kilmarnock. It was a 2-1 defeat but few cared. The attendance was 743.

A pattern had emerged over the course of the past two seasons. To put it succinctly the team had started well then fallen away. 1982/83 was to see a disturbance to that pattern. It would start poorly and remain poorly. Our Premier League history was becoming increasingly remote. This time the opponents in our League Cup section were St.Mirren, Stirling Albion and Queen of the South. Losing 3-1 away to St.Mirren in the opener was in line with expectation. I attended that match in the company of my Paisley Halifax five-a-side team mates. They were enthralled by Lex Richardson's hat-trick but I was as sick as the proverbial parrot. The ensuing midweek match was lost 1-0 at home to Stirling Albion. This was very badly received. The vocal dissent was as loud as could be mustered from a meagre attendance of 1,047. Several days later we had Queen of the South at home and it was watched by a critically low crowd of 968. It was a 2-0 defeat and once again the crowd reacted angrily. The *Ayr Advertiser* was unrestrained by sycophancy: "Form in both of these games was pathetic and inexcusable." Contrary to expectation Premier League St.Mirren were beaten 2-1 in the return at Ayr and the return match against Queen of the South brought a heartening 4-1 victory even although qualification was impossible by then.

The protests receded. For now! The first four league matches comprised a win at home to Alloa Athletic, a draw away to Hearts, a win at home to Partick Thistle then a draw at home to Hamilton Accies. This was tolerable. The four consecutive defeats that followed was a state of affairs that was intolerable. Once more the *Ayr Advertiser* summed up what we all felt. After defeat four (Ayr United 1 Clydebank 3) this was written: "There is almost no adjective strong enough to describe adequately Ayr United's performance on Saturday. They performed like a bunch of strangers." If the reporter was keen enough to find a strong enough adjective he should have stood in the Somerset Road end. There was no shortage of strong adjectives in there although they were probably not printable.

Falkirk 1 Ayr United 3 occurred on 9th October, 1982. It was the club's first away league win since 3rd October, 1981. In that time there had been seventeen winless away league fixtures in a row. It was not the start of a revival. No wins were recorded in the next seven league matches. During that phase I had a diversion from the despondency. As diversions go it was a major one. I got married to Carol and we set up our first home in Irvine. Two days after the wedding Ayr United had a bleak result in bleak surroundings. It was Clyde 3 Ayr United 1. A Paris honeymoon was a vastly better option.

While living in Irvine I used to enjoy visiting Terry McGibbons who lived locally. Mrs McGibbons would roll out a hostess trolley laden with cakes and over tea it was a pleasure to converse with Terry. Between 1933 and 1938 he scored 118 goals in 178 league appearances for Ayr United. All except one of these seasons were in the top flight. He still retained his passion for the club.

Reverting back to 1982/83, wins were sporadic. Too sporadic! After losing at Perth on 8th January we were just three points above the relegation zone. Worse was to come. Losing at Alloa in the Scottish Cup in 1982 was bad enough but getting eliminated at home to Albion Rovers in 1983 was even worse. Once more Jim Robb of the *Ayr Advertiser* availed himself of the opportunity to write a less than glowing report: "It was an embarrassment to everyone with Somerset Park connections. Thousands of fans have already had enough; many more will follow them away from the terracing unless something is done quickly." He deserved to be commended for his gift of prophecy. The next home game attracted 924 for a visit from Airdrie. Four weeks after that just 778 pitched up for a fixture against Clydebank.

Ayr United versus Dunfermline Athletic on 9th April, 1983. The sparsely populated terracing speaks of an apathy for relegation battles.

On 9th April a 3-2 defeat at home to Dunfermline Athletic was catastrophic. It was a relegation four-pointer. With five games left we were now just two points above Dunfermline who occupied a relegation spot. The fans did not meet this result with stoic acceptance. Anger had peaked so much that there was a demonstration in Tryfield Place after the game. I was one of the demonstrators. In retrospect I remain unrepentant. On the Monday Willie McLean resigned. George Caldwell was now in charge. With Queen's Park already relegated we entered the final match one point ahead of Dunfermline Athletic and we had a superior goal difference. The crucial fixtures were Clyde versus Ayr United and St.Johnstone versus Dunfermline Athletic. In the event of a Dunfermline win we would be safe in the event of a draw at Shawfield. Bill McWilliam ran buses to this match at the subsidised price of £1. St.Johnstone had an incentive to win because defeat for them would mean losing the league title in favour of Hearts. Clyde 3 Ayr United 2 was the result which had us all scrambling for news from Perth. 1-0 to St.Johnstone. Phew!

In the summer of 1983 there was no optimism amongst the fanbase and rightly so. The only expectation was that there would be another struggle. Five years earlier there were hopes of getting out of the First Division. Now the hopes were that the club would survive in it. Kilmarnock had now been relegated and they were scheduled to play at Ayr in the opening league fixture. They won 2-0. Apart from the Ayrshire Cup it was their first win at Ayr since 3rd January, 1967. The League Cup had now reverted to a knockout basis over two legs for the first two rounds. Within a week of the derby defeat we lost to Clydebank both home and away.

Times were getting to be desperately disappointing with home crowds barely scraping past one thousand. Based on the individual talent it made no sense. This was a team containing such as Eric Morris, Ian McAllister, Gerry Collins, Derek Frye, Robert Connor and Alan McInally. On 7th October Derek Frye was transferred to Clyde. His new club then became revitalised after a start in which they got three points from the first ten games. Derek Frye was a key player in that transformation. Supporters do not have privy to the internal running of a club but that did not prevent questions from being asked. The most common mode of protest in such times is simply to not turn up. In 1983/84 the terracing admission to Somerset Park cost £1.30 for an adult. Even allowing for inflation this was cheap. Disillusionment rather than cost was the main cause of falling attendances. However decreasing crowds was not a malaise unique to Ayr United. For now, at least, people were falling out of love with football.

January 2nd, 1971, Kilmarnock versus Ayr United –
Crowd = 15,240.
January 3rd, 1984, Kilmarnock versus Ayr United –
Crowd = 2,890.

The New Years of old were a nostalgic memory. I was there in 1971 and 1984 but thousands on both sides had fallen by the wayside. That 1984 derby was badly frustrating. Kilmarnock were given a complete roasting but we contrived to lose 1-0 to a goal conceded two minutes from the end.

There was no repeat of the Scottish Cup humiliations suffered in the two previous years. Losing 1-0 away to Dundee United had to be put into context. Later in the season Dundee United reached the semi-finals of the European Cup, beating Roma 2-0 at Tannadice then losing 3-0 in the second leg. At Tannadice Ayr United ran Dundee United closer than Roma. Moreover the 76th minute goal was scored by Paul Sturrock after Davy Dodds had fouled Ayr goalkeeper Jimmy Brown. I cannot claim to have been there that night but those who did travel had a similar story. It was a tale of snow blizzards so bad that it was a difficult feat even to approach the turnstiles.

One Ayr United team was successful in season 1983/84. Radio Clyde had been running what was known as the Kick-Off Quiz since 1982. League clubs were represented by supporters plus one player. Our player was Davy Armour. The rest of the team comprised Tom Cockburn, Sandra Moore and myself. While this competition lasted we competed at places as diverse as Bearsden, Hampden, Dumbarton, Clydebank and Kirkintilloch. One of our victories was against Rangers in the bowels of Hampden's South Stand. At the time it was a record winning margin for the competition. Beating Rangers at Hampden by a record score was most satisfying. It remains the only time Ayr United have beaten Rangers at Hampden! In 1984 we reached the final where we lost to Hamilton Accies who were the Real Madrid of the quiz world.

On Thursday, 29th March, 1984, our first child was born. This was our daughter Jill. For that reason I was glad to skip the Morton match at Somerset Park on the Saturday. Mother and child just had to be the priority. Morton won 2-1 anyway. One week later the result was Raith Rovers 5 Ayr United 0. Even the family priorities did not allow me to be unaware that a relegation battle was unfolding. A 1-0 loss at Airdrie then left the club in third bottom place, just two points ahead of second bottom Raith Rovers with four to play. The penultimate match was a 3-0 defeat at Kilmarnock watched by just 1,495. This rendered the situation desperate. We were one point ahead of the relegation zone with one to play. The key fixtures were Meadowbank Thistle versus Raith Rovers and Dumbarton versus Ayr United. Alloa Athletic were already doomed. It was assumed that Raith Rovers would win. The assumption proved correct. This meant that we had to win at Dumbarton to stay up. Dumbarton were already assured of promotion to the Premier League but they still had a chance of winning the league. Their hopes were pinned on beating Ayr United and hoping that Morton would lose to Kilmarnock. Morton did win but Dumbarton proceeded on the basis that they might pip them. Gerry Collins scored two headed goals just before half-time but in the second half Dumbarton were relentless. Lawrie McGee got sent off with twenty minutes left and it started to get even more desperate. Then Alan McInally tied it up at 3-0 with a wonder goal minutes from the end. Our fans were ecstatic. On a personal level I had the same kind of feeling as the one experienced in the Scottish Cup quarter-final at Firhill in 1973. The jubilation continued on our way out of Boghead. Yet these last day relegation escapes are bad for the nerves. Why do we put ourselves through it?

Stevie Evans in action against Alloa Athletic on 17th March, 1984. The miserly attendance was 673.

Ongoing there was a danger that things were going to get tougher. Alan McInally was sold to Celtic and Robert Connor was sold to Dundee. There was a fear too of losing Ian McAllister who initially signed a short term contract for one month. It may seem that I have been guilty of over punctuating the text with crowd figures but this is essential since crowd figures are illustrative of trends in relation to the attitudes of fans. After opening the 1984/85 league programme with a 1-1 draw against Hamilton Accies, we proceeded to draw 0-0 at Kilmarnock in fixture two. The Rugby Park attendance was 2,013. Kilmarnock had a player red-carded in the sixth minute so it was not an especially glorious result but it seemed as if football was a matter of supreme indifference to people. Three weeks later our 1-1 draw at Motherwell was watched by 2,069. Even Celtic and Rangers were attracting attendances that were moderate by their own standards.

The League Cup had now reverted to a knockout basis over one leg. We proceeded to eliminate Motherwell 1-0 at Ayr before losing by the same score away to Hearts. The form in the First Division was acceptable for now. Eight matches into the programme the top three were Airdrie (12 points), Motherwell (11 points) and Ayr United (11 points). By the third Saturday in November we were ninth having just lost away to Clyde who got their winner through Derek Frye.

The last two Saturdays of 1984 were occupied in losing at Forfar and Hamilton respectively. With Kilmarnock due at Ayr on 2nd January there was at least an opportunity to lift the mood. The opportunity was taken. John McNiven scored the only goal in the last minute. It was New Year 1984 in reverse. Both Ayrshire clubs were still hovering perilously close to the dreaded relegation zone. Of course football has the propensity to throw up surprises which can be pleasant. In the previous season a run of three consecutive defeats was terminated in a 5-1 win away to Meadowbank Thistle. In February 1985 a 5-0 win at Forfar was similarly termed a freak result. Entering this match Forfar Athletic, although fifth, were two points off the top whereas Ayr United were in what was developing into a virtual default position of just above the drop zone. The Forfar match was played in snow blizzards which worked to our advantage in the second half. It was 0-0 at half-time.

The prospect of playing St.Mirren in the Scottish Cup was formidable, even with home advantage. In 1984/85 they were to finish fifth in the Premier League, beaten for fourth place by Rangers having a better goal difference. It was still enough for European qualification. In that context a 1-0 defeat was just about sufferable.

Football fortunes are cyclical and this is especially true for Ayr United. It is too bad that sometimes the wheel of fortune takes too long to turn. Between March and April 1985 it turned quickly and favourably in a run comprising six wins, one draw and one defeat. It all started with a 4-1 win at Hamilton where most of us looked on in a state of pleasurable amusement at the transformation. During that run we ruined Airdrie's promotion hopes by beating them home and away. The home game was 5-1. Losing at home to the already relegated Meadowbank Thistle in the last game was a luxury we could afford. Relegation fears were long since banished by finishing precisely midway in the fourteen-club First Division.

That Meadowbank game was played on the same afternoon as the Bradford City fire disaster. The tragedy was a major topic of conversation at that evening's Player of the Year function. Future Ayr United player Ross Jack played for Lincoln City at Bradford on that fateful afternoon. In the same month the Heysel Stadium disaster occurred. The headlines generated by it all caused a lot of people to take a sickener to football. A couple of months earlier we had looked on aghast at the television coverage of Millwall supporters rioting at Luton. All this combined to have a generally adverse effect. Football has traditionally created back page headlines. Now the headlines were on the front pages and they were bleak. Going to the football was far from a pleasurable pursuit according to the way it was being portrayed but it could not be denied that it was an accurate portrayal rather than just negativity for the sake of it. The ramifications were there for all clubs.

Ayr United versus Kilmarnock on 31st August, 1985

In August 1985 I left the Halifax Building Society in order to become an insurance agent with the Co-operative Insurance in Kilmarnock. My area was mainly, but not entirely, New Farm Loch. For the next thirteen years I took great care not to mention Ayr United when entering people's homes. It could have had an adverse effect when trying to build up relationships with people who were a potential source of business. Sometimes conversations would take place about the previous Saturday's football and I was able to discuss brief details of the Kilmarnock game based on what I had read. This, and the fact that I could recall being at their big European nights in the sixties, occasionally conveyed the impression that I was a Kilmarnock supporter despite continually answering no to the question: "Were you there on Saturday?" On derby occasions though the answer was yes. Our first two league matches of 1984/85 were a 3-0 defeat at home to Falkirk then a 1-0 defeat at Forfar. Fixture three was Ayr United 3 Kilmarnock 0 so of course I was there. Killie had Blair Millar sent off in the first half. On the Monday at lunchtime I was standing two behind him in a queue at a baker's in John Finnie Street. He worked in a nearby bank. Kilmarnock too were part time then.

Aberdeen 5 Ayr United 0. This League Cup defeat was against the reigning Scottish champions. It was quite telling that goalkeeper David Purdie won the Man of the Match award. Mercifully this was not the standard of opposition on a weekly basis but it still degenerated into a struggle. If the Kilmarnock result was a boost to morale it did not manifest itself in results. Showing no momentum whatsoever, the next two results were a 1-1 draw at Alloa and a 3-1 demise at home to Brechin City.

Any stories you have heard about the eccentricities of Hugh Sproat are almost certainly true. In a match at Airdrie in October 1985 he went on strike after the home team got awarded a penalty. He was raging at the award. When John Millar was lining up to take it Hughie stood motionless on the line with his arms folded. Millar ran up and struck the ball but still he showed no inclination to attempt a save. Then, with rapid reflexes, he unfolded his arms and dived. He nearly saved it but the ball slipped through his hands. I found it extraordinary that the media did not report this incident. The match was lost 4-1. Airdrie had Ally MacLeod in the dugout while out on the field they had Henry Templeton and John Sludden. The world would seem a happier place once all three had switched allegiance. Ally was the first in line. He rejoined Ayr United three weeks later. He was no sooner back when he commented: "There is a lot of work to be done."

On 14th December, 1985, Henry Templeton scored a hat-trick at Ayr inside the first twenty-five minutes. Airdrie got another to lead 4-0 at half-time. Whether through an act of mercy or not it remained that way. In consequence the club sat foot of the table with ten points from eighteen games.

On New Year's Day a 2-1 win at Kilmarnock lifted some of the gloom. It was reminiscent of the year before when a New Year derby win was achieved in the midst of otherwise sad times. Even in view of that win we were foot of the table that evening while Kilmarnock were second top. Forfar Athletic were below Kilmarnock on goal difference only and with a game less played. Brechin City were two points behind Forfar with two games in hand over them. With two going up automatically Forfar and Brechin were realistic promotion contenders. Supporters are liable to argue about their club being bigger than other clubs but the league table will only define clubs by their points total.

In January 1986 we flitted from Irvine to Symington. It was a pleasure to find out that the village had more Ayr United supporters than I had expected. Occasionally supporters' buses originating in Troon would pick up in the village but for what remained of 1985/86 there was insufficient demand and it was little wonder.

The 1980 Scottish Cup visit to Easter Road was replicated in 1986. Again it was a Sunday and again it was nice to have an excuse to visit Edinburgh. It was a defeat again too but losing 1-0 to a stoppage time goal made it a closer tie than expected. Yet it was frustrating to get within seconds of a replay. Including the cup tie we had five consecutive away games, two of which were at Dumbarton. The only win in that spell was 1-0 at Cappielow after which it was reported that: "Ally MacLeod has reminded his players that the search for First Division safety is not yet over."

An unexpected 2-1 win at Falkirk on the evening of 19th March put the club up to fifth place. Sitting above nine other clubs at an advanced stage of the season did not prevent the *Ayrshire Post* from issuing a warning: "Although Ayr United have now pulled away from the bottom places there is still danger due to having played more games than most of the fellow strugglers." The danger was real as evidenced by the fact that no further league games were won in the remainder of the season. It reached the stage where a mathematical miracle was required. The permutation of results required for safety became increasingly improbable. When relegation threatens it is time for the brain to go into overdrive to work out what sequence of overall results will do. To put it more succinctly it is clutching at straws. A final finish of second bottom brought relegation along with Alloa Athletic. In 1978 the aim was to get out of the second tier. Eight years later it had happened but at the wrong end. The third tier now beckoned. For third tier read bottom tier.

Stevie McIntyre, right, at Easter Road on 16th February, 1986.

8. The Fightback

Please do not misconstrue the heading. The fightback referred to is in relation to a return to Scotland's second tier only. Scotland's Premier League existed in some far off place well beyond Ayr United's horizon. These were miserable times to be populating the Somerset Park terraces yet the faith in Ally MacLeod remained unshaken. He had a great knack of knowing the correct thing to say. Our second fixture of the season was a 5-0 defeat away to Raith Rovers which prompted him to express these comments: "We are just as well losing five goals in one game than one every game for five matches. I won't be panicked into making changes." The next game was a midweek League Cup tie at Kilmarnock. Hours before kick-off John Sludden was signed. He had been on loan from Airdrie since February but he was now our player. He proceeded to score in a 2-1 win against Kilmarnock. The visit of Dundee United in the next round was viewed as being an exercise in damage limitation and we succumbed to three second half goals.

Battling in the league was a sobering experience. "We have no divine right to promotion" was a common utterance from the doubters. Defeats away to Albion Rovers and Cowdenbeath caused the doubters to swell in number. At Cowdenbeath the attendance was 260. After that match I wrote a scathing editorial in the next week's match programme. Beyond doubt it would have found disfavour with the directors. I got away with it this time but future misdemeanours of this sort were to solicit a phone call from Helen Nelson to say that the directors would like to see me. It was a bit like an errant schoolboy being called to the headmaster's office. Yet these discussions were constructive and cordial, besides which I was a volunteer rather than a paid employee. Not that any of this mattered in the grand scheme of things. Above all the first team result was the overriding priority. A week after the demise at Cowdenbeath we had a 2-0 win at home to Meadowbank Thistle who were top of the league. There was no fear of relegation. In the three-league structure there was nowhere to get relegated to. It was a moot point anyway. Form increased sufficiently to reach the promotion fringe. With Ally MacLeod in charge there was always the possibility that things would improve. On New Year's Day 1987 Stranraer were beaten 4-2 at Ayr. This was the first of six consecutive league wins. That run concluded with a 4-0 win away to Stenhousemuir which claimed top place. On the way home that night the driver of the supporters' bus I was on kept asking people for directions, even while heading west on the M80. On the Saturday it was the team's turn to lose its way in a 2-0 defeat at Arbroath. Time would prove this to be Ayr United's last away defeat for more than a year.

In consecutive years the Scottish Cup was exited in Edinburgh, this time against Meadowbank Thistle. In the round before Stranraer were beaten at Ayr in a replay but the real excitement was in the original tie. We went a goal down so early that some of our supporters were not yet in the ground and the equaliser came so late that a lot of our supporters had already left the ground. Ian McAllister sent a defence splitting pass in the direction of John Sludden who found himself with only the goalkeeper to beat but with nearly half the length of the field to run. The tension was unbearable as he closed in on goal. Will he? Won't he? He did! The place erupted. There was even a pitch invasion. In retrospect this may seem like an overreaction for a draw at Stranraer but the nature of the goal and it happening seconds from the end combined to make the elation a natural reaction.

In football parlance there is a cliché which describes a close league finish as going down to the wire. On 9th May, 1987, the last round of Second Division fixtures got played. The expression 'down to the wire' was made for this day. We needed a draw at home to Stirling Albion for promotion. A win combined with a Meadowbank Thistle defeat at Alloa would mean that we would be champions. An Ayr defeat and a Raith Rovers win at Stranraer would promote Raith unless Stirling Albion were to win at Ayr by a big enough margin to edge it on goal difference. A Stirling Albion win would promote them in the event of a Raith Rovers defeat. It may sound complicated but the football brain is able to work out such permutations. Since Meadowbank Thistle were expected to win, it was easier to simply ponder that a draw against Stirling Albion was the minimum requirement. A crowd of 4,438 descended on Somerset Park. Anticipation gave way to frustration when a 2-0 deficit was faced at half time. In the second half the responsibility for taking a penalty kick was foisted on Kenny Wilson who had his effort saved. Hopes seemingly vanished when the deficit was stretched to 3-0 with less than half an hour left on the clock. Ian McAllister (67 minutes) and John Sludden (76 minutes) succeeded in setting up a frantic finish in which the excitement was almost tangible. Alas, the final whistle was blown with no further scoring. Meadowbank Thistle stepped up with Raith Rovers. We entered the ground with the possibility of becoming champions and we departed having finished fourth.

Shamefully I have to admit that I should not have been at the game at all and this had nothing to do with the frustrating outcome. For the previous couple of days Carol had been in a maternity ward in Irvine's Ayrshire's Central Hospital. The visiting times were in the afternoon then again in the evening. I had been visiting afternoon and evening until the Saturday. The birth was not due and I said that I would skip Saturday afternoon. Carol was okay with this. However on arrival on the Saturday evening I was not popular and here is why. Since it was a beautiful sunny day the women in the ward were permitted to accompany their menfolk on a walk round the hospital grounds. This meant that she was left on her own, something I still regret and would have regretted even if promotion had been won. Baby David was born on the Monday afternoon. That night Ayr United were playing Kilmarnock at Somerset Park in an Ayrshire Cup semi-final. I was not so callous as to even think about going! Sometimes, just sometimes, there are more important things in life than football.

In retrospect the narrow failure in 1987 was a blessing in disguise. The season ahead was a quite wonderful time of attacking abandon. 1987/88 would remain fondly remembered for decades. Ally MacLeod was back to his inspirational best and, after signing Henry Templeton on the eve of the season, he had just the players to perform his favoured brand of football. In pre-season we had a special treat. It is far from unknown for clubs to advertise glamour friendlies when the opposition could not be thus described other than with a stretch of the imagination. With no reservations at all the visit of Arsenal most certainly did comprise a glamour friendly, especially since they were at full strength. Three days earlier we had won 8-0 at Annan. This time we were on the end of a 6-0 loss. We took heart from the obvious knowledge that such formidable opposition did not await in the Scottish Second Division.

Losing 1-0 at home to Dumbarton in the League Cup was irritating on the night but inconsequential in relation to what was coming our way. Fixture five of the league campaign was a 1-1 draw at Stirling. It was the first league match in Scotland to be played on a synthetic surface. Quite frankly it was an appalling surface. It had the texture of a hall floor. With that result we topped the league with three wins, two draws and no defeats. Brechin City and Queen's Park lurked behind on goal difference but not for long. A week later the result was Cowdenbeath 1 Ayr United 6 and it was magnificent to watch. It was the first time Ayr United had scored six in a league match since the 6-4 win at Montrose on 14th October, 1978. Here in 1987 it was the first of eight consecutive league wins. Having waited nine years to see an Ayr team score six in a league fixture, the wait for it to happen again was merely three weeks. Stenhousemuir 0 Ayr United 6 whipped up so much fervour that Ally MacLeod voiced concern over the number of pitch invasions. Near the end a Stenhousemuir defender slammed the ball against his own post. It really did look as if he was trying to score an own goal but the intention could only have been to lump the ball out for a corner-kick. In all my time watching Ayr United I have only twice seen a referee laugh during a match. This incident at Ochilview was the second time. The first time was on 27th December, 1982, during a home match against Hearts. Alex MacDonald got hurt and he lay on the ground writhing in what was definitely genuine pain. This was just in front of where I was stood. His team mate Sandy Jardine and the referee stood over the scene while the physio got to work on the still distressed player. Then an Ayr supporter shouted: "Ah hope it's sair, MacDunalt." (The severe expletive has been omitted!). At that point Alex MacDonald burst out laughing and momentarily forgot the pain. This had an infectious effect causing Jardine, the physio and the referee to also start laughing. The referee's good humour towards MacDonald did not last. Later in the match he sent him off. It hardly mattered though. Hearts won 3-0.

Having gone off on a tangent let us revisit those glorious days in the autumn of 1987. The team was rampant. Scoring for fun is a footballing cliché but nevertheless it was justified. The essence of it all was captured in the requirement for the appeal for the fans to restrain their enthusiasm. Admittedly these pitch invasions had to stop yet the glee intensified week by week. **W**alker, **T**empleton and **S**ludden were rattling in the goals. The initials gave rise to the phrase **W**e **T**hree **S**trikers. After we had played everybody once the record was Played 13 Won 11 Drawn 2 Lost 0 For 39 Against 6 Points 24. Walker, Templeton and Sludden were the league's top three scorers so far. Away days were the best. On our travels the excitement escalated. Losing 3-0 at home to St.Johnstone was dismissed as a blip. Whether arrogant or not we were correct to dismiss it in this manner. One week later it was party time at Montrose even although the party mood occurred late. We were 1-0 down with less than half an hour to go. Then came a scoring burst of three Ayr goals in three minutes. Ultimately it ended in a 4-2 win but the bonus had yet to come. Back in the car (it was my friend Hugh Cole's car on this particular day) the classified check on the radio issued joyous news. St.Johnstone 0 Cowdenbeath 1. The ground conceded to our nearest rivals had been quickly clawed back.

Promotion celebrations at Stirling on 26th March, 1988

This Ayr United team had flair. It was a typical Ally MacLeod team. Week in week out it was great to watch. It was a team possessed of character too. The fighting qualities displayed at Montrose were repeated when Cowdenbeath were at Ayr on the Saturday before Christmas. Cowdenbeath led by a goal scored in the 13th minute. The teams were still separated by this at a critically late stage. It would have been worse had not Paul Cherry missed an open goal in the 75th minute. The match was won 3-1 with goals by Dougie McCracken (77 minutes), John Sludden (78 minutes) and Henry Templeton (87 minutes). It was a turnaround created by a tactical masterstroke from Ally MacLeod. Dougie McCracken was a defender but Ally pushed him up front ten minutes before his equaliser.

Despatching Stirling Albion 4-0 at home on Boxing Day was the second of seven consecutive league wins. During that run we had a sterner test at cup level. Dunfermline Athletic away was considered winnable even although they were in the Premier League and we were in the third tier. With the assistance of subsidised buses the travelling support was estimated at 2,500 in the overall crowd of 8,484. Conveniently the one I was on departed Symington. When we reached the Forth Bridge word came through that the Raith Rovers versus Rangers tie had been postponed due to waterlogging. In view of the proximity of Kirkcaldy to Dunfermline there was a palpable fear that the same fate would befall East End Park. Jim Leishman was the Dunfermline manager at this time and in his autobiography he mentioned how much he enjoyed the choruses of 'Super Ayr' that afternoon. He claimed it was so catchy that he could not help tapping his feet. As for the serious business of the match, it ended 1-1. On a wet Wednesday night the crowd at Ayr for the replay was 11,712. Dunfermline won 2-0 and they beat Rangers by the same score at East End Park in the next round.

The league form might justifiably have been defined as rampant but shaking off St.Johnstone proved stubbornly difficult. Even in February it was a virtual certainty that both clubs would be promoted so the main focus was now on the title. St.Johnstone 2 Ayr United 0 on 27th February cut our lead to three points. Losing this four-pointer carried a degree of disappointment but it had to be viewed in context. It was Ayr United's first away defeat in all competitions since 14th February, 1987. Defeats in places like Perth, Dundee and Arbroath always had the blow softened by a visit to the great chippy in Auchterarder. Supporters from this time are bound to remember it. Fans of many clubs frequented the place. Nothing completely erases the pain of defeat. It is probably just a case of making the best of a bad situation. Similarly an ice cream at Nardini's is an antidote to losing at Cappielow. Anyway enough of this talk of defeat. This was 1987/88 when defeat was a rare commodity.

Ayr United became plastered over the national news following a *Sunday Post* story the day after the St.Johnstone match. Central to it all was a proposed takeover bid by David Murray. As a shareholder I started to receive correspondence outlining the fine detail of the offer. The question of whether to accept or not was addressed by a shareholders' vote. Only the larger shareholders were permitted to take part in the vote meaning that I was eliminated from the process. Of the sixty involved all except four rejected the takeover proposals.

Boardroom matters are essential to the running of a football club but the life and soul only seriously manifests itself when the first team is playing. That is when we feel the elation, the disappointment or those other emotions that land in between. On the first Saturday in March, Ayr United 5 Cowdenbeath 0 did create elation and there was a bonus when the announcement came over that St.Johnstone had lost 3-0 away to Stenhousemuir. When the announcement was made most of us were clear of the ground but it was still clearly audible and very well received. In taking pleasure at a St.Johnstone defeat there was no element of grudge against the Perth club. Quite simply they were our closest rivals and the prevailing situation was 'them or us'. A fortnight later another goalfest ended Ayr United 6 Albion Rovers 2. It meant that promotion would be ours in the event of getting just one

The Ayrshire Cup final at Kilmarnock on 10th May, 1988. Jim Hughes (3) and Ian McAllister (5).

point at Stirling a week later. In the previous May, Stirling Albion had shattered our promotion hopes. However the situation was not nearly as fraught this time. It is true that we once more needed one point for promotion but this time we had seven games in which to obtain it. After a 2-2 draw the scenes were manic. We all spilled onto the artificial surface to hail the players who had congregated in the Annfield stand. Three weeks later we decanted to that part of the world again. A win would clinch the title at Alloa. Admittedly we had four matches in which to obtain the requisite two points. This did not deter the black and white-bedecked hordes from being fully expectant of nailing it on the day. It happened – Alloa Athletic 1 Ayr United 3. The promotion celebration at Stirling had taken place on terra firma. At Alloa the pitch invasion in celebration of the title had no such luxury. It was a wet afternoon and the pitch had cut up badly. Yet none of us cared about mucky shoes as we squelched around on the muddy surface. It was a truly memorable day. In something of an anti climax just one point was taken from the three remaining fixtures yet sixty-one points comprised a club record points total (at two points for a win).

The season was rounded off with a 2-0 win at Kilmarnock in the Ayrshire Cup final but the post match discussion revolved around it ending as eight versus eleven after Kilmarnock had three players sent off. Excluding the Ayrshire Cup ten opposition players got red-carded against Ayr United in the season. Our own red card count for season 1987/88 was just one. The offender was Jim McCann in a home fixture against Alloa Athletic.

In stepping up a league there was none of the usual talk about consolidation. Confidence was so high that there was a definite belief that the team was capable of kicking on and getting a further promotion. The idea that we would be fighting against relegation did not even occur. There was an attitude of 'bring it on'. We had now been out of the Premier League for ten years. Surely this situation could not persist indefinitely. When taking stock in 1988 this is how it looked, no matter how ill-judged the march of time would prove this positivity to be ill-placed.

On 6th August, 1988, the crowd topped 10,000 for a pre-season friendly. The visiting hordes were attracted by the Souness revolution at Rangers. It remains a record crowd for a Somerset Park friendly. Losing 4-1 to an expensively assembled squad was not critical. Less than a fortnight later we had another stern test, this time away to Scottish champions Celtic in the League Cup. That too was lost by the same 4-1 margin. It was a tie preceded by an appalling piece of gamesmanship. The teams emerged and a short time afterwards the Ayr team trooped off the field and back up the tunnel. To myself and the other Ayr supporters standing on the terracing it was a mystery. We looked on in bemusement. Celtic manager Billy McNeill had complained to the referee about the Ayr strip causing a colour clash. As a player he had often played in the green and white hoops of Celtic against Ayr teams in white shirts and black shorts. What was different this time? Quite remarkably the referee conceded to McNeill's request. The team trooped out for a second time and the change kit was blue. It was an appalling episode designed to create an anti-climax.

The start of the league programme yielded three wins and a defeat. Game three was a 2-0 loss at Kilmarnock that was most unexpected. Neither before nor since has the Ayr United support entered a derby match so confident of victory. It was all just a delusion. Afterwards Ally MacLeod said: "We must learn to adapt when things go wrong."

The First Division was a tight league and this is not being mentioned as a typically clichéd remark. At 3 pm on 10th September, Clyde were in top place. Two hours later they were ninth out of fourteen. After seven matches Airdrie, Dunfermline Athletic and Morton all had ten points at the top. We were fourth, just one point behind. The notion was to stay with the pack or even get ahead of it. It was a notion that we were quickly to be disabused of. The situation was the preliminary to a run of eleven consecutive league matches without a win. In metaphorical terms supporting a football club is popularly described as a rollercoaster ride.

A rollercoaster climbs gradually then descends rapidly. This rollercoaster analogy describes the situation to perfection. Ayr United 3 Morton 1. We were on the way back. Er, no actually! On Christmas Eve we were crushed 5-1 at Dunfermline.

On 3rd January, 1989, the Somerset Park crowd of 8,585 was probably more than the teams deserved. Ayr United and Kilmarnock were on the same points total, uncomfortably close to the relegation zone. The Kilmarnock support got taunted with choruses of 'Happy New Year, Happy New Year' while we coasted to a 4-1 win. Coasted is not an exaggeration. The *Ayr Advertiser* report opined: "Having scored four goals, Ayr proceeded to express their superiority in other ways." The chief tormentors were Henry Templeton and John Sludden. One of my insurance customers from Kilmarnock spotted me at the game. Later that week I made my fortnightly call to his house and he said: "Was that no' an awfu disappointment at Ayr?"

The next match was also at home and it was also 4-1. For Airdrie! In the next again match we were on the wrong end of a 5-1 hammering at Clydebank. A 2-0 win at Dumfries offered some respite before the month concluded in a 4-1 defeat away to Hearts in the Scottish Cup. At Tynecastle we looked on aghast from the terracing at the Gorgie Road end while Hearts went 2-0 up with only eight minutes played. The outcome really could have been worse. I have always believed in the 'sing when you're winning' philosophy. January 1989 proved the value of enjoying it while you can.

In February the 4-1 scoreline emerged for the third time since beating Kilmarnock and yet again it was not in our favour. It was doubly damaging because the deed was done at Firhill and Partick Thistle were fellow strugglers. After the New Year game an Ayr United fanzine had been renamed '4-1' in commemoration of the derby win. Here we were in mid-February looking upon that scoreline as being a matter of dread. Eighteen days later we were back at Firhill because Clyde were sharing that ground. During and after the 1-0 loss the fans vented a lot of anger.

The structure of a 14-club league in which we played each other three times worked in our favour in 1988/89 because two of the three derbies were at Ayr. A week after the Clyde match Ayr United versus Kilmarnock would either have the effect of soothing or inflaming passions. With the score at 1-1 Ian McAllister headed the winner in the 74th minute. Suddenly the ire of seven days earlier seemed like a lifetime away. Yet the league table still had a sobering look. We were one point in front of Partick Thistle and Kilmarnock and two in front of Clyde and Meadowbank Thistle. This just left the doomed Queen of the South at the foot. In a nutshell we were just two points above the relegation zone with nine to play.

St.Johnstone 0 Ayr United 1 was the result of the last match ever played at Muirton Park. Those of us of an Ayr persuasion cared little for the historical significance although I would have had a totally different perspective had I indeed become a Saintee back in 1959. As things stood I considered the two points to be as valuable as gold dust and here is why. Two matches were left and whoever was going down with Queen of the South would either be Ayr United (33 points), Kilmarnock (32 points) or Clyde (31 points). For the penultimate set of fixtures it was assumed that Clyde would lose at Dunfermline. This would mean that Ayr United required a draw at home to Airdrie to ensure safety. Taking things for granted is a reckless activity when it comes to football. Clyde got a draw at Dunfermline thus necessitating an Ayr win. In stunned silence we watched on when Ian McPhee put Airdrie ahead with a goal timed at twenty-eight seconds. Henry Templeton proceeded to play the game of his life. He equalised then we took a first half lead through Tommy Walker. In the closing minutes there was great tension with it still standing at 2-1. Please hold on! Then with seconds to go Henry Templeton broke clear to make it 3-1 thereby creating a racket that lasted to the final whistle and beyond. This illustrates a concept that supporters of larger clubs fail to understand. Why would anyone wildly celebrate an escape from relegation? It would be pointless to define passion. Passion has to be experienced.

The season felt as if it was over but there was the matter of the final fixture at home to Morton. With the pressure off it had the resonance of a friendly. Morton's 1-0 win was not unduly troubling. After the match I got back to the car and put on the radio. West Sound were reporting on the celebrations at Palmerston where the result was Queen of the South 0 Kilmarnock 6. The Kilmarnock supporters were on the pitch. At Firhill the score was Clyde 1 St.Johnstone 0 so Clyde and Kilmarnock were tied on points and goal difference but Clyde were in the second from foot relegation position having scored less goals. However 1-0 for Clyde was a score rather than a result. Quite dramatically West Sound announced that Clyde had just been awarded a penalty which would relegate Kilmarnock if it were converted. It seemed ridiculously late. The game at Ayr had been finished for close to ten minutes. Goal for Clyde – Colin McGlashan! Kilmarnock were down. It was the last action of the game. That evening the Ayr United Supporters' Association had their Player of the Year function and I had the honour of presenting the trophy to Tommy Walker.

By the summer of 1989 Ayr United had been part time for fifty years. At the behest of the Scottish Football Association the club was compelled to relinquish full time contracts one day after the declaration of the Second World War. This restriction applied to all member clubs. When peace was resumed Ayr United did not revert to the club's pre-war status of being full time. The board's decision to go full time in 1989 came as a major, but welcome, surprise.

Due to redevelopment work ongoing at their own ground, Albion Rovers hosted Ayr United at Airdrie's Broomfield Park for the league opener. It was a gala occasion for Albion Rovers. In 1988/89 they had won a league title for the first time in their history and there was some pre-match entertainment involving novelty events. Their mirth continued in a 3-1 win. If full time football was going to make a meaningful change we were going to have to exercise patience. The Ayr support did not take kindly to this performance and the players were made to hear what the fans thought. I was one of the dissenters and a frank editorial in the match programme was the catalyst for another of those calls from Helen Nelson to tell me that the directors wished me to call into the boardroom for a discussion. Within the space of eleven days Hamilton

Accies won 1-0 at Ayr twice, the first time being in the League Cup. Notwithstanding any disagreements about the tone of programme material, it has to be mentioned that the board had ambition. The commitment to full time football was huge. So too was the £40,000 purchase of Tommy Bryce from Clydebank. In the previous season he had scored seven goals against Ayr United.

It took until fixture six to obtain the first league win. This was a 1-0 victory at Falkirk which just happened to comprise Ally MacLeod's 200th league win as Ayr United manager. As with so many of these statistics there is a dependency on my arithmetic being correct. Scrupulous checking and rechecking is the normal procedure before putting such information into the public domain. In the present day people are liable to put a query into a search string and leave themselves at the mercy of AI. When accuracy is at stake there are no substitutes for manual forms of research.

The win at Brockville was a boost to morale. So too was a 3-2 win at home to Clydebank a week later, even allowing for the need to hang on desperately towards the end. Tommy Bryce scoring his first Ayr United goal against his former club could almost have been scripted. Two consecutive wins could not be deemed to comprise a run. What did comprise a run though was one win in the next nine. Even with due allowance for there being five draws in the mix, the fans were restless. Kilbowie Park was a ground that Ayr United supporters entered with trepidation and rightly so. The winless run ended after a 4-1 loss at Clydebank and, once again, ire was volubly expressed. Fickleness is a criticism that supporters get accused of. Being unhappy in defeat and happy in victory is understandable and it might even mirror life itself. When failure transforms into any meaningful success you can count on people taking to the moral high ground. They will say: "Where are the moaners now?" It is a totally illogical line of thought. It is entirely natural to bemoan bad times and be happy to express delight when fortunes change for the better. The principle is the same whether or not the transformation is major or minor. To explain the point major transformation is typically a promotion and a minor transformation is a bad or mediocre run of results followed by a decent run of results. It is quite natural that supporters are liable to change mood. You will have guessed what this is alluding to. The hostile shouting at Clydebank was the preliminary to a run of five unbeaten matches, four of which were won. On Boxing Day a 2-0 win at home to Albion Rovers propelled Ayr United into fourth place. The last Saturday of the year saw a 1-0 loss at Forfar blamed on the pitch. In the *Ayr Advertiser* it was written: "The pitch looked far from playable with players having difficulty keeping their feet." I must confess that I was not at Forfar that day but on 2nd January I was at Hamilton where the pitch was not a contributory factor in a 4-0 hammering. It was horrible to watch. Henry Templeton had a penalty saved and Jim Hughes got sent off.

"We are the luckiest team alive to still be in the Scottish Cup." Those were the words of St.Mirren boss Tony Fitzpatrick after a 0-0 draw at Ayr and you would have struggled to find anyone who disagreed with him. The midweek replay was memorable for being played in snow blizzards. A 2-1 defeat and a hazardous journey home was our lot. In a curious chain of events the Ayr support was complicit in getting a player sent off. Jim McCann got yellow-carded for a tackle on Gudmunder Torfason who in turn was yellow-carded for his reaction. Our fans cheered when Torfason was shown his card. Then he turned round and made a gesture in our direction. A linesman witnessed this and reported it to the referee with the consequence that the Icelander got a second yellow card. His dismissal brought an even bigger cheer but there were no retaliatory gestures this time.

Several days later Ayr United played at McDiarmid Park for the first time. The novelty was unceremoniously ruined at the sight of St.Johnstone winning 4-0. Being a new stadium the acoustics were good. This rendered great clarity to the unsavoury chants and songs hurled at the team and the manager. There was discord in the boardroom too. Bill Barr quit as a director citing that he was "not comfortable with the present policies." The break was not permanent.

Perth was bad enough. A fortnight later though there was an even worse road trip. Airdrie! It was 6-0. This was the club's biggest margin of defeat in a competitive match since losing 8-1 at Easter Road on 16th December, 1972. Competitive? You may hardly think so. It is somehow inappropriate that this description relates to every match in a proper league or cup competition.

Ayr United 0 Albion Rovers 2 on 14th April was our first home defeat since 7th October, 1989. On the face of it this will seem like a creditworthy statistic and it may suggest that the fans had been insensitive in expressing sporadic ire. On further analysis it is an obvious fact that teams only play half of their matches at home. More forensic scrutiny would have revealed that the unbeaten home run extended to twelve matches (including the St.Mirren cup tie), seven of which were draws.

In Scotland's three-league system promotion and relegation between the two lower tiers was on a two-up and two-down basis. Promotion to and relegation from the Premier League was on a one-up and one-down basis. It was too bad that this system of self preservation had not been in force in 1978. In 1989/90 the one promotion place went to St.Johnstone. They clinched the title with a 2-0 win at Ayr. Watching another club's promotion party at your own ground is an uncomfortable experience. If the Sliding Doors episode in 1959 had turned out differently I would still have been at Somerset Park that afternoon but it is nonetheless difficult to imagine. In the grand scheme of things the thought of supporting a club other than Ayr United seems unnatural. As it says in scripture, we are created for a purpose.

Finishing tenth out of fourteen had the considerable consolation of avoiding relegation fears. Was full time football beneficial? Not yet. The improvement was just one league place of a difference.

In June 1990 the Carmichaels flitted to Monkton. Irvine – Symington – Monkton. Mysterious forces were at play. Were these successive house moves created by a mystical force leading to a gravitational pull towards Somerset Park? Probably not. In fact definitely not but it is a nice thought.

9. Life Beyond Ally

The fans had long since assumed ambitions which were less lofty than a return to the Premier League. In this phase of history it would have invited ridicule at the very mention of a hope to return there. The board was not similarly constrained in the matter of ambition. Talk can be cheap, especially when it is empty rhetoric. The Ayr United directors were not of a mind to engage in that way. Direct action was more their way of working. In the summer of 1989 the Family Stand extension was completed and full time football was restored for the first time in half a century. The purchase of Tommy Bryce was a further signal of intent. In the 1990 close season it was reported that Peter Weir had been bought from St.Mirren for £50,000. The truth was even more impressive. £66,000 was the cost to Ayr United.

22nd August, 1990, was an historic date. That evening an Ayr United match was screened live in its entirety for the first time. Moreover it was a satellite broadcast on BSkyB. The result, Celtic 4 Ayr United 0, will hereby be quickly glossed over! I once had the pleasure of interviewing Adam Fullarton in his Prestwick home. Adam had a distinguished career with STV but by 1990 he was overseeing outside broadcasts for BSkyB including this League Cup tie at Celtic Park. He said that it cost BSkyB £25,000 to mount the broadcast. Nine cameras were used. First, the pictures were beamed from Celtic Park to the transmitting station at Kirk o' Shotts, in Central Scotland, by a microwave signal. Then they were transferred to British Telecom who transmitted them to the BSkyB studios, who passed them on to the satellite situated 36,000 kilometres in orbit. The pictures were then retransmitted down to our television sets.

Ned Fullarton is second from the right in the back row. His grandson was a principal member of a team responsible for an historical Ayr United broadcast. This 1893 image is the oldest

Adam's grandfather was Ned Fullarton who played for the pre-amalgamation Ayr FC. The oldest surviving photograph taken at Somerset Park dates to 1893 and Ned is in it. When he posed for that long ago photograph he could not have dreamed of moving pictures being transmitted into outer space. Yet in a manner of speaking Sky News did exist in Ned's day. Ayr FC used to take pigeons to away games in order to send home goal updates!

This historical aside could be interpreted as a distraction from the start of Ayr United's 1990/91 league season. One win, three draws and two defeats yielded five points from a possible twelve. In losing 4-0 against Airdrie, Owen Coyle scored a Broomfield hat-trick against Ayr United for the second time in 1990. After Tommy Bryce had proven to be a consistently formidable opponent when at Clydebank the solution was buying him. Replicating the process with Owen Coyle would have been prohibitively expensive. His February hat-trick against Ayr United had occurred one day after Airdrie had signed him from Clydebank for £175,000.

Falkirk 1 Ayr United 2 occurred on 9th October, 1990. The date has been purposely emphasised because after this we lost every game played at Brockville until winning there on 24th February, 2001. This led to talk about it being a bogey ground. The word 'bogey' hints at superstition. In truth Falkirk simply had better teams for a decade.

Kilmarnock were now back in the second tier having been promoted as runners-up to champions Brechin City. It had been tight. Stirling Albion, in third place, had finished behind them on goal difference. The resumption of the Ayrshire derby drew 9,042 to Rugby Park. Our 1-0 half-time lead looked fragile since Jim McCann had been sent off in the 41st minute. The fears were confirmed when Kilmarnock pressed home their advantage to win 3-1. Whenever a morale boost is required a derby match has the potential to provide it. What now? Where, if anywhere, were the supporters going to get a boost?

Ayr United versus Queen of the South on 23rd October, 1990. Ian McAllister gets a shot away.

Tommy Walker in action at Kilmarnock on 13th October, 1990.

The Centenary Cup was a possibility. This competition was designed to commemorate the centenary of the Scottish League. The eligible clubs were all league clubs outwith the Premier League. It was planned as a one-off competition but it proved to be more popular than anticipated therefore it was restored under various guises to reflect sponsorship.

Ayr United's introduction to the tournament was subdued. For the first round tie at home to Brechin City the crowd was only 1,134. However this was not wholly attributable to fan apathy. The tie was played on a Tuesday night amidst severe rainstorms. Tommy Walker was the first player of any club to score in the competition. A 3-0 win was a fair reward for getting soaked and frozen. A fortnight later, in a 3-2 win at Montrose, Henry Templeton got the clincher in the 118th minute. Ayr United 4 Queen of the South 1 saw a comfortable passage into the semi-finals. Of the Ayr team that night six were Queen of the South players of the future. They were David Purdie, David Kennedy, David Smyth, Alan Gillespie, Tommy Bryce and Henry Templeton. Ally MacLeod was also destined to end up there in a managerial capacity. Clyde were beaten 2-0 at Ayr to take the club into what the media described as our first ever national final. The media were wrong.

To commemorate the Festival of Britain in 1951 there was a competition called the Festival St.Mungo Quaich. The participating clubs were the 'B' Division clubs therefore the criteria was the same as the Centenary Cup of 1990 i.e. competed for by league clubs outwith the top league. It could be argued that neither comprised a major tournament but nevertheless both were national tournaments with a comparable entry criteria. Favoured with home ties, Ayr United battled past Cowdenbeath and Stirling Albion before winning against Hamilton Accies on the toss of a coin. The final was then contested against Dumbarton at Firhill on 6th August, 1951. Dumbarton won 2-1 with a goal scored in the last minute of extra time.

Henry Templeton in the 1990 Centenary Cup final.

On Remembrance Sunday 1990 a crowd of 11,506 converged on Motherwell's Fir Park for the Centenary Cup final. The A77 was thick with traffic heading for the game. It was an enormous buzz. The Ayr support was housed on the terracing at the end that is now the home end of Fir Park. It struck me that a lot of the fans were people who had not been at a match for a long time. Some had scarves that were relics of a decade or two earlier. Ian McAllister scored at the end housing the Dundee support and it was still 1-0 at half-time. Billy Dodds equalised with a penalty then put Dundee ahead. David Smyth made it 2-2 with a crazy goal. His shot cannoned off Colin West. I can remember standing behind that goal and watching the ball deflect skyward. Then it plummeted like a stone and landed in the net. Billy Dodds got his hat-trick and the winner in the closing minutes of extra time. It was a real sickener but the Ayr team got a deserved ovation at the end.

There is an old saying that is sometimes used in a football context: "After the Lord Mayor's coach comes the dustcart." How apt. The sense of occasion and buzz at Motherwell was followed six days later with a 3-1 defeat at Forfar watched by 726. The first home match after the final attracted 1,737 for a 2-2 draw against Hamilton Accies. At Motherwell there was no breakdown on the split between each club's fans. Estimates put the Ayr support at 7,000 and this may have been reasonably accurate based on the amount of black and white in comparison to the amount of navy blue. Yet it would be unfair to criticise people who only appear for big games. We are not all cast from the same mould.

Raith Rovers 3 Ayr United 0. The visiting fans subjected the team to a volley of jeers at the end. Working on alternate Saturday mornings sometimes debarred me from getting to games in the east or north. I experienced no grief at missing this one. The writing was on the wall and it did not make for nice reading. Two days before this I was in the company of Ally MacLeod and Peter Weir for the launch of Volume One of the club's official history. By the time the photographs appeared in the local newspapers Ally was no longer the manager. Chairman Sandy Loudon told him that his contract would not be renewed in June. When a manager departs the expression 'by mutual agreement' is liable to be trotted out when it is really a euphemism for a sacking. In this instance it really was mutually agreed that it would be better to depart straight away. His last game in charge was Ian McAllister's testimonial versus Celtic. He remains Ayr United's most successful manager of all time.

With Davy Wells as caretaker manager five points were taken from a possible six. This was prior to the Ayrshire derby on 2nd January, 1991. With 9,448 inside Somerset Park it was more like the derbies of old. Other than the result! Kilmarnock's 2-1 win gave them their first New Year derby win at Ayr since 1967.

Glad to be in the illustrious company of Ally MacLeod and Peter Weir at a book launch in December 1990.

The question of who the next manager would be was the subject of speculation, some of it wild. It was George Burley. This was satisfactory although no one seemed to have guessed correctly. There was a bonus since he came to Ayr as a player-manager. In mentioning that he was a model professional this should not be interpreted as a cliché. When he applied for the job he had references from Bobby Robson, Iain Munro, Andy Roxburgh, Jim McLean and Tommy McLean. Interviewing well is an important prerequisite to getting a job. How beneficial would his skill set be when it came to the practical reality? That question had still to be answered but the fans had a good vibe. We had hope. Hope is probably the most abundant commodity in the make-up of Ayr United supporters. He selected himself to play in his first match in charge. This was a 1-0 defeat away to Meadowbank Thistle which was considered forgiveable. The requirement to 'hit the ground running' is a common concept in a new job, especially in football management. Notwithstanding the natural impatience for immediate success it was understood that at least some time would be required to make changes. "Burley led by example."

This was a journalistic take on his first home match in which the team had a 4-0 half-time lead against Brechin City, this being the full time result also.

The fans were quick to take a liking to George Burley. For now, at least, it seemed like the good times were on their way back. His stock rose with a Scottish Cup win at Clydebank which was normally a place to induce fear and trepidation. In the next round there was a win at Hamilton in a midweek replay. What a night that was. For many years it would be remembered for Peter Weir scoring a textbook free-kick and a climax in which Ally Fraser did a Roger Milla-style celebration after heading the winner seconds from the end. That evening was the first time I had experienced corporate hospitality at a match. It was a complimentary invitation from a director of Hamilton Accies. Out of respect for the hosts I felt compelled not to react manically at the late winner.

That Saturday Ally Fraser scored four in a 5-3 win at home to Raith Rovers. The good times were rolling. Rolling off a cliff! The next twelve games were winless. They comprised seven defeats and five draws. In the mix was a 5-2 loss away to St.Johnstone in the quarter-finals of the Scottish Cup. This might have been excusable had not the smallest player on the park (Allan Moore) scored a hat-trick of headers in the last ten minutes. One of the draws was 2-2 away to bottom club Brechin City.

The ambition had degenerated into nothing more than escaping relegation and this aspiration was realised without a ball being kicked. On 4th May Ayr United had no game but we had a vested interest when Hamilton Accies beat Clyde at Douglas Park. It meant that Clyde were going down with Brechin City. We had two games to spare, the last of which was a 1-0 win over Kilmarnock. That was on a Saturday. On the Monday Kilmarnock were back at Ayr for a 2-1 defeat in the Ayrshire Cup final.

The rapid back to back wins over Kilmarnock might reasonably have been described as papering over the cracks. Avoiding relegation to the third tier was undoubtedly a matter of relief but most of us harboured loftier ambitions. It was possible to cling to the notion that George Burley had not yet had a pre-season. The annual bout of hope resurfaced albeit that there were still doubters who could foresee nothing other than an eternal struggle.

Success in pre-season friendlies tends to be played down on the basis that teams are at an experimental stage. Yet to beat Coventry City 3-1 was a conspicuous success in the context of the visitors being an English First Division club. Please note that this was when the First Division actually was the **First** Division. It bode well that fitness levels were high. This energy was carried into the start of the season. For the first time since 1958/59 the first four league fixtures were won. Fixture five was a 1-1 draw at Kilmarnock. During this spell similar form was replicated in the League Cup with a 4-2 win away to Dundee being followed up by a 2-0 win at home to St.Johnstone. Hibs, on their way to winning the trophy, won 2-0 at Ayr in the quarter-finals. Significantly the crowd was 8,730. Looking around Somerset Park that night at least afforded a glimpse of better days.

Prior to the north terrace being covered there were hardy souls who would stand there in appalling weather, some with golf umbrellas and some not. In conditions of wind and heavy rain the usual suspects were rewarded for their fortitude with a 7-0 rout of Meadowbank Thistle. The softer creatures amongst us watched on from the refuge of the Somerset Road end. A week later we had the same number of goals which, although more evenly distributed, created even more excitement. Being 3-1 down at Cappielow with twelve minutes to go was a restless experience. Proceeding to win 4-3 with an Ian McAllister goal in stoppage time was a testimony as to why we should have more faith at times.

The Centenary Cup was now renamed the B & Q Cup. Ayr United's love affair with the competition was rekindled. Dundee (away), Stenhousemuir (away) and Stranraer (home) were all beaten by a common scoreline of 2-0. After a 3-2 home win against Queen of the South in the semi-finals, the opposition manager voiced disapproval at some of the refereeing decisions. The manager in question was Ally MacLeod. Once more the final was at Fir Park and once more we were allocated the same terracing areas. It was the first all-ticket match Ayr United had been involved in since 1966. This time the margin of defeat was again narrow – beaten 1-0 by Hamilton Accies. On this occasion there was no ovation from the Ayr fans. The performance was in complete contrast to the year before. It was awful. If I had been playing in goal for Hamilton Accies the result would have been the same! I remember drifting away and moaning about it. Somebody overheard me and said something like. "Give them a break. They did their best." A week-in-week-out fan would never have said that. In the *Ayrshire Post* Sports Editor Mike Wilson opted for a headline of FINAL LETDOWN.

The B & Q Cup ties had been interspersed by league fixtures which made the team's form difficult to fathom. Ayr United 0 Kilmarnock 3 on a Saturday was followed by Ayr United 4 Dundee 1 on the Tuesday night. It was the first time since November 1917 that an Ayr United team had lost a home league derby by more than two goals. After sourcing that statistic and including it in the match programme some older supporters were quick to recall losing 5-0 at home to Kilmarnock in 1938. However that was in the Scottish Cup rather than in the league. Not that this made it any more palatable.

On taking stock it could have been considered satisfactory to be hovering around mid-table. Some were of a persuasion to suffer from 'the bottle half empty' syndrome, a justifiable condition when weighed against the outstanding start to the league programme. It stood to be a long-ish campaign of forty-four fixtures in a league of twelve. By mid-season it had descended into a hotch-potch of brilliant performances laced with mind numbing mediocrity in between. It was inconsistency in its most acute form. Would the real Ayr United team stand up?

Motherwell at home in the Scottish Cup typified the sort of match likely to produce a good performance. We were up against the cup holders. When Duncan George hit an 87th minute equaliser in a 1-1 draw the place erupted. The passion and fervour on the pitch was more than matched on the terraces and in the stand. We then had the temerity to push in hope of a late winner. This tie was an outstanding example of why we love Somerset Park for the sheer partisanship. Inconsistency reared its ugly head when Motherwell won 4-1 in the replay. It was 4-0 by the 34th minute.

25th January, 1992. In the first image Duncan George's shot approaches the Motherwell net; in the second image it hits the net.

It was both difficult and irritating to try reconciling the team's form. Partick Thistle 4 Ayr United 1 got followed by three consecutive wins, the last of which was especially impressive. Raith Rovers 2 Ayr United 4 occurred at a time when the home team was in promotion contention. Ally Graham scored a hat-trick in a performance clearly noted by the home staff. This was 1992 and in 1994 he was in their League Cup winning team. The fans love to have a hero. Ally Graham was Ayr United's hero for now. After the match at Kirkcaldy we were sixth in the league. Three defeats in the next four soon had us all hoping that the basement clubs would continue to struggle. Even the solitary victory in that run failed to generate much in the way of confidence. After beating Forfar Athletic 1-0 at Ayr the *Ayrshire Post* called it "a poor game" then further mentioned that "the crowd booed their displeasure." George Burley commented: "We have 14-year-olds as good as any in Ayrshire but, while we are on the right lines, it will take time for them to come through." This was a plea for patience. Such pleas do not sit well. Supporters are impatient and with due reason. We were not putting our cash down at the turnstiles in return for a promise of better days. The mention of 14-year-olds took no cognisance of the fact that the club's under-18 team contested the BP Youth Cup final in April 1992. It was played at a questionable venue. Playing against their Hibs counterparts at Easter Road did not even have the pretence of a neutral venue. The attendance of 6,562 was a record for any BP Youth Cup final at the time. With the backing of 100% of the crowd the home team won 2-0. Two of the Ayr United youths were destined for a good future. They were Derek Allan and Gregg Hood. Three days later the first team was in Edinburgh to play in front of a contrasting attendance of 310. This was a league fixture against Meadowbank Thistle and it was rehoused to Tynecastle because the Commonwealth Stadium had been requisitioned for an athletics meeting. A 1-0 win was recorded. Two weeks later the season ended with a sixth-placed finish.

When the season finished it was already known that there was going to be a price increase for season 1992/93. An adult ground admission for Somerset Park would now be £4.50. There were few grumbles because the other First Division clubs were raising it to £5.

I had always said that I would not coerce the children into going to watch Ayr United but when the new season did get underway my son David decided that he would like to go. He had not long reached the age of five. His first game was a 0-0 draw against Sunderland. Would he want to go back? Yes he did. In fact he was so keen that I was made to go to matches early because he wanted to watch the players warming up. His older sister Jill became an occasional fan at this time but the years ahead saw her transformed into a regular too. Thus began the Family Stand years.

Somewhat rarely the first two First Division fixtures were at home. Of the ten opening league games in the 1990s there were six 1-1 draws and this one versus Dunfermline Athletic in 1992 was one of them. The run of eight winless opening league games from 1992 until 1999 inclusive is one of those dubious club records. With recourse to statistics the Dunfermline result was likely. Less likely was Ayr United 1 Meadowbank Thistle 2 three days later.

Anyone who has followed football for a while will have numerous memories. Conversations are peppered with them. Sometimes though matches are remembered for all the wrong reasons. In August 1992 a League Cup tie was lost 2-0 at Firhill. Ostensibly the result was not terrible. Partick Thistle had recently been promoted to the Premier League. However the moderate scoreline may have disguised our performance that night. It was simply terrible with not one meaningful shot registered on goal. The *Ayrshire Post* called it "an instantly forgettable tie." My personal thought at the time was: "What am I doing here? Why do we bother?"

The last question will be repeated because it raises an important point. Why do we bother? You will now be told why we bother. Football's propensity for creating a sudden mood change was about to manifest itself. The next home match was against Kilmarnock at Ayr. David Kennedy (49 minutes) and Ray

Montgomerie (52 minutes, own goal) brought about a 2-0 victory. All was right with the world. For now! Fast forward two weeks when Morton came down and won 2-0. In the aftermath we were second bottom with Cowdenbeath at the foot. Cowdenbeath were having a wretched time. Their seven fixtures had yielded a negligible return of zero wins, one draw and six defeats. They had scored seven goals for the loss of twenty. Their next match was at Ayr. With half an hour left they opened the scoring with a breakaway goal. Ten minutes later a Garry Agnew penalty crashed off the underside of the bar and onto the line whereupon future Ayr United goalkeeper Billy Lamont gratefully grabbed the ball. Copious amounts of stoppage time rarely occurred in 1992. However in the fourth minute of added time Gordon Mair replicated Garry Agnew by firing the ball against the underside of the bar and again Billy Lamont smothered the rebound. This was the last action prior to the final whistle which was the cue for booing and an abundance of indelicate remarks being shouted. Chronic luck got blamed and there was some credence to this. Realistically it was time that this Ayr United team made the opposition rue their bad luck. Seven days hence it happened – Dumbarton 0 Ayr United 3.

Not just in football but in life it is possible to witness things which you can hardly believe you are seeing. One of those 'can't believe my eyes' moments occurred when St. Mirren visited for a first round tie in the B & Q Cup. Three days earlier the teams had met in the league. With home advantage St.Mirren had won 2-0. On the Tuesday night at Ayr I noticed Garry Agnew standing nearby on the terracing at the Somerset Road end. Beyond doubt it was him. It is said that we all have a doppelganger but that notion was not entertained. Ordinarily he would be in the team. Why was he standing in amongst us? It transpired that he turned up palpably ill. Food poisoning was suspected. Perhaps through a fear that he had something contagious, he was sent home. He then made his departure from the dressing room but did not go home. Garry was a fan as well as a player so he concealed himself amongst the Somerset Road enders. What a guy! No doubt he was as delirious as the rest of us when Tommy Walker rammed home the winner seconds from the end. Just prior to the goal the St.Mirren staff were pouring out drinks in the belief that their players would require refreshments before the onset of extra time. The next round saw a 1-0 defeat at Kilmarnock. Objectively it had to be admitted that the narrowness of the result was a poor indication of Kilmarnock's superiority.

There were fleeting successes in the league but they were all too fleeting. On the third Saturday of November a 5-3 win at home to Dumbarton was enthralling yet even in the aftermath we were ninth in a league of twelve. The next home match trumped the Dumbarton game for excitement. Watching Ayr United can be dull but this is the exception rather than the rule. St.Mirren's league visit was positively volatile. Ally Graham headed home a George Burley free-kick seconds before half-time. At 1-0 it remained well contested but peaceful until the last ten minutes. Then it all exploded. Paul Lambert, who had already been booked by Joe Timmins, got sent off after a bad challenge on Gordon Mair. The challenge was so bad that Mair's shinpad was broken in two (82 minutes). Barry Lavety got sent off for elbowing Gordon Mair (84 minutes). It was now eleven versus nine in our favour and full advantage was taken when Tommy Walker made it 2-0 (86 minutes). Chic Charnley got sent off for spitting at Duncan George (89 minutes). It therefore ended as eleven versus eight. When Charnley played for Ayr he was known as Jim. Why or when Jim became Chic was immaterial. Some of the St.Mirren supporters staged a demonstration after the match. The scene was one of mayhem. As if to illustrate football's propensity for contrast there was no threat of mayhem three days later. How could there be? Merely 284 watched our 2-2 draw at Cowdenbeath on a Tuesday night. Less than a fortnight later there was another contender for one of the lowest crowds at an Ayr United match. With due allowance for it being the last Saturday before Christmas it was appalling that our match at The Commonwealth Stadium attracted merely 339. All the fewer to tell the tale of a 1-0 loss against Meadowbank Thistle!

Win, lose, or draw, George Burley was thorough with his planning and preparation. In post match interviews he spoke well and was generally a good ambassador for the club. On Christmas Day 1992 the players were called in for training in preparation for a match at Kirkcaldy on Boxing Day. Whether the players appreciated such thoroughness may have been a matter of debate yet such exacting standards were to be commended. Raith Rovers were the league leaders and in the whole of 1992 Ayr United were the only visiting team to win a league game at Stark's Park. In a 1-1 draw that accolade was very close to being repeated. Right at the end Tommy Walker had a goal disallowed for an alleged foul by Gordon Mair on their goalkeeper.

On entering 1993 a survey of the league table indicated that the Ayr support had experienced the joy of victory, the pain of defeat and the ordinariness of drawing in equal measure. It was Played 24 Won 8 Drawn 8 Lost 8 For 29 Against 27. Sitting eighth out of twelve, the most redeeming feature was being clear of the relegation zone. Cowdenbeath were heavily adrift at the foot, their one win in twenty-four being at Ayr.

Losing 1-0 at home in the New Year derby was dispiriting. Raith Rovers had a commanding lead at the top and Kilmarnock were their nearest challengers. With Ayr United well out of contention the clichéd response was used: "We won't go up but we'll have a say in who does." Sabotaging other clubs' promotion aspirations (it was two up automatically) was the height of what could be achieved unless an appreciable impact could be made in the Scottish Cup. Dunfermline Athletic away was the third round draw. Outside the ground before the game I heard an anguished cry from behind. My son David had tripped and fallen into a puddle. This was in Halbeath Road, right behind the stand. It was the only puddle in sight. People were very quickly on the scene. Then we were escorted inside. He was medically checked and they took his wet clothes away to get dried. Once he was sorted we were escorted to a seat in close proximity to the First Aid facility in case there were any problems (my protestations that we had not paid were ignored!). There was a request that we should return after the match for a further check. By then I think that the person needing to be checked was myself. For shock! We won 2-1. The way we were treated was a credit to Dunfermline Athletic Football Club.

On reaching the Forth Bridge we heard the draw for the next round on the radio. It was Rangers at home. The capacity of Somerset Park was 11,548 but the club put forward a case to have the capacity increased. This initiative paid off. The capacity was increased to 13,918 and precisely that number of tickets got sold despite just 13,176 turning up. Rangers won 2-0 and we could reflect on the ticket sales swelling the coffers.

By 1993 Douglas Park had developed into one of those grounds that created undue difficulty for Ayr United. When we pitched up there on 2nd March the statistical analysis was unedifying. There was just one win in our previous eighteen visits there. That one win had occurred in 1985. Bogey, jinx, hoodoo – call it what you will. Hamilton Accies 1 Ayr United 3 – it was rendered a moot point.

In those days when only two substitutes were listed it was extremely rare for one of those slots to be utilised by naming a goalkeeper. What if the goalkeeper got injured? Football managers were not of a mind to consider 'what ifs'. While Ayr United were winning 1-0 at home to Cowdenbeath, Cammy Duncan collided with a post and had to be stretchered off. Consequently outfielder David Kennedy was sent on to replace him. Merely two minutes of the second half had been played at the time. Inexperience of the goalkeeping position caused him to carry the ball outside of the box. A goal was conceded from the resultant free-kick. What now? There was half an hour to go. The pendulum swung in our favour and the match was won 3-1. It looked unnatural to see David kitted out with gloves and a goalkeeper's jersey but he performed well in the circumstances. In the ensuing midweek Willie Spence guarded the Ayr United goal at Dunfermline. A 1-1 draw meant that we had taken six points off Dunfermline from a possible eight and knocked them out of the Scottish Cup as well. This was conspicuously good against a club in promotion contention.

David Kennedy as an emergency goalkeeper on 6th March, 1993.

Cowdenbeath 0 Ayr United 1 – attendance 213; Meadowbank Thistle 1 Ayr United 2 – attendance 277. Note that the word 'crowd' has been avoided. Such small assemblies of spectators could hardly be thus categorised.

With two left to play the title had already been won by a considerable distance. Raith Rovers were dominant. Behind them Kilmarnock and Dunfermline Athletic were on fifty-one points followed by St.Mirren on fifty. The Ayr United versus St.Mirren fixture was therefore vital for the visitors. This raised a very interesting question. Would our fans prefer a St. Mirren win since it would maybe have the potential to prevent Kilmarnock from getting the second promotion place? When they had lost at Ayr in December, St.Mirren boss Jimmy Bone complained about it being officiated by an Ayrshire referee (Joe Timmins from Kilwinning). For this match in May the referee was Kenny Clark from Paisley and one of the linesmen was from Barrhead. Regardless of the implications to the league table our fans showed great partisanship and the team responded. A frenetic match ended 3-3 and at times our own team played with a passion that made it look as if we too were a promotion contender. The result killed St.Mirren's promotion hopes and Jimmy Bone said afterwards: "This is a very intimidating place to come." Kilmarnock ultimately claimed promotion.

The last game of the season was our first at Stirling Albion's recently opened Forthbank Stadium. There was no pressure and the afternoon was a novel experience in the new surroundings. In drawing 1-1 we were able to look back on just one defeat in the last thirteen league fixtures. Even at that the sole defeat was a slender 1-0 reverse at Cappielow. We finished the season with eighteen draws from the forty-four fixtures. This was the most in the First Division. Of Scotland's thirty-eight league clubs we finished nineteenth, right in the middle. In the context of the First Division the final placing was seventh from twelve. 1992/93 was a chequered season in which a semblance of form was captured in the closing weeks.

Ayr United Boys' Club under 16s with the Gothia Cup in July 1981. Colin Calderwood is holding the trophy.

Since the 1970s the club had been successful in bringing through some outstanding young players. The heydays of Ayr United Boys' Club had produced Ian McAllister, Robert Connor, Stevie Nicol and Alan McInally. In the season just finished, there was the extraordinary story of Derek Allan who was registered with the club as a Youth Training Scheme player. On 9th February he made a first team debut. After making five first team appearances he was sold to Southampton on 12th March. On 1st May he went on as a substitute for Southampton at home to Manchester City in the English Premiership. In July 1993 Colin Calderwood was transferred from Swindon Town to Tottenham Hotspur for £1.25m. He had formerly captained Ayr United Boys' Club in winning the Gothia Cup but was not thought worthy of a professional contract.

The question of whether Ayr United's immediate future would have an accent on youth was answered with 'probably not' when Neil McNab, aged thirty-six, was signed. With recourse to an oft-quoted football cliché it could have been argued that a blend of youth and experience was best. In Neil McNab's case the argument was quickly rendered redundant. By August he cited difficulty in commuting from Manchester and he was transferred to Darlington.

Ayr United 3 Coventry City 2 – as in 1991 when they had also lost at Ayr, Coventry had the status of being in England's top sphere. Would this count for anything when the competitive matches started? At the time my heart said yes. If I had consulted my head it would have said no. There is a popular adage to the effect that it is the hope that kills you. In the context of supporting Ayr United this is untrue. When hopes are dashed we survive, albeit in a frustrated state. Admittedly the fringe support may drop away while the rest of us are compelled to stand there and suffer. Why do we do it? To repeat the point made in an earlier chapter, supporting Ayr United is a disease for which there is no cure. That is why. This alludes to Ayr United 0 Motherwell 6. It was a League Cup tie and it comprised our biggest home defeat since the 0-7 Dundee United debacle on 24th September, 1966. One difference between this and 1966 was that this time I saw it through until the very bitter end. The Motherwell rout was three days after losing at Clydebank in the opening league fixture. This combined to have a deteriorating effect on the attendance for the first home league game. It amounted to a miserly 1,503. More important to relate is that Stirling Albion were beaten 2-1.

As always it was important for the supporters to have a hero, the type of player whom the media label a fans' favourite. Whether in good, bad or mediocre times these characters tend to exist. Here in 1993 the hero was Malky Shotton, a solid defender who played football with a smile on his face. A solid defender? How does this square with the 6-0 hammering by Motherwell? He was sent off before some of the worst damage was inflicted. In a perverse way a sending-off in such circumstances can actually enhance a player's stock because it is definitive proof that he is going to go down fighting. Such is the perspective of the fan.

Away wins against Clyde, St.Mirren and Brechin City made a mockery of the concept of home advantage. It was encouraging too that the club had a willingness to pay out money in transfer fees even if they were modest in the context of the wider footballing world. Colin McGlashan made a scoring debut at Brechin two days after being purchased from Partick Thistle for £25,000. He was a popular signing for one particular reason. Prior to Partick Thistle his club was Clyde for whom he scored the goal that relegated Kilmarnock in 1989. Supporters sometimes get accused of having short memories. It can be an unfair accusation. Selective amnesia is the correct diagnosis.

There was additional pressure in this season's league campaign. Ordinarily avoiding the bottom two places was the requirement for avoiding the ugly spectre of relegation. Owing to league reconstruction it stood to be more difficult this time. From 1994/95 the structure was converting from a three-league set-up to a four-league set-up. In order for Ayr United to maintain a place in the second tier it would be necessary to finish at least seventh out of twelve. At the season's end the bottom five would be banished to the third tier. As a peculiar consequence the relegation battle was taking place in the middle of the league rather than at the foot. A 2-1 loss at home to Airdrie plunged Ayr United into the bottom five. Sitting eighth in mid-November was a cause for concern rather than outright panic. By the following week we were back above the cut-off after a 1-0 win away to Morton.

Catastrophic form was pending. A 6-1 debacle at Dunfermline was worrying. Dunfermline had six different scorers. It was a horrible night with no redeeming features. George Burley condemned his players for a lack of fighting spirit. This gave credence to the rumours that he had lost the dressing room. Fan agitation was on the increase and it was about to peak.

Ayr United 0 Falkirk 3 had more ramifications than just dropping below the relegation cut-off. This was just four days after the hopeless performance at East End Park and the hopelessness was repeated. The margin of defeat did not reflect Falkirk's dominance and the crowd did not hold back from venting their anger. Emotions ran far higher than mere disappointment.

Five days later, on Thursday 23rd December, George Burley and his assistant Dale Roberts were sacked. In future years he managed at higher levels in the game thereby causing people (including Ayr United supporters) to say that his sacking was a mistake. Viewed as a neutral or viewed from a future decade it is easy to see why this conclusion could be drawn. The Ayr United supporters of 1993 did not complain. On the contrary. It was considered to be a necessary action. To the outside world this sacking was thought to be inhumane due to the close proximity to Christmas but the psyche of the grizzled football supporter contains no compassion. Sentiment and ambition mix like oil and water. On a personal level I admit to being imbibed with such uncharitable feelings although I must qualify this by mentioning that this is my state of mind only where Ayr United are concerned. Football is eternally proficient in bringing out the worst in people.

Burley's successor was named straight away. The new man came as a player-manager too. It was Simon Stainrod, who was still a highly skilled player. This was a hugely popular choice. He had been in football at a high level and had the reputation of being a great extrovert. Confidence immediately soared. If there were any dissenters they did not make themselves known. His first match in charge was at Clydebank on 4th January, 1994. It could not come quickly enough. The media focus on this match was in connection with Davy Cooper's return to his old club. To the travelling support this was a mere incidental in comparison to the fervour about it being Simon Stainrod's first match. We were 2-0 up by the 13th minute and the vocal backing was in overload. The man of the moment went on in the 83rd minute and the applause was tumultuous. By then we were hanging on for grim death but the 2-0 lead was safely maintained. Morale was through the roof. Within a matter of weeks the Club Shop was selling fedora hats as worn by Simon Stainrod.

The Clydebank euphoria was followed by three draws which preceded a 3-1 win in a four-pointer at home to Stirling Albion. After that match we were in the all important seventh place but just two points ahead of Stirling Albion who had a game in hand. The relevance of our league position was majorly distracted by the third round Scottish Cup draw. Kilmarnock away! The tie attracted 12,856. We lost 2-1 and were left to bemoan the Killie winner in the words 'never a penalty'.

In contrast the crowd at Brechin City's Glebe Park a week later was 483. It was a wet day and the pitch started to get churned up. At one point of the second half the ball got kicked over the touchline and landed almost at the feet of a resplendently dressed Simon Stainrod. Rather than return the ball he stood there flicking remnants of splattered dirt from his clothing. There was no element of time wasting since we were running away with the match at the time. Looking on we began to think that he was oblivious of the ball at his feet. He did eventually kick it back but only after he was sure that his clothing was in order. It was reminiscent of the Simon Templar character who would disarm four thugs then calmly straighten his tie and smooth out his jacket. Brechin scored a late goal which mattered little. We won 4-1. The fans loved Simon Stainrod and his eccentricities. For now!

On a Tuesday evening in Stirling a most important match was played out. Ayr United and Stirling Albion were seventh and eighth respectively in this mid-table relegation battle. The gap between the clubs was one point. There was an Ayr support of 455 in the overall attendance of 1,002. After winning 3-1 Simon Stainrod said: "We went out with a positive attitude." Morton 0 Ayr United 1 on 16th April, 1994, was Ayr United's last away win in a competitive fixture until 23rd September, 1995 (excepting a shootout win at East Stirling). This lapse in away form began too late in the current season to have any effect. With two games to spare it was guaranteed that we would be in the First Division for the season ahead. Finishing seventh was a cause for celebration and the champagne was opened. It seems timely to recall what Willie McLean once said: "To finish fifth or sixth in Division One is a disgrace to a club of our calibre." In consecutive seasons we had now finished nineteenth out of the thirty-eight league clubs. Right in the middle!

A champagne celebration for finishing seventh.

In the final match programme of the season Simon Stainrod wrote: "The days of Ayr United being an insignificant club are over." The *Ayr Advertiser* contained: "Ayr United plan to have a bigger full time squad next season in order to push for a Premier League place." At the time these were just the kind of remarks we wanted to hear. What could be wrong with a cocktail of confidence and optimism? In hindsight quite a lot could be wrong with that. The resources have to be there if such lofty ambitions are to be realised. In retrospect it is possible to view matters with 20/20 vision. That is why we can now look at these remarks from 1994 and treat them with ridicule. Push for a Premier League place? In the season ahead the club would exit the second tier but at the wrong end (sorry for the spoiler!). The bookmakers either ignored or were unaware of Ayr United's Premier League talk. Together with Stranraer we were installed as 40/1 outsiders to win the First Division in 1994/95. This translated to Ayr United and Stranraer being favourites for the two relegation spots and this is exactly what would come to pass. A major change was now being introduced. Henceforth it would be three points for a win rather than two.

In preparation four matches were played in the Republic of Ireland and we had a visit from Bryan Robson's Middlesbrough. Stainrod peddled a narrative that he wished to make Somerset Park 'the land of giants'. In support of this he said that he would be utilising long ball tactics designed to get high balls to his tall players up front. It was all just a ruse designed to delude opponents into expecting a different kind of approach from the one employed. Judging by match reports the ruse worked. These reports were punctuated by mentions of aerial assaults. Notwithstanding the fact that the whole idea was consistent with the physique of several of the new signings, it was still a delusion but people bought into the idea that Somerset Park truly was 'the land of giants'. In a second round League Cup tie Celtic won 1-0 at Ayr and afterwards their manager Tommy Burns said: "Every time Ayr launched the ball into our box I was holding my breath to see if they would get a flick on or a deflection." Quite apart from the tactical ramifications there was the additional benefit of generating publicity for Ayr United. It was publicity of the intimidatory kind. 'Abandon hope all ye who enter here' was the message being conveyed. Therein is a cruel irony. In the season ahead the people most likely to abandon hope on entering Somerset Park were our own fans. The long ball tactic was not persisted with, if it had even existed at all. Stainrod hoodwinked the media, besides which the idea of emulating Wimbledon's Crazy Gang would only have been practical if we had the quality to execute the plan.

Stranraer away is a trip much enjoyed by Ayr United supporters. Chips at Girvan, sweeties at Ballantrae and a nice run down the coast. The quaintness of it all is nostalgically captured by the bandstand outside the ground. Unfortunately the biggest threat to this idyll is the game itself. 27th August, 1994, saw the idyll smashed to smithereens (I have no idea what a smithereen is but there is no more appropriate metaphor!). Stranraer 2 Ayr United 1 was the result. Stranraer 11 Ayr United 8 was the end of match player count. This remains a club record for the number of sendings-off in a game.

Football's propensity for anger is liable to be countered by an equal propensity for humour. Due to a Falkirk versus Rangers fixture on the Saturday, the East Stirling versus Ayr United tie in the first round of the B & Q Cup got shifted to the Sunday. At half-time the Firs Park announcer mentioned that there were no other games that day so he would read out the half-time scores from the day before. So we stood there and listened to the state of play in Scotland at 3.45 pm on the Saturday. When this little joke was getting enacted we were all more concerned at being 1-0 down against a club that had never won a single tie in the competition. Luckily that situation prevailed at the end but only after extra time and a shootout.

24th September, 1994, was an historic date. It was the first time Ayr United collected three points, rather than two, for a win. It was a 3-2 win at home to Dundee. At the season's end Dundee were in a situation where one more point would have got them promoted. They contrived to lose both fixtures at Ayr while the two Dens Park fixtures between the clubs were drawn. It made no sense. In the final table we were thirty-nine points behind them. I can confess to being a strict non-gambler. This is not necessarily for moral reasons. I would not bet on horse racing because I do not know enough about it. As for football I would not bet on it because I know too much about it. Football is only predictable in its unpredictability. In beating Dundee, Justin Jackson scored twice on his league debut. At the end of the season he was our joint top scorer in the league with a total of four.

Indiscipline was a marked feature in the 2-0 loss to Airdrie at the quarter-final stage of the B & Q Cup. The tie was played at Broadwood Stadium, their temporary home pending the construction of their new stadium. Garry Paterson created another of those dubious club records. In this case the accolade was the fastest booking. It occurred nine seconds after the kick-off. He was the first of four Ayr United players to be booked that night.

After we had played every other club once, the points total was seven from the nine league fixtures played. Ignominiously this secured second bottom place. To remedy the situation Simon Stainrod tapped into the foreign market. This practice succeeded in reviving the interest of the beleaguered supporters. The most foreign players on the pitch for Ayr United at the same time is five and it dates to 5th November, 1994.

They were Niclas Nylen (Swedish), Claudio Valetta (Italian), Franck Rolling (French), Bruce Murray (American) and Regis Gorgues (French). Such a radical policy was deserving of success although the occasion was spoiled by a 1-0 loss away to St.Mirren. A week later we had five foreigners in the line-up again. They were the same players who had played against St. Mirren with the exception of Bruce Murray but including Jose Fortes (Portuguese). Again the experiment failed (0-3 versus Airdrie). By the last game in the month (1-1 at Dens Park) on 26th November, Franck Rolling was the only foreigner in the starting eleven. These were times of struggle yet some of the regulars could look at themselves in the mirror with no feelings of guilt. Cammy Duncan, Gregg Hood, Franck Rolling and Duncan George were not complicit in the mediocrity.

John Sharples scoring against Kilmarnock on 17th December, 1994

The visit of Raith Rovers created more interest than usual since they had beaten Celtic in the League Cup final six days earlier. They had not won at Ayr since October 1982 and before that they had not won at Ayr since October 1964. The 1-1 draw was now their fourteenth consecutive fixture at Ayr without them winning. With normal luck they would have been beaten on this occasion. People are quick to point out that you make your own luck but it does not always work out in that way. Still, there was enough encouragement on view to make us all believe that the team could make a fist of it at Dunfermline a week later. Dunfermline Athletic 6 Ayr United 0 – yet again a build-up of confidence proved to be a hoax. Supporting Ayr United plays havoc with the emotions and the Dunfermline result induced panic because the next match, unconventionally for December, was the Ayrshire Cup final at home to Kilmarnock. The sense of fear was not so much on account of the Premier League status of our county neighbours. It was more to do with our own form or rather our lack of form. At East End Park the display did not even reach mediocrity. An embarrassment was pending. The embarrassment materialised but not in the manner we had feared. Ayr United 4 Kilmarnock 1 – a miracle had happened in the Christmas season.

Watching Stranraer versus Ayr United has often been a confusing spectacle due to the number of our former players in the opposing team. At Stair Park, on 2nd January, 1995, that is exactly what it was like. In the blue of Stranraer were Jim McCann, Jim Hughes, Nigel Howard, Tommy Sloan, Lex Grant, Robert Reilly and Tommy Walker. Having Alex McAnespie as their manager merely compounded the notion. When Lex Grant concluded the scoring at 2-0 in the 75th minute, a posse of Ayr supporters decamped from behind the goal and settled at a vantage point more suitable for barracking Simon Stainrod and the Ayr United directors. Posse, with its connotations of the wild west, is the most apt collective noun in description of the group. The anger was justified. Once more the idyll of a trip to Stranraer was shattered. Bottom position was now occupied.

Ayrshire Cup winners 1994/95.

Several days later I took my son and daughter to the Whitletts Community Centre for a Big 'A' Club evening. The Big 'A' Club was designed for young supporters. Bill Barr and Simon Stainrod turned up that night. It was clearly done in the interests of PR. Ayr United's stock was low. Bridges had to be built. Yet the best way to restore public faith was to rectify onfield matters. The remedy came immediately. They say that a week is a long time in politics. That saying might be suitably adapted to apply to football. Ayr United 2 St.Mirren 0 was a six-pointer in view of the opposition being fellow relegation strugglers. This left Ayr United and Stranraer on the same points, the same number of goals scored and the same number of goals conceded. We were off the bottom on alphabetical order. St.Mirren were marginally outside the relegation zone with two points more.

In January 1995 Ayr United received a letter from the Scottish Football Association. The tone of it could not have been described as sociable. Seven other clubs received a similar letter. It was a warning about an adverse disciplinary record. At the end of the season we were able to look back on a campaign in which we had three instances of a goalkeeper being sent off. They were Cammy Duncan twice and Stuart McIntosh. Ironically McIntosh was sent off when he was covering for Cammy Duncan who was working off a suspension for a red card. The tone of negativity will now be maintained to tell you that January concluded with a Scottish Cup defeat away to Raith Rovers and February started with a league defeat at the same ground. Ayr United 1 Dundee (league leaders) 0 went some way to alleviating the suffering, not least since we had now escaped the folds of the bottom two. Alas this situation was temporary. It might have been termed a stay of execution. Form degenerated to the point where we awaited the inevitable.

When the inevitable came it was horrible. The deed was done by Hamilton Accies at Firhill where they were ground sharing. Jim Sherry got sent off after seventeen minutes so for the entire remainder of the game we were up against ten men.

Chance after chance got scorned. Some of these were in the harder to miss category. In stoppage time Hamilton scored the only goal of the game. Merely 1,073 were there to witness the unedifying spectacle. With two games left we were relegated. It was still possible to draw level on points with third bottom Clydebank but it was rightly considered that we had no chance of overturning their goal difference which was superior by fifteen. Getting taunted by Hamilton supporters on the way back to the car merely topped off an awful afternoon. The response to relegation was an announcement that just five players would be offered full time contracts for season 1995/96. They were Duncan George, Cammy Duncan, Franck Rolling, John Sharples and Gregg Hood. The public were also appraised of the fact that the club's part time players would be getting paid £30 per week. It had further been decided to scrap the club's reserve team. Ongoing the ground admission price for an adult was set at £7. Was there any good news? Yes there was. In something of a major coup striker Gordon Dalziel was signed from Raith Rovers. Pertinently he came as a coach too.

Vinnie Moore heading the winner against Dundee on 11th February, 1995.

George Watson makes a save from Owen Coyle at Clydebank's Kilbowie Park.

3rd October, 2024, at the same spot at where the above George Watson photograph was taken.

10. Happy Days Are Here Again

The heading is relative. Anyone with a shred of sanity knew that thoughts of reaching the Premier League were as futile as chasing rainbows. Landing in Scottish football's third tier amidst a welter of economic downsizing initiatives was a bleak portrayal of the club's status. Better days lay in store but not before suffering a bit more pain in the immediate term. Pre-season was the time of year for the fans to replenish our stock of hope. In dropping a league there just had to be hope of a quick return. The opposition would be less daunting after all. You have just read a brief summary of the logic. The reality was different. Even the more partisan amongst us struggled to muster much in the way of positivity in the summer of 1995.

The season began with a 1-1 draw at home to Clyde, this virtually being Ayr United's default scoreline on league opening days in the 1990s. It was watched by a crowd of 1,963. This was the record gate at any Second Division match all season, this statistic applying to all clubs. It was a clear marker of the level we had descended to. Cup involvement was rapidly dispensed with over the period of three days. Celtic won at Ayr in the League Cup (0-3) then Dunfermline Athletic won at Ayr in the rebranded League Challenge Cup (1-2 after extra time). Then, to use a footballing analogy, it all kicked-off. Steve Archibald and Simon Stainrod had opposed each other in the Spurs versus Queen's Park Rangers FA Cup final in 1982. Now they were the respective player-managers of East Fife and Ayr United. When they renewed their acquaintance (albeit that Stainrod was in the dugout due to injury) the attendance at Bayview Park was 748. East Fife won 1-0. After the match the Ayr United Travel Club prepared a statement which expressed "disgust at the performance." Bluntly it also said: "We strongly advise that the manager leaves before the rest of our loyal hard core support does."

It could have been argued that the Travel Club view was not representative of the overall support and that it was merely the opinion of one busload. Yet no such argument existed. You would have struggled to find anyone who was not in accord with the sentiment. One week later you would definitely not have found someone who was not in accord with the sentiment. Ayr United 1 Berwick Rangers 4 had major ramifications. Berwick's only previous league win at Ayr was on 27th February, 1965. The *Ayrshire Post* went with a headline of **DISGRACE**. The beleaguered Stainrod said that his players should get done by the Fraud Squad. Throughout the second half the level of ire from the terraces gradually rose to a crescendo. After the match there was a protest in Tryfield Place and I was one of the dissenters. The word 'mob' has been carefully avoided because it has connotations of disorder and the gathering was commendably peaceable. A policeman approached and said that there was no point in waiting. We realised that he was right so the group dispersed with a feeling of demoralisation. On the Tuesday morning Stainrod told the *Ayrshire Post* that he would not be resigning. Less than three hours later his resignation was announced after a meeting with Bill Barr. Thirteen league wins out of sixty encapsulated the whole sorry situation. In a parting shot he complained that the supporters were moaners. He was correct and I admit that I was one of the moaners. My defence is that there was much to moan about.

I wrote a scathing but constructive piece of programme editorial which was intended for publication in the Forfar Athletic issue a week later. In view of the events on the Tuesday I withheld it. One week after Berwick Rangers got their second ever win at Ayr, Forfar Athletic did likewise. Their only previous league win here was on 30th September, 1967. Ayr United 1 Forfar Athletic 3 caused the club to be sitting second bottom of the league with one point from four games. Then, for the third consecutive week, we had another match that came in for adverse statistical analysis. Stirling Albion 2

Ayr United 0 meant that the club had now gone twenty-two consecutive away league games without a win. This remains the club's second worst such run. It was our first away defeat against Stirling Albion since 5th December, 1964, these games covering the League Cup in addition to league fixtures.

Montrose 0 Ayr United 1 then offered some respite. The date was 23rd September, 1995, and it was our first away league win since 16th April, 1994. The caretaker boss was Gordon Dalziel and in response to a 0-0 draw at home to Stranraer he said: "It was the worst game in the whole world bar none." Alex McAnespie, his Stranraer counterpart, concurred: "Games like this will get football stopped."

In the autumn of 1995 one saving grace was that I was able to wallow in yet more statistical analysis. Queen of the South 0 Ayr United 0 – this was the first ever scoreless draw between the clubs at Palmerston in all competitions. Ayr United 1 Stenhousemuir 2 – this was Stenhousemuir's first win at Ayr since 20th April, 1963. Ayr United 0 East Fife 1 – this was East Fife's first league win at Ayr ever. On the day after the Stenhousemuir match I had a meeting with Bill Barr and his fellow directors. Mr Barr suggested the meeting in order to air my complaints about the direction of the club. It was clear that the infrastructure of the club was very sound.

Three days after the East Fife match Gordon Dalziel was named as the new manager. His first match after his appointment was a 2-1 defeat at home to Stirling Albion. The date was 4th November, 1995. This proved to be our last home league defeat until 14th September, 1996. When Dalziel said: "I'm ready to pull this place upside down" his words were corroborated in results after an indifferent start. Losing 2-0 at Stranraer was a fourth consecutive defeat, three of which were under his permanent managership.

Thereafter the fightback was on. Bill Barr demanded high standards and in Gordon Dalziel he had a man who was willing to work tirelessly. By the end of season 1995/96 forty-five players were used in first team action. This was one more than the previous club record set in 1917/18 when there were extenuating circumstances. In 1997/98 the record would be broken again with forty-six players being fielded. The national press reported that latter statistic as being a British record. East Stirling had used precisely fifty in 1982/83. These statistics are in reference to competitive matches only. The figures have not been manipulated by pre-season friendlies which can carry a proliferation of trialists.

Fan anger subsided although it did make a brief reappearance at the first match of 1996. This was a Scottish Cup tie which resulted Ayr United 0 Ross County 2. Our opponents were then in the fourth tier. As the season progressed confidence was restored. The start to the league programme had created too big a handicap for any future momentum to overcome. Long before the end of 1995/96 we yearned for the season to end in the knowledge that a title challenge was capable of being mounted once the slate was wiped clean. There was a gradual easing away from the relegation zone. The club had introduced an initiative to the effect that bonuses would no longer be paid for draws. Saturdays were not awaited with trepidation any more. Ayr United 5 Berwick Rangers 0 was an unrecognisable spectacle in comparison to this fixture back in September. Concerningly this match was watched by just 903 although in mitigation there was the counter attraction of a major televised rugby international. It would be 29th November, 2003, when Ayr United would next have a three-figure attendance for a competitive match at home. A 2-0 win at home to Montrose lifted the club from eighth to sixth. Stirling Albion came to Ayr on the second last Saturday of March knowing that a win would guarantee promotion for them. After a 2-2 draw their celebrations were deferred. Including this match there was just one league defeat for Ayr United out of the last sixteen. In quoting this statistic you will already have discerned that the next match was lost. The damage was 1-0 at Forfar. One point from a possible twelve was a dispiriting yield against a struggling Forfar Athletic team.

On the last Saturday of April an East Fife win at Ayr would have given them a club record for away wins in a season. It was 1-0 to Ayr. Yet the visitors were already guaranteed promotion along with champions Stirling Albion. Although envious of the top two there was an almost certain knowledge that our time would come in the season ahead. Sixth place in the third tier had the resonance of a moderate season but it masked the substantial progress since November.

Positive vibes coursed through the club and the fans awaited the onset of season 1996/97 with a 'let's get started' attitude. We had suffered from delusion before but this time there were real grounds for optimism rather than a reliance on blind faith. In pre-season Luton Town (1-0) and Millwall (4-3) were beaten. The Millwall game was 4-0 at one stage and Paul Kinnaird would have made it 5-1 if he had not failed with a penalty. Of course it had to be recognised that friendlies can be an unreliable guide. The competitive action began with a match high in incentive. Ayr United versus Livingston was a League Cup first round tie which was played in the knowledge that the winners would be playing at Kilmarnock in the next round. This was 1996 and we had not scored in the competition since 1991. A comprehensive 5-2 win put paid to the drought.

Kilmarnock were two leagues above and they were embarking on a season in which they would win the Scottish Cup. In a 1-0 win Robert Connor scored against the club he had recently been freed by. Late in the game Henry Smith was beaten but Bobby Law rose to head the ball off the line. As he did so I found myself rising from my seat and subconsciously mimicking his action down there on the pitch. Our support was large and noisy. Gordon Dalziel commented: "Tonight they are away home proud of every player who pulled on a jersey."

The League Challenge Cup was soon removed as an impediment to league progress. Ross County 0 Ayr United 4 remains a club record winning margin in the competition (shared with East Stirling 1 Ayr United 5 on 16th August, 2017). That was round one. Ayr United 0 St.Johnstone 4 in round two generated what remains a club record margin of defeat in the competition. It is quite extraordinary that such contrasting records should have occurred in consecutive rounds. Ayr

United 6 Berwick Rangers 0 was the perfect cure for any lingering ills after the St.Johnstone tie. Berwick's win at Ayr a year earlier had caused ructions and their two subsequent league visits had now resulted in them being routed 5-0 and 6-0. The League Cup was exited in a 3-1 loss away to Rangers. Our ticket allocation of 3,000 was sold out and the overall crowd was 44,283. It was manic in the Broomloan Road Stand when Darren Henderson made it 1-1. This was Ayr United's 500th goal in the history of the competition but in the general mayhem you can be assured that none of us were contemplating statistical matters at that time. I failed to see the ball cross the line because people in front stood up seconds before it ended up in the net (not that it spoiled the moment).

Ayr United 2 Clyde 4 was our first home defeat since 4th November, 1995. It was also Clyde's first win at Ayr since 16th October, 1971. Gordon Dalziel called it "a hiccup". He was right. The response was winning the next seven league games. These were great times to be following the team away from home. It was reminiscent of 1987/88. Gordon Dalziel even commented that the team seemed to play better football away from home. At Dumbarton the team turned out in a strip comprising shirts of green and purple halves and shorts of green and purple halves. It was not the only unconventional happening that afternoon. A shot from Isaac English was weakly struck but the goalkeeper let it slip through his hands. From the vantage point occupied by most of the Ayr support it was not realised that the ball had scraped across the line. It was a goal greeted in silence until we noticed the players moving back in the direction of the centre circle. This made it 3-1 and that was how it stayed. These three points were vital because the next two matches were against our nearest rivals. In beating Livingston 1-0 at Ayr we replaced them at the top of the league. On the same day Hamilton Accies 2 Dumbarton 0 made things very tight. The top three were all tied on twenty points. Ayr and Hamilton had the same goal difference but we nudged it at the top by virtue of having scored more goals. Next up we were away to Hamilton Accies who were then ground sharing at Cliftonhilll Park in Coatbridge. The attendance was 1,173 which was just sixty-five short of the restricted 1,238 capacity. Stevie Kerrigan and Isaac English scored in a 2-1 win. Another six-pointer was put to bed.

A curious incident occurred during a 1-0 win at home to Brechin City. Visiting goalkeeper Ray Allan attempted to throw the ball upfield but succeeded only in throwing it out for a corner-kick. We looked on in amazement because he came very close to throwing it into his own net. There was no such hilarity a fortnight later when the winning run crashed to a halt when Stenhousemuir won 2-1 at Somerset Park.

Who present will ever forget the debut of Alain Horace at Stranraer? When we reminisce on Ayr United it is inescapable that the conversation will turn to heroes. Hero was an accolade deserving of the diminutive midfield supremo. With Stair Park once more proving to be a difficult venue the match ground on in a scoreless state. Then, in the 73rd minute, he scored directly from a corner-kick whereupon he was engulfed by fans who had spilled onto the track. It was the only goal of the match.

In the entire league season only two away defeats were suffered, each of them at Livingston. The December match saw the home team score with less than two minutes played and there was no further scoring. Isaac English was stretchered off with a broken leg after twelve minutes and an additional item on the list of woes was a drop to second place.

For the second consecutive year we had a second round failure in the Scottish Cup and again it was 2-0 at home. Clyde were the victors in this our first match of 1997. "It's more important to concentrate on the league" was the popular refrain. That may be true but it is a saying that does not carry much gravitas when the date of elimination is 7th January. Prior to the match I was asked to do an interview for BBC Radio Scotland. Not unreasonably I was asked about Ayr United's lack of a Scottish Cup pedigree. There was no escaping the truth. One semi-final since 1910 was our lot. In 1997 our league form at least provided something in the way of a silver lining.

January was concluded with another six-pointer success when a Robert Scott goal was enough to beat Hamilton Accies 1-0 at home. To have gone top on that evening it would have been necessary to win by four goals. We were now behind Livingston on goal difference only and third-placed Hamilton Accies trailed by eight points with a game in hand. The next fixture was Livingston at home. Again it was a six-pointer and again it was a 1-0 Ayr win. There is a school of thought that teams should be able to take care of themselves and that it is therefore futile to bother about the results of other teams. It is naive to think that way. We had a vested interest in how Livingston and Hamilton Accies were doing and it was simply a natural reaction to watch out for their results. Two would go up automatically and three clubs were in the mix.

In mid-February a 2-1 win away to Stenhousemuir was most productive. It was consecutive league win number six and the fans were in great voice although we felt a bit nervous towards the end when the home team fought furiously to get level. We were now eight points in front of Livingston who had a game in hand and thirteen points in front of Hamilton Accies who had two games in hand. Football can be hard to fathom though. Dumbarton is a case in point. In November they had won 4-1 at Ayr. When they returned in March we were forty points in front of them. Ultimately they were to be relegated with bottom club Berwick Rangers. For this visit we watched on in horror when they took the lead with a shot from forty yards. It was an empty goal with Henry Smith stranded. In the final minute of the first half Alain Horace equalised after exhibiting some of the sublime skill we knew he was capable of. The second half onslaught materialised but it was ineffective and we even came close to conceding a goal at the end. It was 1-1 against a struggling team and it replicated the result when the teams had met at Boghead in January. One win in four against a team doomed for the drop was incomprehensible.

With six games left we had a lead of six points over Hamilton Accies and twelve over Livingston. The next fixture was at Livingston. Again we had a large and noisy support but it was a day of extreme frustration. People will tell you that you cannot blame a referee. If you are an adherent of that persuasion then please look away now. In stoppage time, with the game poised at 1-1, the ball was played through to Jason Young who controlled it with his hand. The handling offence seemed a moot point anyway because when the ball was played to him he was in an outrageously offside position. With no flag raised and no whistle sounded Young was allowed to run on and score. It was too late for a comeback. Being appraised of Dumbarton 0 Hamilton Accies 3 made it an even more unpleasant journey home. With the lead now cut to three points there was little margin for error. Ayr United 2 Stenhousemuir 1 was not the most illustrious of results but this did not diminish our gratitude for the points.

In order to guarantee promotion a point was required in the next match which was against Clyde at Broadwood. It was 1-1 therefore promotion was won. Yet unlike Stirling in 1988 there was no celebration. The atmosphere was flat. I tried to get a chorus of 'Super Ayr' going at the end but quickly stifled the song in its infancy through the embarrassment of it being a solo. In the away dressing room there was a mood of despondency despite bottles of champagne sitting on the table. It was known that Hamilton Accies had won 5-0 at Berwick. This cut our lead at the top to one point. Promotion had been considered a certain contingency for several weeks. The scramble for the title was now too tight for comfort. Ominously the next fixture was Hamilton Accies away.

Ordinarily this match would have been played at Cliftonhill Park but with its 1,238 restricted capacity it was clear that the volume of public interest would heavily overtax that number. In an eminently sensible initiative it was arranged for Fir Park, Motherwell. Gordon Dalziel lived near the ground so regardless of the outcome he would be home in time for tea! Justification of the switch was the attendance of 5,156. Approaching the turnstiles with my friend Brian Johnstone and our sons, we passed a flag seller. His flags bore the legend 'Ayr United FC Second Division Champions 1996/97'. In a good humoured way I said to him that we hadn't won it yet.

He replied: "Shy weans don't get sweeties." It could almost be a lesson for life. There is no rule to say that inspirational quotes have to be pretentious or dripping in sentiment. If you only take one pearl of wisdom from this book then please make it the utterance from that vendor at Motherwell. Great was the rejoicing when Robert Scott scored just before the half-hour mark. With a little over quarter of an hour to go a wayward tackle from Willie Jamieson caused a penalty which was converted for 1-1. A draw would be a better result for Ayr than it would be for Hamilton so it was pleasing when time was called with that scoreline still intact.

The issue was simple. There were two games left and we had a lead of one point but a vastly inferior goal difference in comparison to Hamilton. On the penultimate Saturday the key fixtures were Ayr United versus Brechin City and Clyde versus Hamilton Accies. A Clyde win and an Ayr win would mean that the title was ours. Ayr United 2 Brechin City 0 and Clyde 0 Hamilton Accies 1 shifted the onus onto the final Saturday. The title now rested on a journey to play bottom club Berwick Rangers. Hamilton Accies had it a lot tougher with a final fixture at home to Livingston. We just had to at least match Hamilton. They drew but we had to maintain an assumption that they could win therefore our game had a win-or-else quality to it. Two goals in a minute just before half-time brought about a 2-0 victory. Ayr United had succeeded in clinching a league title in England. This was the day before my son's tenth birthday and you need hardly be told that he had a great weekend. On the way there I detoured into Bathgate to show him my first school. Further on we stopped for a break in Haddington, my place of birth. The theme of nostalgia was maintained on the way home too with a stop at the chippy in Ormiston. However this indulgence into the family roots in the Lothians was secondary to the main purpose which was winning the league.

We had one league defeat in the last nineteen and it was a highly contentious one at Livingston. The club record for consecutive unbeaten league matches is seventeen dating to 1958/59.

The title is won at Berwick on 10th May, 1997

Bad times were so recent that they should still have been indelibly printed on the memory but there were no such recollections on that day at Berwick. "Dalziel there's only one Dalziel" is how the song went. The board were in accord. He was offered a three-year contract which he accepted. This killed the speculation linking him to Raith Rovers. In a statement of solidarity he said: "Things are right for me to continue at Ayr. I feel we can bypass teams like Raith and go on to bigger and better things."

In July 1997 Coventry City made their third trip to Somerset Park in the decade. Their record so far was Played 2 Lost 2. This time they won 3-0. For the challenge ahead Gordon Dalziel was not prepared to rest on his laurels. The first competitive match of 1997/98 was a league fixture at home to Morton. Of our starting line-up only Willie Jamieson and Gregg Hood had been at the club the season before. In fact only Hood had started at Berwick. Morton won 2-1, this result not fully emphasising their superiority. This early we could see that the First Division was a tougher gig. Tougher yet was Dunfermline Athletic away in the League Cup. They were in the Premier League. We were slaughtered 5-1. Some perspective may be added. Dunfermline won a league fixture at Celtic Park a week later.

The carefree away days of 1996/97 were not so carefree in 1997/98. On a beautiful sunny day we went to Brockville to play a Falkirk team who were contesting their first competitive match at home since appearing in the Scottish Cup final. The climatic conditions may have been beautiful but not the result. The margin of defeat was 2-1 and we still sought that first league point.

In the League Challenge Cup Clydebank won at Ayr after extra time. Taking no cognisance of the limited importance of the competition, the crowd voiced displeasure at full time. In response Gordon Dalziel said: "I'm determined to do well and won't let criticism affect me. Nor will I crucify the players and ruin their confidence." By this time the first league point had been picked up (Ayr United 2 Partick Thistle 2) and the real wisdom of Dalziel's thinking was validated when the Clydebank tie was followed up with a 2-0 win away to Hamilton Accies who were still in their temporary home in Coatbridge. This moved the team up to sixth.

Paul Bonar in action against Coventry City on 24th July, 1997

Hamilton Accies were not the only First Division club housed in a temporary home. Airdrie were still sharing with Clyde at Cumbernauld's Broadwood Stadium. In late September our journey there carried bad vibes if we were having recourse to the statistics. Ayr United had failed to win either of the previous fifteen league fixtures with Airdrie, regardless of where the games were played. Airdrie won 1-0 and one more was added to the sequence.

Ayr United had come a long way since the most vigorous means of recruitment was to scout the cream of the Juniors then give them a trial either at reserve level or even at league level. That was why team listings showed such pseudonyms as 'Junior', 'Trialist' or 'A.N. Other'. The net was now being cast somewhat wider than places such as Ardrossan or Annbank. On 4th October, 1997, the Ayr team contained four Frenchmen in a 2-1 win at home to Stirling Albion. They were David Castilla, Luc Sonor, Willie Mainge and Laurent D'jaffo. Sonor had highly impressive credentials having played nine times for France at full international level. This was the precise number of times he was destined to play for Ayr United. Although contracted until the end of the season he was permitted to leave after becoming unsettled. Since Monaco was one of his former clubs it was understandable that he could not settle in Ayr.

Sixteen consecutive winless league games versus Airdrie! This looked to be heading for seventeen when they came to Ayr and ran riot in a torrid opening spell. Poor finishing and brilliant goalkeeping by David Castilla kept it at 0-0 but it looked like a matter of time before we would capitulate. Totally against the run of play Laurent D'jaffo scored with a header. Ian Ferguson and Jim Dick got it to 3-0 by half-time. It beggared belief that a team could be in this position after being outplayed. John Traynor, Laurent D'jaffo and Tom Smith took the final score to 6-0 despite Airdrie continuing to dominate possession. It remains a serious contender for the oddest match I have ever seen. If anyone had walked into the ground near the end it would have had the illusion of Ayr United clinging on desperately for a draw or an odd goal victory. David Castilla did not get the Man of the Match award but many felt that he should have. Ayr United won 6-0 but our goalkeeper was a Man of the Match contender! It was crazy. Without recourse to the actual statistics I would confidently say that we scored every time we were near goal. In the quest for consolidation there was maybe just a slight unease when surveying the league table. Hovering just below mid-table was not so secure as to ignore the teams below. In the meantime we looked not so much safe but more safe-ish.

"Even Stevie Wonder would have seen that was no penalty." This was a comment from Gordon Dalziel after a 1-1 draw at Stirling. He was rightly irked by an incident midway through the second half. With the score at 0-0 Luc Sonor and Gavin Price contested a high ball. Quite clearly Price handled the ball but the referee decided that Sonor had handled it and he awarded a penalty which Alex Bone scored from. Sonor was so enraged that he got a yellow card. In the 74th minute Ally Graham, now in his second spell at the club, levelled it. These away games threatened to lose their recent appeal when, a fortnight later, we played Partick Thistle who were struggling to exist. The 'Save The Jags' campaign was in full swing. Our fans may have been charitably disposed towards the collection tins, especially since it was the last Saturday before Christmas. Unfortunately such charitable sentiments were not reciprocated. Partick Thistle won 3-0.

The theme of moaning about away games will be maintained to relate another tale of woe. On 3rd January, 1998, Hamilton Accies versus Ayr United got postponed at short notice. Too short notice! The pitch at their temporary Cliftonhill Park home was waterlogged. This was hardly surprising since the rain had been heavy since the morning. Any threat to the match could have been anticipated sooner and acted on accordingly. I had barely locked the car when appraised of the news. Flooded roads and diversions on the A77 caused the journey home to take more than three hours. Turning up at an away game then finding it to be postponed is majorly frustrating. In the year of writing it has happened to me four times. These called off games were against Rangers, Meadowbank Thistle and Hamilton Accies twice (including this one at Coatbridge).

The next again away match was subject to no trauma whatsoever. Alloa's Recreation Park was limited to a capacity of 931 with the consequence that our Scottish Cup tie there was rendered all-ticket. It seemed that 931 was an oddly random number, especially since there was plenty of spare space once the tie was underway. Historical precedent told of Ayr United losing at Alloa in the Scottish Cup in 1939 and 1982. Every time Ayr United had been drawn against Alloa Athletic in the Scottish Cup, Britain was plunged into a war later that year. 1939 - Second World War; 1982 - The Falklands; 1998 – Iraq. The precedent of losing these bygone ties was ignored and Ian Ferguson got a hat-trick in our 3-0 win. On the same afternoon Kilmarnock, the holders, won 2-0 at Stranraer. The draw for the next round was Ayr United versus Kilmarnock. Some of my work colleagues in Kilmarnock predicted that it would be a Valentine's Day massacre. An Ayrshire derby on Valentine's Day was a huge irony. Love is a scarce commodity on these occasions. That morning the rain was so heavy that the tie had to be in doubt. Referee Hugh Dallas thought so. At 1 pm he said that the match was in jeopardy. He then allowed the ground staff thirty more minutes to work on the surface. On reaching the deadline the pitch was still heavy but it was declared playable. Jim Dick (83 minutes) and Ian Ferguson (85 minutes) scored in a 2-0 win watched by 9,286. If it was a Valentine's Day massacre it was not of the type that our Kilmarnock counterparts had predicted. Work commitments on a Saturday ensured that my wife Carol only attended Somerset Park occasionally. My daughter Jill only attended occasional matches through choice. Not any more! She was smitten by this match and ever since she has been an avid regular. Amidst all the euphoria it almost went unnoticed that league results elsewhere that afternoon had plunged Ayr United into second bottom place.

"Ghostly Firhill" was used in description of the next match. It was only three days later but the contrast could hardly have been more marked. Floodlighting issues at Cliftonhill had caused the postponement on 3rd January to be rescheduled for Firhill. Hamilton Accies were living a nomadic existence by moving from one temporary home to another. Merely 732 watched a 1-1 draw. Our next visit there would attract more than ten times that number.

Jim Dick maintaining possession against Partick Thistle on 28th February, 1998.

The fear of relegation is not something that it is possible to get used to no matter how many times such battles have been experienced. Prior to a home match with Partick Thistle on the last day of February, the foot of the First Division table had a concerning aspect. Stirling Albion were bottom with twenty-three points, above them were Partick Thistle on twenty-four points and then it was Ayr United on twenty-seven points. We had the same goal difference as Partick Thistle. It boiled down to this. Lose and we will drop into a relegation place. Partick Thistle had a 2-1 lead when the game had just a matter of seconds to run. One last attack was mounted, during which the referee could be seen consulting his watch. The concern was that he could put the whistle to his mouth at any second. Derek Anderson succeeded in making it 2-2. It was an important goal but we would not know just how important it was until the end of the season.

One week later we had the distraction of a Scottish Cup quarter-final against Hearts who were then second in the Premier League. The 4-1 defeat was riddled with refereeing controversy with the only saving grace being a nice morning in Edinburgh. Hearts went on to lift the trophy.

"Be careful what you wish for". Whosoever made up this phrase must have been teeming in intellect and no little foresight. I was reminded of this by my work colleagues in Kilmarnock to whom I had said: "If we beat Kilmarnock I don't care supposing we don't win another game all season." A swift retraction was forthcoming. The fixture list was daunting. When Airdrie returned to Ayr we all knew that they would be smarting from the 6-0 defeat in November. They managed to atone although they did not extract repayment in full. Nonetheless at 2-0 it was damaging enough. We were now second bottom, behind Stirling Albion on goal difference and above Partick Thistle by three points.

Of course life had other priorities such as raising a family and maintaining a job. Ayr United's fight against relegation did not compare. Such would have been the narrative of an outsider looking in. Nonetheless such issues as Ayr United's form are impossibly difficult to dislodge from the mind. It is never far from my consciousness. Would hypnotherapy work? Definitely not!

Stirling Albion 2 Ayr United 0 was enough to induce panic. A 'must win' game had been lost. The consequences were potentially terrible. From being two points ahead of Stirling we were now one point behind and again we were in a relegation place. Partick Thistle were four points behind and five games were left. All season we had scored just eight away league goals. This was the lowest of any club in the Scottish and English leagues. Only one of the eight had been scored in 1998.

When Andy Millen hit an 86th minute winner at home to Hamilton Accies the relief was palpable. Stirling Albion lost at Falkirk so we moved out of the folds of the dreaded bottom two. Four games were left, three of which were away starting with Dundee who had just clinched the title. What a game. In a 1-1 draw Dundee got two penalties, one of which was saved. The goalkeeper facing both was outfielder John Robertson who had deputised in goal since the 34th minute when Kristjan Finnbogason had to go off injured.

In a 1-0 win away to Morton the final whistle was awaited nervously. Surely now we were safe. With two games left we were two points above St.Mirren, three above Stirling Albion and four above Partick Thistle. It was just a matter of winning at home to Falkirk and we were over the line. Even a Partick Thistle defeat at Dundee would do. The Falkirk game had an added complication. They were second in the First Division with a five-point lead over Raith Rovers and two games left. With the advent of the breakaway Premier League for the following season, the club finishing second in the First Division would not have a play-off against the club finishing second bottom of the Premier League. Instead the club finishing as runners-up in the First Division in 1997/98 would receive compensation of £250,000. This money was important to Falkirk and a win at Ayr would guarantee it. They were financially stricken to the point that the receivers had been in. Ayr United 1 Falkirk 3 – they got it. Still, not to worry, Partick Thistle (bottom) would lose at Dundee (top). Or so we thought! It was Dundee 0 Partick Thistle 3. Stirling Albion had lost 1-0 at home to St.Mirren so they were confirmed for relegation. Who would join them? The situation was horrifying. The last match was away to Partick Thistle and the stakes were starkly simple. A draw or better for Ayr United would relegate Partick Thistle and a Partick Thistle win would relegate Ayr United. Many of us could recall last day escapes in 1976, 1983 and 1984. There had also been last day escapes in 1931, 1935 and 1938. In 1998 the heat was intensified by being pitched against the other team in peril, 1938 being the only historical precedent for this. I did not look forward to the Firhill showdown. Alas the week seemed to pass all too quickly. The kick-off had to be delayed for fifteen minutes due to the crowd size which eventually swelled to 8,424. Great were the celebrations when Ian Ferguson scored midway through the first half. Great was the despondency when Gareth Evans made it 1-1 in first half stoppage time. Early in the second half Laurent D'jaffo went on and he transformed the game. He scored a brilliant goal after being on the field for five minutes. It all now hinged on preventing Partick Thistle from scoring twice. Billy Findlay made it 3-1 in stoppage time. 1998 was added to the catalogue of last day escapes. On the way home we were sat in traffic alongside a bus on the Kingston Bridge. There was a Union Jack on one of the side windows. It seemed inconceivable that a Rangers bus could have got back from Tannadice in that time. Closer inspection revealed that it was a Stranraer bus and the occupants were buoyant. They had beaten Clyde 1-0 at Broadwood and in the process were the successors to Ayr United for the Second Division title. Their team contained Paul Watson, Isaac English and Paul Kinnaird all of whom now had the accolade of winning this title in successive years.

That summer I changed employment and I was now absolved of the responsibility of being guarded in football conversations when on my insurance agent beat in Kilmarnock. For the rest of my career I was destined to pass through a variety of jobs based in a variety of places but predominantly Glasgow where there was a strong tendency for people to be Old Firm-centric. I was to discover that my over-enthusiastic ramblings about Ayr United caused work colleagues to look out for the Ayr United score. This was a reminder of my oft-quoted belief that supporting Ayr United is infectious. It was always satisfying to see people adopt Ayr United even if only as a second team.

The club had adopted an air of professionalism at this time. On each of the last five weeks of season 1997/98 the players were taken to a "top hotel" forty-eight hours before kick-off in order to get the preparations exactly right. In 1998 there was a pre-season tour to Sweden. Ayr United had played in

Norway and Sweden in 1928. Getting to Scandinavia back then had involved a choppy crossing from Newcastle to Oslo. It was reported that: "Heads disappeared over the railings at regular intervals until only five of the eighteen-strong party could enjoy a smoke." This is an extraordinary piece of social commentary. By implication we are being told that the entire squad were smokers. In 1998 the squad flew from Prestwick Airport. No smoking was permitted on the flight!

In 1998 Ayr United played in Sweden for the first time since 1928. This Swedish newspaper clipping from 1928 has a caricature of Jimmy Smith with a caption stating "Engelske". He was born in Old Kilpatrick therefore the correct designation should have been Scotsk.

Every generation of Ayr United supporters has had a hero. Heroes fall into two categories. There are those who are the fans' favourite because they are superb players. In the other category are those who do not quite fit the 'superb' criteria but are nonetheless revered because they possess gut determination. The latter are known as cult heroes. In 1998 the hero was Glynn Hurst, he of the rapid pace and cannonball shot. Paired up front with Andy Walker this was just one element in a growing confidence that the team would immediately be challenging at the top end of the First Division. Too many false dawns had been experienced and this should perhaps have countered a confidence that was now bordering on cockiness. However it just felt different. The entire infrastructure had changed for the better.

The importance of getting off to a good league start was put at risk by having to play at Falkirk in the opener. Our adverse record at Brockville would be put right one day. Unfortunately that day was not 4th August, 1998. The scale of the damage was just 1-0 but, for what it was worth, a difficult fixture was out of the way. On trudging out of the ground we might have been forgiven for believing that we were under a gypsy's curse at Brockville.

The Challenge Cup has changed name with the frequency that a chameleon changes colour but for season 1998/99 the competition did not take place anyway, albeit that its absence was temporary. Its loss was barely lamented. No such indifference was accorded to the League Cup. Queen's Park, St.Mirren and Motherwell were all beaten away from home, each quite convincingly. Between cup and league we had seven matches in August, six of which were away from home. At last we got a home draw in the League Cup. It was a quarter-final against Rangers. If everyone with a ticket had turned up the crowd for that tie would have been 12,178 but only 11,198 appeared. During the summer Rangers had spent £27 million to supplement an already expensive squad. No signs of an inferiority complex were shown and it took a late goal for Rangers to seal it at 2-0.

Ayr United 7 Stranraer 1 occurred on what was a beautiful day in more than one way. People will argue that the lack of a competitive edge creates a poorer spectacle. I disagree. If watching Ayr United was like this oftener it would lower the stress levels. It is a luxury to be able to watch and contemplate what's for tea rather than witness the team hanging on for grim death in the hope of a draw or an odd goal victory. Again I can hear a chorus of voices saying that there are worse stresses and strains in the world than anything likely to be experienced at Somerset Park. However at the time it does not seem like it. It is a stomach churning experience when you're a goal up in stoppage time and the opposition gets a corner or a free-kick on the edge of the box. The 'sing when you're winning' philosophy was proven when Airdrie won 2-1 at Ayr a week later. We have always had to enjoy it while we can.

Consecutive weekends in Renfrewshire saw six points being accrued – St.Mirren 0 Ayr United 2 and Morton 1 Ayr United 2. After ten matches the First Division table made for promising viewing. Hibs and Falkirk were first and second respectively with eighteen points, then came Airdrie with seventeen and Ayr United with sixteen. Intriguingly it was Falkirk at home next. That match was won 4-2 despite Andy Millen getting sent off at 2-2. We were now third, just two points behind top-placed Hibs who were at Ayr in the next match. Alas a 3-1 lead was blown when Hibs scored twice in the last five minutes. Yet the idea of reaching the top was not a lost cause and when it did happen the circumstances were bizarre. After beating Clydebank 4-1 at Ayr the hallowed spot was reached because Hibs versus St.Mirren was postponed. The St.Mirren bus got snarled up in heavy traffic in Glasgow and could not get through. In the near certainty that Hibs would have beaten St.Mirren we were at the top of the league by default. Surely enough Hibs reclaimed their place when they won 4-1 in the rescheduled match on the immediate Tuesday. Unexpectedly Hibs drew at Hamilton on the next Saturday while our 2-0 win at nearby Airdrie was enough to claim top spot again although only on goal difference.

The Airdrie win comprised our sixth consecutive away victory in the league. This was just one shy of the record created in 1958/59. The next away game was at Falkirk and there was almost an expectation that the sequence of away wins would founder there. At 3-0 the expectation was comprehensively delivered. A Glynn Hurst hat-trick in a 5-0 demolition of Hamilton Accies added further joy to the festive season. Then came the Boxing Day storm. Metaphorically, it occurred in the afternoon when a six-pointer was lost 3-0 against Hibs at Easter Road.

Hibs at Ayr on 27th February, 1999

Literally, it occurred that night when the gales were severe enough to rip the roof off the Somerset Road end enclosure. Some of the debris crashed into houses in Somerset Road and residents had to be evacuated. Somerset Road! What would it be like to have a football club as a neighbour? There are the obvious impediments such as crowd noise and inconsiderate parking yet on a personal level the thought of living there is quite appealing.

There was an overriding fear at this time. It concerned the matter of winning the league then being denied promotion because of the 10,000-seater rule. Plans had already been drawn up for a 10,000-seater stadium at Heathfield but that ambition was to die a slow lingering death through strangulation by red tape. We need not have feared about being denied promotion. Even solely on a points-based criteria it would prove to be out of reach. For 1998/99 it was one up and one down with no play-offs and this was why SPL was popularly considered to stand for Self Preservation League. In the event Hibs pulled away to win the First Division by a margin of twenty-three points.

In dropping out of promotion contention, interest in Ayr United did not depreciate to any harmful extent. The team was still good to watch. At times there was an attacking abandon which looked to have been borrowed from the era of Ally MacLeod. Oh, and there was the not insignificant matter of the Scottish Cup! We were all a bit incredulous at the third round draw. It was Kilmarnock at home again. Kilmarnock supporters were itching for revenge. They were second in the Premier League at the time so it was considered that they were capable of extracting vengeance. This sentiment was not shared south of Symington. It was an all-ticket tie watched by 10,153 and the anticipation was huge on both sides. Just short of the half-hour mark Andy Lyons scored. I was still in my Family Stand phase and when the ball hit the net I instinctively leapt to my feet only to be confronted by a steward who said: "Would you mind sitting down, sir?"

It was goal time in a derby match. Was I really hearing this? Admittedly I was out of my natural habitat which was the

Somerset Road end. In phases of the second half Kilmarnock probed desperately for an equaliser but to no avail. Then it all exploded in the last ten minutes. Ray Montgomerie got sent off for pulling down Glynn Hurst. Andy Walker made it 2-0 from the resultant penalty. This time there was no caution for the goal celebration. It would have been a hopeless task anyway with the overall level of exuberance within the Family Stand. With the fans still loudly acclaiming that goal, Martin Baker brought down Gary Teale for another penalty. This one remained part of Ayr United folklore. Andy Walker gently chipped the ball down the middle and it seemed to float over the line in slow motion. He later said that he had done it before when faced by Gordon Marshall in training matches when they were both at Celtic. To replicate it in an Ayrshire derby showed a coolness which might have been described as contemptuous. Winning 3-0 made it a fantastic afternoon. For the third consecutive season Ayr United had eliminated Kilmarnock from cup competition. Beating Albion Rovers 1-0 at home in the fourth round was tougher than expected. The outcome brought forth the old statement about 1-0 being enough in the cup. Dundee United at home in the quarter-finals was a great opportunity to reach the semi-finals for the first time since 1973. Alas the opportunity was squandered amidst heartache. With the tie balanced at 0-0 Andy Millen was brought down for a penalty with four minutes left. This time Andy Walker's ploy of hitting it down the middle did not work. Sieb Dijkstra saved it. The replay was lost 2-1. Football had once again revealed its capacity for alternating elation with despair.

On re-evaluating what could now be realistically achieved in what was left of the season, a runners-up spot had to be the aim even although promotion was out of the question. Hibs had pulled up the drawbridge quite apart from the 10,000-seater rule which had clubs going into administration to fulfil. Hamilton Accies, still not in a permanent home, had lost their last seven league games when we went to Firhill to play them in March 1999. Seven became eight. Our

2-0 win was watched by just 729. Even allowing for it being a Wednesday night it was a despairing gate. Gary Teale was now playing the best football of his Ayr United career. This was ringingly endorsed in a 2-0 win at Airdrie which had very positive consequences. With six games left we were now third, two points ahead of Airdrie with a game in hand. We also had a game in hand over second-placed Falkirk who were five points above. The opportunity to finish as runners-up was denied. Falkirk won 2-1 at Ayr and there was a sense of déjà vu. In successive seasons they had guaranteed second place by winning at Somerset Park. To them and others the Premier League was a closed shop. There was ample currency for the argument that the structure was designed to keep the top sphere as an exclusive domain for establishment clubs. What was an establishment club? Mainly it was the type of club still trying to live off past glories and in order to recapture such glories would blindly lapse into financial jeopardy. To lighten the mood a little the spectacle at the Falkirk game was most interesting off the park by courtesy of visiting supporters in fancy dress. If there had been a prize it would have gone to the two people inside a pantomime horse. Galloping (or what passed for galloping) up and down the terracing steps looked like a tough gig.

The lowest ever attendance at a competitive match involving Ayr United (lockdown excepted) did not take place in the despairing days of 1964. Nor did it take place against a background of such mitigating factors as poor form, extreme weather or a remote location. Clydebank versus Ayr United was originally scheduled for 9th January. It had been postponed ten times before getting played on the evening of 27th April. Our opponents were ground sharing at Dumbarton's Boghead Park. By reason of its name it was easy to make cheap jokes about the state of the pitch but now we were in a situation where there was a certain validity to the unkind comments. Clydebank were in a financial mess. For the Ayr game their goalkeeper was Steve Morrison, a coach who was aged thirty-eight. Morrison had not even been a goalkeeper in his playing days. The meagre gathering was 197. Clydebank contrived to win 2-1. It may have been an act of mercy that so few were there to complain. The next game was billed as the last match at Cappielow. The cause of the demonstrations had nothing to do with a 4-1 Ayr United win but everything to do with Morton's planned ground share at Airdrie which, as you well know, did not materialise.

11. New Century New Hope

The heading is a tad understated. It was not just a new century approaching but a millennium. You may recall the fears about the millennium bug. We were told that computers would reset to zero which in turn could cause bank balances to disappear and planes to fall from the sky. The operative word here is 'could'. With the 100% assuredness of hindsight the operative word is 'didn't'. The reference to 'hope' in the heading is not understated though. Ayr United supporters thrive on hope. It is popularly said that it is the hope that kills you. This is a false maxim. Even when hopes are unfulfilled the more rabid in our ranks will continue to return to Somerset Park.

Pre-season in 1999 saw an explosion of goals. On a tour to the Highlands eighteen got scored in four matches. At home Oxford United (1-0) and Wrexham (3-0) were disposed of. The Oxford boss was Ayr United cult hero Malky Shotton who was welcomed with an ovation. This summer goalfest was in stark contradiction to 1997 when no goals at all were scored in the five pre-season matches played (excepting shootout goals in the Livingston Tournament).

A new promotion format was introduced. At the end of the season the Premier League was getting extended from ten to twelve clubs. The First Division champions would be promoted while the bottom club in the Premier League would play in a round robin tournament at neutral venues with the second and third teams in the First Division. Two of the three would play in the following season's Premier League. However promoted clubs would have to fulfil the following criteria by 31st March, 2000. They would require a ground with 10,000 individually numbered seats under the cover of a roof. They would also require to have an adequate pitch protection system. Quite chillingly it was further stipulated that if all of the top three in the First Division were not to meet the criteria there would be no play-offs or relegation and the two highest placed clubs whose stadiums did meet the criteria would be promoted. The possibility existed for a club to get promoted from mid-table. Ayr United's plans to relocate to Heathfield would fulfil the criteria but the chances of it happening by 31st March were nil. We could not be promoted regardless and neither could Falkirk who had finished second in each of the previous two seasons. The whole situation stank.

Ayr United entered the season having scored 4,999 league goals since the club's formation in 1910. As always such statistics are dependent on my arithmetic being accurate but you have the assurance that I check, recheck and recheck again. To whom would go the honour of scoring the landmark 5,000th? It was Alex Bone in a 1-1 draw away to his former club St.Mirren. Earlier that year, on 30th January, Ayr United's 3,000th league fixture had taken place at the same ground. That ground was always referred to as Love Street although its actual name was St.Mirren Park. If ever a match was destined to finish 1-1 it was this one. In an earlier chapter you will have read about the club's proliferation of league openers resulting in that scoreline in this decade. Another statistical tit-bit was that we had now gone eight consecutive seasons without winning an opening league fixture. This remains another of these dubious club records.

Notwithstanding the argued injustice of it all we had a red card in each of the club's first three league fixtures. Losing at home to Raith Rovers in what was now called the Bell's League Challenge Cup did not register terribly high on the scale of disappointment. However this was the first of five defeats suffered against Raith Rovers that season, an issue that could not be so glibly viewed. The League Cup was almost exited by the same 0-1 scoreline. Almost! Mickey Reynolds (85 minutes) and Alex Bone (89 minutes) salvaged a 2-1 win against Hamilton Accies. In football parlance Bone was over the moon about his late winner quite apart from the natural joy of scoring. It was a Tuesday night and he did not drive. The last train from Glasgow to his home town, Stirling, was at 10.33 pm. He asked referee Bobby Orr how long was left and he even said to Orr that he would have to score the winner to catch the last train home. Extra time would have been problematical. The question of extra time did not arise in the next round. It was Ayr United 0 Celtic 4.

You have already been given a spoiler about Raith Rovers. They lost 6-0 at home to St.Mirren and their next home match was against Ayr. In between these fixtures they had won 4-1 at Airdrie. It was too bad that they did not replicate their form from the St.Mirren match. Raith Rovers 5 Ayr United 1 meant a points total of four from the first five games. This was clearly unsatisfactory unless there was a willingness to clutch to those proverbial straws. This is a reference to the club having four points from five games a year earlier when the season became reasonably successful. Even after bouncing back to win 2-0 at home to Airdrie our league position was a modest seventh. On the occasion of winning at Cappielow in May the Morton fans protested against a planned ground switch. In September we were back at Cappielow where the nomadic Clydebank were housed. Again there were protests. John Hall, the Clydebank owner, was the subject of torrents of abuse from his own club's fans. A 2-0 Ayr win did nothing to alleviate their discontent.

To Ayr United supporters of this era, the sight of Owen Coyle was enough to induce panic. He had caused us considerable damage when playing for Clydebank then Airdrie. In September 1999 he was in the Dunfermline Athletic team to face Ayr United at East End Park. He scored in the ninth minute then celebrated by making it 2-0 within a minute of the recentre. Glynn Hurst minimised the damage to 2-1 and we were desperately unlucky towards the end. Nigel Jemson struck the bar with a header with two minutes of the regulation ninety left. Then, in stoppage time, he struck a free-kick which crashed back off the junction of bar and post. In July Thomas Gill had been signed on a two-year contract. He was a Norwegian goalkeeper who had made five full international appearances for his country including a 4-2 win against Brazil. Prior to Ayr United his club was FC Copenhagen. His credentials were of little use at Dunfermline. Much of the blame for the defeat was heaped upon him. It was his last match for Ayr United and it was mutually agreed that he could walk out on his contract.

Ayr United supporters will always reminisce about good times as well as bad times. It may seem a stretch of credibility to associate 1999/2000 with adverse records but here is a statistic from that time which does fall into the negative category. Between October and December 1999 Ayr United scored no goals in four consecutive home league games. This replicated an identical run between November and December 1917. However the run in 1999 was preceded by a home League Cup tie in which the team did not score (0-4 versus Celtic) so this made the overall total five consecutive home games without scoring.

The final match in that run went very badly (0-3 versus Dunfermline Athletic). This prompted a recurrence of the barracking. In these situations the prime target is almost always the manager. There was no exception here. Gordon Dalziel responded: "People shouting at me doesn't matter. I'm not interested. They should get their heads around the facts and look at what is happening. Wait till we get a full team on the park and get it settled with a wee run going. We have ten or eleven players sitting in the stand and for a club of this size we cannot afford that. It is impossible to carry the burden. I feel sorry for the players who had to play out of position. Gary Teale and Glynn Hurst were playing in the middle, Keith Hogg had been out for a year while Andy McMillan, who is a right-back, had to play in the centre." His appraisal was detailed, frank and impossible to argue with. Many times through the years I have witnessed fans turning on the manager in response to a missed sitter. "Ah, but it wasn't the manager who missed the sitter" is a futile counter argument because it is guaranteed that the barracker's comeback will be: "Aye, but the manager picked him."

On the last Saturday before Christmas, St.Mirren 1 Ayr United 2 was a most unexpected gift. St.Mirren were top of the league even after the match and they were previously unbeaten at home all season. Our own form was a tale of no league wins in the previous nine. Glynn Hurst was suspended and Andy McMillan got sent off when the second half was barely underway. The fates were conspiring. Neil Tarrant then hit the winner two minutes from the end.

In the last match of the nineteenth century the pre-amalgamation Ayr FC beat Airdrie 5-0 in a league fixture at Somerset Park. By a great coincidence Airdrie were at Somerset Park for the last fixture of the twentieth century. I mentioned this in the match programme and hinted at the possibility of the coincidence being stretched by a repetition of the scoreline. Here is what happened. Marvyn Wilson (5 minutes) 1-0, Neil Tarrant (12 minutes) 2-0, Glynn Hurst (43 minutes) 3-0, Glynn Hurst (44 minutes) 4-0, Jens Hansen (83 minutes) 5-0, full time 5-0. In reference to the programme spiel Mike Wilson jocularly claimed in the *Ayrshire Post* that I had psychic powers. In practical terms we finished the year (and the century) by leapfrogging Airdrie into seventh place. For a team so rich in individual talent the league table made grim reading.

There can be no doubting that New Years are not at all like they used to be. Postponements excepted we were guaranteed football on New Year's Day provided it did not land on a Sunday. The millennium was supposed to see the ultimate in New Year celebrations yet there was a common view that it was an anti-climax. It certainly was as regards the football. 1st January, 2000, landed on a Saturday but our derby was pushed on to the Monday. Derby is defined here in its loosest sense. It was Clydebank at Cappielow. Yearning for the past was acceptable when drawing comparisons with the 15,240 crowd for our match at Kilmarnock on 2nd January, 1971. This match at Cappielow drew 901. One year later this would be the scene of Glynn Hurst running riot but for now he scored the game's solitary goal.

Successive league fixtures were played in the Kingdom of Fife and they were both lost 2-0 against Raith Rovers then Dunfermline Athletic. Some publicity was accorded to the consequent unlikelihood of reaching a play-off place but this merely highlighted errant media sources which were unaware that we were debarred from the play-offs anyway. The Scottish Cup though carried no such lack of incentive. On being drawn away to Premier League Dundee, the wave of confidence was vindicated in a 0-0 draw. Postponements are frustrating but the frustration was compounded when the replay got postponed despite Somerset Park being perfectly playable. Fifty-five minutes before the scheduled kick-off time it was called off because of the wind. Safety was of paramount importance not just in football but in the big wide world also. Someone might have had their eye taken out by a flying crisp packet! One week later the match did go ahead but there was a threat of an abandonment when the snow got heavier. In the 79th minute referee Jim Herald called for an orange ball. After ninety minutes without a goal, ten minutes got spent sweeping the lines which had since disappeared from view. It was 1-1 after extra time then we had the spectacle of Ayr United's first ever shootout on home soil. John Robertson struck the winner with kick number sixteen. The fourth round draw was awaited with interest. Motherwell away, that would do nicely even although they were third in the Premier League. What a day it was. John Robertson had to deputise in goal for a spell. Four wingers were on the pitch. Mickey Reynolds was sent off. Seven goals were scored in the first half. Andy Goram was in goal for Motherwell. It was Motherwell 3 Ayr United 4 with the second half still to be played. The bullet points were abundant. There was no settling of the pace even although the scoring settled. The half-time score was the full time result. Alliteration of the letter 'T' will now be used to tell you that our scorers were two from Teale and two from Tarrant. Newspaper reports described the action in glowing terms. To couch it in abbreviated terms it was simply a great game.

The quarter-final draw could not have been kinder. It was Second Division (third tier) Partick Thistle at home. The only historical precedent for Ayr United reaching the Scottish Cup semi-finals was 1973 when Partick Thistle had been eliminated at the same stage. Again the hurdle was overcome. It was a 2-0 win in front of 8,365. If 1973 was to be further replicated the semi-final would be against Rangers at Hampden. It was! What happened next? It would be tempting to cite amnesia but that would be a lie. The damage was 7-0 and the experience was awful. It was reported as a record defeat ever in a Scottish Cup semi-final. From the realms of my own research material I knew this to be a wrongful claim. It was not even a record defeat by an Ayr club in a Scottish Cup semi-final. That dated back to 13th January, 1877, when the result at Kinning Park was Ayr Thistle 0 Vale of Leven 9. Admittedly that was very far back in the mists of time but it endorses the need to exercise care when using the word 'ever'.

Craig Nelson missed the Rangers match after getting injured in training therefore the recently signed Marius Rovde made his debut. To quote the most suitable metaphor he was thrown in at the deep end and he was our second Norwegian goalkeeper of the season. By the end of the season we would be able to reflect on five goalkeepers guarding the Ayr United goal. They were Thomas Gill, Craig Nelson, Jens Knudsen, Marius Rovde and John Dodds. If being totally pedantic full-back John Robertson may be added as a sixth after his stint of seven minutes as a deputy at Motherwell.

During the Scottish Cup run Gordon Dalziel had implemented a policy of fielding understrength teams in league fixtures prior to the forthcoming ties. Promotion could not happen anyway even in the event of finishing top while at the other end relegation posed no real threat. Yet no matter the reasons it was unsatisfactory to finish seventh. The new stadium application was still alive and for the foreseeable future it had to succeed if any promotion ambitions were to be realised. After such a mediocre league season it may have sounded fanciful to even hint at the prospect of promotion. Even if the planning issues could be resolved it would still be necessary to build a team capable of challenging.

That summer club administrator Brian Caldwell told me about a telephone conversation he had with Marvyn Wilson who was walking through East Kilbride's Olympia Shopping Centre at the time. Wilson asked him about new signings and he was taken aback by what he heard. Dundee created a flurry of interest when it was made known that strikers James Grady and Eddie Annand were available for transfer. On grounds of affordability clubs considered an 'either or' situation while Ayr United signed them both. John Hughes, Pat McGinlay, Paul Lovering and Michael Renwick were all fixed up on their release from Hibs. The amazement of Marvyn Wilson was matched by the general public. These were quality signings to supplement a player pool that included Neil Duffy, David Craig, Mark Campbell and Glynn Hurst, not forgetting Marvyn Wilson either.

From 1928 it had taken Ayr United seventy years to revisit Sweden. In 2000 the return took place after two years. Brian Caldwell was always a good source of amusing anecdotes behind the scenes. One such was in relation to this latest tour to Sweden. The Swedish hospitality extended to post match meals. A practical joke was created which involved the hosts being told that one of the Ayr United players had been practising his Swedish language skills and that he wished to do a short speech by way of thanks for the hospitality. The Swedes would then listen in amazement while the speech was delivered in perfect Swedish. Peter Lindau was the orator and by now you will have guessed that he was Swedish.

Ayr United 1 Ross County 0 was our first opening game league win since 1991 and the first at home since 1988. It was untidy. The goal came from a penalty and Brian Irvine, the perpetrator, was sent off. Barely twenty minutes had been played. Ross County's second red card was too late to have any impact. The points may have been in the bag but the fans were not deluded. In the ensuing midweek the fan reaction was hostile. Third Division Dumbarton (fourth tier) were tenants of Albion Rovers while their new stadium was getting built. This was a League Cup tie that finished 0-0 after extra time then we had the added indignity of losing the shootout. It went down very badly and the players trooped off under a hail of verbal abuse. A 1-1 draw at Alloa in the next league fixture did little to soothe the angry passions. Then we had a 3-1 defeat away to Brechin City in the Bell's League Challenge Cup. Beaten by a Third Division team again!

A common expression in football is 'kick-start'. It is used in the context of a requirement to kick-start the season in order to correct an indifferent run of form. Pull the finger out is another colloquialism appropriate to such situations. Well, the team did pull the finger out. Home matches on consecutive Saturdays brought victories of 3-1 and 5-2 against Airdrie and Falkirk respectively. This rendered the table most interesting. At the top we were behind Livingston only, the differentiating factor being goal difference. It was Livingston away next. Unfortunately the injury list ruled out Mickey Reynolds, Gary Teale, James Grady, Eddie Annand and John Hughes. In a 2-0 defeat Glynn Hurst got sent off for a tackle on David Hagen. After the red card had been shown he was chased round the field by a posse of Livingston players. It would have been most appropriate if the PA system had blurted out the theme tune from the Benny Hill Show.

We had another comedic episode, this time at Falkirk. Brockville was hardly the cheeriest footballing rendezvous, especially while standing in the pouring rain on an uncovered terracing behind the goal. Late in the match, by which time we were 2-0 down, some fellow Ayr supporters took the opportunity to have a chat with Falkirk substitute Kevin McAllister who answered to the nickname Crunchie. Being close enough to eavesdrop it all sounded quite convivial. Crunchie then broke off the conversation with an apology. "Sorry, got to go, lads." He was being hailed to go on. This was in the 88th minute but he still had time to make it 3-0 from a delicate chip after running almost from the halfway line. He was still difficult to dislike!

Livingston, Falkirk and Ayr United were vying with each other in the top three. That was why Livingston's visit to Ayr was a six-pointer. Yet the importance attached to the match was not reflected in a visiting support of 208 in the overall figure of 3,082. After a 1-1 draw the principal post-match talking point was referee Kevin Toner who was a son of former Ayr United player Willie Toner. In the 86th minute John Hughes and Marino Keith were jostling for position prior to a Livingston free-kick. On the advice of the farside linesman Yogi was yellow-carded. He argued with the referee only to land a second yellow card and therefore a red. Bizarrely, as he walked off the field, the referee followed him. Yogi ignored him until such time as another conversation was ignited which resulted in a second red card. In all the years I have watched football this remains the only time I have ever seen a referee send a player off then accompany him on his way.

At different phases of history Ayr United have seemed fated not to win at certain grounds, typically Brockville, Palmerston and the Caledonian Stadium. Grounds such as Celtic Park and Ibrox are very difficult to win at but it has always been irksome to go for years without a win at grounds which should be winnable at. Inverness Caledonian Thistle 7 Ayr United 3 caused Gordon Dalziel to say that it was the worst day of his managerial career. Not since 12th November, 1975, had an Ayr United team conceded seven in a league fixture (2-7 versus Celtic). The travelling support contributed to Dalziel's discomfort by venting fury. On 2nd January, 2001, the world was a beautiful place once more when Glynn Hurst scored five goals in a 6-0 win away to Morton. This equalled the club record away win at the time. Hurst was the first Ayr United player to hit that number since Peter Price in an 8-1 win at home to East Stirling on 26th November, 1955. What next for Glynn Hurst? What indeed! He did not score for Ayr United again and he stated a wish to move back to England. On 15th February he was sold to Stockport County.

The Scottish Cup third round draw was awaited with great anticipation only to be received by great disappointment. Inverness Caledonian Thistle away! It was a reminder of the old maxim about being careful what you wish for. We wished for a long run in the Scottish Cup but not this type of long run! It was a 410-mile round journey and we had conceded seven there in the previous month. It was Inverness Caledonian Thistle 0 Ayr United 3 by half-time. Then came the capitulation. The result was Inverness Caledonian Thistle 4 Ayr United 3. At the final whistle the fury of the fans was unrestrained. Quite frankly the verbal barrage was deserved. For this particular game I opted to travel with the family in a supporters' bus rather than drive. In contrast to the racket at the end of the match there was total silence in the bus as it made its seemingly interminable way down the A9. On the Sunday I checked my records to ascertain matches in which Ayr United had scored at least three and lost. I then checked the scoring patterns in these games. The result of this exercise showed that Ayr United had never previously lost a competitive match after achieving a three-goal lead. In the year of writing the capitulation in 2001 remains the only incidence of this. We can at least be grateful that no Ayr United team has ever lost a league match after going three up. Gordon Dalziel got the brunt of the fury at Inverness but certain of the players should not have been absolved from blame. Marius Rovde's handling, or lack of it, was a key factor in the whole shambles. When Airdrie visited on league duty a week later the verbal assaults on Gordon Dalziel continued during a 2-2 draw. The Airdrie support inside the ground was small because most of their number opted to stay outside in protest at Ayr United chairman Bill Barr whom they wrongly believed to be responsible for holding up Steve Archibald's ongoing attempt to buy over their club. Barr Limited had built their stadium and remained the main creditor.

The Inverness hangover was eventually cured by the only means possible. Winning matches! Pat McGinlay scored a hat-trick in a 4-1 away win over Raith Rovers and a week later we were back on the road for a 2-1 win at Falkirk. Yes, a win at Falkirk! After losing every game at Brockville since October 1990 it had finally happened. The prospect of catching Livingston at the top was close to a lost cause. They pitched up at Ayr with a lead of eleven points and only eleven fixtures left.

Anything less than a home win would eradicate much of the remaining hope. It was a Saturday afternoon so the visiting support of 185 was inexplicable in the situation they found themselves in. We had to rely on a stoppage time penalty to salvage a 1-1 draw. Despite the late penalty award referee Stuart Dougal was booed off at the end. Marvin Andrews had repetitively been fouling Marvyn Wilson, culminating in a 72nd minute challenge which caused him to be stretchered off with a triple fracture of the cheekbone. Andrews finished the match without even a yellow card against him. In a post match interview Livingston boss Jim Leishman said: "I hope wee Marvyn's okay". He was far from okay.

This was followed by a home match against Falkirk on the Tuesday, just ten days after we had beaten them at Brockville. Work commitments meant that it was nearly half-time when I got into the ground and I was delighted to get an update of "1-0 to Ayr". Five goals in a fifteen-minute burst in the second half created a 6-0 rout. The beleaguered goalkeeper was Myles Hogarth who had experienced an identical demise with Airdrie at Ayr. An early rematch with Livingston brought a 1-0 away win which narrowed the gap to one point. However the elephant in the room was their three matches in hand.

There was yet another recurrence of the word 'hope' as late as 14th April. Livingston had no league fixture because they were playing Hibs in the Scottish Cup semi-finals. All we had to do was to win at Inverness to get a one-point lead at the top then count on Livingston faltering in their two games in hand. Of course with Inverness being in the equation this was easier said than done. After conceding a 1-0 defeat the writing was on the wall. We proceeded to finish as runners-up, seven points off the top. This was the cue to indulge in some end-of-season statistics and the findings were positive.

Highest ever position in the new-style First Division.
Only one league defeat at home.
Only one league defeat in the last seventeen fixtures.
Highest scorers in the First Division with seventy-three.
Fewest defeats of any club in the First Division with five.

In retrospect it was a good season when viewed overall. Fans of course are sensitive and the occasional lapses in form were met by some indelicate choruses from the terracing. Again this could raise the question of fickleness but such an accusation is unfair. It is a perfectly natural state to be happy when you are winning and disappointed when you are not.

In July 2001 the Carmichaels had a week's holiday in Whitley Bay. It was a once mighty holiday resort which looked to be a bit faded when we arrived. Why Whitley Bay and why mention it here? The reasoning was sound. Ayr United were playing in the Blyth Spartans tournament. I offered to cover the matches for the *Ayrshire Post*. This was in gratitude for their help with some photographs in the Ayr United Images book which was very close to publication. We arrived on the Sunday and the first match was against the host club on the Monday evening. After a 1-1 draw we returned to the Guest House and I hand wrote the report which the owner agreed to fax to the paper first thing in the morning (such was the primitive state of communications then). Afterwards it became clear that he had read the report and had disapproved of it, likely because I did not hold back from describing the home team's combative style. Thereafter the owner was a bit cold when indulging in conversation. On the Wednesday evening we returned to Blyth for a 3-2 win against Darlington. When I handed the report to the Guest House owner for faxing he said, in a heavily sarcastic tone: "Is this another wonderful report?" Would I have recommended his place? Yes, actually! On the Friday evening Blyth Spartans beat Darlington 4-1 to take custody of the Absolut Print and Design trophy. On the Saturday morning we journeyed home via Berwick rather than via Carlisle. We had a friendly against Berwick Rangers which was won 3-2. We made up four of the dedicated 212 in attendance.

Beating Wigan Athletic 4-0 in pre-season allowed our opponents to have a look at Gary Teale. We can be sure that they had another look at him and that the scouting reports were favourable because in December they purchased him for £275,000. In time the clauses about appearances and promotion got triggered thereby elevating the deal to a figure in excess of £400,000. It remains the highest transfer fee received by the club.

Somerset Park was liable to be criticised by lazy journalists who would trot out unoriginal clichés such as 'stuck in a time warp' or 'relic of the fifties'. Investment in the facilities was not going to occur beyond what was necessary because the Heathfield project had not yet had the life strangled out of it. Yet it was a safe environment to watch football. Ayr United supporters could testify about the state of Dumbarton's Boghead Park in its last years. Sections of terracing were taped off. Our opening match of the 2001/02 season was a league fixture at Falkirk. On entering Brockville on this occasion it was clear that the end was nigh. After passing through the turnstiles, taped-off crumbling parts were in view. Aesthetic conditions should not really matter to the average football supporter besides which it would have made no sense to invest in a facility when plans for relocation were being formulated. Anyway Falkirk 1 Ayr United 2 was more important than any preponderance towards football ground architecture. We then went clear at the top with a 2-0 win at home to Ross County. No other First Division club won the first two games. Getting off to a flyer is largely preferable to having to give chase but positive sentiments expressed so early will be met with the rebuff: "It's still just August." Fixture three was a 2-1 defeat at Airdrie. It was our second loss in the league since Christmas. Statistically it might have been dismissed as a blip. Only it wasn't a blip! It was the first of five consecutive away defeats. Airdrie, Partick Thistle, Arbroath, Inverness Caledonian Thistle then Ross County – this was a bad time to hit the road to watch Ayr United. Yet when such eventualities occur there is equal grief when staying at home. Score updates on the television can make for a tough watch.

Such gloom was lightened when Kilmarnock were at Ayr for a third round League Cup tie. Our cause was handicapped when Paul Sheerin and Andy McLaren got involved in an altercation. Altercation! Now there is a word straight from the book of footballing clichés. McLaren got a yellow card and Sheerin got a red card. No goals were scored by the end of extra time. We had therefore played with a man short for seventy-eight minutes. There were twelve kicks in the shootout and the tie was won when Killie's Chris Innes blazed the ball into the night sky at the Somerset Road end. Stranraer had been beaten 4-0 at Ayr in the previous round. It was a major turnaround from losing 3-2 at Stranraer in the Bell's League Challenge Cup. Beating Kilmarnock was a source of great satisfaction to the Ayr support. They had now lost to Ayr United in cup competitions in seasons 1996/97, 1997/98, 1998/99 and 2001/02. Four in a row was regaled in song but the elation of it all did not square with league form. On Halloween night the biggest scare was Ayr United 0 Partick Thistle 2. It was our first home defeat in a competitive match since December. A run of fifteen consecutive unbeaten home games was over (thirteen in the First Division and two in the League Cup).

Ayr United 0 Arbroath 1 was met with hostility although this is not a first-hand account. On the afternoon of the match I was travelling to Manchester with an Ayr United quiz team. We were taking part in a competition that was being recorded on the Sunday for some obscure television channel. The host was Simon O'Brien who made his name in Brookside apparently. Coincidentally Ayr Scottish Eagles had an ice hockey match in Manchester on the Saturday night and they won. I had seen Ayr Bruins occasionally in the 1970s, initially at Beresford Terrace and then at Limekiln Road. It was impressive to see ice hockey 2001-style put together as an entertainment package. With Ayr United now second bottom of the First Division it was a useful diversion too. In our absence a petition to get rid of Gordon Dalziel was in circulation at the Arbroath match. It was understandable at the time but would never have happened if the perpetrators had possessed the gift of foresight. To call them perpetrators is to use a connotation that may be interpreted harshly. More moderately they may have been described as concerned fans. Highly memorable days (and nights) were on the way and they would be happening soon.

Our time in the folds of the dreaded bottom two was mercifully brief. Pat McGinlay hit the only goal of the match in the closing minutes away to St.Mirren. Ayr United 3 Inverness Caledonian Thistle 0 then gave further impetus to the climb back up the league. In the immediate midweek our visitors from the north were back at Somerset Park for a League Cup quarter-final. In the ninth minute Ross Tokely headed his team in front. Two minutes later Tokely got sent off. Within five minutes of his departure it was 2-1 to Ayr and we went on to win 5-1. For the fourth time in the club's history we were in the League Cup semi-finals. League progress was steady although not absolute. Ayr United 1 Airdrie 3 prompted the *Ayr Advertiser* to state: "Any realistic chance Ayr United had of winning the First Division championship this season all but disappeared on Saturday." It was a sad truth but it did not diminish the pleasure of winning 2-0 at Falkirk a week later. That was win number three at Brockville in 2001. The ghosts had been exorcised.

2001 had opened with a 6-0 away win and so did 2002. Deveronvale away in the Scottish Cup brought forth the predictable pre-match clichés chief of which was 'potential banana skin'. That potential did not materialise. At 6-0 James Grady had a penalty saved. A special guest at this tie was Willie Grant whose two goals for Elgin City had knocked Ayr United out of the Scottish Cup in 1967. Was his presence ominous? Judging by the result the answer is no. The next round draw was Dunfermline Athletic at home. Their Premier League status counted for nothing and they were swatted away 3-0. Football fans are notorious for having a wicked sense of humour and the Somerset Road enders are hard to beat in this regard. Our second goal was an own goal by Gus MacPherson and it was greeted by choruses of "There's only one Gus MacPherson." This was solely on account of him being an ex-Kilmarnock player.

Cup football continued to be the source of the main thrills. Beating Hibs at Hampden in the League Cup semi-final was an incredible experience. Ayr United had never played in a major final before and I was desperate to hear the final whistle.

Eddie Annand scored the only goal from the penalty spot in extra time. By the closing minutes I was pacing the concourse area in a nerve, a bit like an expectant father in a Maternity Ward. When the final whistle blew I ran back down to where my family were sitting. Hibs supporters were leaning over to shake my hand. They could see from my excited demeanour just how much it meant. Their graciousness in defeat was quite touching.

These important cup games came apace. The next hurdle was Dundee United away in the Scottish Cup quarter-finals. It hardly seemed to matter that we were up against a Premier League club. After the Dunfermline win my daughter was very chilled about the outcome and she explained that she expected Ayr United to beat Premier League clubs. Her attitude was not born out of arrogance. It was born out of the experience of recent years. A 2-2 draw at Tannadice moved the issue to a midweek replay. I was working that night so I knew that I would miss all or most of the first half. While getting off a bus at Tam's Brig I overheard someone say that it was 1-0 for Ayr. On a breathless arrival at the ground marginally before half-time, I learned that this was the happy truth and that the scorer was Scott Crabbe from a penalty. Ten minutes from time Paul Sheerin made it 2-0 and so it remained. For the third time in our history we were in the Scottish Cup semi-finals and it had now happened twice in three seasons. Had it not been for a missed penalty in 1999 it would have been three times in four seasons.

It was quite staggering to survey the schedule of forthcoming matches. On 17th March we had the League Cup final versus Rangers and on 23rd March we had a Scottish Cup semi-final against Celtic, both matches at Hampden. Prior to the final it was tempting to visualise an open-topped bus parading along Prestwick Road. A major obstacle to such daydreaming was an expensively assembled Rangers squad. Eleven of the thirteen Rangers players who played that afternoon benefited from EBTs. These were Employee Benefit Trusts which were aimed at minimising tax liability. The ensuing controversy was so great that there was talk of Rangers having to forfeit competition wins that occurred while they were operating this scheme. That's all it was. Talk! Our 4-0 defeat had little chance of being overturned. The Ayr United ticket allocation of 12,000 was sold out and there were many recollections of what people termed 'a great day out'. Personally I shared no such sentiment. I could think of better days out than losing 4-0 to Rangers. Still, at least the Rangers supporters gave up time from their St.Patrick's Day celebrations to attend the match! Our Scottish Cup semi-final ended 3-0 to Celtic. The one redeeming feature was that we were afforded a glimpse of the big time. When the teams take to the field on such occasions it is sometimes described as the type of moment when the hairs on the back of your neck stand up. I must absolve myself from such a claim because, in the year of writing, a barber told me that I was the first bloke he had ever come across with no hairs on the back of the neck.

When the climax to the league season occurred the events were extraordinary. At home to Airdrie, Stewart Kean scored with twenty-one minutes played. This was the cue for a gang of Airdrie supporters to walk onto the field. Referee Bobby Orr took the teams off while the police ushered the invaders back towards the railway end terrace. On the way back some of them swung on the crossbar until it snapped. Bobby Orr then abandoned the game because the crossbar could not be repaired immediately. This has been the only abandonment in Ayr United's history in which the score stood. Within days of the match Airdrie went out of business despite finishing second in the First Division. Partick Thistle were the champions and Ayr United finished third. After a match I would depart Somerset Park with my son and daughter then we would head to the High Street to meet my wife who finished her work there at 5 pm. On the day of the Airdrie abandonment people in the High Street were confused by the fact that we were wearing Ayr United colours and were in the town centre before 4 pm. The story rendered them incredulous. That summer Airdrie re-emerged as Airdrie United and the new club took the place of Clydebank who dropped from the league on going defunct.

12. The Descent

Great cup runs and a third-placed finish in the First Division left the fans with memories to cherish for decades. Admittedly it had been tortuous at times but it now looked as if there was a good springboard for the future. Yet the passage of time was to prove that how it looked was at odds with how it was to pan out. Fourteen players departed at the end of season 2001/02. They included such talent as John Hughes, Neil Duffy, Scott Crabbe, Marvyn Wilson, Pat McGinlay and John Robertson. William Hill's odds to win the First Division for the season ahead saw St.Johnstone installed as favourites and Ayr United as second favourites. The odds of 3/1 had clearly taken no cognisance of the mass clearout.

After losing the first two league games (Falkirk at home and Clyde away) some comfort might have been drawn from the argument that "it's still only August." It is in the nature of the provincial football fan to grasp at anything that might alleviate the suffering. Alas, the suffering intensified after the Clyde defeat. On 13th August, 1952, a League Cup tie had resulted Ayr United 11 Dumbarton 1. Precisely fifty years afterwards the Golden Anniversary coincided with the clubs meeting in the Bell's League Challenge Cup. Inauspiciously the occasion was marked by a result which read Dumbarton 3 Ayr United 0. Ex-Ayr United players in the home team were David Stewart (their captain), Craig McEwan, Neil Duffy, Mark Crilly and John McKeown. Their manager was an ex-Ayr United player too, David Winnie. In relative terms this was an unimportant competition but that much was not apparent from the intensity. It ended up as ten versus nine. We had Aaron Black and Iain Nicolson red-carded then Craig McEwan of the home team suffered a similar fate.

Thereafter a run of three consecutive league wins occurred for the first time since April 2001. The second of those was 2-1 away to Queen of the South. Note the date well. It was 24th August, 2002. In the year of writing it was the date of our last league win at Palmerston. It is another on the list of grounds we have had to approach with fear and trepidation. The spectres of Falkirk and Inverness were laid to rest eventually. Not so the spectre of Dumfries. A League Challenge Cup win there in a shootout in 2006 hardly counts. On an individual basis there was the spectre of Owen Coyle. He had scored against Ayr United when playing for Dumbarton, Clydebank, Airdrie and Dunfermline Athletic. Now he was coming to Ayr to play in a League Cup tie for Falkirk. The feat of preventing him from scoring was achieved but it was a case of winning the battle and losing the war. In the ensuing weeks there was an early rematch in a league fixture at Brockville. The match was lost 3-0 and Owen Coyle scored twice despite being anonymous for most of the game. Discipline was a problem. Paul Lovering was sent off at Alloa. Allan McManus was sent off in this match at Falkirk. Neil Murray was sent off at home to Clyde a week after the Falkirk match. The next match after Clyde was at Arbroath where Paul Sheerin and Marc Smyth were both sent off. Including the Bell's League Challenge Cup match at Dumbarton the total of red cards for the season was seven by 5th November. At last we did manage to finish with eleven men but Queen of the South won 1-0 for their first league win at Ayr since 1967.

The prospect of an away fixture against St.Johnstone was none too alluring. On that particular afternoon my wife and I were at a wedding. The best man was an Ayr United supporter who had a betting slip in his sporran. St.Johnstone 0 Ayr United 2 was the bet. St.Johnstone 0 Ayr United 2 was the result. He deserved to be rewarded for his faith. Four days later it was announced that Gordon Dalziel had stepped down as manager. At Perth it had been a brilliant result with a performance to match. That was why this development caught everyone by surprise. Why quit now? He could reflect on an Ayr United career in which he was the club's second best manager of all time. Football managers habitually depart in acrimonious circumstances which, in the rhetoric of club statements, get dressed up as being "by mutual consent." Gordon Dalziel was able to step down with head held high.

The new incumbent had already been arranged. It was Campbell Money who was stepping up from his youth development role at the club. The importance of a good start was obvious and it materialised in a 3-1 win at home to Alloa Athletic. On retracing our steps to Somerset Park a fortnight later the challenge was more difficult. Inverness Caledonian Thistle were top of the league. After taking a 3-0 lead in the 52nd minute the delight was more restrained than would normally be expected with that scoreline. At that point I heard one of our fans shout mockingly: "Come on Ayr. We can still get a draw out of this." The origin of this sarcasm just had to be in relation to a recollection of the infamous capitulation at Inverness the year before. In retrospect the barracker may have possessed second sight. Anxiety levels gradually increased as 3-0 transformed to 3-1 to 3-2 to 3-3. Would history repeat itself? At 3-3 there was still plenty of time left and the final whistle eventually came as a relief. Football is supposed to be an entertainment. To an outsider looking in it would be a peculiar irony that a supposed source of entertainment could cause anxiety. Against Inverness there was anxiety on the pitch too. Our already indefensible red card count for the season was enhanced by the dismissal of James Grady. Once more the stock of footballing clichés was plundered to use the word 'altercation' in description of the offence. This particular altercation was with Russell Duncan who was also sent off.

A crowd of 1,663 watched the Inverness game. The next home match drew an attendance of 1,664. It was never revealed who the additional spectator was! Campbell Money was a good tactician and he knew the capabilities of the club's youth players in forensic detail. Those two virtues were on the point of dovetailing to spectacular effect and the victims were Arbroath. The team he sent out remains the youngest ever Ayr United team in a competitive fixture. A 4-0 win was achieved in an exhibition of attacking abandon. Three of the scorers were teenagers with Mark Campbell scoring the other goal. The young scorers were Stewart Kean (19 years 299 days), Mark McColl (two days after his eighteenth birthday) and Andrew Ferguson (17 years 279 days). In the 85th minute Boyd Mullen (five days short of his seventeenth birthday) went on to replace Scott Chaplain (19 years 80 days). The starting line-up also included Marc Smyth who had only just ceased to be a teenager (it was the day after his twentieth birthday) and Willie Lyle (18 years 258 days). It was a fabulous match to watch. We departed with a strong confidence that a decent future was assured.

On 1st January, 2003, the crowd of 2,921 for a Queen of the South versus Ayr United fixture was considered to be quite good. Old people, with some justification, are liable to be criticised for harping on about how much better things used to be. Nonetheless there is a justification for harping on about olden day football crowds. New Year 1935 saw the equivalent fixture draw 11,278 and in 1966 there was a crowd of 7,180 for our New Year fixture at Palmerston. Viewed from a different perspective the old days did not always compare favourably. The 1-1 draw in 2003 was more palatable then the 7-1 debacle in 1935.

Inverness Caledonian Thistle 0 Ayr United 1. The date was 18th January, 2003. Our next win at Inverness did not occur until 19th February, 2022. In the interim barren years the only thing to commend going to Inverness was a nice stop at Pitlochry. Paul Lovering got sent off in this 2003 win. The red card count to this point of the season was beyond ridiculous.

Peterhead at home was a favourable Scottish Cup draw. In future years Peterhead would be a considerably more daunting prospect but for now a 2-0 win was vindication for being glib. The cockiness evaporated when drawn at home to Rangers next. Yet confidence was restored when the tie got underway. Rangers won 1-0 with a 79th minute goal but the match finished with Ayr United on the offensive in vain pursuit of an equaliser.

In the present day copious amounts of stoppage time gets applied. Historically this rarely happened. In the event of injuries the referee's watch would be stopped and the game would be frozen but you would never see a goal timed at 90+8 for example. If '89' appeared beside the scorer's name you could be sure that the goal was scored at the death. I did not attend this particular match at Arbroath so I sat at home watching the score updates. With the score standing at Arbroath 1 Ayr United 0 time was running out but occasionally the screen would flicker with a goal update from somewhere. It got to the stage where it was so late that I gave the game up as being lost so I headed into Prestwick with the family. In the town centre I met my brother in law who said: "That was a good win for Ayr today" to which I replied: "No Jim we lost 1-0". To my great delight he assured me that I was wrong. Right at the death Stewart Kean had scored twice within a minute.

Ayr United 0 St.Johnstone 1 illustrated that no momentum had carried on from the euphoria at Arbroath. James Grady striking the crossbar from a penalty was regretful. Even more regretful was the fact that Ayr United's next penalty came one year and two days later. The St.Johnstone game was followed by two more home fixtures. Those were lost too; firstly against Queen of the South then Alloa Athletic. A run of home games had yielded three 0-1 results. Things got no better when we were back on the road. In a 3-0 loss against Clyde at Broadwood the name of the referee just happened to be George Clyde. He gave Clyde two penalties, both of which were converted by our former player Andy Millen. The season had already turned into a red card-fest and the total grew again with the dismissals of Willie Lyle and Allan McManus at Broadwood. These were red cards nine and ten for the season. The roll of indiscipline now read Paul Lovering (two), Allan McManus (two), Aaron Black, Iain Nicolson, Neil Murray, Paul Sheerin, Marc Smyth and James Grady.

It was getting so desperate that Stephen Whalen was selected to play at Alloa despite having suffered food poisoning. If there were any lingering effects they were not visible. In a 3-2 win he scored a hat-trick. Broadly speaking the expectation is that home and away games are played alternately with due allowance for postponements and cup fixtures disturbing that neat arrangement. Yet as this season wound on we had eight home games out of nine followed by no home games at all over the next six Saturdays. It was convoluted to the extent that the Stephen Whalen-inspired win at Alloa occurred ten days after Alloa had won 1-0 at Ayr.

Brockville Park was a wonderfully traditional Scottish football ground. Back in 1903 my grandfather had played there in Falkirk's first ever league season and down through the years I had been there many times to experience the elation of an Ayr United win or, more likely, the disappointment of an Ayr United defeat. There were draws in the mix but these were not so memorable. 26th April, 2003, saw the occasion of Ayr United's last ever visit there. The home club were already guaranteed the First Division title so there was a possibility that we could exploit their lack of incentive. That possibility should have been viewed as an improbability. Falkirk won 3-0 and, based on results, we were glad to see the back of the place.

At the other end of the table Arbroath were fated to relegation. Entering the last game it was a question of whether Alloa Athletic or Ross County would join them. Ross County would be safe only in the event of winning at home to Ayr United. Even a draw would have put them down. Our team was composed mainly of young players, the only exceptions being Craig Nelson, David Craig and Neil Murray. This team selection was no doubt to the chagrin of Alloa Athletic who beat St.Mirren 4-0 that afternoon but got relegated anyway because Ross County beat Ayr United 4-1. In defeat the curtain was brought down on a finishing place of sixth.

In July 2003 Bristol Rovers won 5-0 in a pre-season friendly at Somerset Park. The mere staging of this game was to have some unexpected personal consequences. Via social media my son David got to know some Bristol Rovers supporters who had attended the match. Bristol Rovers had a league fixture at Carlisle in August and it was suggested to him that he should go to the match. Including that one and excluding the one at Ayr, he has been to thirty-seven of their matches at the time of writing and I have accompanied him on twenty of those occasions. His sister Jill loves going to these matches too and for some of them all four of us have been there. I have written up an account of all thirty-seven trips, albeit that I was not on them all. The record is Won 11 Drawn 8 Lost 18. There was a phase where twelve trips had produced one win. The highlights have been the journeys to Bristol. People found it hard to believe that we went to London specifically to see Leyton Orient versus Bristol Rovers. Visiting lower league grounds has been an education and it has often been possible to do this while minimising disruption to attending Ayr United matches. One test of fortitude was watching a 2-0 defeat while standing on an uncovered terracing during a sleet storm at Accrington Stanley. The 'Two Clubs' Ayr United/Bristol Rovers flag has always been admired. When people identify themselves with an English club they get labelled as glory hunters. From personal testimony you may be told that there is no glory in watching your adopted team losing at Hartlepool. However it is good to know that there are people from in and around Bristol who now look out for the Ayr United result.

Pre-season was dreadful. As well as being routed by Bristol Rovers there were further routs against Partick Thistle (1-6) and Motherwell (1-4). Pre-season form is not necessarily an indication of how the season will unfold. Not necessarily perhaps, but in 2003 it was an indication. It was shameful to lose at home to Third Division (fourth tier) Stirling Albion in the first round of the Bell's League Challenge Cup. On the scale of shame it was a little less severe to lose at home to Dumbarton in the first round of the League Cup. This was a Second Division club. Stephen Ferguson was red-carded against Dumbarton. Marc Smyth was red-carded too but this was after the match for an outburst against the referee that was probably justified. What about the more important priority of the league? Clyde 3 Ayr United 0 heralded the opening of the league season.

The 'Two Clubs' flag at Accrington Stanley.

In 2002/03 Falkirk won the First Division by a nine-point margin and, pending their relocation, they proposed to ground share with Airdrie in 2003/04. The proposal was dismissed after a vote by SPL chairmen. This was hypocrisy on a grand scale. Celtic had been permitted to ground share at Hampden in season 1994/95. Falkirk had therefore to remain in the First Division while Motherwell, foot of the Premier League, were spared from relegation. The situation was appalling. This is being mentioned to put context on why Falkirk were at Ayr for our first home league game of the season. In a 1-1 draw Stewart

Kean's equaliser came two minutes from the end. There was great elation and goalkeeper Ludovic Roy ran the length of the pitch to join the celebrations. There were no such celebrations when we retraced our steps to Somerset Park a fortnight later. When the damage settled it was Ayr United 1 Queen of the South 4.

It took until fixture six to get the first league victory. Ayr United versus Brechin City was second bottom versus bottom. Brechin had beaten Kilmarnock in the League Cup in the prior midweek so this was a warning that there could be no complacency. In a 3-2 win Michael Dunlop struck the decider in stoppage time. Such determination to fight to the end was crucial again a week later. At 1-0 down away to St.Johnstone Michael Dunlop was sent off. Thus handicapped, Stewart Kean equalised with only two minutes to spare. It was a valiant effort to fight back for a draw but the first away win was still sought. In the next away fixture it came. Falkirk 0 Ayr United 1 was played at Ochilview Park, the temporary home of the club denied promotion in abhorrent circumstances. Campbell Money's accent on youth was highlighted by the fact that John Hughes, at the heart of the Falkirk defence, was aged thirty-nine while the players up front for Ayr United had a combined age of thirty-eight. They were Stewart Kean, aged twenty, and Andrew Ferguson, aged eighteen.

At times this team could be good to watch. These young players were pacey and could inject excitement. This much was proven in a 2-2 draw at home to a Clyde team who would remain heavily in title contention right up until the end of the season. It is cynically said that light at the end of a tunnel is sometimes a light on an approaching train. Five consecutive defeats followed. A loss against Queen of the South was Ayr United's first defeat at Palmerston since 1978, a statistic that has since been turned on its head. The margin was only 1-0 and it was a result that put the home club back on top of the league but any optimistic plaudits were futile. Losing 3-1 at Brechin a week later left not even the slightest chink of optimism. It was bottom versus second bottom. This remains the only time I have witnessed crowd disorder caused by Ayr United supporters fighting with each other. It took so long for the police to arrive that a fragile peace had been restored by the time they got there. The trouble had been caused by some fans taking exception to a song that was being sung. It was a saving grace that there were no press reports of the trouble. Having the club name tarnished by results was more than enough.

Following on from the defeat at Brechin, the crowd (if it could have been thus termed) for a home fixture against Ross County was 977. It was the first three-figure home attendance for a competitive match since 2nd March, 1996, when Berwick Rangers were at Ayr. These matches were in the midst of the run of defeats mentioned but we could at least be grateful that five straight defeats did not become six. While 1-0 down at home to St.Johnstone, Dougie Ramsay scored with a vicious drive from thirty-five yards. This development set Somerset Park alight. After the recentre the game lasted for fifteen seconds. A lot of fans were probably on their way over Hawkhill bridge when the goal was scored.

From the perspective of the fan, relegation haunted football induces stress no matter how often it has been experienced before. The only cure is winning, especially the six-pointers. When Raith Rovers called on the last Saturday of 2003 it was one of those win-or-else games that are so often lost. Andrew Ferguson scored in the middle of the first half and we clung on grimly all the way through to the end. The second half pressure was intense and every conceivable means was employed to run down the clock. It meant that we were now level on points with third bottom Raith Rovers but it would have taken a 3-0 win to pass them by on goal difference. The stakes had shifted since the halcyon times of 2002 which now seemed light years away.

Any New Year cheer quickly deflated itself in January. Two league points from a possible twelve and knocked out of the Scottish Cup at home to Falkirk! Ayr United 1 Brechin City 2 on the last day of the month was a wretched spectacle. Brechin were the bottom club and two red cards reduced them to nine men. An Ayr win would have lifted the club out of the bottom two because the Raith Rovers game was postponed that afternoon.

On the Sunday the depression from the Brechin game worsened considerably. That afternoon I got a phone call from John Dalton with the news that Ally MacLeod had died. I am not often stuck for words but I was then. It was devastating. At the age of seventy-two he had passed away after suffering from Alzheimer's. The funeral service was held in St.Columba's Church and it was conducted most ably by Fraser Aitken. A distraction was caused by the temptation to look round and spot some true legends of British football. In attendance were several of Ally's Blackburn Rovers team mates including such illustrious names as Ronnie Clayton, Bryan Douglas and Dave Whelan. The even more illustrious Alex Ferguson was there too despite Manchester United having a match the next day. It was quite ironic that, in 1901, the Rev. Millar Patrick had loudly denounced football from the same pulpit, even going so far as to caution people against attending Somerset Park. His argument was that "the fierce excitement unfits people for the spiritual interests of life." It would be convenient to say that he was suffering from religious psychosis but it was true that the Somerset Park of 1901 was not a model of moral rectitude.

In relation to the relegation plight there was a popular wave of feeling that gaining safety would be "doing it for Ally." It was a strong sentiment but the practical application of it was an altogether different matter. Our first game after the funeral was a 3-0 defeat away to St.Johnstone which meant plunging to the bottom of the league. The *Ayrshire Post* report was scathing. "On the evidence of this display it is hard to see Ayr picking up another point all season." Fortunately the next match bore no evidence of that display. Ayr United 2 St.Mirren 0 occurred on a day when our relegation rivals, Raith Rovers and Brechin City, lost. On goal difference we were at last out of the bottom two but Raith Rovers had a game in hand. Brechin, at the foot, were just one point behind.

Two games later we were bottom again after losing 2-1 in a six-pointer away to Raith Rovers. A player called Ramon Pereira went down in the box for a penalty when challenged by Lee Hardy in this match. From where I was sitting it was a clear and obvious dive. Pereira got up and converted the penalty.

You may think that the diving accusation is prompted by Ayr United bias. However in November of the same year, by which time Pereira was playing for Hearts, he was disciplined by his club for diving. Manager John Robertson said: "If players are being brought down by being tripped you can live with it, but where no contact is made, like in the incident with Ramon on Saturday, it's disappointing."

Injustice, whether actual or perceived, does not have the capacity to overturn anything once the final whistle has blown. With six games left the gap from safety was six points and with four games left it was seven points. By the second last game the issue was painfully clear. There would only be a chance of avoiding the drop if, on the penultimate Saturday, the team were to beat Falkirk away from home and Brechin City were to win away to Raith Rovers. Both games were drawn and relegation was the consequence. It was hard to think of any redeeming features. Maintaining an upbeat tone in the face of footballing adversity is to risk being labelled as a happy clapper. I have seen Ayr United supporters applaud the team off after being relegated or suffering a heavy defeat. The attitude is "I'll be there win, lose or draw." Win, lose or draw, I'll be there too because supporting the club has become ingrained but it does not necessarily follow that I have to like it all the time or to applaud failure. Expressing negativity, even when it is appropriate, will risk being called a moaner. If the team wins after a couple of defeats you can be assured that someone will go online to post the message "Where are the moaners today?" This overlooks the fact that moaning can be a perfectly natural state of mind in adverse circumstances. In England the psyche is different, although this view is admittedly based on an assumption that Bristol Rovers represent a microcosm of the English game in general. The distance between Carlisle and Bristol is 282 miles which represents a colossal return journey for an afternoon's football quite apart from the considerable expense. I have seen Bristol Rovers win, lose and draw at Carlisle but at the end of the match the response has always been the same. The players will always come over to the fans at the end and there will be mutual applause. It is a situation that pertains even in a heavy defeat.

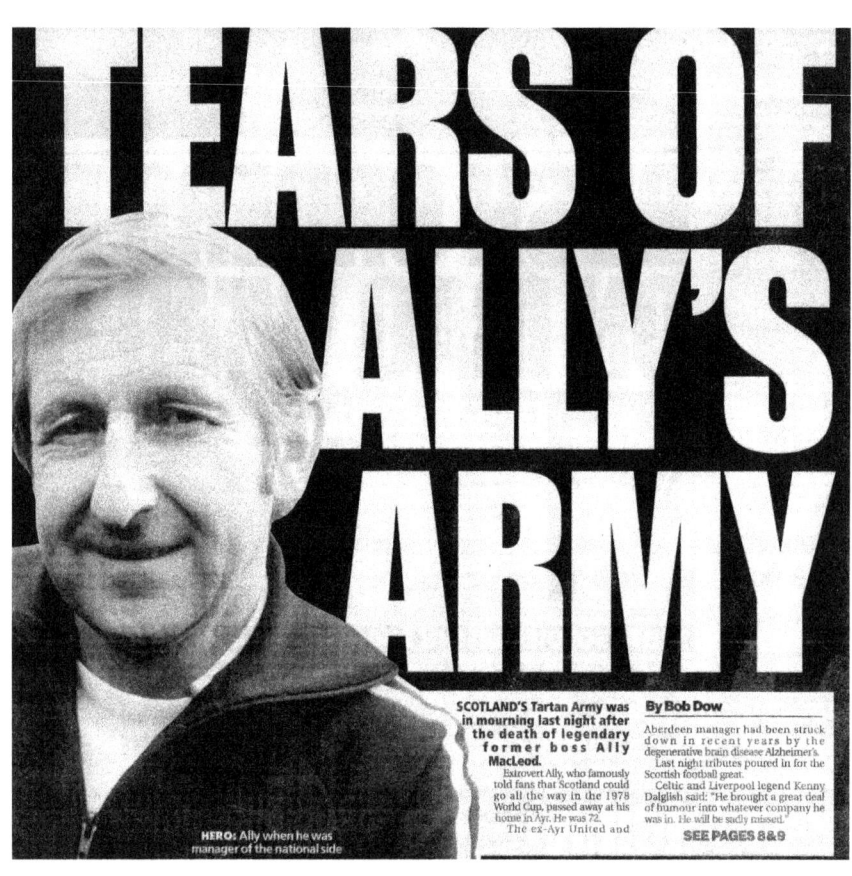

When Ally MacLeod passed away it was front page news

13. The Seaside League

The chapter heading may prove to be a little difficult to digest. Where or what is the Seaside League? The Seaside League is a mythical place known only to cynics. It is a term of reference for the third tier of Scottish football. To an outsider with little or no knowledge of football, the name could imply a league comprised of clubs based in coastal towns. However the true implication is obscurity. You will be left to contemplate a suitable moniker for the even greater obscurity of Scotland's fourth tier.

In pre-season there was a bit more interest than normal on account of a visit from Kilmarnock. At stake was the West Sound Big Match Trophy. West Sound Radio, of course, publicised the match heavily. It was all-ticket although, with a crowd of 3,166, this was overkill. With Kilmarnock winning 2-0 and dominating the match, no one could have been faulted for drifting towards the exits. Against the run of play Stewart Kean (78 minutes) and Graeme Brown (82 minutes) hauled it level. No extra time was played and Ayr United won 5-4 in the shootout. It was hardly the most prestigious of trophies but, in such times, we have to nurture every conceivable seed of positivity. Just when the season was getting properly underway I was saddened to hear that Davy Armour had died from cancer at the age of fifty-one. He had signed for Ayr United in 1979 and I had got to know him through being a colleague in the Ayr United quiz team in those competitions staged by Radio Clyde.

Losing 0-3 to Falkirk in the Bell's League Challenge Cup was met with dismissive acceptance. The league had yet to start and the 'better out of the Challenge Cup' attitude was largely prevalent. With the season barely more advanced the same may have been said of the League Cup (Hamilton Accies 4 Ayr United 1). On last being relegated to this league it had been a two-season job to get promoted back out of it. This time it would be a five-season job. Luckily we were not possessed with the mystical powers to know it at the time.

The opener was at Dumbarton and the kick-off was delayed, not because of the crowd size (1,016), but because of traffic issues creating delays on the road. In warm weather it was uncomfortable for the Carmichaels to have arrived early only for the game to start late. The discomfort was on the point of getting worse. Barry McLaughlin had been suffering from a shoulder injury so he had to go through a fitness test. He passed it then got sent off just after the half-hour mark. We were 1-0 down by then and so it remained. There was a dawning realisation that the so-called Seaside League could be a tougher prospect than we had realised. Beating Berwick Rangers 2-1 at home did little to raise hopes since it had been necessary to cling on desperately towards the end.

League fixture three was to have radical repercussions. It was another of those bewitching road trips to Stranraer in beautiful weather. Then the game started! The game approached the late stages with the score tied at 1-1 much to the discontent of the travelling support. More was expected. Then, with seven minutes left, the roof caved in. David Graham picked up possession in his own half then powered forward. All attempts to impede his progress failed. Just as he was approaching the penalty area he unleashed a tremendous drive. In the still summer air it was possible to hear the ripple as the ball hit the back of the net. It was one of those goals that had to be seen to be believed and it was certainly worthy of winning any match. It was just unfortunate that it won this one. Within the week Campbell Money resigned. There was no delay in announcing our former player Mark Shanks as his successor. Shanks quit his managerial role at Kilwinning Rangers to take up the post. Rumours circulated that Ayr United were in financial difficulty. These rumours gathered enough currency for the club to issue a statement of denial.

The expression 'new manager bounce' was not in vogue in 2004. If so it would have been used prolifically in description of Mark Shanks. He won the first two games; Morton 2-0 and Alloa Athletic 1-3. However nature dictates that a bounce has its limitations. Then the law of gravity takes over. We had one win in the next six and even that was the closest of close shaves when Stewart Kean scored the only goal of the match in stoppage time at Berwick. During that run a 0-0 draw at Arbroath gave the home team their first league point of the season. Indiscipline had also reared its ugly head. We had a player sent off in each of four consecutive games during the winless spell. They were Ludovic Roy versus Forfar Athletic, Willie Lyle versus Arbroath, Stewart Kean versus Brechin City and Jamie Doyle versus Stirling Albion. Marc Smyth versus Dumbarton made it five red cards from six games. By way of contrast only one red card had been administered to an opposition player so far in the season. Ludovic Roy's misdemeanour was contrary to his good nature. He was the victim of a nasty challenge from Forfar's Alan Rattray and he retaliated by headbutting his assailant. Upon his dismissal Graeme Brown was sacrificed to get goalkeeper John Hillcoat on to replace the void left by Ludo. The game restarted with a penalty that Hillcoat saved. Just thirteen minutes had been played at the time of the flare-up. Jamie Doyle's red card at Stirling also carried an interesting tale. He had been freed by Ayr United at the end of the previous season and he was listed as a trialist for this match.

After a one-match ban Ludo was reinstated to the team for the next four fixtures whereupon he was called to a meeting at which he was banned for six more games. Peter Cherrie was hurriedly signed from Kilsyth Rangers and he saved a penalty in each of his first two games (Morton 0 Ayr United 1 and Ayr United 4 Alloa Athletic 3). Peter Cherrie's third match was a 3-2 win at Forfar so his personal record so far was three victories out of the three played. Successes, although savoured at the time, were too occasional. The apathy from the public was evident from the crowd figures. The two home matches in November 2004 drew 1,275 (Alloa Athletic) and 1,236 (Arbroath). Negative financial vibes have the propensity to make the supporters nervous. In early December the public were left to put their own interpretation on the following piece of news. "Ayr United have slashed their running costs by 25% and have reached agreements with two major creditors. It means that the club won't have to seek a Creditor's Voluntary Agreement (CVA) as had been originally feared." The last word was chilling.

Of course the fans are predominantly concerned about what is happening on the field. Ostensibly everything is okay if the team is winning. If! Days after these financial details were made public we were all horrified by being on the wrong end of a 5-0 rout at Brechin. At least Stewart Kean was able to opt out. On the following Saturday he made a debut for St. Mirren against Falkirk.

The league season had started at Dumbarton in weather conditions which could, with only a little stretch of the imagination, have been described as tropical. On returning on 27th December the weather was a vile mix of strong gusts and heavy rain. Both goals in a 1-1 draw came early. Ordinarily, when Ayr United are playing, my focus on the match is so absolute that I sometimes even dread getting drawn into a conversation. For most of the second half at Dumbarton my main worry was driving home, such were the conditions. You will now be appraised of some more meteorological misery. I have watched football at grounds reputed for cold weather, including leading contenders Arbroath and Oldham. Yet Somerset Park is the ground where I have experienced the most intense cold and I can even pinpoint the date to New Year's Day 2005 when the match against Stranraer was played in a storm. Standing at the Somerset Road end was a reminder of the days when there was no roof there. The roof only offers protection when the rain or sleet is coming down. On this particular day it came horizontally. Numerous layers of clothing failed to keep out the penetrating cold. It was painfully intense quite apart from the other discomfort of vain attempts to stay dry. Good football can divert the mind away from such conditions. Unfortunately good football was a scarce commodity. The result was Ayr United 0 Stranraer 1 and it was lost to a Michael Dunlop own goal. Michael Dunlop had a habit of going over to applaud the fans after a match. Since the match had turned on his own goal I wondered whether he would forego his ritual this time. It was business as usual for him and it was admirable that he had the courage to approach fans who were soaked, frozen and dejected.

Two days later we were back at Somerset Park and it was an act of mercy that the storm had abated. Tempers were abated too. Ayr United 2 Morton 1 pushed the club into third place. Alas, we were soon cast back to whence we had come. Even in Scotland's third tier there was an acceptance that some matches would be lost. 'Some' is indefinite and might have been tolerated. What could not be tolerated was a run of three league defeats comprising 5-1 at Alloa, 2-0 at Arbroath and 2-0 at Stirling. The sequence was broken with Stranraer 1 Ayr United 3. By then we were already out of the Scottish Cup after losing 0-2 to St.Mirren. That tie was irritating on several counts. Kick-off was delayed for thirty minutes (the crowd was only 4.748), Darren Henderson was sent off, their second goal was scored by our former player Stewart Kean and referee Kenny Clark was from Paisley. When eventually getting a league fixture on home soil it was a 1-0 defeat against bottom club Berwick Rangers. The humiliation was compounded when the Man of the Match announcement was greeted with laughter. Three days later Mark Shanks quit. After a further passage of three days there was an announcement that the new manager was Robert Connor with Robert Reilly as his assistant. In common with his predecessor, Robert Connor was a former player and he carried a lot of respect. Yet also in common with his predecessor he would have to work with limited resources. His first match in charge was against another club operating with limited resources. Alloa Athletic pitched up at Ayr and listed no substitutes at all. Such poverty of resources did not unduly hinder them in achieving a 1-1 draw.

One win in the season's final twelve fixtures was a damning statistic. Even the isolated win did little to stir enthusiasm. It was a 1-0 result at home to Forfar Athletic and Andrew Ferguson was sent off for the club's eighth and final red card of the season. Sometimes my obsession for statistics can attract criticism. This is liable to occur when the statistic is negative. The default accusation is that it is 'wrong to kick them when they are down'. Yet it is important to draw the distinction between an opinion and a fact. On the Tuesday evening of 15th March, 2005, Ayr United 0 Brechin City 1 was watched by an assembly of 742. It was the lowest attendance for a competitive match at Somerset Park since 17th March, 1984, when 673 turned up for the visit of Alloa Athletic. These were facts and the lowest attendance for more than twenty years was deserving of being called out. Our finishing position was eighth in the ten-club Second Division. The 'goals for' column showed thirty-nine. It was the worst scoring record in the division.

Something radical needed to happen and it did. Eleven players were released. Freeing players who were surplus to requirements was not as big a concern as the loss of players who declined terms. Marc Smyth and Scott McCulloch went to Partick Thistle, Paddy Connolly went to Stirling Albion, Willie Lyle went to Raith Rovers, Michael Dunlop went to Queen's Park, Ludovic Roy went to Livingston and Andrew Ferguson had already signed a pre-contract agreement to join Dundee. The deduction could be drawn that the offer of reduced terms did not have universal appeal. To redress the balance an attempt was made to sign the cream of the Juniors. In the summer of 2005 eight players were signed from the Junior ranks. With contract offers now being on a part time basis, new players would require to make a living outside of football. This formula had worked for Ayr United in the 1970s but even the illustrious Ally MacLeod's motivational skills would have had insufficient capacity to bring success to the squad of 2005. The popular view was that inexperience would be a handicap.

After drawing 1-1 against Hibs, the match went to a shootout which Ayr United won for custody of the Ayr Guildry

Cup. A week later the West Sound Big Match trophy vacated the trophy cabinet after a 4-0 loss at Kilmarnock. It was one trophy in, one trophy out. Then, for the third consecutive July Saturday, we had cup action. Losing 1-0 at home to Stirling Albion after extra time put paid to any ambitions there may have been in the Bell's League Challenge Cup. In retrospect it is unlikely that any such ambitions were harboured.

In defiance of most expectations the season started well. The first two league fixtures were won (2-0 versus Dumbarton and 1-2 versus Forfar Athletic). In the midweek between we had a 2-1 win away to Morton in the League Cup. Progress was stalled a little when Peterhead visited for the first ever league match between the clubs. Yet 1-1 was not a great failing. The home league fixtures to date had drawn attendances of 1,274 and 1,283 which made it self evident that the public had yet to be convinced. Winning 2-1 away to Ross County in the League Cup just may have convinced some.

Seven days after our first ever league match against Peterhead came our first ever league match against Gretna. We went to Raydale Park in the knowledge that the home club had won their last twenty-two home league matches. Midway through the first half my daughter Jill felt light-headedness. Two First Aiders promptly appeared. In the minutes that they administered treatment Ayr United scored twice. Naturally my focus was not on the game and I did not see either goal. When people all around were jumping about in wild celebration I felt a compulsion to remain restrained. The treatment worked and she was fine after that. Gretna fought back for a 2-2 draw and there was a reprieve seconds from the end of stoppage time when a Kenny Deuchar header hit the Ayr post. It was a great result against a heavily bankrolled team. Maybe, just maybe, the season would not be all that bad. Even on losing 2-1 at home to Hibs in the League Cup there were signs that the future may be bright.

The first league defeat of the season occurred at home when Morton scored the only goal in the 88th minute. It meant a drop to fourth place. Winning the league was beyond reach.

Gretna would go on to win it by a margin of eighteen points. They would also go on to qualify for Europe while still in the third tier. This village-based team would end the season by losing in a shootout in the Scottish Cup final.

A run of draws was unceremoniously halted at Dumbarton. While driving there, news came over the car radio that George Burley had been sacked as manager of Hearts. Whereas his sacking from Ayr United was unlamented, his dismissal from Hearts was hugely different. They were top of the Premier League at the time with eight wins and two draws from the ten games played. Thoughts then turned back to the match in prospect. To blame a catastrophe on the officials is to induce accusations of club bias but, even if viewed objectively, the conclusion still had to be drawn that the worst team was the team with three in it, namely the referee and his two linesmen. Dougie Ramsay and Raymond Logan were both sent off for incidents in the build-up to a Dumbarton penalty. In Logan's case it was a second yellow, his first having been when he was the victim of aggression and he got the same punishment as the perpetrator. His second yellow was for a tackle which resulted in no foul being given. Many more bewildering decisions could be cherry-picked from my notes and from personal memory but a line will now be drawn under a 6-0 defeat. Even the recollection of it is enough to induce anger. It was the club's first defeat by a six-goal margin since an identical result at Dunfermline on 10th December, 1994.

A fortnight later we plunged to third bottom after losing at home to runaway leaders Gretna. The next match was also at home and it had to be a matter of concern that it drew a three-figure attendance. Even with due allowance for it being a Tuesday night in November it did not bode well. It was a 2-1 win over Raith Rovers. The Raith striker was our former player Eddie Annand and he got a yellow card for making a hush gesture to the home support. It was hardly necessary. A crowd of 930 was always going to seem hushed anyway. Nevertheless it was an improvement on the 488 who attended our next match, a 4-0 win at Alloa,

It is a curious feature of Scottish Cup draws that clubs get drawn against each other for a tie scheduled around the time they are due to play in the league. Hence we had Morton 2 Ayr United 1 on a Tuesday night in the league followed by Ayr United 3 Morton 2 in the Scottish Cup on the Saturday. The cup tie was a torrid affair with three red cards (Jason Walker and Derek Lilley of Morton plus our own Paul Weaver).

At this time I was working in Stirling to which I commuted daily. Ayr United 2 Stirling Albion 5 may have caused some embarrassing conversations when I returned to work on the Monday. Only it didn't. My work colleagues who did have an interest in football were armchair fans of Rangers or Celtic. In mentioning this I am reminded of a particular day when I worked in Glasgow. Celtic had a European tie that night and my colleagues were having a conversation about where they would be watching the game. At home, at a friend's house and at the pub were the answers proffered. I was too constrained by politeness to suggest that Celtic Park would be the best place to watch it. Nonetheless I was seldom, if ever, looked down on by fans of these clubs. A Partick Thistle supporter, in relation to the Old Firm dominance, once remarked that it is easy to swim with the tide. Supporters of big clubs know that to be true but sometimes they are deluded if they believe that the success of these clubs is reflected in themselves. This is especially true of those who watch only on television. I really do believe in the adage that football is something that you go to and not a television show. It is quite amusing that people can look you in the eye when telling you that they support Manchester United. In fact I even find it amusing that people choose a club to support. My relationship with Ayr United occurred by way of a force of nature. It simply happened.

Ayr United 2 Dumbarton 0 on Boxing Day at least erased the memory of the 6-0 debacle when the clubs had last met. This was a classic illustration of the old saying about making hay while the sun shines because there was a strong feeling that 2006 would start badly. Instincts were correct. Gretna could not be stopped and the margin of defeat down there was

3-0. For what it was worth it was one each for red cards. There was a similar sense of foreboding about going to Inverness in the Scottish Cup five days later. Inverness Caledonian Thistle were going strong in the Premier League quite apart from the memory of the Scottish Cup collapse there in 2001. For once the drive there did not seem too daunting. The commute to Stirling ensured that I was conditioned to being behind the wheel. Our support was hyperactive when the tie got underway and the backing barely subsided until Dennis Wyness scored for Inverness (52 minutes). The bedlam was immediately restored when Gareth Wardlaw scored after a move initiated straight from the recentre. The replay was the first ever Ayr United home match to be televised live. In contentious circumstances goalkeeper Mark McGeown was sent off with the consequence that Eric Phillips made his senior debut at the advanced age of 36 years 17 days. Rather than harp on about a catalogue of refereeing catastrophe let it just be said that history recorded a result of 0-2.

The winless run at the start of 2006 ultimately extended to thirteen matches, comprising eleven league fixtures and the two Scottish Cup ties. Chronic luck can be used as the grain of an excuse to explain losing an isolated game but league form over a sustained period of time is the true indicator. This rendered the league table a matter of concern. The team had now crashed to third bottom place, just four points ahead of Dumbarton who had a game in hand. One more slip down the table and we would be facing play-offs to avoid landing in the fourth tier.

The first win of 2006 came when it was not expected. Morton were comfortably ensconced in second place, albeit well behind the rampant Gretna. With home advantage against a struggling Ayr team the proceedings might easily have been considered a foregone conclusion. Morton 0 Ayr United 4 had the aura of a miracle. Just before the end Paul Weaver nearly made it five when he chipped the ball against the bar. It had taken until 25th March to win a game in 2006. The wait for the second win was merely one week and it happened in handicapped circumstances. Referee Willie Collum sent off David Lowing with just twelve minutes played. Winning 3-0 at home to Stirling Albion required a herculean effort through being a man short for the overwhelming majority of the game. This remains the only time I have experienced Ayr United fans boo a referee off after a comfortable win. In practical terms we were nearly clear of the relegation threat. A fortnight later Dumbarton 4 Ayr United 5 ensured safety. At different stages it was 3-0 and 4-1 to Ayr then it was 4-4 before Chris Robertson's goal won it. The season's close happened at Peterhead. Conceding an equaliser in stoppage time was momentarily disappointing but only until Gareth Wardlaw made it 2-1 even deeper into stoppage time. Despite the pleasure of the score updates I considered it a matter of regret not to have been there, partly on account of hearing that our fans formed a conga line at the end. It was a neat distraction from the mediocrity of finishing sixth.

Barely had season 2005/06 finished when the club announced that there would be no reserve team operating at a competitive level in 2006/07. Instead friendlies would be arranged for the fringe players. Despite being trapped in mediocrity the stewardship of the club was sound. Donald Cameron had become chairman in 2005, a position he would hold until 2008 when succeeded by his son Lachlan who was the incumbent until 2021, thereby making him the club's longest serving chairman in one stint. It was generally recognised that the Cameron family had the club's best interests at heart.

A third attempt would now be made to get out of what was still being uncharitably called the Seaside League. On opening the season with a league fixture at Stirling the fans turned up in buoyant mood. It was a beautifully sunny day and there was enough enthusiasm to convey a feeling of invincibility. During a 3-1 win the goal celebrations even spilled onto the track. When there is any pretence at success it is mandatory to have a hero. For now the player who fitted that profile was striker Jerome Vareille who scored twice at Stirling. It was a great start yet the passage of a further week was to prove the wisdom of enjoying things when you can. Fixture two ended Ayr United 0 Cowdenbeath 4. The modern nickname for Cowdenbeath was The Blue Brazil. It suited. Their football would have been a joy to watch had it not been against Ayr United. It was a sobering experience after the frivolity at Stirling. In future, when erratic results got treated to the 'it used to be worse' argument, this match against Cowdenbeath had a habit of being cited. Just ten days later it looked as if we would be hosting an even tougher challenge against a Fife club. Dunfermline Athletic were in the Premier League and we had to face them in the League Cup. With four minutes of the regulation ninety left and the match scoreless there was great excitement when a penalty was awarded for a challenge on Gareth Wardlaw. The excitement dulled considerably when Ryan Caddis's weak spot kick was easily saved. It was still 0-0 after extra time and the shootout was lost 7-6. Nonetheless it was considered that matching a Premier League team over 120 minutes was more than an indication that life in the third tier should not be unduly troubling. Cowdenbeath was just a blip wasn't it? This theory was put to the test four days later. It did not hold water. Ayr United 0 Stranraer 2 was the unhappy outcome and it did not escape notice that three former Ayr United players were in the opposition line-up. They were Willie Lyle, Dougie Ramsay and Mark Crilly. The recently released James McKinstry also went on as a substitute for them.

Brian Reid was a significant signing. Surely this was a player who could shore up defensive deficiencies. In a similar manner to the signing of Gordon Dalziel in 1995 it could not have been foreseen that he would one day occupy the manager's chair. After signing he made a debut that night. In the League Challenge Cup we had already ousted Livingston (home) and Queen of the South (away), both clubs being from a league above. Brian Reid's debut was in a quarter-final away to Clyde, also from a league above. In losing 1-0 it was our first away defeat since February. Quite apart from the result it was a depressing spectacle at Broadwood. An attendance of 682 in an all-seater stadium created the illusion of watching a training match. Onfield shouts of 'man oan' or similar were clearly audible. At smaller grounds low crowds did not detract from the spectacle in the same way. Following on from the Clyde tie were away games at Alloa (556) and Brechin (509). In the absence of large banks of seating such crowds had more of a semblance of normality. More importantly both games were won 0-1 and 0-2 respectively. All thirteen league points had been gained away from home.

Privileged to be in the company of Peter Price and Robert Connor at a book launch in November 2006.

At last a home league win happened but our family missed it. We regularly holidayed in the Lake District and bookings were made without close scrutiny of the football fixtures. In our temporary home in Ambleside the score update flashed across the television screen – Ayr United 1 (Pettigrew 81) Raith Rovers 0. The joy of being on holiday stepped up a notch. There was even greater pleasure when it flashed up again with the FT suffix to denote full time. The amended league table now showed Ayr United to be third, separated from second-placed Stirling Albion on goal difference. Morton were at the top. With Stirling Albion due at Ayr in the next fixture there was the opportunity to cement second place. In the event it was a 0-0 draw which drew criticism. The bone of contention was playing defensively at home. It was a 4 : 5 : 1 formation with Jerome Vareille as the lone striker. Even the game's greatest managers attract criticism for team selection, substitutions and tactics. Do the fans really know best? Robert Connor's decisions were based on experience at a high level including playing for Scotland. If he thought it expedient to adopt a defensive approach, we terracing dwellers should have had no substance for argument.

Spirits were raised when it was revealed that Ryan Stevenson was joining on loan from St.Johnstone. He was a native of Drongan and had been a boyhood Ayr United supporter. As a youth he was a much sought-after player. He even declined an offer to go down to Manchester United, opting for Chelsea instead. His reputation as an attack-minded midfielder caused a stir when it was known that he would be making his debut at Cowdenbeath that Saturday. As early as the first minute he was in the thick of the action. Chris Strain hit the equaliser in a 1-1 draw but all the talk was about Stevo's performance. With the 4 : 5 : 1 now ditched, his home debut was a scoring one in a 5-0 rout of Forfar Athletic. It was our biggest league win for more than five and a half years. In Ryan Stevenson there was a new hero already but his status was tempered by the knowledge that the loan period was merely one month. Then, by some smart negotiation, it was extended by two months. Happy days! Within the extended period he was purchased from St.Johnstone for "a five-figure fee". Even happier days! His contract was for three and a half years. A hazard of supporting Ayr United is seeing a bubble burst. Ryan Stevenson consistently turned in an impeccable performance yet he could not be expected to carry the team. Six consecutive league defeats marked the departure from 2006. It took until 2nd January, 2007, for the rot to stop and even then it was far from convincing. In the third minute of stoppage time Gareth Wardlaw scored the only goal of the match at home to Stranraer.

In the early part of 2007 watching Ayr United was a habit rather than an enjoyable experience. Even the hope was ebbing away. Depending on the psyche of the individual, poor performances would be greeted with either stoic acceptance or loud expressions of anger. To the diehards it was not considered an option to stay away. We were in it for better or worse. Success is cyclical but the wheel showed no sign of turning.

St. Johnstone away in the Scottish Cup provided a McDiarmid Park return for Ryan Stevenson but only as a spectator. At Peterhead, in the previous round, he got a yellow card for encroachment during stoppage time. It was his second of the tie. Ironically his dismissal occurred when the game was as good as won at 2-0 with so little time left. After a 0-0 draw at Perth, Stevenson scored in the replay which was lost 2-1 to a goal in the 116th minute. The ability to perform well against clubs from a higher division did not translate to league fare. In February we had two home league games and the attendances were 864 (0-2 versus Raith Rovers) and 872 (0-2 versus Cowdenbeath). The public of Ayr had no taste for such poor fare. Neither did Robert Connor. On the Monday after the Cowdenbeath match he quit and so did Robert Reilly, his assistant. They had won just one of their last fourteen league games and even that was by a stoppage time goal against Stranraer.

A temporary management team was put in place comprising players Mark McGeown and Brian Reid as well as club director and former player Alex Ingram. It is commonplace for people in a new role to be told that they will have to hit the ground running which, in consequence, means that there will be no allowance for a settling-in period. In the context of Ayr United this was now a harsh truth. It was Stranraer away in the next match and they were second bottom, just two points behind us and with a game in hand. The risk of getting sucked into play-offs at the wrong end was real. Fears were allayed in a 3-0 win. Including this one, our last three league wins had all been against Stranraer.

The interim management team succeeded in hitting the ground running by winning all three games under their charge. Reaching the promotion play-offs remained a forlorn hope. Speculation was rife on the topic of who the new manager would be. The majority of opinion favoured Neil Watt but it was tinged with wishful thinking. When he was the manager of Stranraer he had declined the offer of managing Dundee. Since quitting Stranraer eleven months earlier he had been out of football. There was general delight when he was appointed as the next Ayr United manager. At a 'meet the fans' event he was candid when fielding the questions posed to him. His work commitments meant that he was taking the Ayr United job on a part time basis. He was a partner in a Glasgow-based factoring firm and he assured the assembly of fans that this would present no impediments because he had enough autonomy to be able to drive down to Ayr at short notice if required to do so.

In his first match it took a stoppage time equaliser to get a 2-2 draw at Peterhead. Neil Watt then endorsed what we already knew. "As far as the play-offs go they are a long shot. We would have to win our last five games and hope that the teams above us lose most of theirs and that is unlikely." To reach the last play-off position the requirement was fourth place. Brechin City and Raith Rovers were third and fourth respectively and we were ten points behind both. Ten points were gained in these last five matches but the season concluded with the gap between fourth place still showing as ten points. Finishing fifth was hardly worth brooding about. Now that Neil Watt was here season 2007/08 would be a promotion winning campaign. Or so we thought!

It was a busy summer for signing activity. Players acquired included David Hamilton, Michael Moore, Murray Henderson, Stephen Swift and Craig Higgins. They did not all have Stranraer as their previous club but they had all played for Stranraer under Neil Watt. Pre-season matches ordinarily fulfil the function for which they are intended but, one way or another, the results should not be taken too seriously. Yet occasionally there are exceptions to the apathy of such matches. One such was in the Brewers Cup semi-final against

Queen of the South at the ground of tournament hosts Annan Athletic. It ended Queen of the South 7 Ayr United 1. A Queen of the South player at this time was Neil McGowan, a future Ayr United player. A work colleague of mine was Neil's brother Chris who then played for Cumnock Juniors. Chris told me that Neil and his colleagues had been taken aback at how bad this Ayr team was. Stephen Dobbie scored six.

There is a sound logic in claiming that, if anything is going to go wrong, pre-season is the best time for it to happen. This works on the principle of identifying the faults then still having time to work on them to prevent a recurrence. Entering the third tier for a fourth consecutive season would have been a cheerless prospect had it not been for a feeling that Ayr United were on the way back. Ross County 2 Ayr United 0 did not get the league season off to a flyer yet the disappointment was tempered by knowing that our toughest fixture was out of the road.

On arrival at Livingston for a League Cup tie on a Tuesday night, the steward overseeing the car park asked me if I was a player. At the age of fifty-four I did not consider it worthwhile to play along with such a deception so I made a u-turn. I wish I had made it a complete u-turn and just headed for home. Livingston 5 Ayr United 0 was the sorry tale. The misery just kept on coming. Ayr United 2 Queen's Park 3 was hard to accept because Alan Trouten got the decisive goal in the third minute of stoppage time.

'Ah'm no' gaun back tae Somerset' is a time-ravaged grumble. This can occur when the complainer has taken issue with such tenuous things as inadequate toilets or a price increase for the pies. There can be personal reasons too such as taking a dislike to someone at the helm of the club. Yet the commonest reason for this ultimatum is adverse results. It is a reminder of the old saying about the straw that breaks the camel's back. Most of them break their resolution and do indeed come back to reclaim their old seat or standing point when things get better. On a personal level I believe that it is a mistake to desert Somerset Park, even on a temporary basis. You just never know what is going to happen.

This is a preamble to what even neutral opinion labelled the greatest goal ever scored. Admittedly it is a big claim but footage on YouTube went so far as to use that title. On 1st September, 2007, a 1-0 lead was being clung onto in a home fixture against Alloa Athletic. Ryan Stevenson collected the ball roughly halfway inside his own half. He eluded his first opponent by selling him a dummy then started to hare upfield. On crossing the halfway line he eluded his next opponent with his trademark stepover. On advancing towards the penalty area he had two defenders in front of him and a scene reminiscent of the Keystone Cops behind him. He then stole between the two defenders and now just had goalkeeper Raymond Jellema to beat. It was boyhood Ayr United fan versus boyhood Ayr United fan. Stevo then struck the ball inside the goalkeeper's right hand post for 2-0. It was beyond magnificent. Digesting what had happened made it difficult to concentrate on the four remaining minutes. It was an illustration of why people should resist the urge to stay away. The point is worth repeating. You just never know what is going to happen.

It was indicative of this level of Scottish football that the wonder goal was witnessed by 1,239 and this was considered to be a decent crowd at this level. On the following Tuesday night Forfar Athletic 0 Ayr United 2 drew in just 333. Forfar plied their trade in the fourth tier. It was a League Challenge Cup second round tie. This progression brought Partick Thistle to Ayr for a quarter-final. Alex Williams scored twice in a 2-1 win after extra time. The winner was so late that the tie lasted for no more than a matter of seconds after the recentre. Form in this competition was proving to be conspicuously good, having eliminated First Division Hamilton Accies, Third Division Forfar Athletic and First Division Partick Thistle. It was a competition shrouded by apathy but this progression changed the mindset. The prospect of winning anything was enough to whip up interest. Alas, the path to the final was blocked with a 1-0 loss at Dunfermline.

Even against a background of lowered expectations, there was a welter of barracking when Ross County came to Ayr and took a 4-0 lead by the 31st minute. A lot of barracking from the terraces is little worse than good-humoured banter. This was neither good-humoured nor banter. It cut to the bone. At half-time, goalkeeper Barry John Corr caught the brunt of it when vacating the Somerset Road goal. At half-time he was replaced by Mark McGeown. The rarity of substituting an uninjured goalkeeper was emphasis of the prevailing desperation. In the manner of a politician it could have been said that we won the second half since the final damage was 1-4. Ayr United greats Sam McMillan, John Murphy and Henry Templeton conducted the half-time draw on this day. It was not hard to guess what they thought. Neil Watt quit on the Monday and Brian Reid was named as the new manager on the Tuesday. Barry John Corr did not return to the club and he was released from his contract a fortnight later.

Neil Watt had been expected to weave some kind of magic. It was not in his nature to make outlandish boasts. The existence of overblown hopes was down to the fans. I readily admit to being one of those caught up in the hype at the time of his arrival. The appointment of Brian Reid was a welcome development but experience had cautioned the fans to be more restrained in our aspirations. Ayr United 2 Brechin City 1 was a satisfactory start. The date was 27th October yet it was the team's last win in 2007. Throughout this we had the unwelcome novelty of being eliminated from the Scottish Cup in November but at least the 2-1 defeat away to Partick Thistle was close. Some of the league form at this time was beyond horrendous. Look at these results from December and judge for yourself. Ayr United 1 Cowdenbeath 4, Peterhead 3 Ayr United 0, Ayr United 0 Raith Rovers 3 and Brechin City 5 Ayr United 1. Just one league point was taken all month. That was in a 1-1 draw against Queen's Park at Hampden but the result was sullied by dropping to second from the foot of the table. There were other factors to compound the December misery. Mark Casey was sent off against Cowdenbeath, Gareth Wardlaw was sent off against Peterhead, Ryan Stevenson was stretchered off against Raith Rovers and David Lowing got sent off against Queen's Park.

Brian Reid

New Year 2008 saw none of the excitement of the New Years of old. Being first-footed by Berwick Rangers was by not a derby by any stretch of the imagination. Nonetheless wallowing in nostalgia was a secondary consideration in comparison to winning 4-0. Happy days? Not quite! It was nothing more than a happy day. This was on Wednesday 2nd January. On Saturday 5th January we were at Cowdenbeatth, playing in front of an assembly of 297. The home team was below strength and had to draft in young players. Inside the first ten minutes a debut striker, signed from Dundonald Bluebell, scored. With the game eventually petering out on a 2-0 defeat the travelling support vented fury on the away dugout. The revulsion was captured by the *Ayrshire Post*: "Gutless, spineless and clueless. After the false dawn of their New Year win over Berwick, Ayr United are back to their wretched worst." These words flew in the face of the contention that local newspapers avoid criticism lest they risk their harmonious relationship with a club they rely on for stories. The words were accurate though. Had the report been sycophantic we would all have seen right through it.

There is an argument that barracking players is wrong because they are doing their best and they want to win just as much as the fans do. It is said that players do not need to be reminded when mistakes are made because they already know. In polite society such utterances would be commendable. Football though is driven by passion. It is not like tennis or golf where the public have to obey the instruction 'silence please'. Those with a heavy emotional commitment to the club are justified in complaining when it is all going badly. In the 1950s fans were heard to express the view that a trier is always forgiven. The modern game does not always work on that principle. Historically a trier is a player who runs himself into the ground. Nowadays a player may do precisely that but to little or no effect. The modern fan will accuse said player of "running around like a headless chicken."

Despite seeing out January with two home wins we were soon having to survey the league table with a sense of dread. In a home defeat against Peterhead, passions were so inflamed as to require stewards to hold back enraged spectators. Why the anger? Here is why. In the 89th minute Peterhead got a penalty for a handling offence committed by their own player, Bobby Mann. With the fans still raging about it Peterhead got another penalty in the next attack. Murray Henderson was running shoulder-to-shoulder with an opponent who suddenly fell over. Both these penalties were converted to take the damage to 0-3. The situation was further aggravated by Eddie Forrest getting sent off for complaining about the award of the second penalty. Team captain Murray Henderson said: "It was one of the worst refereeing performances I have ever seen and how he is a referee at senior level I have no idea." It can take a while for the anger and frustration to get out of the system when it is elevated to such heights. There was further horror on looking at the updated league table. Second bottom!

An illustrious visitor attended our next match. It was Gordon Brown, the reigning Prime Minister. He had supported Raith Rovers since his boyhood but it is a reasonable guess that he did not enjoy the nostalgia of a return to a familiar ground. It ended Raith Rovers 1 Ayr United 2 with Alex Williams scoring twice. Was this the cue to start an assault on the league table? No it was not! One week hence we had to witness Brechin City winning 3-0 at Ayr and the frustration was compounded by David Lowing getting sent off and Alex Williams having a penalty saved by Craig Nelson who was formerly a fans' favourite at Ayr.

Ross County at Dingwall on a Tuesday night was a worrying undertaking, most especially because they were the league leaders. By the 51st minute it was Ross County 0 Ayr United 4, Ryan Stevenson having scored a hat-trick. At the end it was 2-4. Avoiding a relegation play-off was now highly likely. It was not possible to bask in this unexpected success for long because four days later we were scheduled to play Ross County at Ayr. Jocularly it was said that the outcome on the Tuesday would have riled them. Credence was added to the old saying that many a true word is spoken in jest. Ross County extracted repayment with a 2-0 win.

The Somerset Park boardroom on 7th September, 2008

Eight days after beating the league leaders on their own patch we had the pleasure of beating the second-placed club on their ground. That club was Airdrie United, a phoenix of the original Airdrieonians. Despite their lofty position, the home club had been afflicted by poor gates. There was no mystery as to why the people of Airdrie did not support their club in appreciable numbers. The adult admission price was £15. For third-tier football in 2008 this was considered exorbitant. Our 2-0 win was watched by just 737.

Queen's Park 1 Ayr United 3 created a positive statistic in a season that was disappointing overall. It amounted to the club's sixth away win out of seven. To put this into context, the club record for consecutive away league wins is seven which dates to 1958/59. Then the final fixture of 2007/08 generated a statistic that made a mockery of the recently found form on the road. Ayr United 1 Airdrie United 2 was the club's tenth home league defeat of the season. Brian Reid was left in no mood to mince his words: "Yet again we lost cheap goals at home and that's why there will be big big changes in the summer." Note the emphasis in his comment. There would not just be big changes but *big big* changes. A seventh-placed finish was mortifying. The next campaign would be the fifth consecutive season in the Seaside League. It felt like entrapment. If there was to be an escape it seemed within the bounds of possibility that it would be at the wrong end.

When the Challenge Cup got underway the tournament had not attracted a sponsor. The first round ties were therefore deemed to be in the League Challenge Cup. When the competition was in progress a sponsor was found and it was renamed the ALBA Challenge Cup. For Ayr United the name change was a moot point since we were eliminated before it was implemented. The first round tie was against East Stirling who were then sharing Stenhousemuir's Ochilview Park. In anticipation of a low crowd the terracing behind the goal was closed off. Yet even the figure of 761 was more than expected and we had the novelty of being shepherded round the track to the hastily opened terracing. At 1-0 up a visible complacency set in. East Stirling exploited this by scoring twice in the last four minutes to win the tie. The predictable excuses got an airing. It's only July! It's only the Challenge Cup! In the previous season East Stirling had finished second lowest of Scotland's forty-two clubs, just one point off the bottom of the pile. On drifting out of the ground on that Sunday afternoon the mood of the fans was nonchalant.

Ayr United 0 Raith Rovers 0 brought a nice opportunity to indulge in statistics. In the club's history there had only been two previous occasions when the league season had started with a scoreless draw at home. The years were 1924, 1966 and now 2008. Each time the gap was forty-two years. I could claim a personal recollection of being there in 1966 but not in 1924! Winning at Alloa then preceded a 2-1 win at home to Arbroath. It was our first home win since January. Ryan Stevenson and Bryan Prunty both got yellow cards for the same offence which was running onto the track after scoring. You will hear people talking about daft bookings but in scenarios like this daft bookings are forgivable. Although these were early days there was immense satisfaction at being top of the league.

On being drawn against Aberdeen in the League Cup there was a sensation of novelty. It was the first time we had played Aberdeen since August 1985 and the first time at Ayr since November 1978, these matches also being in the League Cup. In this 2008 visit the only goal of the tie was scored by Aberdeen's Chris Maguire who was to become an Ayr United player in the far distant year of 2023. By mid-September top spot had been maintained. However the competition at the top was intense. Morale was dented with a 3-0 loss at East Fife which had the consequence of descending to third place. In the psychology of football it is important to respond to defeat in the right way. Mistakes must be learned from and a negative mindset has to be avoided. The expression 'false dawn' could have been written for Ayr United based on past experience. This time it seemed different. There had been enough early season promise to suggest that a promotion push was viable. Second place was quickly reclaimed with a 2-0 win at home to Peterhead in vile weather. Such inclemency is easily sufferable when the result is favourable. Top-placed Brechin City were merely one point in front.

Football is riddled with frustrations. One such is experiencing the elation of a late goal only to concede an even later goal. In the grand scheme of things Raith Rovers versus Ayr United was a six-pointer. At 2-1 down there was elation when Scott Walker equalised in the 88th minute. Two minutes later there was a corresponding level of despair when the winning goal got scored at the opposite end. A hard fought draw at home to Stirling Albion then preceded five consecutive league wins. Those who were imbibed with a more pessimistic nature were quick to urge caution in the time-honoured manner by stating that we should not get carried away. In retrospect the guardedness was more attributable to experience rather than pessimism. Yet a purple patch amidst bleak times is a welcome release and it is a natural reaction to live for the moment.

Lochee United away was a favourably received Scottish Cup draw. This was not due to any leanings towards arrogance but rather the liking for attending a ground hitherto unvisited. The Thomson Park pitch was iced over thereby causing five postponements. It eventually got played with a 1.30 pm kick-off on a Wednesday afternoon. In my mind I had already ticked the ground off as a new one visited but when the match was in progress I was in an office in Glasgow city centre, relying on texts from my son David. These were '1-0 Ayr Williams' followed by '1-1'. With only two sleeping nights left before Christmas the replay was won 3-1. The stakes were high because it was already known that the winner would be at home to Kilmarnock in the next round. When broadcasters summarise a cup draw they have a strong tendency to talk about the home club welcoming the visiting club. For example they will say "Ayr United will welcome Kilmarnock". Yet anyone with a vestige of knowledge of Ayrshire derbies will be aware that the tone of cordiality is wayward.

Ostensibly it appeared that a fixture at Brechin on the last Tuesday of the year would pale into insignificance in comparison to the impending Scottish Cup tie. Yet the 1-0 win was of considerable importance. We were now five points clear of third-placed Brechin City and one point behind Raith Rovers at the top. A postponement at Stranraer led to Kilmarnock being our first opponents of 2009. 10,185 tickets got sold although just 9,280 turned up. The obvious reason for this was the weather. It was an afternoon of driving rain and blustery wind. Kilmarnock had not beaten Ayr United in competitive action since 1994. Moreover we were chasing our fifth consecutive cup win against them. Objectively we had to take cognisance of the two-league gap. Or did we? Not much is viewed objectively on these occasions. When Manuel Pascali scored for Kilmarnock he looked outrageously offside. It seemed as if he was sheltering from the rain under the crossbar. Dean Keenan levelled it with a flying header. With twenty minutes to go Kilmarnock got a penalty for the chance to put them 3-1 up. Stephen Grindlay not only saved it but he held it too. In stoppage time a Chris Aitken corner-kick was punched out in the direction of Alex

Williams who made it 2-2 with the outside of his right boot. In frantic scenes he got a yellow card for taking his shirt off. The referee then prevented him from running onto the track thus preventing him from a second yellow card. Williams, on realising that the referee had done him a favour, planted a kiss on him. For the avoidance of doubt this will be repeated. Alex Williams kissed the referee. Kilmarnock boss Jim Jefferies afterwards blamed the weather for his team not winning. Told you that not much is objective on these occasions! The replay was lost 3-1 after having a 1-0 half-time lead. This was the first Ayrshire derby to be televised live in its entirety.

When the excitement of cup football reverts back to league football it is commonly said that we are getting back to the bread and butter. Although it is an odd metaphor it still conveys the meaning graphically and it is all the more potent when the cup football has doubled up as a derby. Quite apart from the Sky television audience, the replay on that Thursday night was watched by 11,563. Then, on the Sunday afternoon, 1,256 watched our 2-1 win at home to Arbroath. After selling out our ticket allocation for Rugby Park this was disappointing. The win was of primary importance though. At the top of the Second Division there was little margin for error. We next had to contend with a visit from Raith Rovers. Once more this fell into the category of a six-pointer. On going 2-0 down in the ninth minute all manner of horrors were envisaged. The fears were groundless and it ended 2-2. It was just as well. It meant that we were now five points behind top-placed Raith Rovers with two games in hand. Fortunately we did not have to ponder the ramifications of defeat.

A week later, at Alloa, we again found ourselves 2-0 down and again it was clawed back to 2-2. In the 88th minute the home team got their second penalty of the match and it ended in a 3-2 defeat. Losing is a frustration but on this day at Alloa the frustration was worse than normal. It was riddled with 'if onlys' and controversies. Such frustrations are not left behind at the game and the drive home gets riddled with irritation through innocuous things like red traffic lights.

The experience of being 2-0 down threatened to become a habit when, for the third consecutive match, it happened again. Again we got it back to 2-2, this time going on to win 4-2 at home to Brechin City. With Raith Rovers only drawing at home to Stirling Albion we were now just three points off the top with a game in hand. Queen's Park 0 Ayr United 3 replicated a result from November. With Queen's Park due at Ayr in the immediate midweek, a home win was a foregone conclusion but 1-1 was the actual conclusion.

Ayr United versus Stranraer was top versus bottom. At 5-0 the gap was apparent. Then came the big one. Raith Rovers away! The clubs were tied on points at the top but our goal difference was superior. As the match progressed it appeared as if neither team would break the deadlock, besides which a draw would not have been wholly disastrous. In the 84th minute David Gormley scored with a shot that rolled over the line agonisingly slowly. It was the cue for bedlam behind that goal. The final whistle was the cue for further bedlam. It was a fantastic win and our big support was elated. I tended to be a bit overbearing in the workplace when Ayr United were doing well. A colleague of mine in Glasgow had recently had ear wax removed. He said: "If yez win that league ah'm gaunae get the ear wax injected back in."

There was an undercurrent of belief that the title would be won. It was still March but, to use another of those metaphors, we were in pole position. During the run-in our hopes perished on two results. These were 0-0 at home to Peterhead and a 1-0 loss at Brechin. The latter match meant being two points off the top with three games left. We ran out of straws to clutch so, on finishing second, promotion would depend on the play-offs. All season we were unbeaten at home in the league. This was just the fifth time it had happened in the club's history. Extraordinarily just two of the five occurred in a title-winning season.

Short work was made of Brechin City in the play-off semi-finals. It was 5-2 on aggregate. Promotion now rested on two legs against Airdrie United. Both legs were televised live on BBC Alba with a Gaelic commentary. Language of a different kind was heard at Somerset Park when we went 2-0 down in the first half. Of course to this point of the season we had a conspicuous proficiency at coming back from 2-0 down. Could it happen again? Yes! Mark Roberts scored twice. Chris Aitken then missed a penalty which could have made it 3-2 and we had the further misfortune of a second yellow card for Neil McGowan.

The action then decamped to Airdrie. With it level at 2-2 it was a final in the true sense of the word. The tension was as high as the stakes. Ryan Stevenson's first half goal was the cue for scenes that were beyond euphoric. This was not a quiet Sabbath. It was the only goal of the game and the final whistle saw jubilation on and off the pitch. The uncharitably-named Seaside League was now departed. To understand the joy of promotion it has to be experienced. Right there at that time it felt fabulous to be supporting Ayr United. It transpired that Airdrie United retained their place in the First Division anyway. This occurred due to a reshuffle caused by Livingston being relegated to the Third Division due to financial misdealing. We would therefore have been promoted even in the event of losing on that day at Airdrie. Was it still worth it? Most certainly.

Post war Scottish Cup crowds at home

Highest

18th February, 1956.	Ayr United 0 Celtic 3	24,100
10th March, 1951.	Ayr United 2 Motherwell 2	22,152
5th February, 1949.	Ayr United 0 Morton 2	21,462
12th March, 1960.	Ayr United 0 Clyde 2	est 18,000
13th March, 1974.	Ayr United 1 Hearts 2	16,185
6th February, 1993.	Ayr United 0 Rangers 2	13,176
2nd March, 1977.	Ayr United 1 Celtic 3	13,100
1st February, 1958.	Ayr United 1 St.Mirren 1	est 12,500
3rd February, 1988.	Ayr United 0 Dunfermline Athletic 2	11,712
27th February, 1960.	Ayr United 4 Airdrie 2	11,226

Lowest (Covid excepted)

1st November, 2014.	Ayr United 1 Alloa Athletic 1	784
2nd November, 2013.	Ayr United 3 Queen's Park 2	879
27th November, 2021.	Ayr United 2 Albion Rovers 1	986
19th November, 2011.	Ayr United 2 Montrose 2	988
3rd November, 2012.	Ayr United 2 Clachnacuddin 1	1032
20th November, 2010.	Ayr United 5 Sunnybank 0	1069
18th January, 2010.	Ayr United 1 Brechin City 0	1139
20th January, 2018.	Ayr United 4 Arbroath 1	1151
11th December, 2004.	Ayr United 3 Edinburgh City 0	1183
21st January, 2017.	Ayr United 0 Queen's Park 0	1326

14. The Centenary and Beyond

There were no illusions that, after a five-year absence, life in the First Division would be anything other than tough. In pre-season the squad stayed at a training camp in Austria. This reeked of thoroughness. The preparations continued with a Somerset Park friendly against Unirea Urziceni, the Romanian champions. It was a close match too. The Romanian team won 2-1 via an own goal inside the last ten minutes. In the Alba Challenge Cup the first round result was Ayr United 0 Albion Rovers 2. In consecutive years we had now been eliminated by a Third Division team at this stage of the competition. The outcome was barely grieved over.

Partick Thistle were at Ayr for the league opener and with five minutes played there was one of those goals that makes you doubt your own eyesight. Partick goalkeeper Jonny Tuffey made a hash of a kicked clearance and it fell for Mark Roberts who was near the touchline. Marko noticed that Tuffey was out of his goal so he audaciously had a go from about fifty yards and at an angle. We watched in amazement as the ball found lodgement in the net. It ended 1-1 which was satisfying enough. In comparison to where we had been for the past five years the fixture list always looked daunting. Inverness Caledonian Thistle were newly relegated from the Premier League and since they had home advantage it was considered that we did not have a ghost of a chance in fixture two. Not that our boisterous support was worried. Escaping with a 0-0 draw was another good afternoon's work.

The reality of life in the second tier soon became painfully apparent with just one point taken from the next four league matches. During that run further pain was inflicted by St. Mirren who won 2-0 at Ayr in the League Cup. When left to survey the wreckage it could be seen that we were kept off the foot of the First Division table only by Morton who had already won 2-0 at Ayr. Where or when would the first win come? Maybe an 'if' should have been thrown into the mix. Patience was rewarded when Raith Rovers were beaten 1-0 at Somerset Park. It was their first league defeat since Ayr United had won at Kirkcaldy on 14th March. The table now had a far healthier complexion. In order we were now above Dunfermline Athletic, Morton and Airdrie United. There was an element of firefighting. One aim existed and it was a simple one. Avoiding relegation was the sole ambition. Optimism became an increasingly diminishing quality during a run of eight games yielding five losses and three draws. Much of it was brutal to watch, especially being routed 5-1 at home to Inverness Caledonian Thistle. Who could have known that they would return to administer an even bigger rout by the season's end?

Deveronvale away in the Scottish Cup was an opportunity to bag a win at last. It happened. At 1-0 it was far from replicating the 6-0 win there in 2002 but Brian Reid was rightly unconcerned when he commented that the result was never in doubt. Would the team now oblige by following it up with a long overdue league win? Ayr United 1 Dunfermline Athletic 0 was a relief yet the situation was still fraught with peril. Only Airdrie United were lower placed. The date of the Dunfermline match was 5th December, 2009, but our next home league game did not take place until 6th March, 2010. Between those dates Somerset Park hosted only a Scottish Cup tie against Brechin City. It was won 1-0. The winter of 2009/10 was comparable to that of 1962/63, hence the multitude of postponements.

Ayr United's first league fixture of 2010 took place on the advanced date of 23rd January and even then it was in Dingwall. At this time there was a scheme offering £15 return rail travel to anywhere in Scotland. The condition for eligibility was being aged fifty-five or over. On reading the small print in the terms and conditions I could not see any restrictive clauses. Surely enough I was able to buy a Prestwick to Dingwall return for the bargain price but I felt a bit irked at not being asked for proof of age. Okay, I was over fifty-five but I was deluded into believing that I did not look it! The match was lost 1-0 so there were a few gloomy ruminations on the way back.

The run of predominantly away matches continued with a Scottish Cup tie at Dens Park. During the game there was an altercation between fans and stewards. In basic terms the dispute was over fans being told they had to sit down but they insisted on standing. I tend to have tunnel vision when a game is in progress but the commotion did make me turn round to see a flurry of bodies tumbling down the steps in the manner of the human snowballs you see in cartoons. There was excitement on the pitch too when Tam McManus scored. Alas Dundee fought back to win 2-1. On the eve of the match I was made redundant by an ailing company. To put it succinctly it was a rotten couple of days. Onwards and upwards is an inspirational phrase utilised to lighten the mood but there are times when it does not resonate in the intended manner.

Relegation fears deepened at Palmerston on an afternoon when goalkeeper Craig Samson was sent off. We had an able deputy in Stephen Grindlay but not able enough to stop Queen of the South winning 3-0. His first act was to retrieve the ball from the net after our former player Stewart Kean had scored with the penalty awarded for the red card offence. It was the proverbial bad day at the office, to quote another of those phrases which get drawn into a football context.

The wheel of fortune swung once more. Unbeaten in the next eight! This comprised four wins and four draws. It was so close to being seven wins and one draw. In consecutive away fixtures against Inverness Caledonian Thistle, Airdrie United and Raith Rovers, we had the severe misfortune to concede an equaliser in stoppage time. Oscar Wilde once said: "To err once is human, to err twice is careless." By deduction we can draw the conclusion that he would have considered it to be beyond careless to err three times. Yet this run was still enough to escape the clutches of the bottom two. The escape was followed by a recall. Eight defeats in the last nine fixtures was fatal. The final fixture was away to Morton. Winning by at least a three-goal margin would have meant finishing safely in eighth place. To have won by a lesser margin would have secured a play-off place which would have allowed a fighting chance of escaping relegation. While leading 1-0 hopes were alive only for Morton to draw level (77 minutes) then hit the winner (86 minutes). In consequence we finished bottom. It was devastating. Our 'goals for' column was the lowest in an Ayr United league campaign since 1966/67. On the previous Saturday it had been painful to watch Ayr United 0 Inverness Caledonian Thistle 7. It equalled our record home defeat in all competitions by replicating the 0-7 versus Dundee United in September 1966. In 1966 I cleared off before the end but in 2010 I remained until the very bitter end. I overheard a very interesting conversation during the first half of the Inverness rout. Near my stance in the Somerset Road end two elderly supporters were justly bemoaning the manner in which the persistent attacks were cutting through the Ayr United defence with ease. The conversation then turned to Ayr United hard men of the past who would not have been brushed aside in this way. Then one of them said: "Ah've been coming here since 1952 and in aw that time the hardest Ayr United player ah've seen wis..........". While he was finishing his sentence I momentarily guessed that he was going to say Stan Quinn or Sanny McAnespie. The scenario was deserving of a twenty-five second pause and a drum roll. However without hesitation he said Gordon Brice. The word of a veteran Somerset Road-ender just had to be taken as binding. Gordon Brice was marginally before my time but I had heard about him. Moreover his reputation was in complete accord with my own research. During the war he had been a Commando so straight away it is obvious that he would not have been daunted by anything he experienced while playing at centre-half for Ayr United. He was born in Bedford and in turn he played for Luton Town, Wolverhampton Wanderers, Reading then Fulham from whom he joined Ayr United in December 1956.

The date of Ayr United's centenary was 9th May, 2010. There are instances of clubs undergoing uncertainty about when they were founded. For example Berwick Rangers claimed to be founded in 1881 until changing it to 1884. Setting aside the 2012 argument, Rangers claim 1872 to be their year of foundation despite celebrating their centenary in 1973. The precise date of our own foundation carries no doubt whatsoever. It was a Monday evening and the historic event occurred in the Masonic Hall, Nile Court. A lot of preparation went into the Ayr United centenary event and Andrew Downie was worthy of being singled out for special praise. The centenary dinner took place on 8th May, 2010, in the Ayrshire Suite at Ayr Racecourse. At midnight there was a countdown to the actual date. It had been hoped to avoid relegation in this of all years but football has no truck with such sentiment.

The Scottish Football Association imposed a £2,000 fine for the club's disciplinary record over the season. There would be no sign of repentance with an even worse record looming. Three red cards were accrued by the end of July. William Easton and Dean Keenan were sent off in a friendly at Annan and Jonathan Tiffoney had the same fate in a League Cup tie at Elgin. The Annan match was lost 4-0 although we could file it as 'only a friendly'. However there could be no similarly glib dismissal on losing 3-2 at Elgin where the killer goal was conceded thirty-nine seconds before the end of extra time.

At least my period of unemployment was now at an end. Working in Glasgow it was a bonus to have fellow Ayr United supporter Allan Clark for company. I had worked in Glasgow before but this particular privilege was hitherto unknown to me. It has to be admitted that we were in an extreme minority. Would we have a promotion winning season to discuss? That was still in abeyance. Scottish Football's third tier still existed under the decoy-esque title of the Second Division. The previous relegation had resulted in a five-year exile at this level. It was too depressing to contemplate a repeat. With the start of the league programme came the annual wish to get off to a flyer.

Jill Carmichael presenting her cross stitch to Alex Ingram.

The wish was denied when Brechin City came to Ayr and won 2-0. Prior to the match my daughter Jill presented the club with a work of cross stitch which she had made to commemorate the centenary. Then I received the award of a beautiful piece of glass suitably inscribed to commemorate forty years of service to the match programme. The boardroom hospitality extended to the family made it a very pleasant afternoon in all aspects except the football.

A week later we were well on course for the first league win when 2-0 up at Airdrie. Then the roof fell in with the loss of two goals in the last ten minutes. Tempers were frayed to the extent that it finished up as nine versus ten. The first league win came in fixture three and it was a match that was never going to linger for long in the memory. At home to Dumbarton a Scott McLaughlin corner-kick landed for Paul Maxwell who fired it into the net. If you do not recall Paul Maxwell playing for Ayr United it is not down to a lapse of memory. It was an own goal as well as the only goal. My obsession for collating Ayr United statistics extends to maintaining pedantic details of own goals in the club's favour so this was a welcome bonus.

We continued to scratch and claw for league points. Diehards barely care how results are obtained whereas purists are mainly preoccupied with a desire to be entertained. On that basis the Dumbarton win only appeased the diehards. It was a similar story when we retraced our steps to Somerset Park a week later. It took a stoppage time penalty to scrape a 1-1 draw against Peterhead.

Having eliminated Airdrie United (played at Alloa) and Cowdenbeath in the Alba Challenge Cup, a 2-1 loss away to Partick Thistle was treated with the usual nonchalance so familiar to this competition. However there was no such nonchalance after losing 4-1 at Alloa on the Saturday. Five of our former players were in the starting line-up. They were Michael Dunlop, Billy Gibson, Scott Walker, David Gormley and Bryan Prunty. Disconcertingly Brian Reid said that it was the worst Ayr United performance since he had taken over as manager. It could hardly have been a more scathing condemnation.

A week later Mark Roberts scored a hat-trick of penalties. In the year of writing he remains the only Ayr United player ever to have achieved this feat. It occurred in a 3-2 win away to East Fife. The winning kick came in stoppage time and there was an odd finale when Stuart Cargill of the home team decided to involve himself in the goal celebration. His involvement cost Marko a red card. This was the start of a phase when the trepidation ebbed away. The win over East Fife commenced a run in which six wins were notched up out of seven. There were extenuating circumstances for the one defeat in the midst of it all. In the year of writing it remains the only match in our history in which an Ayr United team has conceded four penalties. The beneficiaries were Forfar Athletic on their own ground. Three of the four were awarded in a six-minute spell.

Two of the four were converted and David Crawford saved the other two. We had two players sent off and the match was handled by a different referee in each half due to the late arrival of the nominated official. The eventual result was a borderline tongue twister. It was 4-1 for Forfar!

Neutral opinion seemed unanimous in the view that Livingston would win the league therefore it was a conspicuously good result when they were beaten 3-1 at Ayr. There was an indomitable spirit in the team and this was vital during the successful spell. At home to Airdrie, for example, the 1-0 win came from a goal scored so late that the final whistle was blown immediately upon the recentre.

The accumulation of eighteen points from seven games had a hugely beneficial effect. Livingston were top and Brechin City and Ayr United were just one point behind but our goal difference was inferior. Football's propensity for the unlikely then kicked in by virtue of a 3-2 loss against the bottom club at Dumbarton. The date was 13th November, 2010, yet our next league match would not materialise until 2nd January, 2011, also against Dumbarton. Between those dates the only match was a tough-tackling Scottish Cup tie at home to Sunnybank, a Junior club from Aberdeen. At one stage in the second half the visitors had six players on yellow cards. They finally accumulated two red cards. It finished 5-0 despite the intensity of it all. Two of the goals were from penalties.

Frozen pitches blighted the country. After the Sunnybank tie six weeks elapsed before the thaw permitted the next match to be played. Ayr United 2 Dumbarton 0 made it a happy New Year. The top of the table remained tight. We were now two points behind Livingston and one point behind Brechin City. The league was temporarily shelved with the fourth round of the Scottish Cup pending. Hibs away brought recollections of the Scottish Cup visits to Easter Road in 1980 and 1986. Six days earlier the crowd for our home match with Dumbarton had been 1,224 yet we headed east with a support in excess of 1,400. After a 0-0 draw it was a contented journey home. In the build-up to the replay Hibs manager Colin Calderwood spoke about how difficult it would be at Somerset Park. In this phase of history it should not have been too daunting for a club of that stature but on a personal level I derived confidence from his belief that it was going to be tough. He was now returning to the club he had been released from despite being the captain of a successful Ayr United youth team. His fears were vindicated. Mark Roberts scored an exquisite goal to win the tie 1-0. We have had a history of Scottish Cup wins against clubs from a higher league but this was the first Ayr United team to achieve the feat against a team from two leagues above. Not even in our wildest dreams could we then envisage the Scottish Cup being paraded along Prestwick Road in an open-topped bus. The issue at stake was just how far we could proceed. In the next round St.Mirren won 2-1 at Ayr. It can be a futile exercise to draw too many positives from a defeat yet it was inescapably apparent that, once more, the team had belied its third-tier status.

The hordes from Paisley swelled the cup crowd to 5,997. A week later there were no such hordes from Livingston. Merely 1,614 were here for a win-or-else game. Ayr United 0 Livingston 3 was the first home league defeat since the opening game back on 7th August. It rendered our title hopes fragile. Ten points off the top was tantamount to a promotion Everest even with two games in hand. The gap with second-placed Brechin City was just one point. If any title hopes did still exist it was not apparent to the public. A midweek visit from East Fife drew in just 789. It seemed that the team too had thrown in the towel. East Fife secured their second ever league win at Ayr and it was accomplished in convincing fashion at 4-0. In the vernacular it was being said that the team had 'chucked it'. Bewilderingly the result ten days later was Airdrie United 0 Ayr United 5. Ambition to finish second was suddenly reignited. Livingston were disappearing from sight at the top. The rout of Airdrie was the first of three consecutive wins. We were starting to enjoy our football again and we had a new hero in Michael Moffat. The story of supporting Ayr United is a marathon tale of peaks and troughs. One point was taken from the next five matches despite the run of fixtures not looking too tough. The four defeats in the mix were against Forfar Athletic home and away, Stenhousemuir away and East Fife away.

With five games left, second place was occupied but Livingston were nineteen points in front. In the completed table Livingston's lead was twenty-three points and our second-placed finish was preserved by reason of having a better goal difference than Forfar Athletic and two points more than Brechin City. Before contemplating the possibilities there was a major story which increased the excitement by a notch or two. The *Ayrshire Post* covered it in these terms: "In a sponsorship deal that has made headlines around the globe, Ayr United will carry the name of the world's largest online betting brand, Bodog. The company founder was Calvin Ayre. His spokesman Ed Pownall said: 'We are going to have some fun with this and try to make Ayr United everyone's second team. We have some heavy resources and we'll use them to make Ayr's name known globally. From hockey fans in Canada and basketball supporters in China, everyone wants a second team to support. Let's make that team Ayr United. We have big plans to unveil and we're going to try and give the team a big push. We are genuinely excited about the deal and we are looking forward to a long term relationship and want to build a love for the club.'"

Experience prompted an 'I'll believe it when I see it' school of thought yet it was difficult to escape a 'supposing it's true' attitude. The hockey fans in Canada and the basketball supporters in China were oblivious to Ayr United winning 4-1 at Forfar in the first leg of the play-off semi-finals. The 3-3 result in the second leg was the subject of an equal lack of global awareness. When Brechin City arrived for the first leg of the play-off final the eyes of the world were still averted. There were too many armed conflicts and political shenanigans going on. If the promise to make Ayr United a globally-known name was going to be fulfilled it would have to be deferred to another day. The Ayr support can be unkind in the treatment meted out to former players who return to play for opposing clubs. Goalkeeper Craig Nelson was a definite exclusion. He was assured of a cordial reception but this did not weaken his resolve to keep a clean goal. Although Michael Moffat succeeded in beating him we were consistently denied a second goal which was considered to be well nigh essential. Against the run of play Brechin made it 1-1 four minutes from the end. Escaping the Seaside League was now dependent on winning at Glebe Park on a Sunday afternoon. It was a nice day for a drive until the idyll got disturbed on the Dundee ringroad. From the rear of the car there was a sound like a small explosion followed by a clatter and the sound of scraping. The exhaust looked as if it had given up the ghost. A Google search revealed the whereabouts of the nearest exhaust centre. The distance was mercifully short because the racket from the car would have wakened the dead. Once it was fixed I asked how much I was required to pay whereupon I was told: "See that man ower there. Jist gie him £20 or £30." I gratefully obeyed and the man 'ower there' was given £20. Grateful to have got this done on the cheap, the Carmichaels were soon on the way with a refreshed vigour.

It may seem ridiculous to suggest that 2,404 was a massive crowd but, in the confines of Glebe Park, the place seemed packed. By a rough estimate the Ayr support must have been about 2,000. Exchanges were tentative. Then we conceded an own goal a minute before half-time. There were chaotic scenes when Mark Roberts made it 1-1 (77 minutes). The game could not resume until the pitch was cleared of fans. Craig Nelson was in no mood to be beaten again but eventually he was. Michael Moffat made it 2-1 on the day and 3-2 on aggregate (88 minutes). The place was frantic with joy and once more some of the fans scattered onto the field. Such scenes were replicated at the final whistle but this time there was a far bigger mass of humanity on the pitch. We were back in the First Division.

On compiling my end-of-season notes there were some compelling statistics.

> Penalties. Nineteen awarded. Mark Roberts scored fourteen and had two saved. Andy Rodgers scored two and Alan Trouten scored one. Of the sixteen penalties conceded, fourteen were scored and two saved.
> Red cards. Nine received (eleven including friendlies) with one overturned. Ten opposition red cards.
> Own goals. Two in Ayr United's favour. Three in the opposition's favour.

It was a season of varying emotions yet here is the evidence that it was far from dull. Promotion in 2009 had been followed by relegation in 2010. Promotion in 2011 gave rise to some talk about the recurrence of instant relegation. Even those of us who entertained the possibility of survival had to admit that it would be tough going.

Great interest was generated by the news that Manchester United had agreed to send a team to Ayr for a pre-season friendly. It was a young team therefore our opponents were designated Manchester United xi. After holding out until the 54th minute Oliver Norwood scored the only goal of the night. One player stood out above all others. This was Paul Pogba, then aged eighteen. Even in a summer friendly it was possible to see that he was destined for the top. The pinnacle of his long list of accomplishments was winning the World Cup with France and scoring in the final. At Ayr a ball came to him at head height and he managed to kill it stone dead with his heel. If I had not witnessed it I would have considered it a physical impossibility.

With the start of the league programme came the moment of truth. Maybe now we would have an inkling as to how tough the First Division would be. Hamilton Accies provided the answer with a 2-1 win at Ayr. The action then switched to Cappielow on the Tuesday night but the home club was not Morton. It was Ayr United. This was a Ramsdens Challenge Cup tie against Raith Rovers. It could not be played at Ayr because the new floodlighting system was incomplete. A comprehensive 3-0 win was watched by a paltry attendance of 227. In the first round we had beaten Queen of the South 2-0 at home after extra time. The challenge spluttered with a 1-0 defeat at home to Annan Athletic in the quarter-finals. On resuming league duty the schedule looked frightening. The forthcoming fixtures were Dundee away then Falkirk at home. In drawing 1-1 at Dens Park the critics were silenced. As for the Falkirk match we had an amusing finale. With it poised at 2-2 Higginbotham headed the ball into the Ayr net in the second minute of stoppage time. He then earned himself a yellow card for jumping into the crowd to celebrate. After extricating himself from his own fans he was just in time to find out that his effort had been chalked off. Immediately the free-kick for offside was taken, the referee blew the final whistle.

"Most of my players were at work today while Inverness relaxed in their hotel, so it's great and we are delighted." This was Brian Reid's response to a 1-0 win over Inverness Caledonian Thistle in the second round of the League Cup having already won 3-0 away to East Stirling in the first round. This was the year after the 0-7 horror show. Reid was right to emphasise the club's part time status. Caley Thistle were in the Premier League but they would not be the only club in that hallowed sphere to fall victim to Ayr United as the competition progressed. The momentum carried over to the home game on the Saturday when Ross Robertson headed a stoppage time winner against Raith Rovers.

To support a club like Ayr United is to become well versed in the concept of realism. The realistic outlook was that every point gained was a potential buffer against relegation. Consolidation in mid-table was the loftiest ambition of those who did allow their mind to wander. Morton 4 Ayr United 1 and Partick Thistle 4 Ayr United 0 were consecutive results which plunged the club into bottom place. This was a bigger dose of realism than we could digest. Next up we had Hearts at home in the League Cup. What hope was there? Statistically there was a vestige of hope. To this point of 2011 Premier League clubs Hibs and Inverness Caledonian Thistle had lost at Ayr. So had St.Mirren but that was in a friendly. The Hearts tie was played in conditions of high winds and heavy rain. It was 1-1 after extra time and we won the shootout. In season 2011/12 the only teams to beat Hearts in cup competitions were Ayr United and Tottenham Hotspur. Working in Glasgow it was commonplace to be asked how Ayr United were getting on. Although this was just intended as polite conversation it was a bit disconcerting to reply, for example, that we had just been hammered at Forfar. That was why I went out of my way to say to anyone who would listen: "We beat Hearts last night." Being conceited about Ayr United is a nice but lamentably rare feeling.

Prior to playing Queen of the South a most interesting ceremony took place. The *Ayrshire Post* sponsored the Ally MacLeod Suite and Mike Wilson, the Sports Editor, publicised the names of twelve greats who had played under Ally. It was then put to a public vote with a view to naming the hospitality boxes after the top five. The chosen names were Cutty Young, Stan Quinn, Henry Templeton, Davy Stewart and John Murphy. They were all there for the ceremony with the exception of John Murphy who had work commitments. It was a great pleasure to be there, a personal highlight being the opportunity to have a good chat with Davy Stewart. A good afternoon got even better. Queen of the South were beaten 1-0 by an 84th minute goal from Mark Roberts who got shown a yellow card for jumping into the crowd in celebration. It meant a move from tenth to eighth. Queen of the South were ninth and Dundee were bottom but they were on the brink of a resurgence that would bring them promotion. Ross County 4 Ayr United 0 then had the dispiriting consequence of being at the foot of the table a week later. It was just on goal difference though. There was no need to abandon hope.

The League Cup quarter-final draw offered another crack at Premier League opposition but the difficulty was exacerbated by it being an away tie. League fare in the First Division was testing enough. The time served question was whether the team could rise to the occasion at St.Mirren Park. With nine minutes left Chris Smith scored with a header.

Could the 1-0 lead be protected? With seconds of the three minutes of stoppage time remaining, Graham Carey struck the Ayr crossbar with a header. The final whistle came as a merciful relief. For the fifth time in our history an Ayr United team would be playing in the semi-finals of the League Cup. Patience was necessary since the big occasion was not taking place for a further three months. The opposition? Kilmarnock!

I had to work on occasional Saturday afternoons. Quickly and discreetly I would check the Ayr United score updates. With 4.45 pm having come and gone the state of play on this particular afternoon was Hamilton Accies 2 Ayr United 2. While busy on a phone call someone slipped a piece of paper onto my desk. Scribbled on it was "Hamilton 2 Ayr 3 Smith 90". It left me with the impression that my work colleagues appreciated that, to me, Ayr United was a way of life.

Four days after losing 1-0 at home to Morton, a club statement appeared on the official website. It was a lengthy condemnation of fan behaviour. To cherrypick one sentence: "The behaviour of some Ayr United fans lately, both at home games and away, has gone beyond the acceptable legal parameters." At half-time in the Morton match the standside linesman intervened to restrain Brian Reid who was responding to a supporter who had shouted at him.

Brian Graham is a name most closely associated with Partick Thistle yet in November 2011 he scored the only goal in a Raith Rovers versus Ayr United match. Fortunately for us it was an own goal. This meant that Raith now took our place second from the foot with Queen of the South bottom. The date was 12th November, 2011. Our next league win was on 25th February, 2012, which in turn was our first home league win since 24th September, 2011. These times were rendered tolerable by some good cup form. Third Division Montrose were eliminated in a third round Scottish Cup replay at Links Park. It is commonly said that getting through is all that really matters in cup football. This saying implies struggle. It was very close to being a losing struggle. In the 2-2 draw at Ayr we had to endure the sight of Montrose missing two gilt-edged chances late on. The next round brought some excitement but it was not all for football reasons. It was at Livingston. If asked to name Livingston's ground in a football quiz it would be difficult to get the correct answer due to the ever changing name. In 2012 the moniker was the Braidwood Motor Company Stadium. The start of the game was delayed because the fire alarms went off. Fire engines arrived and there was a sweep of the stadium. Consider yourself to be forewarned of a pun. The only thing on fire was Ayr United. We won 2-1.

Ayr United versus Kilmarnock at Hampden had no historical precedent. The occasion was a League Cup semi-final. Supporters of both clubs indulged in a lot of online posturing in the build-up. Having an opportunity to air thoughts on football was no longer the sole domain of journalists. However social media posts were hardly noted for impartiality. The attendance of 25,057 was the second highest for an Ayrshire derby, beaten only by the figure of 27,442 for a Scottish Cup quarter-final at Rugby Park in 1938. Kilmarnock got the tie's only goal. It was scored in the 109th minute. Our attacking capability did not manifest itself until the last ten minutes of extra time. Brian Reid bore the brunt of criticism for the cautious tactics. Opinion was divided as to whether this was fair. It might have worked if just one of the counter attacks had been productive or if we had held out for a shootout. On the way back to the car I stopped and spoke to a lone figure standing at a bus stop. He was wearing an Ayr United scarf and smoking a cigarette. It was Henry Templeton, one of the most popular Ayr United players of all time.

Interest was still alive in the Scottish Cup. When Falkirk came to Ayr for a fifth round tie it was already known that the winners would be at home to Hibs in the quarter-finals. Falkirk's early goal caused them to become relaxed to the point of complacency. We won 2-1 and Brian Reid made a most telling comment: "I thought we were wonderful in the second half and we showed we can pass as well as Falkirk. Hibs will be aware of what happened last season so they will not underestimate us." Pundits summed up our chances with the old cliché about lightning not striking twice in the same place. Depressingly they were right. Hibs won 2-0. Just as depressing was the resumption of the league programme being a re-acquaintance with the fight to avoid relegation. It is impossible to mention these foot-of-the-league scraps without using combative words like 'fight'. Watching football should be a recreational pursuit but it differs from other forms of entertainment through its propensity to cause anxiety. Brian Reid was empathetic. He understood the fans. After losing 2-1 away to Queen of the South he said: "The fans came here in numbers and we could hear them all game. We are so disappointed for them."

Hibs versus Ayr United on 10th March, 2012. The Carmichaels from the east meet the Carmichaels from the west.

Disappointment at Palmerston was far from an unknown experience but Queen of the South were the bottom club. The perspective was not lost. A week later there was another telling comment after Partick Thistle had won 3-1 at Ayr. Mark Roberts said: "Two years ago we lost eight of the last nine games. We're on a dire run and it kind of stinks of that right now." Five games were now left but the principle was the same. A lapse in form could be potentially fatal. The next game was a Wednesday evening visit from Ross County. On the previous evening Dundee had drawn 1-1 at home to Queen of the South. This clinched the league title for Ross County. They were graciously applauded onto the field by the Ayr players. On the face of it this was a fortuitous development. Having won the league already our opponents would have no incentive. Well if they did have no incentive somebody must have forgotten to tell them. They departed with a 3-1 win.

Livingston 0 Ayr United 1 comprised our fourth win against Livvy thus far in 2012. With three games now left it was a time for cool heads. Heads were anything but cool at Hamilton. Eddie Malone got sent off three minutes into the second half and it became even more calamitous when Hamilton Accies won 3-2 with a goal scored in the 89th minute. One week later we had a mirror image of that game when Ross Robertson scored in the 89th minute to beat Dundee 3-2. I was in the boardroom when Jackson Longridge got the Man of the Match award. Or rather he didn't! He had turned seventeen earlier in the month so the bottle of champagne was handed to his father. Keigan Parker's 84th minute equaliser won the SFL Goal of the Season award. It came from a spectacular scissors kick. Dundee's late collapse marred their commemoration of becoming champions of Scotland precisely fifty years earlier. They even turned out in retro 1962 shirts. On the same afternoon Raith Rovers 3 Queen of the South 1 meant that we were consigned to the play-offs. Queen of the South went down automatically. For the final fixture the squad was supplemented by players from the Youth Academy. Losing 3-2 at Falkirk had no consequence.

The thought of playing Airdrie United in a play-off semi-final carried no dread. They had finished fourth in the Second Division and had only just scraped into the play-offs because Stenhousemuir had failed to beat Forfar Athletic on the last day. However the midweek away leg was a chastening experience even although it finished 0-0. The home team hit the post and crossbar as well as having a goal disallowed and a penalty saved by Kevin Cuthbert. Despite their misfortune it was expected that they would be picked off in the second leg on the Saturday. With seventeen minutes played, Jackson Longridge tackled Ricki Lamie who went down and remained on the ground. A red card was shown. This was a complete shock. Thereafter Lamie got booed whenever he was in possession. Unfortunately the numerical advantage was made to count. In stoppage time Jonathan Tiffoney was shown a red card but by then we were just seconds away from a 3-1 defeat. The resultant relegation was badly received. Brian Reid was in tune with the public mood and he quit on the Tuesday. He was immediately replaced by Mark Roberts with David White as his assistant.

Objectively it could have been argued that, as a part time club, the third tier was the rightful place. This was at odds with the public perception. Under Brian Reid the training nights were Monday and Wednesday. Mark Roberts changed it to Tuesday and Thursday nights. Before a ball was kicked he issued a statement of intent: "There's no reason why we can't win this league, so I can assure everyone we'll be trying to do it." It did not seem like an outrageous claim. We had a new manager who was young and enthusiastic as well as being possessed of a good work ethic. In a pre-season friendly Motherwell were beaten 4-0 at Ayr. Motherwell had finished third in the Premier League and were soon to be playing in the qualifying rounds for the Champions League. In a further friendly we had a 1-1 draw against Bolton Wanderers who had got relegated from the English Premiership in the previous season.

Would the early signs of promise translate to the pending competitive action? Not immediately! East Stirling 3 Ayr United 1 reinforced our recent history of getting knocked out of the Challenge Cup by Third Division opposition. What happened next was extraordinary. Ayr United 6 Clyde 1 was the result in the first round of the League Cup. It was 0-0 at half-time. With the league programme starting a week later the mood was reinvigorated. Stenhousemuir at home just had to be winnable. Yet it transpired that the team got booed off after a 1-1 draw. Stenhousemuir's equaliser was so deep into stoppage time that the re-centre coincided with the final whistle. For the fifth consecutive year we had started the league programme with a home match and none of them had been won. Neither of our previous four promotion winning campaigns had started with a win. By recourse to statistics it is often possible to put a positive spin on a bad situation. I am sure that political spin doctors work to this principle. Losing 4-2 at Arbroath could not have been excused even by the most tenuous statistics. Ayr United 2 Forfar Athletic 3 was the result in fixture three. The fatal goal was conceded one minute before the end of the ninety regulation minutes. Things were getting desperate.

For the fourth consecutive season we were drawn against St.Mirren in a cup competition. We had won at Paisley in the League Cup the year before but the chances of replicating that feat this time were negligible. The 5-1 trouncing surprised nobody. Anger was simmering and it was on the point of boiling over. Once more Stranraer was to set the scene for Ayr United supporters voicing angry passions. The home team contained six of our former players. Their 2-0 win did not fully represent their superiority. In the second half they struck the post and the crossbar. When Adam Hunter got sent off near the end it just put the lid on a horrible afternoon. We were now foot of the table with one point from four fixtures. The fans were enraged. In the trim confines of Stair Park the players, manager and directors would have heard the outbursts too clearly for their own good. That evening a banner was left on the wall near the main gate at Somerset Park. Emblazoned on it was the message NOT GOOD ENOUGH. The players saw it when the team bus arrived back at the ground.

Strong language was employed at Stair Park and a week later at Somerset Park it was equally indelicate during a 4-2 loss against Queen of the South. Why do people get so angry over football? No explanation will suffice for those who do not know. How long would the situation persist? In Scotland's third tier we had one point from the fifteen possible. On a Monday morning my work colleagues in Glasgow would ask how Ayr United got on at the weekend. It was no more than polite conversation on their part but sometimes I wish I could have been stricken by selective amnesia. True support of a club means sticking with it in good times as well as bad and there are many of us who will do that but that is not to say that loyalty will not be strained.

The elusive win arrived with an 88th minute clincher away to East Fife. This did not wholly convince the public as evidenced by a gate of 993 at Somerset Park a week later. After overlooking his team's 3-0 defeat Jim Weir was sacked from his manager's job at Brechin City. Winning a third consecutive game at least warded off some danger. In beating Albion Rovers 2-1 at Ayr it took two penalties, one of which was in the third and final minute of stoppage time.

A consequence of playing at this level was having to compete in the Scottish Cup at a ridiculously early date, 3rd November to be precise. The opposition club was Inverness Clachnacuddin who had played at Somerset Park just once before. They had lost a Scottish Cup tie 7-1 against the olden-day Ayr FC on 28th September, 1895. All of 117 years 36 days later their defeat here was eminently closer at 2-1. Four weeks later our Scottish Cup interest got terminated at Forfar. It was the first time the clubs had met in the competition. Whatever lay in store would not now be constrained by the distraction of cup football. The philosophy that 'we can now concentrate on the league' was wearisome.

I do not know who coined the phrase that 2-0 is the most dangerous score in football but it is an undoubted pearl of wisdom. In season 2012/13 Ayr United failed to win three league fixtures after attaining a 2-0 lead. Ayr United 2 East Fife 3 was the first of those. A win would have meant attaining third place. The actuality was eighth place after East Fife got an 89th minute winner. Afterwards Mark Roberts said: "Although I'm angry with the result there are plenty of positives to take from the game, particularly the way we created chances. I honestly think that the first forty-five minutes was about the best performance I've seen here for a long time. We could have scored ten goals and that's not an exaggeration." It definitely was an exaggeration to express that we could have scored ten in the first half.

Emboldened by Christmas cheer it was expected that we would win at Coatbridge on Boxing Day. How could we fail against Albion Rovers, the bottom club? By losing 2-0, that is how. At the end there was no evidence of any festive spirit. The verbal barrage was most unseasonal. As the teams left the pitch Mark Roberts got involved in an argument with a supporter. In his defence he said: "I know the fans are frustrated but I can guarantee I'm more frustrated than them. It's my livelihood that's on the line. If things don't improve it could be curtains for me. These guys will go on websites and forums and say what they like but I've got to come back, get these players on top of their game and get out of this position." He also mentioned that if any fans had grievances they should arrange to go in and talk to him. Being a discontented fan I did precisely that. We had a chat over a cup of tea in his office. He made no rash promises and it was clear that he was committed to resolving the unhappy state of affairs. On being questioned about then team's tendency to fall away from winning positions, he admitted that it was a mystery. I could understand that once the players crossed the white line his powers were limited.

It was a sign of the times that a 0-0 draw at home to Alloa Athletic was considered to be an improvement even although the visitors were second in the table. An equal sign of the times was the attendance of 927. Traditionally matches at the New Year drew larger than normal crowds. The next fixture was at home to league leaders Queen of the South on 2nd January, 2013. Yes, the crowd was larger but not by much. However with due allowance for the away support, the home support was lower than it had been for the Alloa match. The result was Ayr United 1 Queen of the South 5. It was our worst start to a year since losing 4-0 at Hamilton twenty-three years earlier. In the year of writing Ayr United have started a calendar year with a defeat by four or more goals on eleven occasions. This one in 2013 has been the only one at home. On taking stock we were eighth out of ten. Top-placed Queen of the South had twenty-nine points more. By the season's end they had fifty-one more.

The horrible start to the year might have induced panic about going to Stranraer for the next match. Stranraer were second bottom and we were separated from them by goal difference only. By a supreme effort a 1-0 half-time lead was preserved. During the second half the home team hit the crossbar, had a goal disallowed and a penalty claim denied. Showing early intent Stranraer twice had headers cleared off the line in the first four minutes. Yet the manner of victory was of little concern. We did not have the luxury of being discerning. Besides, the vocal displeasure was back in evidence when losing at Forfar the next week.

East Fife 3 Ayr United 3 : Alloa Athletic 2 Ayr United 2. Postponements at home created a run of four consecutive away matches. These were the third and fourth respectively and they had something in common. We had taken a 2-0 lead in each. When we went 2-0 up at Alloa I said "aw naw" to the people I was standing with. I was joking. Or so I thought! Amidst the drudgery were there any redeeming factors? There soon would be. Michael Moffat was on the brink of hitting some great form. In a 5-2 win at home to Albion Rovers he scored a hat-trick. The last Ayr United hat-trick at home had been scored by Glynn Hurst against Clydebank in March 2000. In a 4-1 win at Arbroath Moffat scored all four. The last Ayr United player to score at least four in a competitive match was Glynn Hurst away to Morton in January 2001. Either side of the Arbroath win were Tuesday fixtures in which we incurred home defeats against Stenhousemuir and Brechin City. Alarmingly the respective attendances were 821 and 631. In his time as Ayr United manager Mark Roberts had no midweek wins at all.

The curse of the 2-0 lead lingered when Stranraer were at Ayr. Just eleven minutes had been played. Midway through the second half it was trimmed back to 2-1. The fans were already conscious of the vulnerability of 2-0 so there was a general unease. In the closing minutes two extraordinary incidents occurred, both of which were unlike anything I have ever witnessed in all the years I have watched football. Ayr United got a free-kick to the side of the penalty area on the stand side at the Somerset Road end. Stranraer set out their stall to defend but confusion was caused because not one Ayr United player was in the box. Instead the ball was played back towards the touchline to run down the clock. Soon after we got a corner-kick at that same corner of the ground. Ordinarily defenders and attackers would be jockeying for position. The bemused referee had nothing to sort out and the defenders had no one to mark. There was the spectacle of a corner-kick with no attacking players in the penalty area. The ball was played short then recycled back in the direction of the corner arc in order to waste time. It was all quite legitimate and the 2-1 lead was preserved.

The end of the season just could not come quickly enough. A day trip to Belfast ensured that I was well out of the way when the team lost 4-0 away to Stenhousemuir. The Titanic Museum could have been symbolic of Ayr United sinking towards the depths. Central defender Darren Brownlie had now disappeared from the team after telling a newspaper that it was a mistake to sign for Ayr United. The 1-0 loss to Arbroath in the final home game could have been worse. Graeme Smith saved two penalties. Darren Brownlie was reinstated for this match. A week later he got sent off in a defeat at Forfar. It was our eighteenth consecutive game without a clean sheet. A painful season was over and the final placing was seventh.

In the summer of 2013 there was no talk about winning the Second Division in the forthcoming season. Wretched form was only part of it. The other problem was the very large elephant in the room, namely Rangers. A big club with a vast support had been newly promoted from the fourth tier. How this all came about was none of our business. It was a virtual certainty that they would romp through a league containing eight part time clubs. The certainty materialised. For nine clubs the biggest aspiration was reaching a play-off position. In a rebranding the league formerly known as the Second Division would now be called League One. It was an even more deceptive name for the third tier.

There was some early positivity when a club record was broken right at the start of the season. At Hampden an 89th minute goal from Alan Forrest was the winner against Queen's Park in the first round of the Ramsdens Challenge Cup. At the age of 16 years 321 days this made him the all-time youngest scorer of a competitive goal for Ayr United. After extra time we lost at home to Falkirk in the next round of this unloved competition.

Not since 2007 had we commenced the league programme with an away fixture but the broken trend in 2013 was not a handicap. On the contrary. Arbroath 0 Ayr United 3 was the club's biggest away win in an opening league fixture since 1921. An early exit from the League Cup (Partick Thistle 2 Ayr United 1) had occurred even before a ball had been kicked in league action. A further tentative step was taken in the league on beating Forfar Athletic 2-0 at Ayr. Progress was then stalled with four consecutive draws,

Tough fixtures at this level tend to be relative. However in 2013/14 formidable fixtures were real. Dunfermline Athletic 5 Ayr United 1 was a calamity that was unlikely to be followed by immediate redemption because the next game was against Rangers. We had the novelty of a match at this level being broadcast live on Sky. The crowd of 8,968 comprised a Somerset Park record for a Sunday game. Oddly enough all 9,900 tickets had been sold. Refereeing controversy, sectarian singing and a 2-0 defeat rendered it a depressing afternoon. A saving grace was that fourth position had been retained. This was the right side of the play-off cut. East Fife away was eminently more winnable and so it proved. At 4-1 it was the biggest winning margin by an Ayr United team at Methil although this would be surpassed within the season. One week later there was movement from fourth to third on winning 2-0 in the return fixture versus Arbroath. After the passage of a further week a 1-0 win at Airdrie caused a further upward trajectory to second. With Rangers still maintaining a 100% record this was as near to the pinnacle as we could get.

On the evening of 12th November, 2013, the Carmichael family was absent from Ayr United versus Stranraer. We were in the Lake District on holiday and were part of the 162 attendance at Kendal Town versus Chorley in the Doodson

Sport Cup. The home team played in black and white so our Ayr United scarves blended in beautifully. A friend had arranged to send goal texts from Somerset Park. They came through with unexpected frequency and they brought equally unexpected despair. The final horror was Ayr United 3 Stranraer 6. In front of us Chorley beat Kendal Town 3-1 but these texts had us watching on in a virtual trance.

One of the most simplistic expressions in football is the saying that 'it's all about goals'. In the Scottish vernacular veteran fans would even say 'nae goals, nae fitbaw'. It is a premise I have not always agreed with. Matches with no goals can generate excitement because the outcome is in doubt until the end. In November 2013 though it would have been a futile argument for Somerset Park regulars. Ten days after the Stranraer match we had Ayr United 4 Stenhousemuir 3. This meant moving into third place while Stenhousemuir dropped from third to fifth. Stranraer were fourth.

It is disappointing when the Scottish Cup draw throws up a pairing with a club from the same league. The disappointment intensifies when the tie is scheduled close to a time when the clubs are due to meet in a league fixture, In the space of a fortnight we had Ayr United 1 Dunfermline Athletic 1 (Scottish Cup), Dunfermline Athletic 1 Ayr United 0 (Scottish Cup replay) and Ayr United 2 Dunfermline Athletic 4 (League One). In the latter match the curse of the 2-0 lead inflicted itself once more. Brian Gilmour scored the opening goal from several yards inside his own half. It was one of those incidents which leaves you wondering whether it really happened.

On the Saturday between the Dunfermline cup ties we had a match at Ibrox. The crowd of 45,227 was the second biggest in Britain that day. It was eclipsed only by Manchester United versus Newcastle United. The Ayr United ticket allocation of 950 was sold out. Our fans were very vocal, much to the annoyance of the overwhelmingly large Rangers support. Choruses of "You're not Rangers any more" got persistently repeated because of the effect it was having. The big crowd had the illusion of being consistent with an international match.

It was so surreal for Scotland's third tier. Prior to the fixture some of our fans expressed a wish that Gordon Pope would score in order to see the name 'Pope' on the Ibrox scoreboard. Unfortunately it had Rangers 3 Ayr United 0 emblazoned on it at the end.

Football will never lose its propensity for being misreported. Yet there are times when reporters have a good reason for getting things wrong. On the last Saturday before Christmas a 90th minute substitution was made at Forfar while running down the clock on a 1-0 lead. Mark Shankland went on for Michael Moffat but some reports said that the player who went on was Jackson Longridge. On the team lines Shankland was number twelve and Longridge was number eighteen. Shankland went on with number twelve on his shorts and number eighteen on his shirt.

My liking for statistics can sometimes draw criticism because a negative fact can be perceived as having a dig at the team. Yet at Stranraer on 4th January, 2014, you would have found no one deluded enough to proffer any redeeming feature. Stranraer 4 Ayr United 0 was the club's second largest defeat against Stranraer ever (I could still remember the 7-2 on Easter weekend 1963). This was the eleventh time that Ayr United had started a calendar year with a defeat by four or more goals but 2013 and 2014 was the first instance of it happening in consecutive years. Yet again Stair Park set the scene for angry outbursts. Mark Roberts said: "You've got to be thick-skinned as a manager but I find it very disappointing that some of our support, who are the most knee-jerk by a mile, want me out." It went to 4-0 just four minutes into the second half.

With home gates hovering around the 1,000 mark there was a clear display of public apathy. It was a state of affairs compounded by the remaining attendees harbouring resentment strong enough to manifest itself in verbal hostility. In diminishing crowds such oratory can be even more potent. A lone voice in a 60,000 crowd will not be heard but in a crowd of 1,000 it will be heard to thunderous effect. This should not imply that only a minority were unhappy. Even the 'it used to be worse' argument was close to being redundant. It took an effort of memory to recall a time when it truly was worse.

Ayr United 3 Airdrie 0 was the response to the shambles at Stranraer. Was this the start of a revival? A week down the line the answer was Ayr United 1 Brechin City 3. Throughout these turbulent times a play-off position remained within reach. A 3-2 win at Arbroath even meant stepping up into third place. Arbroath is a trip beloved of Ayr United supporters. The nearby Tuttie's Neuk has a welcoming ambience and the various fish restaurants in the town are superb. I also like to bask in reflection of childhood holidays there in the summers of 1958 and 1959. However the wind is liable to spoil the spectacle of watching football there. After the match on 1st February, 2014, Ayr goalkeeper David Hutton said: "It was without doubt the worst conditions I've ever had to play in." With the North Sea as a next door neighbour, the waves battered against the ground wall, some even making their way onto the terraces. At 3-0 up within half an hour, it was far from won. Unsurprisingly Arbroath scored twice in the second half and it was necessary to hold out frantically against both the Arbroath attack and the wind. The goal that trimmed it back to 3-2 was extraordinary. A cross from Bobby Linn was suspended in the air. It was starting to look as if the law of gravity would have to be rewritten. With all eyes looking skyward the ball eventually did find its way back to Mother Earth whereupon Leighton McIntosh drove it into the net.

The 'coming back down to earth' theme will now be maintained. Ayr United proceeded to come back down to earth, albeit metaphorically, with a run of four consecutive defeats. These were Rangers at home (excusable), Dunfermline Athletic away (excusable), Airdrie away (inexcusable) and Forfar Athletic at home (highly inexcusable). What happened next defied all expectations (with due allowance for expectations being low). The only historical precedent for Ayr United having consecutive 5-0 wins dated back to February 1979. For it to happen in March 2014 was nothing short of magical. Yes, magical! Was some form of wizardry afoot? Ayr United 5 Stranraer 0 preceded East Fife 0 Ayr United 5. Before these matches we had a goal difference deficit of ten. From one week to the next the deficit was cleared. It was our biggest ever away win over East Fife, eclipsing the 4-1 previous best which had occurred in the same season.

"It's the worst I have felt after a game in a long time." Why did Mark Roberts have a sudden mood swing? Ayr United 2 Stenhousemuir 3 was bad enough but the manner in which the game was lost increased the angst. Stenhousemuir had equalised in the 87th minute then got the winner in stoppage time. Blips can happen but time would prove this not to be a blip. It was the first in a run of five matches in which one point was taken. One point in total lest there be any ambiguity! The three away defeats in that run were at Brechin, Ibrox and Forfar. Respectively the attendances were 507, 40,561 and 532. The imbalance created by Rangers was unnatural. In losing 2-1 at Ibrox the scorer was Alan Forrest who was still a schoolboy. It was his fourth goal in consecutive games.

The final fixture was crucial. In order to finish fourth and secure the last play-off place nothing less than a win was enough. Ayr United 4 East Fife 1 was the happy outcome although it could not disguise that these were problematic times. Seven home league defeats replicated a statistic from the year before despite playing at this level. In the season ahead it would be even worse. The notion of Fortress Somerset was long forgotten.

In losing 2-1 at home to Cowdenbeath the result was highly flattering. To progress in the play-offs a drastic transformation would be required in the second leg. It did not materialise. At Central Park a goal was conceded after nine seconds. This created another of those unwanted club records. No Ayr United team in history had conceded an earlier goal. Hitherto the earliest had been scored after ten seconds by Aberdeen's George Mulhall at Ayr in 1956. To the optimists of 2014 the early strike availed itself of ample time for a comeback. It ended 3-1 on the day and 5-2 on aggregate. Yet again wrath was expressed. Regardless Mark Roberts had his contract extended for a further year.

Lachlan Cameron, in his capacity as chairman, said: "He succeeded in achieving the desired play-off position and, although there were definitely results that were horrendous along the way, he reached the target laid out for him. There is a section of our support who may not agree that keeping Mark on for next year is acceptable but, as far as I am concerned, he reached the target and deserves the chance to improve on that."

Losing Michael Moffat to Dunfermline Athletic was hard to accept. Dunfermline had lost to Cowdenbeath in the play-off final so he was not even stepping up a league. Lachlan Cameron shared the disappointment: "It baffles me how a club that, a year ago, was on the brink of extinction with no assets and debts far outweighing any reasonable chance of getting out of, can offer such a rewarding package for any single player."

Losing 2-0 away to Clyde in the first round of the Petrofac Training Cup maintained the tradition of elimination by fourth-tier opposition. Ordinarily it may have been quietly forgotten about but much publicity was accorded to the fact that it was Barry Ferguson's first game as a manager. In the ensuing weeks the gloom lifted. The first three league games were won for the first time since 1991/92. It has to be admitted that in 1991/92 we were playing at a higher level and the run extended to four but here in 2014 we were glad to cling to anything that had an inkling of being positive.

Having swatted aside East Stirling in the first round of the League Cup (0-4) there was great anticipation about playing at Kilmarnock in the next round. It was the first Ayrshire derby played on an artificial surface. The team responded to the outstanding vocal backing. In sustaining a 1-0 defeat neither the performance nor the effort could be faulted. Mark Roberts won the League One SPFL Manager of the Month award for August. News of this had a mixed reception because of a commonly held belief that such awards are tainted by a curse. This virtual assumption is based on perception rather than research. Nonetheless the first match after the award was Ayr United 0 Stranraer 2. The perception was reinforced. More practically we were off the top of the league for the first time this season. The margin was goal difference only and top place was quickly reclaimed with a 4-2 win at Brechin. A conspicuous name on the team sheet at this time was Craig Beattie who had a very recent history of playing at a high level. He was a Scottish internationalist who had played in the English Premiership. As lately as 2012 he had played for Hearts in their Scottish Cup winning team. Was he over the hill? Was he still capable of scoring goals? The obvious questions were asked. He was aged thirty but he was still willing to play for part time Ayr United in League One. In the Brechin win he scored twice but this achievement in front of 537 fans was a considerable distance from being a career highlight.

Ayr United 2 Airdrie 3 was sickeningly reminiscent of Stenhousemuir's visit in March. On that day we had blown a 2-1 lead by conceding in the 87th minute then again in stoppage time. Precisely the same thing had happened again. The consequence was a drop from first to third. Forfar Athletic now topped the table with Dunfermline Athletic in second place.

Morton 0 Ayr United 1 occurred on 18th October. We were destined not to win another match until 14th February. The descent started with Brechin City winning 2-0 at Ayr which meant that four consecutive home league games had been lost. This remains the club record worst in the third tier. In 2009/10 there were five consecutive home league defeats in the second tier and in 1966/67 we had seven consecutive home league defeats in the top tier. Despite the level we were playing at the 1966/67 statistic came very close to being equalled. In a 2-2 draw at home to Stirling Albion Craig Beattie equalised in the 90th minute to prevent seven consecutive home league defeats. However number five (2-3 versus Peterhead) got declared void due to a registration offence. The Scottish Cup involvement was similarly bleak. A 4-0 replay defeat at Alloa was the club's heaviest defeat in the competition since the 2000 semi-final. The *Ayrshire Post* ran a triple headline: NO DESIRE NO PRIDE NO BOTTLE.

Ayr United 2 Stenhousemuir 3 (for the second time in 2014) sparked the outrage that had become well versed. The attendance figure of 646 gave further cause for alarm. Second bottom was the position now occupied. After the match Mark Roberts was in the dressing room for seventy minutes. This now made it one win in the last eleven games, this figure excluding the voided defeat against Peterhead. Mark Roberts had his contract terminated on the Monday.

New Year is the time when we apply the concept of 'out with the old, in with the new'. For Ayr United it was 'out with the old, in with the old'. We signed off 2014 with a 3-0 defeat at Airdrie and signed into 2015 with a 2-0 defeat at home to Stranraer. After that New Year match Stranraer were top of League One and Ayr United were second bottom. Was there any shred of hope at all? Yes there was. The Stranraer match was on a Saturday and even before a ball was kicked it was known that a new manager had been appointed but the name would not be revealed until the Monday. There was little apprehension because the media had already named Billy Stark as the successful applicant. The bookmakers even declared it as a closed book. On the Monday there would be confirmation that Stark was the new incumbent. The announcement duly came. It was Ian McCall. All the supposed insider information was wrong. On being appointed he said: "One of the things I remember as a player and a manager coming to Somerset Park is that it was such a difficult place to come and get a result. The fans behind the home goal made a huge effect on the Ayr players and we need to try and get that back."

It was a popular appointment and he was quick to arrange a public meeting with the fans. One of his predecessors, Neil Watt, had similarly conducted a fan engagement event. Ian McCall answered his questions in a manner that was devoid of rhetoric and heavy on substance. The event took place after the first match had been played under his reign. It was a 2-1 loss at Brechin and he expressed that he would ideally have liked a less formidable start than Brechin City away. It was a fair point. Glebe Park being a difficult venue bore testament to Ayr United's status in 2015.

We soon had signs that the rot, if not quite stopped, was receding. At least there was a definitive aim which was quite simply to avoid a relegation play-off then put our trust in Ian McCall to build solid foundations in the summer. However the expression 'quite simply' maybe comes across as an underestimation of the task in hand. It was wise not to get too carried away with outlandish illusions. Even a 4-1 win at Stirling had to be tempered with caution because the opposition were at the foot of the league.

On 28th February the first home win was achieved since 23rd August. The start and the end of the run were both marked by victories over Forfar Athletic. This was considered to be the spark that would reignite the season. It did not work out that way. The remainder of the season was incompatible with such a positive metaphor. After the Forfar win we had a run of nine winless matches comprising six defeats and three draws. For the penultimate fixture the adult entry price was reduced from £15 to £5. The crowd figure of 1,608 was about 600 more than would normally have been expected. Happily a 4-0 win over Stirling Albion rendered it even better value.

The final Saturday was approached with a sense of worry. Stirling Albion were already confirmed for relegation. Still at stake though was which club would require to compete in a play-off. Stenhousemuir were second bottom but we had just two points more. The pertinent fixtures were Forfar Athletic versus Ayr United and Stirling Albion versus Stenhousemuir. Forfar were tied with Morton at the top of the league but had an inferior goal difference. To win the league they had to better Morton's result at home to Peterhead. Being pitched away from home against a team high in incentive was a contrasting situation to Stenhousemuir facing a team already doomed to the drop. With seven minutes played Forfar took the lead with a penalty. Six minutes later Peterhead took the lead at Cappielow so here at Station Park we were up against a team who had a three-point lead at the top. More importantly Stenhousemuir had taken the lead at Stirling. The situation was chronic. It was the final game and we were in the bottom two. With enormous relief we kicked on to win 3-1. Morton beat Peterhead 3-1 so Forfar Athletic would not have won the league anyway. Stenhousemuir contrived to lose 3-2 after conceding goals timed at 89 and 90 so we would have been safe regardless.

There were celebrations after the final whistle at Forfar with the fans singing choruses of "We are staying up, we are staying up." At the time it did seem cause for celebration but from the perspective of the present day it can only be considered mockingly. The cause of delight was the avoidance of a play-off carrying the potential to land in the fourth tier.

In seasons 2012/13, 2013/14 and 2014/15 we had suffered an aggregate of twenty-three league defeats at Somerset Park. It was rendered shocking by the fact that this was third-tier football. This figure takes no cognisance of a play-off defeat against Cowdenbeath nor the voided defeat against Peterhead.

15. The Revival

You may be familiar with the Four Yorkshiremen sketch which was played out by the Monty Python team. The premise of the sketch was simple. Four men were sitting chatting about how poor they were in their childhood, each trumping the other with tales of grinding poverty. In comparative terms Ian McCall was in a position of luxury. He had managed both Clydebank and Airdrie when these clubs were on the brink of being tipped over the edge. It was not edifying to view Ayr United's position in Scottish football's hierarchy but we had a manager who had experienced challenging situations. In the nature of a mission statement he said: "I have a clear picture of what we need. We have a lot of good footballers but require a different type of player. I want to play a brand of football that the fans will love and would urge them to go out and buy their season tickets." This was more than a sales pitch for season tickets. Ian McCall was the type of character who, when he spoke, was to be believed.

Despite such sincerity the opening league fixture was a disaster. The team was 1-0 down inside the second minute and the final damage was Albion Rovers 3 Ayr United 0. We filed out of the ground under a cloud of depression. There is a contradictory expression about expecting the unexpected. The unexpected happened by proceeding to embark on a run of fourteen league games unbeaten. None of us who were present at the Albion Rovers debacle could have foreseen this. Getting detached from cup involvement in August may have helped. It was Ayr United 0 Rangers 2 in the Petrofac Training Cup and Ross County 2 Ayr United 0 in the League Cup. With Rangers in the Championship and Ross County in the Premier League the opposition would be less daunting in League One.

Ayr United 5 Stenhousemuir 2 had more relevance than the obvious pleasure of victory. The date was 1st September, 2015, and it was the club's first midweek win since a 2-1 league victory at Livingston on 6th March, 2012. A 3-3 draw at home to Peterhead on 3rd March, 2015, ended a run of thirteen consecutive midweek defeats. Even then it had taken an 88th minute equaliser in a reprieve match. Up until this win over Stenhousemuir the club endured a sequence of twenty midweek matches comprising eighteen defeats, a draw at Airdrie in a play-off and the draw with Peterhead referred to. In compiling these figures I ignored midweek matches with an afternoon kick-off (technically holiday matches and all lost within this timeframe). It was a malaise affecting evening matches in general. During this phase we had one Friday evening game. It comprised a defeat against Dunfermline Athletic but has not been included in these 'midweek' statistics. The Stenhousemuir result was the first midweek win at home since a 2-1 Scottish Cup victory over Falkirk on 15th February, 2012, and the first midweek league win at home since beating Partick Thistle 1-0 on 10th March, 2010. It was only by a quirk of luck that the midweek misery did not stretch even longer. The Stenhousemuir fixture was scheduled for Saturday 5th September, only to be rescheduled due to an air show locally.

On resuming the relative comfort of weekend football, wins at Dunfermline (0-2) and Airdrie (1-2) on consecutive Saturdays meant going one point clear at the top. There was a growing belief that the league could be won. This was reinforced when Cowdenbeath were slain 5-0 at Ayr. However the feelgood factor that had been building in October 2015 was shattered with the news that Peter Price had passed away at the age of eighty-three. He remains the greatest Ayr United player of all time. This claim is not open to debate. Moreover I had the privilege of being able to count him as a friend. On the day after his death we had an away game against Stenhousemuir. The supporters had a plan to commemorate Peter Price's shirt number by singing "There's only one Peter Price" in the ninth minute. This was duly carried out and by a happy coincidence Ross Caldwell scored right then. The 1-0 lead was preserved. If Greg Fleming had not saved a second half penalty the result would have had a familiar look. Five of our last six matches away to Stenhousemuir had finished 1-1 including the previous four.

Ayr United 3 Stranraer 1 took the points total to twenty-seven. The date was 31st October. In the previous season it had taken until 14th March to reach that amount. This latest win also took the team to the top of the league with a one-point gap. Three weeks later a 3-0 win at home to Airdrie meant that the 2014/15 complete total had been reached. For now the lead at the top had been extended to three points. To call these good times would allude to past glories. More accurately these were improving times.

In 2013 we had bemoaned playing Dunfermline Athletic in the Scottish Cup because it was in close proximity to meeting them in a league fixture. It happened again in 2015. Consecutive games at home to Dunfermline resulted 0-1 (Scottish Cup) and 1-2 (League One). The latter match was the more damaging of the two. In losing this six-pointer we were now three points off the top with a game in hand. The disappointment was tempered by a belief that it was forgiveable since the team had gone fourteen consecutive games unbeaten in the league. When this was followed up with a 3-0 loss at Peterhead there was no such silver lining. Well not immediately anyway. On the Tuesday Ryan Stevenson was fixed up on a 28-day loan from Partick Thistle. On hearing the news the fans trotted out all manner of superlatives. Here was a player who meant it when he kissed the badge. Beyond doubt he was glad to be back. He said: "If you support Barcelona you want to play for them and with me it's no different with Ayr." On the expiry of his loan Partick Thistle released him whereupon he agreed to stay at Ayr until the end of the season.

His Boxing Day return marked a narrow home win over Brechin City but we departed 2015 with a 4-2 defeat at Cowdenbeath then began 2016 by losing 1-0 at Stranraer. Second place was still occupied but Dunfermline Athletic were nine points ahead. It was significant that the Stranraer fixture marked four league defeats out of the last five. Regaining lost ground was frustrated by a series of postponements. Albion Rovers 1 Ayr United 3 was our only other match in January.

When Peterhead won 2-1 at Somerset Park I became acutely conscious that this was a club with a startling record at Ayr so I started to delve into some minutiae. Including the voided game our home league record against Peterhead now read: Played 15 Won 1 Drawn 7 Lost 7. One win in fifteen! In thirty-nine home league games against Celtic there were eight Ayr wins which was marginally better than one in five. In forty-one home league games against Rangers we had eight wins which was a ratio of marginally less than one in five. Statistically, therefore, our chances of beating Celtic or Rangers at home were three times higher than beating Peterhead at home.

In compiling statistics it is essential to have an obsession with accuracy. A particular anathema is estimated attendances. In February 2016 the attendance for our fixture at Airdrie was given as 1,000. Yet the Ayr support was stated as 332 which was very precise. That was the first clue that what had the illusion of being an estimated attendance was indeed the actual attendance. It was. The pedantry on this topic will be prolonged a little more. I went through the turnstiles six minutes after the game started and, since there were no other fans in sight outside the ground, I claimed responsibility for the crowd figure being this round number! Aside from such frivolous detail Ayr United won 1-0.

A referee getting booed off at half-time at Somerset Park is a run-of-the-mill occurrence. On this particular night the circumstances differed from the normal in these situations. The score at the time was Ayr United 3 Cowdenbeath 0. Ultimately it was 4-1. The Saturday action resumed with a 1-0 loss at Brechin. It was an especially bad result in the context of it occurring against the bottom club. In a fit of depression I looked for any kind of consolation in the statistics. This exercise proved to be positive. Brechin City 1 Ayr United 0 had only occurred three times in our history. The dates were 3rd

March, 1956 (promotion season), 18th April, 2009 (promotion season) and 7th May, 2011 (promotion season). It was a good omen.

Title hopes soon had to be abandoned. Beating Dunfermline Athletic at home would have meant being within eight points of them. On that basis the 0-2 result transformed a thin hope into no hope. The run-in started to cause concern with defeats at Forfar and Cowdenbeath as well as at home to Albion Rovers. Form was then regained with 4-0 wins away to both Stenhousemuir and Peterhead. In the certain knowledge that we would soon be facing Peterhead in the play-offs this bode well.

The final match was a virtual dead rubber. Even a 3-0 defeat at home to Airdrie did not prevent a second-place finish. The play-offs were looming. Ten days after a comprehensive win there we were back at Peterhead. At 4-1 it was another comprehensive win. After the second leg it was 6-2 on aggregate. It had been expected that Livingston would be our opponents in the play-off final. Most of us had underestimated Stranraer who had won through in the other semi-final. On a Wednesday evening we decanted down the coast for the first leg. It proved tougher than anticipated. At 1-0 down it was indicated that there would be a minimum of four additional minutes. After the four minutes had expired and most of us having drifted towards the exit, Ross Docherty scored his first senior goal. The goal came in time added on to the added time. Right at the death it was 1-1. It had been torrid with nine yellow cards (six Ayr, three Stranraer). Promotion now hinged on whether Stranraer could be beaten on the Sunday. With the overwhelming bulk of the 4,581 crowd in our favour there was an early sense of unease when the balance of play indicated that losing was a possibility. It proceeded scoreless into extra time and this was still the state of play after 120 minutes. Greg Fleming saved three in the shootout and amidst great celebration we had escaped from the Seaside League. In the history of Ayr United this was our seventh Somerset Park shootout, six of which had now been won. On emerging from the ground I noticed a man with two boys, both of whom were wearing Stranraer colours. They looked as if they were aged about ten and seven. The smaller one was crying. It was difficult not to feel a pang of sympathy. The scene spoke of genuine loyalty to a club rather than the more distant affiliation that people show towards Scotland's big two.

Ian McCall was named as the League One Manager of the Year whereupon he agreed a contract for the next two seasons. For season 2016/17 anything better than survival would be satisfactory. There was a realism that the Championship would be challenging but that did not prevent a range of differing predictions. We had a faction saying "they'll come straight back down" and a faction who entertained hopes of achieving consolidation. When people said that the Championship was a tough league they were not saying so for the sake of saying it. Earlier in 2016 the Scottish Cup final had been contested between two Championship clubs, Hibs and Rangers. My two brothers were at Hampden when Hibs lifted the trophy. On the next day I was on the pavement outside the Hing Sing Chinese Supermarket in Leith Walk when the Hibs open-topped bus came past. Notwithstanding Hibs being the Scottish Cup holders, we would have them for company in the season ahead.

The League Cup had traditionally been an attractive draw to a public who had been starved of football during the summer. In 2016 the sectional system was reverted to but it did not appeal in the time-served manner. Season tickets had been valid for all home matches in days of old but they were now excluded for cup matches. Rather than ruminate further on the reasons for it, Hamilton Accies, of the Premier League, opened the season in front of a sparse Somerset Park attendance of 994. It was a 2-1 win. On the conclusion of the group Hamilton Accies, Ayr United and St.Mirren all had nine points, the odd club out being Edinburgh City. Hamilton progressed as winners on goal difference and by the same means we edged out St.Mirren to go through as one of the best four runners-up. Ayr United 1 Aberdeen 2 was the result in the clunkily named round of sixteen.

The early season promise shown in the League Cup could not mask the fact that the principal focus was on the league. We were now competing in a more testing sphere and the team's capability of coping would soon be put to the test. There were the usual utterances about the importance of getting off to a flyer. It did not materialise in this way. Ayr United 0 Raith Rovers 2 caused a revulsion of refereeing standards but the complaints, though justified, would not erase the result. The prospect of getting early points on the board was not enhanced by fixture two being away to Queen of the South. Our record at Palmerston in recent history was awful. Yet Queen of the South away is a fixture which the Carmichaels looked forward to because we loved the Moore's Chippy in Castle Douglas. Win, lose or draw it was well worth the detour afterwards. Both inevitabilities manifested themselves. The team lost 4-1 and the chippy was excellent. When it comes to football I like to be objective but overwhelming partisanship towards Ayr United is liable to be a barrier to objectivity. Club bias apart I recognise that devotees of other clubs are the same as myself but their devotion, albeit similar, is just for a different club. After this particular match at Palmerston an elderly Queen of the South supporter approached me in the car park and said: "What are your views on the game from an Ayr United perspective?" He was polite, articulate and altogether had the aura of a retired head teacher. After offloading my analysis in minute detail he probably regretted asking. He then said: "We have Falkirk here next Saturday. That will be a better yardstick for where we are at." I considered this to be particularly wounding. The implication was that beating Falkirk would be an achievement but a 4-1 win over Ayr United was neither here nor there. We were not rated. In supporting Ayr United I have never had an inferiority complex. Even in adversity I have adopted a mindset that our day will come.

There was a growing anxiety about when our first points would be registered. The idea of going to Tannadice did nothing to alleviate that anxiety and, surely enough, we were beaten 3-0 by Dundee United. Having played three and lost three there was considerable moaning about refereeing standards. Consistent complaints about referees can induce accusations of paranoia. Yet in our heart of hearts we all really know that they are not out to get us. It just seems like it.

We had a cult hero in Jamie Adams. He was possessed of the one quality required to attain such status. That quality was toughness. Against St.Mirren he scored a headed goal at the Somerset Road end and the 1-0 lead remained intact until the 89th minute. At 1-1 it was a major frustration to concede late. With the clock edging towards quarter to five we were eighth in the league. Minutes later we were tenth. Foot of the league! Would the black clouds drift away? Crowd figures are always a reasonable indicator of how the public perceive Ayr United. With just 1,441 in the ground for the visit of Morton we had evidence that the team was not well rated. Winning 2-1 had a vastly invigorating effect. At last we could dare to look at the league table. On the strength of this one fixture there was movement from tenth to seventh. Yet there was a fear lurking in the background because the next match was against Hibs at Easter Road. A suitable analogy would be youngsters playing football and one of the kids is conspicuously bigger than the others. The crowd at Easter Road was 15,056 which was disproportionately large for this league. Admittedly Rangers had commanded triple this in the lower leagues but we probably all knew that they were passing through and would not return. There are times when we should have more faith in the team. The result was Hibs 1 Ayr United 2. Ian McCall said: "We were very disciplined defensively and scored a couple of good goals." He was being modest. The winning goal came from a move in which the ball was played the entire length of the pitch without a Hibs player touching it. Brian Gilmour applied the finish. We were now sixth. Before the match Hibs had a 100% league record. The top club was now Queen of the South.

A good run of form caused the fear of relegation to recede a little. After a 1-0 home win against Queen of the South in October I did an analysis of the last six league games in terms of how we compared with our fellow Championship clubs in that time. We had taken eleven more points than Dumbarton and St.Mirren, nine more than Dunfermline Athletic, six more than Raith Rovers, five more than Queen of the South and four more than both Hibs and Morton. Over that period we had taken the same number of points as Dundee United and Falkirk.

Morton 2 Ayr United 1 deserved to be placed into context. Up until that match we had lost one in the previous nine (seven league, two Irn Bru Cup). When Morton equalised in the 73rd minute it broke Greg Fleming's run of 463 minutes without losing a goal. The Irn Bru Cup was the most recent reincarnation of the oft-renamed competition popularly known as the Challenge Cup. After beating Airdrie then Falkirk at Ayr an exit was made away to St.Mirren. This elimination was met with the habitual indifference reserved for this competition.

Greg Fleming remains Ayr United's most prolific penalty saver of all time. In a 1-1 draw at Dunfermline he saved a penalty in the 83rd minute. Less than ninety seconds later Dunfermline got another penalty. He saved that too. To this point of the season he had faced five penalties and he had saved them all. This was far from the end of his penalty saving heroics. Statistically we were in more danger of conceding a goal from a corner than a penalty. Every league point accumulated was considered to be a buffer against the threat of relegation. There were no delusions. It is true that there was an ambition to become established at Championship level in the course of time. In the immediate term survival would be considered a success. A 1-1 draw away to St.Mirren had the effect of dropping to ninth thereby putting survival in the balance.

Christmas Eve in 2016 was a very windy day in the west of Scotland. Ayr United versus Dumbarton had the illusion of being played with a beach ball. The vagaries of the gale caused corner-kicks to have the potential to be lethal. On taking a 2-0 lead two minutes before half-time there was still uncertainty about how the game would pan out. The virtual inevitability of a goal being scored directly from a corner-kick manifested itself in the 84th minute. From being 3-2 up it was now 3-3. A minute later we took a 4-3 lead but an 88th minute corner for Dumbarton induced panic. Predictably, when the ball came over, it looked in danger of curling straight into the net. However Ryan Stevenson was there to make it 4-4 with a header from point blank range. Yes, Ryan Stevenson. Conscious of his passion for Ayr United I once mentioned this goal to him when conducting an interview for a Football Memories event. He admitted that after he scored it he thought to himself "What have I done?"

On the last Saturday of the year a scoreless draw away to Queen of the South made it five draws from the last six league matches. Draws were not so crucial in the bygone days of two points for a win. The change to three points for a win was primarily to incentivise attacking football. To that end it could be argued that, to a degree, it was a successful initiative. Yet a further consequence was that four-pointers got transformed into six-pointers. This heaped yet more pressure on teams battling relegation. Simply not losing was not necessarily going to guarantee safety.

Ayr United started 2017 with a defeat (0-2 versus Dunfermline Athletic). The years 2012, 2013, 2014, 2015 and 2016 also started with a defeat. It was a cheerless six-in-a-row. It was the second worst such run in our history, eclipsed by the eight in 1929, 1930, 1931, 1932, 1933, 1934, 1935 and 1936. A week after the Dunfermline match we had a 1-1 draw at Falkirk in which Greg Fleming saved a penalty. Thus far in 2016/17 Ayr United had conceded seven penalties and Fleming had saved six. The one he did not save had been driven wide by St. Mirren's Lawrence Shankland. On saving the one at Falkirk he pushed the ball out for a corner from which a goal was conceded when it came over. It was a further endorsement of the statistic that we were more in danger of conceding from a corner-kick than a penalty kick. Ridiculous though it sounded, there were statistics which proved the claim. Next up a 0-0 draw at home to Queen's Park in the Scottish Cup was disappointing but confidence was high after the replay was level at 2-2 after extra time. Greg Fleming saved two in the shootout and we progressed.

A threat to the club's heritage had started to play out. The ancient court of the Lord Lyon had accused Ayr United of having a badge which contravened the Lyon King of Arms Act of 1672. When the story broke it was greeted with hilarity. It had the resonance of an Ealing comedy. A sequel to Passport to Pimlico? The capacity for humour was tireless. Online comments sarcastically spoke about ending up in the stocks or being chained up in a dungeon. Oscar Wilde famously said that sarcasm is the lowest form of wit. On this point I disagree with the esteemed Mr Wilde. In Scotland sarcasm is an art form and the Ayr United badge issue saw it practised with glee and abandon. Very quickly it ceased to be funny. The threat to the badge was serious. At issue was the saltire inside a shield. This was deemed to be an infringement of the law of arms. It was ironic that people who had a responsibility for protecting heritage were trying to destroy an integral part of Ayr United's heritage. Petitions were futile. They were simply ignored. I indulged in correspondence and telephone calls with the procurator fiscal dealing with this case. It was a waste of time and effort. I even wrote to the Lord Lyon (not Lord Lyon but *the* Lord Lyon!). The reply left no scope for ambiguity. Eventually I got another of those 'the directors need to speak to you' requests. This occurred because the club had asked the public to come up with a new badge design and I was going online urging people to take no part in this initiative. It transpired that the directors were equally devoted to retaining the club badge. However the club was not being asked to comply with a request. It was made clear to Ayr United that there was no scope for negotiation. Protestations were quickly closed down. It was necessary to accede. From the following season there would be a new badge. I have tried as far as possible to remain loyal to the old badge. Many items in my wardrobe are in breach of the legislation drawn up in 1672. I live in constant fear of suffering a punishment devised in those primitive times!

Meanwhile, in the world of 2017, Ayr United's form was difficult to make sense of. A 1-1 draw away to Hibs came a week after losing 4-1 at home to Morton. Hibs would kick on to win the league by an eleven-point margin yet we managed a win and a draw at Easter Road. The concept of home advantage was turned on its head because the home games against Hibs resulted 0-3 and 0-4.

The Scottish Cup became a distraction and it was just as tortuous as the Queen's Park tie. Against Clyde a 2-1 replay win was achieved at Broadwood Stadium. The winner came three minutes from the end of extra time. This cup form was unconvincing but it was essential to regroup for the trip to Dumbarton on the Saturday. The date was 18th February but the team had not won a league game since October. On the bright side we had not lost an away league game since October. These statistics, although accurate, seemed to be a contradiction. We entered the game four points behind Dumbarton with a game in hand. At the very least it was important not to lose. With just less than half an hour played Ross Docherty got sent off. The home team heavily dominated possession and they scored twice (62 minutes and 75 minutes). Even at 2-0 the score was flattering. There was every indication that the damage would get worse. By the closing minutes our support was deserting the place in their droves. The stairs were choked with fans queuing to get out. They had seen enough. Occasionally I will travel to an away game with a bus pass but this is only when no other family members are going. Due to the bus times I did not join the queues to leave because I would have had too much time on my hands. Then, in a rare attack, Michael Rose scored with a free-kick (90+1). It hardly seemed to matter. I expected the final whistle to be blown immediately after the recentre. Yet there was still time to regain possession and launch one more hopeful attack. Quite sensationally Jamie Adams was brought down for a penalty which Craig Moore converted (90+3). It was 2-2 and this time the final whistle did get blown just seconds after the recentre. The minority of us who had stayed back were in raptures. Many only learned of the sensational finale after putting on their car radio.

St.Mirren were the bottom club. Victory over them at Ayr would have meant being eleven points ahead of them. It can be a natural tendency to get ahead of yourself and again it proved to be an impulsive thought. After losing 2-0 Ian McCall said: "We didn't deserve anything from the game."

Three days later we were launched into yet another six-pointer, this time at home to Raith Rovers. The SPFL had refused Raith's application for a postponement. They had claimed that they had no match fit goalkeepers. In consequence they played the entire ninety minutes with a midfielder in goal. This was no ordinary midfielder. It was our old friend Ryan Stevenson. His goalkeeping style was unconventional but effective. He kept a clean goal until the 62nd minute when Alan Forrest crossed for Farid El Alagui to score with a header at the back post. It was the only goal of the game and it was crucial. We were now one point behind Raith Rovers and two behind Dumbarton.

Our good record at Easter Road was put to the test with a return there in the Scottish Cup quarter-finals. When 2-0 down Craig McGuffie scored with a strike so marvellous that it was later voted 'goal of the round'. Twelve minutes later Scott McKenna got sent off for an off-the-ball challenge on John McGinn. Hibs proceeded to win 3-1 but McKenna was the main topic of post match conversation. He was on loan from Aberdeen and in four of the five previous matches he had been an unused substitute. His form at Ayr was erratic at best and had it not been for the injury situation he would probably not have played in this tie. He did not kick a ball for Ayr United again and he returned to his parent club before the expiry date of his loan. When he said that he was going back to fight for a first team place our support seriously doubted that he would be successful in his aim. Not only did he get a first team place but his career blossomed. He has since played in the English Premier League and La Liga in Spain. At international level he achieved the Scotland captaincy. Ayr United supporters were incredulous at his meteoric rise. He did not play at all well here and we were glad to see the back of him. Football never fails in its capacity for surprise.

League results were erratic thereafter with two wins and two defeats in the next four. Then came the mother and father of all six-pointers. We were four points ahead of bottom club St.Mirren. When playing them at the quaintly named Paisley 2021 Stadium there was an opportunity to increase that lead to seven. Even with a game extra played this would have enormous potential to avoid the one automatic relegation spot. The date was 1st April but in mentioning that St.Mirren were winning 4-0 at half-time it is not a joke. The ultimate damage was 6-2. I tried to join in with the half-time booing. This was a mistake but not for moral reasons. It was just that I was not very good at it! One week later we were bottom of the league after Queen of the South won 2-0 at Ayr. It was quite damning that the team had the appearance of lacking desire.

As a reward for preparing a monthly newsletter at my work I was given a couple of tickets for Celtic versus Rangers in a Scottish Cup semi-final at Hampden. My son and I went but did not feel the buzz. Twenty-four hours earlier we had been at Cappielow where we underwent a lot of tension in a 1-1 draw against Morton. With two games left we were at the foot of the table, two points behind St.Mirren. Hopes were pinned on overtaking St.Mirren and winning in the play-offs. Hibs were at Ayr in the penultimate fixture. Since they had already won the league it was considered that they would be in relaxed mode and therefore beatable. Hibs won 4-0! What were the chances now? Raith Rovers were now second bottom and we were playing them at Kirkcaldy in the final match. We could reach second bottom and therefore a play-off but only by winning by a five-goal margin. The fantasy was stoked when the Raith Rovers goalkeeper got sent off with less than five minutes played. The reality was relegation after a 2-1 defeat against ten men. Ian McCall said: "Since starting out I have never been relegated as either a player or a manager. It's an awful feeling but I take the blame and feel the heat for it."

The board quickly confirmed that the club would be full time in 2017/18. Part time in the Championship but full time in League One seemingly told a tale of putting the cart before the horse. In the fullness of time this measure would bring its rewards.

Michael Moffat and Andy Geggan returned to the fold having been released by Dunfermline Athletic. Craig Moore was now a signed player rather than a loanee from Motherwell. Alan Forrest signed on for a further season. The squad would have a capability for firepower.

In the League Cup we were pitched into a section with Kilmarnock, Dumbarton, Clyde and Annan Athletic. It began with a 1-0 win at home to Kilmarnock. When Andy Geggan scored I jumped up without realising that I was half on and half off the terracing step. I twisted my ankle and was in a bit of pain. By the next morning it had swollen so badly that it took a supreme effort to get my left shoe on. When the doctor asked me what happened I resisted the temptation to describe the fine detail of the goal. "I tripped" was the easy explanation. The team was rampant in the section, winning 3-1 away to Dumbarton, 5-1 at home to Clyde and 6-1 away to Annan Athletic. At Annan Ross Docherty broke the club record for the fastest goal. It came fifteen seconds after the kick-off. I had to work on that particular afternoon and I checked the score during a break. It was showing as 2-0 to Ayr United but only three minutes had been played. I was informed by my family that a lot of fans missed the first two goals due to congestion at the turnstiles. After winning the group we had a somewhat sobering 5-0 defeat against Hibs at Easter Road.

The elimination from the League Cup was not overly lamented because the first league match had been played on the Saturday prior and we were imbibed with genuine confidence that a good season was in store. Albion Rovers 1 Ayr United 5 comprised the club's second biggest opening away league win in history. It was eclipsed only by Queen's Park 1 Ayr United 6 in 1921. The importance of progress was embraced. Winning 3-0 at home to Forfar Athletic then 4-3 away to Stranraer effectively piled on the goals as well as the points. Sandwiched between those fixtures was a 5-1 win away to East Stirling in the Irn Bru Cup. With nine games played between cup and league thirty-two goals had been scored. The excitement was on the point of being temporarily curtailed with one point taken from the next three fixtures. Even that one point was a fortuitous one. In a 3-3 draw at home to Alloa Athletic the equaliser came in the fourth minute of stoppage time. Compounding the unease was a shootout defeat at home to Montrose in the Irn Bru Cup.

By now Lawrence Shankland was at the club. He was a September signing who, not having a club, had been doing his own training. Aberdeen had loaned him in turn to Dunfermline Athletic, St.Mirren and Morton. Supporters of these clubs were quick to say that he was out of condition. To put it succinctly they were wrong. He became the first Ayr United player to score in four consecutive matches starting with a debut. The previous best was Charlie Howe in the first three matches of the club's history back in 1910.

By the end of October fifty-two goals had been scored between cup and league. It was just the third season ever in which an Ayr United team had exceeded fifty by this time. In a 4-1 win at Arbroath, Shankland's two goals took him to nine in eight matches. In context it was a great win, Arbroath having beaten Airdrie 7-1 in their previous home game. The excitement of supporting Ayr United was restored in all its glory and it was about to get even better. Having regained the top spot from Raith Rovers on goal difference, the next match was at home to them on the Tuesday evening. The 3-0 win permitted some daylight at the top but this development was tempered by the knowledge that Raith had a game in hand.

Thirty-eight goals so far was the highest in the British leagues, a record shared with Manchester City.

The Scottish Cup third round draw brought a trip to new territory, Spain Park in Aberdeen to be precise. Host club Banks O' Dee had won 10-0 the week before but Ayr United pitched up and won 6-2. Lawrence Shankland's first goal was scored after thirty-two seconds which made it the earliest ever recorded time for a Scottish Cup goal by Ayr United. This was in the midst of a run of nine consecutive wins (including the cup) which was the third best run in the club's history. Ian McCall said: "I can't remember a squad that has scored so many goals. Our players are so clinical and they never give up." Alas the sequence ended with a 2-0 loss at Airdrie.

There was a gilt-edged chance to recover from what happened at Airdrie. Ayr United versus Forfar Athletic comprised top versus bottom. At 2-0 up it was all in line with expectation. Then Forfar scored three times (75, 83 and 88). Losing had hardly seemed credible but it was a reality. There was a quick chance to atone. Stranraer 1 Ayr United 5 was atonement enough on 2nd January, 2018. This was our biggest ever league win at Stranraer, shared equally with an identical result on 26th March, 1966. Yet some of us had a recollection of the 7-1 Scottish Cup win there in 1974. Nonetheless the situation at the top of League One was perilous. We had a two-point lead over Raith Rovers who had two games in hand. A matter of days later Arbroath won 2-1 at Ayr with the killer goal coming in the 88th minute. It felt like watching a replay of the Forfar game seven days earlier. The consequence was a drop to second place. Our next match was against our rivals for the title. Raith Rovers 1 Ayr United 1 – no ground lost and no ground gained.

Ayr United 4 Arbroath 1 was a fourth round Scottish Cup tie which took the goals total to ninety for the season. This match was heavily publicised for reasons that had nothing to do with the result. At 2-0 Arbroath boss Dick Campbell was enraged when he felt that his team had been denied a penalty. He then walked onto the pitch to confront the referee. It was widely considered to be a humorous incident and people were quick to praise Dick Campbell for being a right good character. I could not bring myself to sharing the supposed humour of it all. A pitch incursion by a manager is an inflammatory action and it should have been reported as such. The next round certainly did nothing to induce humour. Alan Forrest scored the opening goal at home to Rangers. By the time the final goal went in I was crossing over Hawkhill Bridge. It was a 6-1 mauling.

A week before the Rangers tie we dropped to second place on losing 2-1 at home to Alloa Athletic. Three consecutive 3-0 wins had a huge impact. Each of those games were at Ayr. The victims were East Fife, Airdrie and, most significantly, Raith Rovers. The first goal against Airdrie meant that Ayr United were the first team in the British leagues to score one hundred goals in 2017/18. More importantly, winning the six-pointer against Raith Rovers meant that we were one point behind them with a game in hand and a superior goal difference. The game in hand was played in the ensuing midweek. It was a previously postponed fixture at Arbroath. The conditions were very windy, even by the standards of Arbroath. It took an 86th minute goal from Craig McGuffie to salvage a 1-1 draw. Luckily enough Raith Rovers had lost at Forfar the night before so we were top on goal difference and still with a game in hand.

Four of the next five fixtures were away from home. All five matches were won. The vocal backing in these away games was magnificent therefore the locals in Forfar, Coatbridge, East Fife and Airdrie had their eardrums assailed.

With three games left we had a five-point lead over Raith Rovers and a vastly better goal difference. The title could be won by beating Stranraer at home provided that Raith Rovers got nothing better than a draw at home to Queen's Park. In a sensational development Lawrence Shankland got sent off against Stranraer with barely more than half an hour played. Yet more consternation was visited upon the anxious support when Stranraer won 2-1 by virtue of an 89th minute penalty. Raith Rovers won 2-0 so the lead was now two points with two games left. We departed Somerset Park in sombre mood but high spirits were revived at that evening's Player of the Year function.

Our penultimate game, at Alloa, was switched to the Sunday in order that it could be broadcast live on BBC Alba. Raith Rovers were at Stranraer on the Saturday and we hoped upon hope that they would drop something. The home team just had to replicate their form at Ayr. A Stranraer win would mean that the title was ours in the event of at least a draw at Alloa. We started to reminisce about winning the title there in 1988. As if life was not complicated enough I had another difficulty. I was scheduled to work on the Sunday. After some desperate pleading a compromise was reached and I was allowed to finish at lunchtime. On the Saturday Raith Rovers did not follow the script. They won 3-0. From being seemingly uncatchable we were now a point off the top but we had two games left to Raith's one. On the assumption that Raith would win their last game we needed four points. Hurrying from work on the Sunday I got to Stirling by a rail replacement bus then on to Alloa by a local bus. The pubs were packed by Ayr supporters in celebratory mood. This was premature. We lost 2-1. Craig Moore missed a penalty in the 78th minute. The ball soared over the heads of those of us housed behind that goal but even as it headed in the direction of the Ochil Hills it was impossible to be critical of a player who had been having a fantastic season.

Ayr United versus Albion Rovers and Raith Rovers versus Alloa Athletic. It was all down to this on the final day. After having the title in our grasp we were now a point off the top. It was a disconsolate journey home from Alloa. Provided Raith Rovers did not win all we had to do was beat Albion Rovers. The assumption however was that Raith Rovers would win. At half-time we had a 1-0 lead and there was no scoring at Kirkcaldy. In the 86th minute we made it 2-0 but it hardly seemed to matter because it all still hinged on Raith not winning. At full time it was still 2-0 but they were still playing at Kirkcaldy and it was still 0-0. The home crowd remained and for about four minutes we constantly refreshed score updates. It was a horrible tension. Quite remarkably Raith struck the inside of the post in what was virtually the last action of the game. Then Somerset Park erupted with the confirmation that 0-0 was the result at Kirkcaldy. There was a pitch invasion, a trophy presentation then another pitch invasion. I scaled the wall less athletically than I did when acclaiming the Second Division title in 1966. My brother and I joined the happy throng. This was a great moment to be an Ayr United supporter.

What a season! 124 goals were scored. This was the highest number of domestic goals of any club in the British leagues. Manchester City were close with 123 (106 league, 6 FA Cup, 11 Carabo Cup). No visiting team left Somerset Park with a clean sheet. The statistics were impressive but the title was won by such a narrow margin. In those last seconds at Kirkcaldy it was merciful that the ball rebounded out when it struck the inside of the post. The chances of it rebounding in must have been 50%.

LAWRENCE SHANKLAND	29	
CRAIG MOORE	27	
DECLAN McDAID	13	
MICHAEL MOFFAT	13	
ALAN FORREST	9	
ANDY GEGGAN	6	
JAMIE ADAMS	5	
ROBBIE CRAWFORD	5	
CRAIG McGUFFIE	4	
CHRIS HIGGINS	3	
MICHAEL ROSE	2	
STEVEN BELL	1	
PADDY BOYLE	1	
ROSS DOCHERTY	1	
BRIAN GILMOUR	1	
LUKE McCOWAN	1	
LEON MURPHY	1	
ANDY DOWIE (DUMBARTON)	1	OWN GOAL
DAVID GOLD (ARBROATH)	1	OWN GOAL
TOTAL	**124**	

Lawrence Shankland leads the 124-goal table

16. Championship Consolidation

Promoted in 2009 relegated in 2010. Promoted in 2011 relegated in 2012. Promoted in 2016 relegated in 2017. Promoted in 2018.........now what? In 2017/18 Lawrence Shankland had scored twenty-nine and Craig Moore was close behind with twenty-seven. Declan McDaid and Michael Moffat both scored thirteen. Could such firepower be unleashed after this step-up? Or would we assume the default position of fighting relegation at this level?

Our League Cup section involved Morton, Albion Rovers, Stenhousemuir and Partick Thistle. It was won with a 100% record. Twelve goals were scored and just one conceded. Michael Moffat's goal at Firhill put him into the list of Ayr United's top ten scorers of all time. Lawrence Shankland's goal in the same match became an online sensation. It was a quite phenomenal half-volley from thirty-five yards.

On a beautiful sunny day the League One title flag was unfurled by director Lewis Grant. Ayr United 2 Partick Thistle 0 proceeded to make it a beautiful day metaphorically as well as literally. Top of the league after game one, it was a case of so far so good. In the context of having Daniel Harvie red-carded after half an hour a 0-0 draw at Inverness was satisfactory. Ian McCall proceeded to make seven team changes for an Irn Bru Cup tie against Queen's Park at Hampden. After a 0-0 draw no extra time was played and Queen's Park won the shootout. Involvement in this competition was generally considered to be a nuisance.

The knockout stages of the League Cup was treated with no such contempt. Dundee 0 Ayr United 3 made outsiders take notice, the host club having Premier League status. This tie saw Ross Doohan making a seventh consecutive shutout.

The club record of eight was set by Sprigger White in season 1912/13. Ayr United 4 Dunfermline Athletic 1 meant reclaiming top place but denied Ross Doohan equalling Sprigger White's record. Things were going well but there was a concern that Lawrence Shankland would be sold before the expiry of the transfer window. Bids were received but rejected. The window closed at midnight on 31st August and it was a great relief to know that he would be in the team at Palmerston on 1st September. The team was playing well and our adverse form there was banished from our minds. It was a good feeling to go there brimful of confidence. It is not unknown for confidence to be a hoax when supporting Ayr United. Assuredly it was a hoax. We looked on in horror at a 5-0 defeat which could have been worse. Stephen Dobbie scored four and had a penalty saved. The complaints about the standard of refereeing were justified but it really was a bad day at the office. Office? Where do such sayings originate?

The consequence of the debacle at Dumfries caused a drop to sixth place. Seven league wins out of the next eight restored our place at the top. The football during these weeks was a delight to watch. The all-pink strip drew unfavourable comments at Palmerston. In contrast it was favourably commented on later in the month when the team beat Morton 5-1 at Cappielow. A week later Dundee United were beaten 2-0 at Ayr. The title challenge was real. In the midweek prior to the Cappielow win we had a 4-0 defeat away to Rangers in a League Cup quarter-final. In the section where the visiting fans were housed there seemed to be more people than seats and the stewards did nothing to remedy the situation. I did not mind standing for the whole match because I am accustomed to doing so at Ayr but it was inconsistent with the narrative peddled by work colleagues that Ibrox was a marvellous stadium.

Consecutive home games on consecutive Saturdays brought consecutive draws (1-1 versus Queen of the South, 0-0 versus Morton). Yet it was a measure of progress that we still had a five-point lead at the top albeit that Ross County had a game in hand. The Morton match was on 17th November,

2018, and it was the first time a visiting team had managed a clean sheet at Somerset Park since Hibs on 29th April, 2017. A distraction though was the Scottish Cup. It was very much a distraction. Few of us were even aware that Beith Juniors were in the draw. It was an away tie too. With the in-laws living close to the ground the parking and the pre-match cup of tea were sorted. In the build-up to the tie there was mention of Beith's Bellsdale Park being on a slope but only on arrival at the ground was there an awareness of just how pronounced the slope was. From one goal to the other the drop was eight feet. In winning 3-0 all of the goals came in the second half when we were literally playing downhill.

Six days later we had a Friday evening match away to Dundee United. I was working that night but when I departed my work shortly before 9 pm it was Dundee United 0 Ayr United 2. On the way down from Glasgow on the X77 I kept abreast of what was happening and it was like a dream. 0-3, 0-4, 0-5. It took a supreme effort not to burst into choruses of Super Ayr. Lawrence Shankland scored four. If Dundee United had won by four they would have gone top and some of their fans predicted that they would manage to do this. On the Saturday morning I had a great time working on the statistics.

> Our biggest win at Tannadice ever. The previous best was a 4-0 league win there on 15th November, 1952.
> Five Ayr United goals at Tannadice for the second time ever. There was a 5-2 League Cup win there on 14th August, 1954.
> Lawrence Shankland now on 55 Ayr United goals from 55 starts.
> Finn Ecrepont became the first player born this century to make a competitive appearance for Ayr United.
> The first four-goal haul from an Ayr United player since Michael Moffat at Arbroath on 2nd March, 2013.
> Ross Doohan's fifteenth shutout of the season.
> Biggest away winning margin in the second tier since Morton 0 Ayr United 6 on 2nd January, 2001.

When I went to work on the Monday morning my boss asked me if the game had finished 2-0. I lapsed into so much detail that he probably regretted asking! The next three fixtures yielded draws. Then we had a run of three defeats, the last of which was a Scottish Cup tie at Auchinleck. Yes Auchinleck! This was a good Ayr United team yet we lost 1-0 to a goal scored by Craig McCracken who was formerly an Ayr United Academy player. I felt numb rather than angry. It was like having an out-of-body experience. On the following Friday night a 1-0 win at home to Dundee United put the team back on top of the Championship. There are times when it is impossible to make sense of football. Yet it was written in the statistics that Dundee United would not win because the date was 25th January, 2019. In the year of writing no visiting team has won a league game at Somerset Park on Burns Day ever. It is a record which dates back to the pre-amalgamation Ayr FC and the origin of league football here in 1897. Rabbie is looking over us!

No visiting team has won a league game at Somerset Park on Burns Day ever. Thank you Rabbie.

Slade famously performed the song 'I wish it could be Christmas every day'. On the basis of the statistics I wish it could be Burns Day every day. The mystical protection in home league matches on 25th January does not apply itself on other dates. The next four home fixtures yielded one point from twelve. Inverness Caledonian Thistle (twice) and Dunfermline Athletic won at Ayr in that period and a solitary home point was taken in a 1-1 draw against Morton. In away games during this phase there were wins at Alloa and Dunfermline but it was now difficult to deny that the title push was faltering.

At a time when our title hopes were still alive (with a little optimism) I was invited to a television studio to do an interview on BBC Alba. The principal topic was the possibility of returning to the Premier League for the first time since 1978. It was far from a ridiculous possibility at the time of the interview but hopes started to ebb away as we progressed into April whereupon conversations became centred on our chances in the play-offs. With three games left it was already known that we would be playing Inverness Caledonian Thistle in the play-offs. In the final match a 1-1 draw at home to Alloa Athletic meant a fourth-place finish whereas a win would have secured third place. We would therefore be at home for the first leg. The failure to beat Alloa had ramifications other than the loss of money by not finishing a place higher. Defeat for Alloa would have relegated them and that is why their players and fans were ecstatic at the end. Their escape meant relegation for Falkirk who were destined to take five years to get out of League One.

The train of thought amongst the supporters was that qualifying for the promotion play-offs was an achievement in itself. It was a change of heart brought on by a dip in form since February. The first leg of the play-off quarter-final was lost 3-1. It was Inverness Caledonian Thistle's third win at Somerset Park this season. Luke McCowan pulled one back in the away leg. Inverness squared it at 1-1 in the 79th minute so we were eliminated on a 4-2 aggregate.

Lawrence Shankland was now a free agent although the fans were grateful that he had stayed at Ayr for a season more than expected. The speculation about where he would go was wide and varied. This worked on the media's propensity to make something up if they do not know. Dundee United declared an interest but we all dismissed this as optimism in its wildest form. We had beaten them three times in the previous season and for the season ahead the clubs would be in the same league. To the surprise of everyone the wild optimism materialised and he joined Dundee United on a three-year deal.

Islay House in Pencaitland. My paternal grandparents moved into this house in 1923. I took the opportunity to pose in front of it on the way to our game at Berwick on 13th July, 2019.

Some days are perfect. One such was 13th July, 2019. We had a League Cup tie at Berwick and the family set out early so we could do some shopping at the Almondvale Shopping Centre at Livingston on the way. By a massive coincidence we met Lewis and Shirley McRoberts there. Shirley's father was

Willie Japp who was one of Ayr United's all time great players. Coincidentally he had played for both of the clubs we were going to watch that day. I had met the McRoberts when they travelled from Grangemouth to Ayr for a short stay and I had the pleasure of showing them round Somerset Park so that Shirley could see the scene of her father's great triumphs. Further on in the journey we had a detour into Pencaitland where I had a look at the house my paternal grandparents had moved into in 1923. After that there was time for a brief stop in Haddington, the town of my birth. I was beginning to forget that we were even on the way to a match. The result was Berwick Rangers 0 Ayr United 7 which was a club record away win in all competitions (eclipsed at Broxburn in 2025). The section proceeded with a defeat at Livingston, a home win over Falkirk and a draw at home to Stranraer. After the draw with Stranraer the shootout was lost and so too was the bonus point required to qualify as one of the best runners-up.

Struggling against Stranraer could have been interpreted as ominous for the imminent start of the league programme. Such fears would prove groundless. We had six league wins out of the first seven. During that run we also had the novelty of a third round tie at Wrexham in what was branded the Tunnock's Caramel Wafer Challenge Cup. Walking along the street in Wrexham I met lots of people I knew but one day later I walked the length of Ayr High Street and met nobody I knew. Was there an explanation for this strange phenomenon? The Ayr support was raucous. When Wrexham scored mid-song our fans kept singing anyway. After a 1-1 draw we lost the shootout. The Ayr team was understrength due to three players being on international duty with the Scotland under-21 squad. My son David did the driving but he was a veteran of such trips. Port Vale away and driving back after the game is just one example. Notwithstanding the elimination at Wrexham, this Ayr team was worth travelling to watch and at home we were recapturing the essence of Fortress Somerset. Dundee United were considered to have the best chance of winning the league but they were beaten 2-0 at Ayr. It seemed unnatural for Lawrence Shankland to be wearing a Dundee United shirt but an excellent team performance was complicit in blunting his considerable attacking threat.

Then came the day when I went flat out to watch Ayr United. Literally! On this particular Saturday I was scheduled to be working until 5 pm. At lunchtime my kindly bosses at Tesco Bank allowed me to offset the afternoon against my annual leave allowance so I got away at 1.15 pm. My son and daughter had already set out for the match but they agreed to divert to Falkirk so I could meet them there after getting a train from Queen Street. In my hurry to get to the station I tripped over a paving stone outside Buchanan Galleries. I went down faster than Didier Drogba. Falling face down I broke my fall with my hands and I was immediately surrounded by a crowd of people wishing to assist. The people of Glasgow really are wonderful but apart from some minor grazing and a broken strap on my shoulder bag the only thing affected was my pride. Face down on a city centre pavement at lunchtime on a Saturday has to register somewhere on the scale of embarrassment. The rest of the plan fell (pun alert!) into place. With half an hour played the team was 4-0 up. Ultimately there was a slackening of pace and it ended in a 4-1 victory in which the standard of football could only be described by recourse to superlatives. After six games we had fifteen points and a goal difference of eight. Dundee United had fifteen points and a goal difference of nine. On emerging from the ground at Alloa it was disappointing to hear that Dundee United had come from behind to win 2-1 in their home match with Arbroath. Lawrence Shankland's goals were timed at 88 and 90+2.

That night stories emerged online about Ian McCall being on the verge of quitting in order to take over the manager's job at Partick Thistle. As always people claimed to be in the know. The internet is a breeding ground for nonsense but there was a degree of unease when the comments started to escalate. Why would he go to Partick Thistle anyway? They were at the foot of the Championship with just two points. The brand of football exhibited by Ayr United at Alloa had been exhilarating at times. Surely these online stories were nonsense. They weren't! On the Sunday he accepted the Partick Thistle job.

With Sandy Stewart and Mark Kerr in interim charge we were at Arbroath in the next fixture. The first half hour was like watching a film you had seen before. As at Alloa that was all the time it took to go 3-0 up and again the football was scintillating. Shortly after the third goal went in an Arbroath supporter standing next to me (no segregation) went off his head at a chirpy PA announcement that the pie stalls were still open. Here is a rough summary of his loud outburst (heavily censored to delete the considerable number of expletives). "Three nuthin' doon. Who cares if the pie stalls are open? Ah couldnae care less supposin' they were ge'in the pies away. We've mair tae worry aboot than pies." I sympathised with his pain. It finished 3-0 and it was one of those perfect days. We detoured through Fife there and back to give the day a touristy feel. Lunch in a divine fish restaurant close to Arbroath harbour was another high spot.

Following Ayr United was a sublime experience in those early weeks of 2019/20. The word 'experience' will now be reused to tell you that experience of supporting Ayr United is an alert to enjoy it while you can. Yet despite a run of three defeats second place was still occupied. Dundee United losing at Alloa and Dumfries kept them within sight. Mark Kerr was now the manager. Once again the speculation surrounding such appointments was wayward. Mark Kerr got his first win in a 3-2 victory away to Morton on a Tuesday night. Then, on the Saturday, Ian McCall was back at Ayr with his Partick Thistle team. It had to be acknowledged that McCall had been a good manager at Ayr but that did not prevent the fans resenting his departure. Without question this was viewed as a grudge match. With an extra edge added to the proceedings the result was Ayr United 4 Partick Thistle 1.

The Carmichaels have a great love of the Lake District and it is to be thoroughly recommended at all times of the year. Our holidays there in November can conflict with Ayr United's fixtures but it does not always necessarily work out in that way. In 2019 the last day of the holiday coincided with Ayr United playing away to Queen of the South. This was perfect because we had to go home through Dumfries anyway. The car, bristling with luggage, got parked outside the ground whereupon we entered to watch a 3-1 defeat in which Luke McCowan got sent off. It could be said that the holiday was good but it might have ended better. Postponements and international call-ups deferred the next fixture until twenty-four days later. This was ample time to regroup but a 1-0 loss at home to Dunfermline Athletic caused a drop to third. The excitement prevalent earlier in the season was wearing off judging by the public perception. Merely 1,361 passed through the turnstiles that night. By virtue of the points stored thus far, it was possible to reclaim second place by winning the next match. Unfortunately it was Inverness Caledonian Thistle away. Our record there was well documented and it made for grim reading. A 2-0 defeat added to the sum total of grimness and the mood was hardened further by a drop to fourth place. Ordinarily this would have been considered a respectable position in the Championship. In the context of the form dip and subsequent slide it was correctly not viewed as such. Maybe fourth place would be temporary. After all we were at home to Arbroath on the Tuesday. It was a game in hand which, if won, would reinstate third place. Such hopes receded when we saw the weather. It was an atrocious night of high winds and heavy rain. The sensible people stayed at home while the 777 of us in attendance watched a farcical spectacle. Stephen Kelly scored directly from a corner-kick in conditions conducive to such a feat. Two minutes into the second half we conceded a penalty which levelled it at 1-1. In the 90th minute Ross Doohan pulled off a quite miraculous save. Seconds later Arbroath's Thomas O'Brien rattled the post with a shot. O'Brien's team mate Michael McKenna had earlier struck the bar. We were lucky to even draw. On the Saturday, by which time it was safe to venture outdoors again, Alloa Athletic were beaten 2-1 at Ayr and third place was restored.

Before the next match a very significant development took place. David Smith was named as a new director. He was a managing director and majority shareholder of Ashleigh Building. Moreover he was a lifelong Ayr United supporter. In the years ahead he was to become a driving force behind massive improvements to the infrastructure of Somerset Park

In losing 4-0 away to Dundee United third place was still clung onto. The grip was tenuous though. Ayr United 1 Queen of the South 2 required the grip to be released altogether so we passed over from 2019 to 2020 in fourth place. On 4th January we went third again with a 1-0 win at Dunfermline. It seemed as if we were moving between third and fourth with the frequency of a table tennis ball. That goal at Dunfermline was one of the best in the club's history. By courtesy of YouTube it could be viewed without seeing it in real time and I found myself watching it back repeatedly. The goal involved all ten of our outfield players and twenty-six passes culminating in an Alan Forrest shot which Craig Moore stretched towards to divert into the net. It was technically perfect.

Caught on the BBC on 18th January, 2020. On the far right are three Carmichaels: my daughter Jill, myself and brother Peter.

With Ross County at Ayr in the Scottish Cup fourth round we were in line for a tie described as a free hit. 'Free hit' is one of the vast number of curious expressions used in football. It implies that the match will probably be lost and anything better will be a bonus. Ross County were in the Premier League so they were accorded this kind of respect. We won 1-0 through a Steven Bell goal. The national media adopted the default position and called it an act of giant killing. Not even Ross County supporters could have perceived their club as being giants. Their rivals Inverness Caledonian Thistle suffered the same fate at Ayr a week later, notably a 1-0 defeat. Inverness remained second but we were now just one point behind them. The result also preserved the 'Burns Day' statistic. Good performances were back as well as good results. Even the *Inverness Courier* admitted: "Ayr looked more threatening for nearly the entire match."

Partick Thistle snatching Ian McCall created a grudge that intensified whenever the clubs met. On a wintry Friday night we were at Firhill and it all reared its ugly head again. This remains the only occasion when I have walked to an away game. Okay, I only walked from my work in the city centre. Does that still count? An ill-tempered match finished 1-1. With the aim now diluted to getting a play-off place, the dropped points were not unduly detrimental. Then we had the challenge of a Scottish Cup fifth round tie at home to St.Johnstone. Ross County were beatable so St.Johnstone were surely beatable too. The belief was reinforced when Aaron Drinan, on loan from Ipswich Town, scored inside the first five minutes. Aaron Muirhead then scored an own goal (18 minutes) and got himself sent off (26 minutes). The St.Johnstone free-kick from the red card tackle then led to a goal. In acrimonious circumstances the match proceeded with no further scoring so we were out. Before the match I did a pre-arranged interview with the BBC. It lasted for close to fifteen minutes but it got edited to half a minute. This was always going to happen because it was geared towards an Ayr United win or, at worst, a draw.

Dog bites man – not a story! Man bites dog – this is a story! Windy weather at Arbroath – not a story! Calm weather at Arbroath – this is a story! On 22nd February, 2020, the conditions at Arbroath conformed to the stereotype. Playing against the considerable wind Aaron Drinan scored. Arbroath's equaliser came in the manner not uncommon in matches played in a gale, directly from a corner-kick. With it tied at 1-1 at half-time, the match would surely be won with wind advantage in the second half. If only! Half-time became full time when the referee abandoned the match. My son and I were marked absent from Arbroath. On that afternoon we were more than 200 miles further down the east coast at Sunderland. The programme seller was quite chatty and, yes, he did remember Dick Malone. Inside the Stadium of Light we were most surprised to see a man in the concourse wearing Bristol Rovers colours and a hat with an Ayr United badge. It was the real badge too rather than the imitation imposed by the row over heraldic law. It transpired that his father had been brought up in Alloway. We watched on while Bristol Rovers lost 3-0. In the second half, of course, it was no longer necessary to check up on the Ayr United updates. Unknown to us we were watching two Ayr United players of the future. They were Chris Maguire (Sunderland) and Jayden Mitchell-Lawson (Bristol Rovers).

The ping-pong between third and fourth continued. Ayr United 1 Morton 2 – now fourth. Alloa Athletic 0 Ayr United 2 – now third. Then Dundee United came to Ayr as league leaders. After a 0-0 draw it was possible to reflect that Dundee United had failed to score in their last five matches at Ayr and in their last eight matches here they had mustered just one goal. Four days later their neighbours Dundee were here to replicate a 0-0 draw. With Inverness Caledonian Thistle losing at Alloa that afternoon a win would have meant a shift into second place so we were left to rue Aaron Muirhead's penalty being saved. The fixtures looked crazily familiar. After Dundee United at home on a Tuesday then Dundee at home on the Saturday the next fixture was Dundee away on the next Tuesday. Losing 2-0 caused a drop to fourth.

Rabbie Burns famously wrote: "The best laid schemes o' mice and men gang aft agley." On Friday, 13th March, 2020, Queen of the South versus Ayr United was scheduled with a

7.05 pm kick-off time and it was to be screened live on the BBC. This was the scheme. Start work in Glasgow at 8 am and finish at 4 pm : Make the short walk to Buchanan Bus Station to catch the 4.15 pm X74 bus to Dumfries : Arrive at Dumfries 6.25 pm : Chippy : Enter Palmerston in nice time for the kick-off : Three points in the bag : Lift home with the family. That morning the SFA announced that all SPL and SPFL matches were postponed until further notice due to the coronavirus crisis. Ours was the first game to fall victim to the blanket ban (Motherwell versus Aberdeen was scheduled for a later kick-off that night). As if to compound the frustration I got the X77 home from Glasgow and it departed at the same time as the X74 and from the next stance.

Ultimately it was announced that the current positions in the Championship, League One and League Two would be the final positions with a decision on the Premier League pending. Twenty-seven of the thirty-six fixtures had been played. Finishing fourth would have been good enough to qualify for the play-offs but these were scrapped. No one knew when football would resume.

For season 2020/21 it was agreed that only the Premier League would have an August start. As for the rest there would be a curtailed programme of twenty-seven fixtures commencing on 17th October with the League Cup getting underway a fortnight earlier. No paying spectators were to be permitted. We would need to sit at home and watch on a live stream. Other restrictions included the players having to get their kit washed at home and we had matches where two team buses were used in order to accommodate social distancing. The Ally MacLeod Suite was pressed into use as one of the dressing rooms with the consequence that one team had to wander down the steps of the north terrace in order to gain access to the field. Simultaneously the other team emerged via the traditional route. The home team initially changed in the Hospitality Suite but the arrangement was eventually swapped round. The atmosphere at matches was surreal. It was more consistent with bounce games during training.

Essential staff were permitted entry so that was me ruled out. I have never been Ayr United staff in any capacity. The point was irrelevant anyway. There would have been no pleasure in attending an event devoid of atmosphere. An Albion Rovers versus Ayr United League Cup tie on 6th October was our first competitive match since playing at Dundee on 10th March. The time gap of 210 days was the longest the club had gone without a game since the Second World War. These live streams were on a pay-per-view basis. The volunteers who put this technology together deserved to be commended for their expertise but watching in this manner was a wholly unsatisfactory experience. Albion Rovers 2 Ayr United 5 was our first match under this arrangement. The other clubs in the group were Hamilton Accies, Annan Athletic and Stranraer. On winning the group our fate was a 4-0 thumping at Livingston in the knockout stage. It was 3-0 by the 12th minute and 4-0 by half-time. This was not good value for a tenner!

Ordinarily we would have looked forward to the first league fixture of the season but the mood was dulled in these times. I like the argument that football is not a television show but something you go to. Now, of necessity, it was a television show. The campaign began with a visit from Queen of the South. Some supporters trampled over the rough ground adjacent to McCall's Avenue then managed to view the game from a vantage point in the north-west corner in what was formerly Walker's yard. Michael Miller scored twice inside the first twenty minutes, each goal originating from a Joe Chalmers corner-kick. There was the illusion of watching a television repeat. Stephen Dobbie scored with a penalty ten minutes into the second half. Queen of the South's James Maxwell got sent off and it ended up ten versus ten when Luke McCowan got sent off. In these times of restriction they did not even have the luxury of an early bath. In the fifth minute of stoppage time Viljami Sinisalo pulled off a magnificent save to preserve the 2-1 lead. In some degree it was a television thriller but it was an occasion tempered by empty terraces. The run of four consecutive opening day league wins was a club best since the six achieved from 1967 until 1972 inclusive.

On Boxing Day 2020 we had a fixture away to Hearts. Six days earlier Hearts had lost to Celtic in a shootout in the deferred 2019/20 Scottish Cup final. You have read that correctly. The 2019/20 Scottish Cup final was played on 20th December, 2020. This was further proof, as if it were needed, that these were strange times. The result was Hearts 5 Ayr United 3. We had gone 2-1 up in the 60th minute. Amidst the blandness of it all there were still some tensions when watching from the living room. On 2nd January, 2021, a 90th minute own goal squared it at 2-2 away to Queen of the South. Then, one minute into stoppage time, we conceded and the match was lost 3-2. There really were times when it was tempting to bin the television. After that New Year match we were sixth in the league, one point in front of Inverness Caledonian Thistle who had two games in hand.

Lockdown did have some advantages, notably working from home. In the world of Scottish football though the eccentricities escalated. On 9th January our Scottish Cup tie at Elgin got postponed on account of a frozen pitch. This would have been no more than a minor frustration had it not been for an announcement made two days later. All Scottish football below Championship level was to be suspended for three weeks. With Elgin City being in League Two the tie could not now be played on the rescheduled date of 12th January. The three-week suspension was later extended further and it would not take place until 23rd March which was an extraordinarily late date for a second round tie. That date of 12th January was significant for a reason far more important than our non-appearance at Elgin. It was the date on which it was announced that David Smith was the new owner of the club. Outgoing chairman and owner Lachlan Cameron said: "I have transferred 51% of the total shareholding to David and also forgiven the majority of my debt." Lachlan always had Ayr United's best interests at heart and his successor was similarly minded.

Ayr United 0 Hearts 1 was proof that it was possible to suffer frustrations even when it was only on a television screen. This was broadcast live on the BBC and the irritation was compounded by televised replays proving that a Hearts penalty was a travesty. The sense of injustice was stoked further when it was converted. It was a mockery of a season anyway. The sooner it was finished the better. We just wanted to see it through safely then hope that spectators would be readmitted in the season ahead. Wintry conditions frustrated the progress. Dundee versus Ayr United was called off four times and a further call-off was Raith Rovers away. With Somerset Park being okay we therefore had three consecutive home games including the Hearts fixture. All three were lost. Inverness Caledonian Thistle (0-2) and Arbroath (0-1) took it to one win in the last ten games. On the Sunday morning after the Arbroath game a board meeting was held. Then a statement was issued to confirm that Mark Kerr had left "by mutual agreement." Losing to Arbroath had plunged the club to second bottom. One win in the last ten games had rendered his position untenable.

    David White and Derek Stillie took temporary charge. In retrospect Ayr United have had a good record whenever David White has been involved in interim managership. Morton 0 Ayr United 2 immediately put the home team second bottom instead. Raith Rovers away then offered a more daunting challenge against the second-placed club. A scoreless draw hinted at the possibility that stability would be restored. The speculation over the next manager was put to bed when David Hopkin was named as the new incumbent. He was thrown in at the proverbial deep end. Appointed on a Thursday, Hearts away on the Saturday followed by Dundee away on the Tuesday! Hearts 2 Ayr United 0 highlighted a statistic of no goals in five of the last six matches. Dundee 1 Ayr United 3 highlighted another statistic. It was our first league win at Dens Park since 31st January, 1981, but we had had three cup wins there since that date. Mark McKenzie scored twice, one of which was a thunderous strike into the top corner from twenty-five yards. This was almost enough to rekindle a love of football regardless of the mode of viewing. It could have been argued that home advantage did not exist when the action was played out in these empty grounds. To the players it might also have been a useful reprieve from barracking. They could play their natural game without a crowd being there to howl abuse at a misplaced pass.

The embarrassment of 1967 was avenged with a 4-0 win at Elgin in the Scottish Cup. Grimmer viewing was Ayr United 0 Clyde 1 in the next round. Very quickly the league situation became a matter of serious concern when a six-pointer was lost 4-0 at Arbroath. David Hopkin was quite candid: "You can coach and do whatever you want but changing people's mentality is another thing. I need to know who wants to be at Ayr United next season. I'll find out on Monday at training who wants this." In these days of lockdown we all had plenty of time to sit at home and study the league table. With two games left Alloa Athletic were in an inescapable position at the foot. Their automatic relegation was confirmed. Morton were next from the foot with twenty-six points and Ayr United sat just above them with a point more. However Morton had three games left to our two. The prospect of finishing in the relegation play-off position was all too real. Morton then drew their game in hand and we were above them in goal difference only.

In the penultimate round of fixtures the key matches were Ayr United versus Queen of the South and Morton versus Alloa Athletic. Several hours before kick-off a drainage issue at home meant that we had to vacate our house. All four of us ended up staying in the Travelodge at Whitletts for six weeks. It was a strange experience to be working from home but not really from home! The unexpected flitting was a major distraction from what was happening at Somerset Park. Anyway it was 0-0. It was the first ever 0-0 result between the clubs at Ayr despite this fixture dating back to 1925/26. Morton 1 Alloa Athletic 1 preserved the status quo. The final round of Championship fixtures were played on the following Friday night. Inverness Caledonian Thistle versus Ayr United and Arbroath versus Morton were now the key fixtures. The requirement was to at least match the Morton result. We twice went a goal down at Inverness and twice drew level. The second equaliser was scored by Josh Todd in the 67th minute. At 2-2 this was satisfactory because Morton were drawing 0-0 at Arbroath. All too slowly the minutes ticked by. The earnest hope was that neither Inverness Caledonian Thistle nor Morton would score in the time left. Then Morton captain Sean McGinty got sent off. In these situations it is necessary to cling to any shred of hope. It was a massive relief when the respective scores were maintained to the end. The relegation play-offs were avoided on goal difference. By virtue of finishing eleventh in the Premier League, Kilmarnock had to play Dundee over two legs to prevent relegation. They failed! In 2021/22 the Ayrshire derby would be restored at league level.

In 2020/21 the club did not issue a match day programme for the clear and obvious reason that there were no paying spectators there to buy it. In 2021/22 the commercial risks still existed. There were indications that spectators would be allowed back in but that did not remove the likelihood of attendances being limited or matches being postponed or cancelled at short notice should there be an escalation of the virus. The prospect of no programme for a further season induced an element of cold turkey in me. I had been involved with the programme since 1970 and I felt driven by an urge to do something. The solution was to produce my own copy in pdf format and distribute it free of charge. I was most grateful to David Sargent for permitting his photographs to be used. Over the course of the season I produced twelve issues. The distribution on its own was a big job and since I was still working full time it could not be produced for every match.

Gradually the Covid restrictions were relaxed. In successive seasons we got started away to Albion Rovers in the League Cup and a restricted attendance of 150 was permitted. An insipid match was witnessed by the few. The result was even more insipid. After a 0-0 draw the shootout for the bonus point was lost. Then came the long awaited day (or night to be precise). For the first time since 7th March, 2020, there would be paying spectators at an Ayr United home game. It was not wholly good news since the limit was set at a derisory 500 for a League Cup tie against Edinburgh City. The match was won 3-0. For the next League Cup match, at Hamilton, the limit was set at 900 (600 home, 300 away). Merely 801 of us were there for a 1-0 win. The limit was then set at 2,000 for the visit of Falkirk (1,600 home, 400 away). However as a result of positive Covid tests Falkirk could not field a team and we got awarded a 3-0 win. The section was won without a ball being kicked. At the knockout stages we lost at home to Dundee United in a shootout after extra time had left it squared at 1-1. This sparked a pitch invasion from a significant faction of the visiting support. A week earlier they had given Rangers their first league defeat in forty-one matches but there had been no incursions onto the field. We were left mystified as to why their contentious win at Ayr had sparked euphoria on such a scale.

Kilmarnock away was the first league fixture. The attendance was to be restricted but Kilmarnock did not stick to the convention of allowing a percentage of away fans to have tickets. They were able to get away with it but it was wrong on so many levels, not least because admitting home fans only gave them an unfair advantage. It was shown live on BBC Scotland and the commentator kept praising the Kilmarnock fans for their vocal support. He seemed oblivious to the fact that they had a free hit. Every one of the 3,692 crowd supported Kilmarnock. A derby match of this magnitude should have been scheduled for a later date and most certainly not for a league opener. A later date would possibly have seen further relaxation of the restrictions. Nonetheless Kilmarnock Football Club really should have allowed at least some Ayr support into the ground. Other clubs had the good grace to adopt a spirit of compromise. In the 43rd minute Jason Naismith wrapped his arms round Tomi Adeloye and pulled him down. No penalty! In the 86th minute Jack Baird blocked a Blair Alston shot with his chest. Penalty! The penalty was converted for 2-0 and so it remained. I felt so bitter about the snub to the Ayr support that I resolved not to go to Ayr United's next match at Rugby Park. This resolution was broken of course.

Unconventionally the Kilmarnock match was on a Monday evening. Five days later we had Arbroath at home. Again a 2,000 limit was set which included 400 for visiting fans. The Arbroath allocation was higher than they needed but it had to be pitched at that level on account of the segregation arrangements. With four adults in our house it was well nigh inevitable that one of us would eventually test positive for Covid. In consequence the entire household had to self isolate so I had to miss the Arbroath match. I could not blame Kilmarnock Football Club this time! A 2-2 draw was considered to be a poor result even in light of coming from 2-0 down. The fullness of time would prove that a draw against Arbroath was actually a very good result.

With the crowds being back it was easier to gauge the public mood. In fact for an evening visit from Raith Rovers it was very easy to gauge the public mood. David Hopkin was heavily barracked. There was a 6 pm kick-off because Scotland had a World Cup qualifying match against Austria later. We were 2-0 down inside half an hour and in a five-minute spell near the end there were three red cards which rendered the contest nine versus ten. There was no further scoring. Two days later the club announced a statement: "Ayr United can confirm that we today have parted company with manager David Hopkin." He had been in the job for 182 days which was a close comparison to his 175-day tenure at Bradford City. Jim Duffy was put in interim charge. Three weeks later the job was his.

On 11th September, 2021, Ayr United 3 Dunfermline Athletic 1 was our first home league win since 30th January. It ended a run of five defeats and four draws in the previous nine home league games. Since beating Dundee on 21st November, 2020, our home league record prior to the Dunfermline game was Played 12 Won 1 Drawn 6 Lost 5. Hamilton Accies 0 Ayr United 2 then Ayr United 0 Morton 0 continued the progress under Jim Duffy. On the basis of this he was given a contract until the end of the season. The first match under his permanent charge was a 4-0 defeat away to Partick Thistle. His body language told its own story. Throughout the sorry proceedings he stood there persistently shaking his head. His discomfort was shared by those of us sitting in the stand behind him.

The team rallied in a 2-1 home win over Queen of the South but the next again home game was more eagerly awaited. Alas it was a night of frustration when Kilmarnock scored the only goal of the game with an 89th minute penalty. This was the start of a run of five games which yielded four defeats and a draw. Some of it was alarming, not least losing 4-0 at home to Partick Thistle and 3-0 away to Dunfermline Athletic. Even a Scottish Cup tie at home to Albion Rovers was a less than alluring spectacle. A 2-1 win was achieved after trailing at half-time.

The Scottish Football Association traditionally attracts criticism from supporters who feel that their club is being unfairly picked on. This could be interpreted as paranoia but there are times when complaints are legitimate. Goalkeeper Aidan McAdams got a two-match ban in December for an incident against Kilmarnock in October. After Kilmarnock had converted their 89th minute penalty a visiting supporter threw a toilet roll onto the pitch. McAdams merely threw it back in the direction from whence it had come. The interpretation was that he had thrown a missile and that this was in breach of rule 77. Only a warped mind could classify a toilet roll as a missile. If this were true we would be left in a state of fear when carrying out lavatorial functions.

The Championship had developed into a league of two halves with a yawning gap between fifth and sixth. We went to Cappielow while occupying seventh place. Morton scored so we went bottom. Steven Bradley equalised and we were seventh again. Then Tomi Adeloye scored and we were sixth. Morton made it 2-2 and we were seventh again and so it remained. These persistent changes of league position amply illustrated that we were dealing in fine margins.

A 3-0 loss away to Queen of the South on the Saturday had a sequel on the Monday when it was announced that Jim Duffy was no longer the manager. Excluding his time as interim manager he had been in the job for eighty-one days. Then we had a recurrence of Covid restrictions. For the visit of

Raith Rovers on Boxing Day the attendance was limited to 500 based on eligibility for season ticket holders on a first come first served basis. Positive Covid tests caused some tickets to be returned and the attendance was 472. A 2-0 win reinforced the good record enjoyed whenever David White has been in charge. Could he employ his magic in the Ayrshire derby? There was no opportunity to do so. Due to an attendance limit of 500 both clubs requested a postponement and it was rescheduled from 2nd January until 9th February. Ayr United 1 Arbroath 0 on 8th January was an exceptional result against the league leaders. It brought David White's second spell of interim management to a conspicuously good end. Fraser Bryden went on as a 77th minute substitute against Arbroath. He was an Ayr United season ticket holder at the time. Three weeks earlier he had been in the crowd at Palmerston as a fan.

The media reported that the next Ayr United manager would be Marvin Bartley. It was a done deal supposedly. Of course we could still recall the reporting of a done deal with Billy Stark prior to Ian McCall being appointed. In 2022 it was indeed another case of misreporting. Lee Bullen got the job. He was appointed on the eve of the Arbroath game. Albeit that he was tracksuited and supervising that day the win was generally credited to David White. We could only hope that Lee Bullen would bring stability. His predecessor's tenure was the second shortest in the club's history, eclipsed only by Bobby Flavell's seventeen days between November and December 1961.

Postponements had the consequence of getting home advantage for three consecutive league fixtures but all three suffered from the imposition of a 500 lid on the attendance. More positively Raith Rovers and Arbroath had been beaten and there was a confidence that Morton would suffer the same fate. Yet Morton, in front of the compulsorily paltry attendance, won 2-0. The run of home games then extended to four when St.Mirren came to Ayr and won 2-0 in the Scottish Cup. It was watched by an uncapped crowd of 3,342. It may seem that I am overly indulging in matters relating to crowd figures but Covid was the reason for such a preoccupation. Can we go to the football at all? If so how many? These were valid questions in those eccentric times.

The fixtures schedule for February 2022 made for uncomfortable reading. Kilmarnock away followed by Inverness Caledonian Thistle away! Yet our fans tend to have a gung ho attitude towards derby matches. The Rugby Park fixture was on a Wednesday night and the Carmichaels had already planned to go to Oldham Athletic versus Bristol Rovers on the Tuesday. Or, rather, three of us planned to go to Oldham. Carol could not get the time off. We set off from Monkton at 10.40 am and the destination was the Travelodge we had booked in Bury. Food is an essential component of longish football trips and experience will always take you to the tried and trusted eateries but in Bury we were working blind. Lorde's Fish and Chips was rated as one of the top three chippies in Bury. As accolades go it was good enough for us. While seated at Boundary Park awaiting the kick-off Chris Gibson, a Bristol Rovers director, came round and personally greeted every travelling fan with a handshake. He immediately discerned that we did not have Bristol accents so he was immediately regaled with the tale of why we were there. Oldham Athletic 2 Bristol Rovers 1 was the outcome on a freezing cold night. On checking out on the Wednesday morning we paid a visit to the nearby Gigg Lane then headed for home. Recounting all of our Bristol Rovers trips would probably require to be the subject of a separate book but this one is being specifically mentioned because it was back-to-back with an Ayr United game. On arriving home it was not so long before we were setting out for Kilmarnock. With just seven minutes played we were a goal down . James Maxwell (14 minutes) and Paddy Reading (80 minutes) turned it around for a 2-1 win. These two days had been a whirlwind. The week was capped off by a 2-1 win at Inverness, our first there since 18th January, 2003.

The Ally MacLeod Memorial Plaque.

Prior to a visit from Queen of the South an Ally MacLeod memorial plaque was unveiled in Tryfield Place and I felt most privileged in being invited to speak at the ceremony. It was a fitting fixture since he had managed both clubs. It was a fitting date too. 26th February would have been his birthday. Not so fitting was a 1-0 defeat against the bottom club. Then a 4-0 win away to Raith Rovers induced the clichéd analogy of a rollercoaster. Ayr United had last won 4-0 at Stark's Park on 19th February, 1916. Would the momentum carry over to our home match with Kilmarnock on the following Friday night? My wife finished her work at a time coinciding with the kick-off time. She walked over from M & S in the High Street and arrived at Somerset Park just as Kilmarnock went 3-0 up. Their goal times were 3, 12 and 16. She didn't go in and neither did some more late arrivals. Markus Fjortoft went on for Mark McKenzie with twenty minutes played. Ten minutes later he was sent off for a last man challenge. In losing 3-1 it most certainly could have been worse. This was the first of seven games without a win. Particularly damaging was a 2-1 defeat at Dunfermline. A 1-0 lead was blown through goals conceded in the 79th minute and the 86th minute. After the match Ayr

United and Dunfermline were in a dead heat in the eighth and ninth positions. The games played, points total, goals for and goals against all matched identically and we were off second bottom place in alphabetical order only. At the Player of The Year Awards that evening Lee Bullen said that we would get over the line. With two games left it was nervy.

At Palmerston, Euan East opened the scoring by putting the ball in the Ayr net in the 80th minute. He scored again in the 87th minute but this time he put the ball in the Queen of the South net. His own goal concluded matters at 1-1. By drawing Queen of the South were confirmed for relegation. It was a great relief to find out that Dunfermline Athletic had lost 1-0 away to Partick Thistle. With one game left we now had a one-point lead over Dunfermline and a goal difference which was one better. The crucial fixtures to be played on the concluding Friday night were Ayr United versus Partick Thistle and Dunfermline Athletic versus Queen of the South. The question of which club would be in a relegation play-off had yet to be resolved. There was a hope that Partick Thistle would be lacking in incentive because they were soon to be playing Inverness Caledonian Thistle in the promotion play-offs regardless. This argument was balanced by the possibility that Queen of the South would lack incentive at Dunfermline because they were already condemned. Some of the pressure was eased after taking a 2-0 lead with half an hour played. In the second half it got extended to 3-0, ultimately finishing 3-1. Due to Queen of the South winning 2-1 we would have been safe anyway. The eighth-placed finish was gratefully received.

Lee Bullen oozed positivity when interviewed and his oratory was based on substance rather than rhetoric. Season 2022/23 would exceed expectations notwithstanding the fact that the League Cup competition left us all with a contrary impression. The finishing order of our group was Annan Athletic, Queen of the South, St.Johnstone, Ayr United and Elgin City. Who would have bet on Annan Athletic winning the group? It was alarming to lose 3-0 at home to the recently relegated Queen of the South. It was disappointing too to concede an equaliser at Annan from a penalty that was the final kick prior to a shootout which we lost. Of course we lost the shootout. The Annan goalkeeper was Greg Fleming. He saved two and scored one. People are liable to discuss the coldest they have ever been at a football match but that night at Annan had to be a contender for the hottest. The heat was extreme. It was reminiscent of a match I had been at in 1978 between Hibernians and Valletta. Please note that this was the Maltese version of Hibernians and not the Leith version! There was a violent altercation in that game when spectators threw stones at players only for the players to reciprocate by throwing them back. I was there with my friend Hugh Cole and brother Douglas and when we mentioned this back at the hotel we were told that it was nothing compared to the level of violence at water polo matches. If you learn only one thing from this book you could make it a resolution never to watch water polo in Malta! Reverting to topic, our solitary group win at home to Elgin City was by default. After a 0-0 draw the shootout was won for a bonus point. It transpired that Darryl McHardy had gone on as a first half substitute for Elgin when he was supposed to be serving a one-match ban. The result was therefore declared void and we were awarded a 3-0 win.

In the previous season Arbroath would have won the Championship title if they had kept their nerve in the closing minutes in the penultimate fixture at Kilmarnock. Ayr United 0 Arbroath 0 was, in that context, not too bad in the opening league fixture of 2022/23. Fixture two was away to Queen's Park on a Friday evening. With Lesser Hampden under renovation the venue was Stenhousemuir's Ochilview Park. In the first half our defence was ripped apart by Dom Thomas and Simon Murray. We were very lucky to be only 2-0 down at half-time. In the first minute of the second half Dipo Akinyemi scored. Fortunately for some the action was visible from the pie queue. It had taken him until half way through his sixth game to get his first goal. At half-time there had been talk of him being hopeless and there were a few other ungracious epithets. Sean McGinty equalised with a bullet header then

Dipo hit the winner with a stoppage time penalty. There are few better ways to create exuberance than a comeback win with the clincher at the death. Dipo was now on the point of establishing a reputation as the most dangerous player in the Championship. In the next match he scored in the third minute at home to Hamilton Accies although he also had the misfortune to have a penalty saved in a 2-2 draw.

Cove Rangers away was a fixture I was desperate to go to. It would be a new ground ticked off. Unfortunately I was working from home until 2 pm that Saturday. The family had therefore to head for Aberdeen without me. I considered the option of hiring a private jet from Prestwick Airport to Dyce then hiring a limo at the other end. Frustratingly I discovered that a South Ayrshire Council bus pass is not valid for such journeys! Cove Rangers 1 Ayr United 2 was the host club's first home league defeat in fifteen months. When David Bangala went on as an 86th minute substitute he got a fantastic reception. This was the player whose visa problems were so prolonged that we had started to wonder whether we would see him at all. During his absence he was nicknamed The Ghost.

With two wins and two draws in the first four games we were the only unbeaten team in the Championship and we topped the league. On the following Friday night we had a 3-1 win at home to Dundee. Dipo scored twice, the second of which came when he had his back to goal in a packed box whereupon he turned and found the net with a vicious shot. A television audience also had the pleasure of seeing it. At halftime in that match I had the honour of receiving an award for fifty-two years of service to the match programme. The fifty-year milestone had not been marked due to Covid.

Winning 2-1 away to Morton was the perfect preliminary to a home match with Partick Thistle. This was first versus second. Or rather it would have been. A postponement occurred due to the death of the Queen on the Thursday. One week later a 3-2 defeat away to Raith Rovers had the consequence of dropping to second. The SPFL Trust Trophy did not have a reputation for intensity but our third round tie at Cappielow ended in a contest of nine versus ten. It was 1-1 so it had more red cards than goals. The shootout was lost.

Statistics are interesting but even when they are ostensibly favourable they do not always reflect in the result. For example at home to Inverness Caledonian Thistle we had twenty corner-kicks to their three but lost the game 1-0. A week later we had six shots on target at home to Queen's Park and won 5-0. Dipo got a hat-trick, one of which was a header. By the season's end his total would be twenty-four and this was his one and only headed goal. He was lethal if the ball was played to him on the ground. It became so tight at the top of the league that we had a proliferation of six-pointers. Ayr United 4 Partick Thistle 2 was one such. There was great delight because this took the club to the top again but just one point separated the top four.

'We wuz robbed' is the war cry of the embittered football fan. Perceived refereeing injustices or the state of the pitch are common means to solicit such a response. Yet are we ever able to admit that the opposition team was robbed? On a Friday evening at Hamilton our travelling support was unanimous in agreeing that the points in our 3-2 win were stolen. Those watching on BBC Scotland would have been similarly minded. It was bottom versus top but it did not look like that despite Dipo scoring in the fourth minute. The home team responded well to that setback and the flamboyantly named Jean-Pierre Tiehi struck the underside of the bar with a shot. The BBC proved that the ball was over the line when it bounced down and a goal was even announced over the PA system. Although sitting behind that goal I really could not tell whether it had crossed the line because the ball bounced down with great rapidity. However the goal announcement just had to be conclusive. Then came a realisation that they were playing on. No goal! Luckily they did not have VAR in the Championship. With the game poised at 2-2 Hamilton pressed furiously for a winner in the late stages. Then, in the 83rd minute, we got a contentious penalty in our favour. Even after Ben Dempsey converted it the game was far from won. Hamilton redoubled their efforts in a tense finish. Lee Bullen said what we already knew: "We were a very lucky team tonight."

The blackest date in Ayr United's history is 19th November. In the year of writing it remains the only date within a conventional football season when no Ayr United team has won. Our record on this date is Played 19 Won 0 Drawn 5 Lost 14. On 19th November, 2022, Dipo established an 82nd minute lead at Inverness. Established? Maybe not. This is a word with an air of permanency. Nathan Shaw squared it at 2-2 five minutes later therefore 19th November remained a seemingly cursed date. It may have seemed cursed as a separate entity but on a personal level November 2022 was a good month. At all dates in that month Ayr United topped the Championship. The month also included a week's holiday in Keswick, our Ruby Wedding, my landmark 70th birthday and my retirement. Ceasing work gave me the opportunity to join the Ayr United Strollers walking group. Eric Belton, Andy McInnes and John Gemmell were tireless in their efforts in organising the walks and carrying out administrative functions. During those Tuesday morning strolls Jim O'Neil could always be relied upon to regale us with his poetry. His support for Ayr United dates back to 1946. Some of his poetry was related to Ayr United or football in general and some of it was about his experiences in life. Unlike modern poetry it all rhymed and it was highly humorous. He also had the ability to recite it with perfect diction.

The idea that Ayr United would collapse after Christmas was a view popularly held by our rivals. They were wrong. We collapsed before Christmas. Losing 3-2 away to Partick Thistle on 17th December was not enough to topple the club from top position. Losing 2-0 at home to Dundee on the night of 23rd December did, however, render the position untenable and we dropped to third. Yet the collapse was not total. We remained in contention with Queen's Park and Dundee.

The Our Wullie Chippy was a convenient food stop when playing Cove Rangers.

A Scottish Cup tie away to Cove Rangers got postponed on the Saturday morning due to a frozen pitch. Some of our fans had already travelled to Aberdeen on the Friday in order to make a weekend out of it. On the following Friday night the result was Cove Rangers 0 Ayr United 5 in the league. Then, on the Tuesday, it was Cove Rangers 0 Ayr United 3 in the Scottish Cup. In consequence we had supporters who had travelled to Aberdeen three times in eleven days. We had seven scorers over the course of these two wins and we were left just one point behind Queen's Park at the top. The next fixture was against Queen's Park at Ochilview Park. Visions of reclaiming top spot were to evaporate in a 2-0 loss.

Having eliminated Pollok (home) and Cove Rangers (away) in the Scottish Cup, we now had Elgin City at Ayr. At approximately 4.50 pm I was stood outside Lincoln Cathedral frantically refreshing updates on the score. It was still 0-1 and I was now expecting to see this come up appended by FT for full time. I tried once more in desperation. 1-1 Bryden 90. Being in a holy place as well as a public place I kept my elation silent. We won 4-1 after extra time.

One point from the next nine dropped the club to fifth in the Championship. Morton 1 Ayr United 3 – we were back to third. People are largely correct when they say that the league is the priority but the Scottish Cup was starting to create some fervour. Falkirk away in the quarter-finals was eminently winnable. They were still in League One and it was earnestly believed that we would reach the semi-finals for the first time since 2002. With the score at 1-1 Chris Maguire hit the post with an 81st minute penalty. Two minutes later there was a goal at the other end when a shot found the Ayr net via a wild deflection. It is possible to get conditioned to losing but this was a tough one to take. There was a chance for atonement away to Dundee. A win would mean a return to second place. We lost 2-0. The Scottish Championship was turning into the Wheel of Fortune. Win at Firhill and we will be third. It was a 1-1 draw and we were fourth.

Fraser Bryden – sponsored by the Ayr United Strollers.

A 1-0 win at home to Raith Rovers in the penultimate fixture created a myriad of complex possibilities. The final round of Championship games took place on a Friday night once more. Occupying fourth place was just enough for a play-off and that was where we were. However finishing there was far from guaranteed. Entering this final game we stood to finish anywhere between second and sixth. Tension was so high that I did not want to go to Inverness. It was the kind of night to hide under the bed until it's all over! However Carol was keen to make the trip because she had been resolving to visit Fort George (twelve miles from Inverness) in order to research some family history there. We did the typical touristy stuff by stopping in Pitlochry in the morning and visiting Fort George in the afternoon. Nonetheless it was difficult to remain laid back about the evening in prospect. David did the driving. Earlier in the week he had driven to Shrewsbury and back to watch Bristol Rovers lose 2-1. The combined return journeys amounted to 962 miles.

The Carmichaels are still smiling after watching
Bristol Rovers 0 Barnsley 0

Bristol Rovers versus Barnsley on 4th March, 2023.

Inverness Caledonian Thistle required a win to reach the play-offs and a draw would prevent both clubs from reaching them. Nine of the ten Championship clubs had something to play for that night in terms of promotion and relegation. In the first half our league position went from fourth to fifth to second to third then back to second. On the previous Saturday Inverness Caledonian Thistle had beaten Falkirk 3-0 to reach the Scottish Cup final so they were formidable opponents. Josh Mullin's goal ten minutes before half-time was vital but the second half, as expected, was nervy. In the 81st minute Inverness equalised and we dropped from second to fifth. There was total bedlam when Mark McKenzie scored in the 88th minute. With that goal we were second again. Then, in the last attack of the game, Inverness had the ball in the Ayr net. A roar went up from the home end and it was immediately followed by a roar from the away end when an offside flag was spotted. Charlie Albinson took the free-kick and the final whistle blew immediately. This was the cue for even greater bedlam. In finishing second it was our highest second tier finish since 2000/01 and our highest second tier points total since then. We got home at 2.30 am still feeling wide awake. Against Dundee we had won one and lost three. If one of those three had been won we would have won the league by one point rather than finishing five points behind them.

In the play-off semi-final we lost 8-0 on aggregate against Partick Thistle. Quite why the team had such a spectacular fall from grace will remain a mystery. It was only partly explained by Dipo sitting out the first leg through injury then getting sent off in the 25th minute of the second leg. The sending off was a source of mystery too. He was red-carded for freeing himself from a headlock. The game even restarted with a free-kick for Ayr United. It was the biggest aggregate defeat in our history. The nearest comparison was 8-2 which had occurred twice, both in the League Cup; in September 1958 versus Hearts (the reigning Scottish champions) and in September 1967 versus Celtic (the reigning European champions). In 2023 Partick Thistle were the reigning champions of nothing.

Without wishing this to sound like an anthropological study, I have long since observed that the female of the species likes to indulge in retail therapy. The first match of 2023/24 was a League Cup group tie at Stirling. My lady wife said: "Stirling's fairly handy for the Almondvale Centre isn't it?" "Barely" was my vague answer. She considered 'barely' to be near enough so our trip to Stirling was via a 'not as the crow flies' route through Livingston. Not that there is any harm in doubling up a football trip to accommodate another function. When the children were young we once took them on a visit to Stirling Castle on a day when Ayr United were playing Stirling Albion. If by chance the football disappoints such excursions allow the chance for some vestige of satisfaction to be retained. Anyway at Stirling we had an 84th minute equaliser in a 1-1 draw which was followed by a bonus point for winning the shootout. With Somerset Park being reseeded we then had the novelty of playing Stenhousemuir at Townhead Park, Cumnock. A 1-0 win was less than convincing. Beating Premier League St.Johnstone 2-1 in Perth was, in contrast, wholly convincing. We could even afford the luxury of missing a late penalty. Ayr United 6 Alloa Athletic 0 was enough to win the group and it was nice to be back at Somerset Park. In the knockout stages we had a 2-0 loss at Livingston. For the Carmichaels the only redeeming feature was the proximity of the Almondvale Centre!

A year earlier a poor League Cup campaign had been the preliminary to a decent league campaign. Here in 2023 a decent League Cup campaign was the preliminary to four defeats in the first five league fixtures. A defeat is bad enough in itself but the scale of it was concerning in a couple of those matches (0-3 versus Dundee United and 0-4 versus Partick Thistle). Losing at Cappielow and Arbroath was equally unpalatable. There was another defeat in the mix, 0-1 versus Falkirk in the SPFL Trust Trophy. Ayr United 1 Inverness Caledonian Thistle 0 was the one blossom in the dust.

Again few grieved for the elimination in the SPFL Trust Trophy but the form in the Championship hinted at a relegation fight. On social media people who complain are commonly branded as haters. Hatred and constructive criticism are completely separate entities and there is no logic in seeing a co-relationship. When a bad run of form transforms into a good run of form we can expect the retort: "Where are all the haters now?" In truth the haters probably did not exist in the first place. Unarguably they did not exist when the team produced a 5-2 win against Queen's Park at Hampden. It was the first of three consecutive away wins, the others being at Airdrie (1-2) and Dunfermline (0-1). It was very much a case of enjoying it while you can. We then had a run of Played 5 Won 0 Drawn 2 Lost 3 For 5 Against 9. This is in relation to the league. In the midst of it was a Scottish Cup tie at Peterhead. In a similar fashion to the Elgin City tie earlier in the year we had a late equaliser after being 1-0 down. Sean McGinty scored in the sixth and final minute of stoppage time. Then Fraser Bryden struck the winner four minutes from the end of extra time.

15th July, 2023, at Forthbank Stadium, Stirling

25th July, 2023, at McDiarmid Park, Perth.

Sean McGinty was loved by the fans. He was a captain who was willing to lead by example yet he would find himself being released at the season's end. On a Friday night shortly before Christmas his wholehearted style got him a 43rd minute red card at Kirkcaldy. Two minutes later Raith Rovers went 2-1 up. It was a formidable prospect to face the league's top club in the second half while a goal down and a man down. In the 85th minute we went 4-3 up and it ended 4-4 after conceding in stoppage time. The team made a mockery of playing with ten men. It was an outstanding team performance.

From the onset of 2024 such combative performances were a memory. Losses to Morton (3-0) and Inverness Caledonian Thistle (1-3) preceded a 0-0 draw at Arbroath. With twenty fixtures played we were second bottom, just two points above Arbroath. Just one win had been registered in the last eleven league games. That match at Gayfield was Lee Bullen's last for the club. On the Monday it was announced that he had "parted company". The club statement read: "Ultimately onfield results over a sustained period of time have not been good enough and it is with real regret that we have come to this decision." At Ayr we have had many instances of managers leaving with angry shouts from the fans echoing in their ears but with Lee Bullen it was a lot different. Notwithstanding the 'one win in eleven' statistic he was popular. There was plenty of support for the argument that he could have turned things around. Nevertheless the board deserved to be commended for taking decisive action.

Somerset Park on 24th October, 2023.

David White now entered his third spell of interim management. His record in that role even had people suggesting that he deserved to be the actual manager. Could he maintain his success? His two matches in this stint were Ayr United 3 Kelty Hearts 0 (Scottish Cup) and Ayr United 2 Arbroath 0 (Championship). On aggregate his spells of interim management now read: Played 6 Won 5 Drawn 1 Lost 0 For 10 Against 0. The Arbroath win was watched by Scott Brown who had been named as the new manager that morning. Steven Whittaker came as his assistant. Understandably they took a back seat that night. As a player Scott Brown was a born winner. He and Whittaker made their names on different sides of the Old Firm divide but they were good friends of each other as well as being professional colleagues. Brown was possessed of a winning mentality and the optimists in our ranks were imbibed with a faith that his psyche would bring success. What would constitute success? It means different things to different people. In the immediate future a reasonable measure of success would be steering clear of relegation danger. Defeat in the Arbroath match would have had the consequence of landing at the foot of the table. However with David White in charge few, if any, would have contemplated losing.

Somerset Park on 13th February, 2024

It was something of a coincidence that Scott Brown's first match in charge was at Hampden, the scene of so many of his great triumphs. Queen's Park 1 Ayr United 2 would rank as one of his more modest triumphs but from our perspective it was all important at that time. "Broonie, Broonie" echoed across Hampden. There was renewed hope. Hope, more than anything, sustains the average Ayr United fan and we departed Hampden feeling that emotion in abundance.

Ayr United 1 Dundee United 2. Pitch invasions are understandable in certain circumstances but no one exceeds Dundee United when it comes to partaking in incursions onto the field. Yet again their fans encroached onto the Somerset turf in celebration of a single-goal win. It was hardly a league decider. The date was 3rd February. Then came a Scottish Cup 5th round tie at Ibrox. Naturally Scott Brown was not going to receive a cordial welcome at this of all places but that did not excuse the tone of some of the online comments in the build-up. Criminal investigation would have been an appropriate response. The people who displayed hatred on such an excessive scale would have been better advised to ditch football altogether. Scott Brown was the manager of Ayr United but now we were being sucked into the bile that exists between Rangers and Celtic. The tie was lost 2-0 and even the Old Firm-centric media agreed that Rangers should have been reduced to nine men. Fabio Silva, scorer of the second goal, committed a very bad tackle on George Stanger while already on a yellow card. There was equal consensus that Connor Goldson should have been dismissed for an over the top tackle on Roy Syla. Goldson was only saved by Syla staying on his feet.

Modern football has a reputation for players writhing about and feigning injury. Yet there are cases where the grounded player is clearly suffering from a serious knock. While leading 3-1 at Airdrie, Robbie Mutch made an exceptional save from a free-kick but the rebound was cut back into the danger area whereupon Airdrie scored. It was the 84th minute and the initial concern was about maintaining the lead. Straight away there was another concern. In attempting to keep the ball out Mutch had collided with a post. Viewed from behind that goal it was possible to see that his pain was extreme and that the source of that pain was his shoulder. His season was over. Charlie Albinson came on and we preserved the 3-2 scoreline. Anton Dowds scored a hat-trick but this was not the last time he would prove to be a scourge of Airdrie. We were now fifth in the league. At half-time we were ninth.

Anton Dowds was in great form but he was on loan from Partick Thistle. There was a fear that he could be recalled yet that was unlikely for as long as Brian Graham was on form at Firhill. Ten days after the win at Airdrie we had a home fixture against Partick Thistle and Dowds was ineligible to play against his parent club. Kurt Willoughby, on loan from Oldham Athletic, scored twice in the few remaining first half minutes but the flow of the game indicated that the 3-1 lead could not be taken for granted. Our former striker Tomi Adeloye trimmed it back to 3-2 (78 minutes) then Jack Sanders scored an own goal for 3-3 (83 minutes). By now we all felt crestfallen but not for long. In a move initiated from the recentre Harry McHugh, on loan from Wigan Athletic, concluded the scoring at 4-3 (84 minutes). Fifth place was maintained for now but points remained vital. Losing 2-0 at Dunfermline was quickly atoned for by winning 2-1 at Inverness. The referee was Iain Snedden and the last time he had handled an Ayr United match was also at Inverness. In that previous match he had awarded Inverness Caledonian Thistle a penalty timed at 45+3 and Billy Mckay had scored from it. Precisely the same occurred in this match. Mercifully the coincidence did not stretch to the same result which was a 3-1 defeat,

Ayr United 2 Airdrie 1 brought a haul of twelve points against a club whom we seemed to hold an Indian sign over. The run of wins against this club was far from over. This was a Friday night fixture which was screened live on BBC Scotland which was handy for the Carmichaels. We were on holiday in a beautiful apartment in Keswick. It turned out that broadcasting the match was not as handy as we thought because the action kept freezing. Trying to watch it on a phone had a similar result. The team winning was all that mattered. With six games left we were one point away from a promotion play-off spot and six clear of a relegation play-off spot. Worryingly the injury list included eight squad players. A further worry was that we had away games looming against Raith Rovers (second) and Dundee United (top). These matches were lost respectively with scorelines of 2-1 and 1-0. On the Saturday between those games we hosted Arbroath who were bottom of the league and had been showing every indication of throwing in the towel. The potentially important goal difference was given a boost with a 5-0 win with five scorers. A 0-0 draw away to Partick Thistle in the penultimate league fixture meant that we were mathematically safe from the relegation play-off position. However the final match did have some incentive. In the event of beating Dunfermline Athletic at home we would finish fifth. After a 3-3 draw the final position was seventh. Between 27th January and 6th April Ayr United's ten league fixtures were won and lost alternately. This statistic told a tale of alternate joy and despair. Fifty-three league goals were scored in 2023/24.

These goals came from a total of nineteen players. In the year of writing this is a club record for the number of league scorers in a season.

"By a country mile this is the proudest moment of my professional life." These were the words spoken by David Smith in response to the completion certificate being issued for the North Stand. He was correctly proud of this most handsome adornment to Somerset Park. It was the biggest capital investment in the club's history. The infrastructure had already been greatly enhanced with the construction of Cameron's Bar together with the adjacent shop and offices collectively known as The Hub. Somerset Park was gradually becoming more aesthetically pleasing and David Smith was the main man. The new stand was formally opened before a friendly against Celtic. More than 9,000 tickets were sold. In a 1-1 draw Ayr United used twenty players to Celtic's twenty-three. Such copious substitutions were to be expected in this type of match. Six nights later we were back for a 3-2 friendly win over Kilmarnock.

In the League Cup we had three group wins out of four. These were Falkirk (home), Stenhousemuir (away) and Buckie Thistle (home). Dundee United, Falkirk and Ayr United all finished on nine points. The top two went through but we were edged out on goal difference. Stenhousemuir 1 Ayr United 4 was the only time in our history when an Ayr United team has scored four in a match and they have all been from headers. A further consequence was that three generations of the one family had all scored for Ayr United; Alex McAnespie, Darren Henderson and now Jay Henderson. There was no historical precedent for three generations of the one family scoring for Ayr United.

In pre-season and in the League Cup we had seen enough glimpses of an attacking brand of football to form a belief that we could be a contender for the Championship title. Without wishing to rewrite the dictionary it would seem reasonable to define belief as a step higher than optimism. When we talk about optimism the context is very often blind optimism. The belief was strengthened when Ayr United won the first four league fixtures of 2024/25, a feat last achieved in 1991/92. There was an element of déjà vu. In 1991 and 2024 fixture four was a home win over Raith Rovers. In 1991 and 2024 fixture five was a 1-1 away draw (Kilmarnock and Dunfermline respectively). In 1991 and 2024 the Ayr United manager was a former Scotland internationalist (George Burley and Scott Brown respectively). In 1991 and 2024 fixture six was at home to Partick Thistle but there the run of coincidence ended (1-3 in 1991 and 1-1 in 2024). In these early weeks of the 2024/25 season Airdrie were hammered 5-0 at Somerset Park and the entire spectacle was witnessed by an audience on BBC Scotland. Anton Dowds had now scored eight goals in the five matches in which he had played for Ayr United against Airdrie. Catastrophically his season was close to being terminated. No longer a loanee, he was eligible to play against Partick Thistle at Ayr. In the 66th minute he slumped to the ground despite there being no form of contact. Ordinarily when a player goes down in such circumstances there can be accusations of simulation. In this instance it was a cruciate ligament injury. Not too many football fans will have a medical degree but we all know that this is a long term injury. It was a devastating development. He had scored nine goals to this point of the season and it was only 14th September. Together with George Oakley the strike partnership had been lethal at times. In drawing 1-1 we dropped to second place.

When Scott Brown had his name linked to the managerial vacancy at St.Johnstone, our fanbase hoped that it was simply media speculation. Hope implies doubt. Media sources were exonerated because the Ayr United board reluctantly gave him permission to speak to St.Johnstone. On the same day he spoke to them he said that he wished to be withdrawn from the running. One day later the Ayr United board issued this statement: "Ayr United can confirm that Scott Brown and Steven Whittaker have signed extended contracts at Somerset Park until 2027."

A 2-0 defeat at Falkirk did not dislodge Ayr United from the top. Our position was fragile though. The lead was on goal difference only and Falkirk had two games in hand. On the Tuesday afterwards they had a 0-0 draw at home to Livingston so they went one point clear with one game in hand. Ayr

United 1 Livingston 2. Successive six-pointers were lost and there was a further drop to third. Losing 2-0 away to Raith Rovers made it three defeats from four, the trend broken only by a 1-0 win at Airdrie. It was a sign of progress that a 1-1 draw away to Morton was considered to be a disappointment. Losing 3-2 at East Kilbride in the SPFL Trust Trophy was a further disappointment. The habitual indifference to this competition was less in evidence in 2024. Having eliminated Raith Rovers and Peterhead in home ties there was a stirring of interest due to a realisation that we were capable of winning the competition.

16th November, 2024, was unique in Scotland's second tier. The Championship fixtures comprised first versus second, third versus fourth, fifth versus sixth, seventh versus eighth and ninth versus tenth. People who take an interest in the minutiae of football statistics are termed anoraks. There is nothing denigrating about this and I will happily admit to belonging to that category. This was a happy day for the anoraks. It was a happy day for Ayr United too with a 3-2 win at home to Queen's Park (third versus fourth).

In relation to a game at Ayr, Dunfermline Athletic put out a club statement urging their fans not to travel. The issue was the weather but 104 of them defied the statement. These fans arrived more punctually than the team. Admittedly the weather was bad but the team's tardiness was largely attributable to diverting to Troon for lunch. The only league fixtures played in Scotland on this day outside of the Premier League were at Ayr and Montrose. The Dunfermline squad arrived at 2.50 pm and the kick-off took place at 3.45 pm which was forty-five minutes late. In weather conditions that were okay the match was won 1-0.

On losing 1-0 away to Partick Thistle there was a storm of post match controversy about the award of the match winning penalty. Yes, it was a dubious award and the complaints were valid but we had to live with it. However in the field of complaining about referees we were amateurs compared to the fans of Falkirk. On losing 5-2 at Ayr they had Luke Graham red-carded. Their fans were adamant that they would have won in the absence of what they considered to be a red card wrongly awarded. Quite how one player would have created a four-goal turnaround is baffling. The match ended with Ayr United pressing for a sixth goal. Even in victory we remained third, seven points behind top-placed Falkirk. Defeat would have left a yawning gap of thirteen points. Livingston 0 Ayr United 1 gave the home club their first home league defeat of the season. These back to back six-pointers left us all ebullient. With Livingston losing away to Raith Rovers a home win over Morton on the last Saturday of the year would reinstate Ayr United to second place. It was 0-0 and even the *Greenock Telegraph* opined that "Morton rode their luck."

On the first Saturday of 2025 George Oakley scored a hat-trick in an emphatic 3-0 win at home to Raith Rovers and second place was reinstated. Falkirk's lead at the top was four points which was whittled down to two after our 2-0 win at Dunfermline. We had played a game more but the momentum was with us. Or, rather, it would have been had it not been for the distraction of the Scottish Cup. Having won 2-0 at home to Morton in the third round we now had an away tie against Broxburn Athletic. They played in the Lowland League, Scottish football's fifth tier. People were quick to point out that in the SPFL Trust Trophy we had lost to East Kilbride of the Lowland League. Past experience indicated that any such warning was worth listening to. It transpired that the warning was not worth listening to. At 8-0 it was the biggest away win in the club's history. Hibs at home in the next round threw up a tie against a team who were in rampant form in the Premier League. Losing 0-1 to an 87th minute goal was creditable.

Winning the first four league fixtures of 2025 had the consequence of reclaiming top place on 1st February. The lead was just one point and we had played one game more. Tantalisingly the next match was at Falkirk by which time they had won their game in hand. In drawing 2-2 it felt like a defeat after having a 2-0 lead. Falkirk, Ayr United and Livingston were now on fifty, forty-eight and forty-six points respectively, all having played the same number of games. Livingston were at Ayr the following week. These six-pointers were unabated. Alas it was lost 2-1 with a goal scored directly from a free-kick in the sixth minute of stoppage time. Looking at it objectively it was a sublime strike from Robbie Muirhead but it was nonetheless a heartbreaker. The final whistle was blown immediately upon the recentre.

Winning the league still remained a possibility. Following on from the Livingston disappointment Airdrie were easily beaten 4-1 at Ayr on a day when our two title rivals only drew. Falkirk, Livingston and Ayr United were now respectively on fifty-four, fifty-three and fifty-one points with Livingston having played a game more. It was so tight that a 2-0 deficit against Queen's Park at Hampden was potentially fatal. Then came the spirited fightback to win 3-2. Once more we were second and just three points off the top. What happened next could almost have been scripted. On consecutive Saturdays we had defeats at Cappielow and Firhill. Then, on the next again Saturday, Ethan Walker scored at home to Hamilton Accies in the fifth minute of stoppage time to nick a 1-1 draw. One point from nine was fatal. The only route to the Premier League now would be via the play-offs.

Yet the run-in was far from dull. Neil Lennon's first match in charge of Dunfermline Athletic was at Ayr and his team contained Victor Wanyama who was making his debut after being announced as a marquee signing. He went on as a substitute and got sent off twenty minutes later after seemingly getting it into his head that he was a goalkeeper. The result was a more than comfortable 3-0 victory. Falkirk visited for the next home game which had a live screening on the BBC on a Friday evening. Victory on the night would have taken the visitors to the brink of winning the league. Their fans were in celebratory mood until Ethan Walker made it 1-1 in the 90th minute. Walker finished the season with four league goals. They were timed at 90, 90+5, 90+4 and 90. On the next Friday a 5-0 defeat at Livingston was the outcome of an uncharacteristically bad performance. The season concluded with a 1-0 win at Airdrie in what was our tenth consecutive victory against them (all league). It hardly mattered. Regardless of the result that night it was known that we were going to finish third. Sixty-three points was our highest total in the second tier since obtaining sixty-nine in 2000/01.

There was a popular view that third place would have been satisfactory if it had been offered at the start of the season. Yet would people have considered it satisfactory in mid-February when we were 2-0 up at Falkirk and top of the league? Rather than persist in an uncharitable tone it would be fair to state that, on balance, it was a good season. With the play-offs pending it had the possibility of getting even better. Alas what happened next remains fresh in the memory. A 1-0 first leg win at Firhill had us all on a high. Cautiously it was pointed out that it was merely half-time. Partick Thistle, as you know, went into the play-off semi-finals on a 2-1 aggregate. Yes it was dreadfully disappointing but it could not mask the fact that we have witnessed vast improvement both in relation to team matters and the infrastructure in and around Old Lady Somerset.

What next? Not having the gift of prophecy we cannot know therefore we must rely on hope. There it is again, the recurring message of hope. Due to wise governance Ayr United Football Club has been built on strong foundations. We can be assured that all efforts are being made to ensure that our hopes will be fulfilled.

This image of the Somerset Road End shows my favoured spot behind the crush barrier at the front.

Index to the Iliad: the places

A

Aberdeen 14, 46, 53, 56, 65, 85, 87, 95, 105, 107, 108, 109, 113, 114, 115, 121, 122, 126, 143, 283, 297, 318, 329, 336, 339, 340, 357, 371, 374
Accrington 252, 253
Airdrie 56, 61, 90, 95, 96, 97, 124, 134, 138, 140, 141, 143, 144, 147, 157, 158, 159, 160, 163, 166, 188, 193, 212, 213, 217, 222, 226, 227, 230, 232, 236, 238, 239, 241, 243, 245, 247, 253, 288, 295, 297, 314, 317, 320, 321, 324, 325, 326, 327, 328, 332, 339, 340, 341, 379, 384, 385, 387, 388, 390
Alloa 27, 32, 33, 50, 53, 56, 114, 132, 133, 134, 138, 139, 143, 145, 148, 156, 214, 215, 236, 247, 248, 250, 251, 261, 262, 263, 264, 266, 271, 276, 282, 285, 288, 296, 311, 312, 320, 339, 341, 342, 348, 351, 352, 353, 356, 361, 378
Alloway 356
Annan 20, 150, 275, 294, 302, 338, 358, 369, 370
Annbank 46, 213
Arbroath 24, 32, 33, 56, 61, 62, 67, 70, 119, 123, 148, 154, 241, 242, 247, 248, 250, 251, 261, 262, 263, 282, 285, 288, 309, 312, 313, 314, 317, 339, 340, 341, 346, 351, 352, 353, 355, 356, 360, 361, 362, 364, 366, 370, 379, 381, 382, 385

Ardeer 39
Ardrossan 213
Argentina 105, 119
Armadale 13, 18, 20, 27
Auchinleck 347
Auchterarder 154
Ayr *passim*

B

Ballantrae 192
Barcelona 93, 326
Barnsley 376, 377
Barrhead 184
Bathgate 13, 17, 18, 19, 20, 22, 23, 24, 25, 26, 27, 209
Bearsden 37, 38, 137
Beith 54, 346
Belfast 313
Berwick 50, 52, 57, 58, 68, 123, 201, 203, 205, 207, 208, 209, 210, 211, 240, 255, 260, 261, 263, 279, 294, 349, 350
Birmingham 103, 106
Blackburn 64, 72, 256
Blyth 240
Bolton 72, 308
Bo'ness 13
Bonnyrigg 36, 42
Bradford 141, 364
Brazil 231
Brechin 54, 56, 68, 143, 144, 150, 166, 169, 173, 187, 189, 206, 209, 236, 254, 255, 256, 257, 261, 262, 264, 271, 274, 277, 280, 283, 284,

286, 288, 291, 295, 297, 298, 299, 300, 310, 312, 317, 318, 320, 322, 326, 327
Bristol 251, 252, 257, 356, 367, 376, 377
Broxburn 13
Buckie 53, 386
Burntisland 12
Bury 10, 46, 367

C

Cambridge 93
Canada 109, 299
Carlisle 240, 251, 257
Castle Douglas 330
Chorley 314, 315
Cleland 40
Clydebank 56, 93, 109, 112, 113, 114, 115, 122, 132, 134, 136, 137, 158, 161, 162, 166, 173, 187, 189, 198, 199, 211, 212, 222, 226, 227, 230, 232, 245, 247, 312, 324
Coatbridge 2, 3, 206, 212, 214, 311, 341
Copenhagen 231
Coventry 174, 186, 211, 212
Cowdenbeath 53, 56, 61, 86, 87, 101, 147, 148, 150, 151, 153, 154, 169, 179, 180, 181, 182, 184, 270, 272, 273, 277, 296, 318, 319, 323, 325, 326, 327, 328
Crossgates 36
Crosshill 40
Cumberland 101
Cumbernauld 212
Cumnock 378

D

Darlington 186, 240
Darvel 51
Derby 106
Dingwall 280, 291, 292
Douglas Water 22
Drongan 40, 272
Dumbarton 20, 46, 50, 54, 56, 70, 96, 99, 102, 123, 137, 138, 145, 150, 169, 179, 180, 205, 207, 208, 226, 235, 241, 246, 247, 252, 260, 261, 262, 265, 266, 267, 268, 269, 295, 296, 297, 332, 333, 335, 336, 338
Dumfries 71, 108, 158, 247, 345, 352, 353, 357
Dundee 46, 56, 70, 108, 109, 121, 122, 123, 128, 140, 154, 170, 174, 175, 192, 193, 197, 198, 218, 233, 235, 264, 274, 292, 302, 303, 307, 344, 356, 358, 360, 362, 364, 371, 373, 375, 377
Dundonald (Ayrshire) 101
Dundonald (Fife) 36, 279
Dunfermline 39, 54, 56, 64, 82, 84, 135, 136, 153, 157, 158, 159, 178, 181, 182, 184, 188, 195, 200, 211, 230, 231, 233, 243, 244, 247, 266, 270, 276, 288, 290, 291, 314, 315, 317, 319, 320, 325, 326, 328, 332, 333, 338, 339, 345, 348, 353, 354, 364, 365, 368, 369, 379, 384, 385, 387, 388, 389, 390

E

East Kilbride 235, 388, 389
East Lothian 3, 9, 10, 11, 36, 48, 123
Edinburgh 11, 12, 36, 39, 40, 42, 74, 90, 111, 124, 144, 148, 177, 217

Elgin 65, 66, 243, 294, 359, 361, 369, 370, 374, 379

F

Falkirk 4, 5, 6, 24, 25, 54, 56, 89, 96, 134, 143, 145, 161, 166, 188, 192, 211, 218, 221, 222, 226, 229, 236, 238, 239, 241, 243, 246, 247, 251, 253, 254, 255, 257, 259, 262, 302, 305, 307, 314, 325, 330, 332, 333, 348, 350, 351, 363, 375, 377, 379, 386, 387, 388, 389, 390, 391
Fisherton 24
Forfar 49, 50, 52, 68, 70, 71, 96, 114, 140, 141, 143, 144, 162, 171, 177, 201, 203, 261, 264, 265, 272, 276, 296, 297, 299, 303, 307, 309, 310, 312, 313, 314, 316, 317, 318, 320, 322, 323, 328, 339, 340, 341
Fort George 376
France 10, 29, 101, 109

G

Galston 25
Girvan 40, 192
Glasgow 16, 67, 78, 85, 90, 96, 105, 106, 126, 127, 219, 222, 230, 267, 274, 284, 286, 294, 303, 309, 346, 351, 357
Grangemouth 69, 350
Greenock 51, 53
Gretna 265, 266, 267, 268

H

Haddington 3, 9, 209, 350
Halifax 72
Hamilton 56, 119, 133, 138, 140, 141, 160, 162, 169, 171, 173, 175, 182, 197, 198, 205, 207, 208, 209, 212, 214, 215, 218, 222, 225, 229, 260, 276, 301, 304, 307, 311, 329, 358, 363, 364, 371, 372, 390
Harthill 14
Hartlepool 252
Hull 105
Hurlford 101

I

Inverness 53, 64, 95, 237, 238, 239, 241, 243, 247, 248, 249, 268, 290, 292, 293, 302, 344, 348, 353, 355, 356, 359, 360, 361, 362, 367, 369, 372, 373, 376, 377, 379, 381, 385
Ipswich 355
Irish Republic 191
Irvine 66, 83, 85, 134, 144, 149, 163

J

Johnstone 53

K

Kelty 382
Kendal 314, 315
Keswick 373, 385
Kilbirnie 101
Kilmacolm 39
Kilmarnock 21, 30, 40, 51, 52, 54, 56, 57, 59, 60, 66, 77, 82, 83, 84, 86, 87, 90, 94, 96, 97, 98, 99, 105, 107, 111, 112, 113, 121, 122, 130, 132, 133, 136, 137, 138, 140, 142, 143, 144, 147, 149, 155, 156, 157, 158, 159, 160, 166, 168, 171, 173, 174, 175, 178, 180, 181, 184, 187, 189, 194, 195, 204, 215, 217, 219,

224, 225, 232, 241, 242, 243, 254, 259, 265, 284, 285, 304, 305, 319, 338, 362, 363, 364, 365, 367, 368, 370, 386, 387
Kilsyth 3, 66, 261
Kilwinning 101, 184, 260
Kirkcaldy 79, 90, 133, 153, 177, 181, 290, 337, 342, 343, 381
Kirkintilloch 137
Korea 12

L

Lanarkshire 22
Larbert 6
Largs 90
Leeds 94, 98
Leicester 99
Leyton 252
Lincoln 141, 374
Liverpool 4, 18, 24, 47, 84, 103, 129, 130
Livingston 13, 204, 205, 206, 207, 209, 228, 236, 237, 238, 239, 264, 270, 275, 287, 297, 298, 299, 305, 307, 325, 328, 349, 350, 358, 378, 379, 387, 388, 389, 390
Loanhead 36
Lochee 284
Luton 141, 204, 293

M

Madrid 14, 51, 106, 138
Malta 370
Manchester 23, 186, 242
Mansfield 99, 106
Methil 314
Middlesbrough 191
Midlothian 36
Monaco 213

Monkton 163, 367
Montrose 51, 52, 61, 107, 121, 122, 150, 151, 153, 169, 202, 203, 288, 304, 339, 388
Motherwell 5, 26, 29, 40, 69, 70, 71, 91, 103, 106, 107, 109, 113, 121, 122, 123, 127, 130, 132, 133, 140, 170, 171, 175, 176, 186, 187, 208, 209, 221, 233, 234, 252, 253, 288, 308, 338, 357
Muirkirk 22

N

Newcastle United 10, 82, 94, 99, 109, 110, 220, 315
Nigeria 109
Northern Ireland 93
Norway 101, 220
Nottingham 77, 99, 110, 111

O

Oldham 262, 367, 384
Ormiston 10, 36, 37, 38, 39, 41, 48, 209
Oslo 220
Oxford 228

P

Paisley 66, 126, 133, 184, 263, 298, 309, 337
Paris 14, 127, 134
Pencaitland 9, 10, 12, 13, 15, 38, 41, 349, 350
Perth 23, 24, 66, 77, 91, 134, 136, 154, 163, 247, 273, 378, 380
Peterhead 56, 249, 265, 269, 273, 274, 277, 279, 280, 283, 286, 296, 320, 321, 322, 323, 325, 326, 327, 328, 379, 388

Pitlochry 249, 376
Pollok 374
Polmont 3, 4, 6
Ponfeigh 22
Prestwick 14, 62, 69, 117, 164, 220, 244, 250, 292, 298, 371

R

Reading 293
Redding 3,4,5, 6, 9
Roda 105
Rome 137
Romania 20, 107
Roxburghshire 3

S

Sedan 30
Shrewsbury 376
Southampton 186
Stenhousemuir 3, 44, 49, 50, 56, 62, 69, 148, 150, 154, 174, 202, 206, 207, 208, 282, 299, 307, 308, 312, 313, 315, 318, 320, 321, 322, 323, 325, 326, 328, 344, 370, 378, 386
Stevenage 93
Stirling 46, 56, 70, 71, 121, 123, 128, 133, 148, 149, 150, 152, 153, 156, 166, 169, 184, 187, 189, 190, 201, 202, 203, 204, 208, 213, 214, 216, 217, 218, 230, 252, 261, 263, 264, 265, 267, 268, 269, 270, 271, 272, 283, 286, 320, 322, 323, 342, 378, 380
Stirlingshire 3, 4, 6, 11
Stockport 237
Stranraer 21, 33, 47, 48, 49, 56, 59, 68, 101, 148, 149, 174, 191, 192, 195, 197, 202, 206, 215, 219, 221, 242, 260, 262, 263, 270, 272, 273, 274, 284, 286, 309, 312, 313, 314, 315, 316, 317, 318, 320, 321, 326, 327, 328, 329, 339, 340, 341, 342, 350, 358
Strathaven 38
Sunderland 22, 89, 178, 356
Sweden 24, 219, 220, 235
Swindon 186
Symington 109, 144, 153, 163, 224

T

Tranent 41, 42, 43
Troon 144, 388

U

Urziceni 289

V

Valletta 370

W

Wallacestone 4
Wallyford 12
West Lothian 13, 34
Whitburn 42
Whitley Bay 240
Wigan 240, 384
Wishaw 18, 22
Wolverhampton 293
Wrexham 228, 350

Y

Yoker 42

Index to Illyria: the football

8th Ayr Boys' Brigade 51, 63, 98, 108

15th Scottish Reconnaissance Regiment 10

A

Aberdeen 14, 46, 53, 56, 65, 85, 87, 95, 105, 107, 108, 109, 113, 114, 115, 121, 122, 126, 143, 283, 297, 318, 329, 336, 339, 340, 357, 371, 374

Absolut Print and Design Trophy 240

Accrington Stanley 252, 253

Adams, Jamie 331, 335

Adeloye, Tomi 363, 365, 384

Advocaat, Dick 105

Agnew, Garry 179

Airdrie 56, 61, 90, 95, 96, 97, 124, 134, 138, 140, 141, 143, 144, 147, 157, 158, 159, 160, 163, 166, 188, 193, 212, 213, 217, 222, 226, 227, 230, 232, 236, 238, 239, 241, 243, 245, 247, 253, 288, 295, 297, 314, 317, 320, 321, 324, 325, 326, 327, 328, 332, 339, 340, 341, 379, 384, 385, 387, 388, 390

Airdrie United 245, 281, 286, 287, 290, 291, 292, 296, 298, 307

Aitken, Chris 284, 287

Aitken, Fraser 256

Akinyemi, Dipo 370, 371, 372, 373, 378

ALBA Challenge Cup 282

Albert Park 39

Albinson, Charlie 377, 384

Albion Rovers 2, 32, 50, 134, 147, 154, 160, 162, 163, 225, 235, 288, 289, 310, 311, 312, 324, 327, 328, 339, 342, 344, 358, 362, 365

Alexander, Gordon 118

Allan, Derek 177, 186

Allan, Ray 206

Allan Stevenson Sports 67

Alliance League 20

Alloa Athletic 27, 32, 33, 50, 53, 56, 114, 132, 133, 134, 138, 139, 143, 145, 148, 156, 214, 215, 236, 247, 248, 250, 251, 261, 262, 263, 264, 266, 271, 276, 282, 285, 288, 296, 311, 312, 320, 339, 341, 342, 348, 351, 352, 353, 356, 361, 378

Ally MacLeod Suite 88, 303, 357

Almondvale Centre 349, 378, 379

Alston, Blair 363

Ancell Babes 26

Anderson, Derek 217

Anderson, Jock 7

Anderson, Tester 7

Andrews, Marvin 239

Anfield 119

Anglo Scottish Cup 99, 106, 109, 110

Annan 20, 150, 275, 294, 302, 338, 358, 369, 370

Annand, Eddie 235, 236, 244, 266

Annbank United 46, 213

Annfield 128, 156

Annpit Road 26
Anton, George 21, 47
Arbroath 24, 32, 33, 56, 61, 62, 67, 70, 119, 123, 148, 154, 241, 242, 247, 248, 250, 251, 261, 262, 263, 282, 285, 288, 309, 312, 313, 314, 317, 339, 340, 341, 346, 351, 352, 353, 355, 356, 360, 361, 362, 364, 366, 370, 379, 381, 382, 385
Archibald, Steve 114, 200, 238
Argentina 105, 119
Armadale 13, 18, 20, 27
Armour, Davy 124, 137, 259
Arsenal 18, 150
Ashleigh Building 354
Auchinleck 347
Auchterarder 154
Ayr Academy 62, 63, 79
Ayr Advertiser 24, 33, 34, 46, 50, 68, 123, 127, 133, 134, 158, 162, 191, 243
Ayr Albion 98
Ayr Bruins 242
Ayr Charity Cup 164
Ayre, Calvin 299
Ayr FC 4, 164, 166, 232, 310, 347
Ayr Guildry 264
Ayr Racecourse 294
Ayr Scottish Eagles 242
Ayrshire Cup 55, 60, 87, 107, 133, 136, 149, 155, 156, 173, 195, 196
Ayrshire Post 111, 115, 145, 175, 177, 178, 201, 232, 240, 256, 279, 299, 303, 321
Ayr Thistle 234
Ayr United *passim*
Ayr United Boys' Club 185, 186
Ayr United Strollers 14, 373, 375
Ayr United Supporters' Association 96, 160
Ayr United Travel Club 200

B

Baird, Jack 363
Baker, Joe 18,
Baker, Martin 225
Bangala, David 371
Banks O' Dee 340
Barcelona 93, 326
Barnsley 376, 377
Barr, Bill 162, 197, 201, 202, 238
Barrhead 184
Bartley, Marvin 366
Baseball Ground 106
Bathgate Thistle 13, 17, 19, 22, 24
Bathgate West 25
Bayview Park 200
BBC Alba 286, 342, 348
BBC Radio Scotland 206
BBC Scotland 363, 372, 385, 387
Bearsden 37, 38, 137
Beattie, Alec 6, 71
Beattie, Craig 320
Beith Juniors 54, 346
Bell, Brian 99, 100
Bell, Steven 353
Bellsdale Park 346
Bell's Sports Centre 66
Belton, Eric 373
Beresford Terrace 242
Berwick Rangers 50, 52, 57, 58, 68, 123, 201, 203, 205, 207, 208, 209, 210, 211, 240, 255, 260, 261, 263, 279, 294, 349, 350
Big 'A' Club 197
Birmingham City 99, 103
Black, Aaron 246, 250
Blackburn Rovers 64, 72, 256
Black & White Shop 88, 89
Black & White Whisky 88
Blane, Bob 50
Blue Brazil 270

Blyth Spartans 240
Bodog 299
Boghall Primary 25
Boghead Park 70, 96, 138, 207, 226, 241
Bolton Wanderers 72, 308
Bone, Alex 214, 229
Bone, Jimmy 184
Bo'ness 13
Bonnyrigg Rose 36, 42
BP Youth Cup 177
B & Q Cup 174, 175, 179, 192, 193
Bradford City 141, 364
Bradley, Steven 365
Bradley, Willie 34
Braidwood Motor Company Stadium 305
Brazil 231
Brechin City 54, 56, 68, 143, 144, 150, 166, 169, 173, 187, 189, 206, 209, 236, 254, 255, 256, 257, 261, 262, 264, 271, 274, 277, 280, 283, 284, 286, 288, 291, 295, 297, 298, 299, 300, 310, 312, 317, 318, 320, 322, 326, 327
Brewers Cup 274
Brice, Gordon 293
Bristol Rovers 251, 252, 257, 356, 367, 376, 377
Broadwood Stadium 193, 208, 212, 219, 250, 270, 335
Brockville Park 4, 5, 6, 161, 166, 211, 221, 236, 237, 238, 239, 241, 243, 247, 251
Brogan, Jim 67
Broomfield Park 61, 160, 166
Brown, Craig 121
Brown, Gordon 280
Brown, Jimmy (Ayr United) 137
Brown, Jimmy (Pencaitland Amateurs) 37
Brown, Scott 382, 383, 387

Brownlie, Darren 313
Broxburn 13
Broxburn Athletic 350, 389
Bryce, Tommy 161, 164, 166, 169
Bryden, Fraser 366, 375, 379
BSkyB 164
Buckie Thistle 53, 386
Bullen, Lee 366, 369, 372, 381
Burley, George 172, 173, 174, 177, 180, 181, 188, 266, 387
Burn, Ramsay 28, 34
Burns, Kenny 105
Burns, Robert 347, 356
Burns, Tommy 191
Burntisland 12
Bury 10, 46, 367

C

Caddis, Ryan 270
Calderwood, Colin 185, 186, 297
Calderwood, Jimmy 105
Caldwell, Brian 235
Caldwell, George 121,132, 136
Caldwell, Ross 326
Caledonian Stadium 237
Callaghan, Myles 119, 130
Cambridge United 93
Cameron, Donald 269
Cameron, Lachlan 319, 359
Cameron's Bar 386
Campbell, Dick 340, 341
Campbell, Ian 92
Campbell, Mark 235, 249
Canada 109, 299
Cappielow Park 84, 90, 145, 154, 174, 184, 227, 230, 232, 301, 323, 337, 345, 365, 371, 379, 390
Carey, Graham 304
Cargill, Stuart 296
Carlisle 240, 251, 257

Carmichael, Andrew (5 x great grandfather) 3
Carmichael, Archie (great grandfather) 6
Carmichael, Carol (wife) 134, 138, 149, 215, 245, 247, 367, 368, 376, 378
Carmichael, Claire (niece) 306
Carmichael, David (son) 3, 149, 178, 181, 251, 284, 306, 350, 376, 377
Carmichael, Douglas (brother) 10, 15, 16, 18, 74, 306, 329, 354, 370
Carmichael, Jill (daughter) 3, 138, 178, 215, 252, 265, 295, 306, 354, 376
Carmichael, Margaret (5 x great grandmother) 3
Carmichael, Margaret (mother) 10, 41, 74, 91.
Carmichael, Margaret (sister-in-law) 306
Carmichael, Peter (brother) 10, 15, 16, 18, 41, 74, 306, 329, 343, 354
Carmichael, Peter (father) 7, 10, 11, 12, 13, 14, 18, 21, 23, 25, 38, 39, 40, 41, 67
Carmichael, Peter (grandfather) 3, 4, 5, 6, 8, 9, 11, 251
Carnegie Library 81
Cashmore, Ian 126
Castilla, David 213
Celtic 14, 20, 22, 26, 30, 33, 62, 67, 69, 71, 74, 77, 90, 91, 95, 97, 101, 103, 108, 112, 113, 114, 125, 126, 127, 140, 157, 164, 171, 191, 195, 200, 211, 225, 230, 231, 237, 244, 245, 253, 267, 288, 327, 337, 359, 378, 384, 386

Celtic Park 26, 33, 93, 111, 112, 114, 126, 164, 211, 237, 267
Centenary Cup 169, 170, 174
Challenge Cup 200, 204, 211, 221, 229, 236, 242, 246, 247, 252, 259, 265, 270, 276, 282, 289, 296, 301, 308, 314, 332, 350
Chalmers, Joe 358
Championship 324, 329, 331, 332, 338, 344, 347, 351, 353, 357, 359, 361, 365, 370, 371, 372, 373, 375, 376, 377, 379, 382, 386, 388
Charlton, Bobby 55
Charlton, Jack 55
Charnley, Chic 180
Chelsea 14, 272
Cherrie, Peter 261
Cherry, Paul 153
Chorley 314, 315
Christie, Gerry 129, 130
Clachnacuddin 288, 310
Clark, Allan 294
Clark, Kenny 184, 263
Clayton, Ronnie 256
Cleese, John 69
Cleland Miners Welfare 40
Cliftonhill Park 2, 206, 208, 214, 215
Clough, Brian 111
Clunie, Jim 130
Clyde 18, 32, 52, 56, 69, 77, 79, 115, 119, 121, 122, 134, 136, 140, 157, 158, 159, 160, 169, 173, 187, 200, 205, 206, 208, 209, 212, 219, 246, 247, 252, 254, 270, 271, 288, 308, 319, 335, 338, 361
Clyde, George 250
Clydebank 56, 93, 109, 112, 113, 114, 115, 122, 132, 134, 136, 137, 158, 161, 162, 166, 173, 187, 189, 198, 199, 211, 212, 222, 226, 227, 230, 232, 245, 247, 312, 324

Coatbridge 2, 3, 206, 212, 214, 311, 341
Cochran, Andy 20
Cockburn, Tom 137
Cole, Graham 124
Cole, Hugh 124, 151, 370
Coleman, David 53, 65
Collins, Gerry 136, 138
Collum, Willie 269
Combined Reserve League 46
Commonwealth Stadium 177, 180
Connolly, Paddy 264
Connor, Robert 124, 128, 136, 140, 186, 204, 263, 271, 272, 273
Conroy, Mike 126
Cooper, Davy 189
Co-operative Creamery 13
Co-operative Insurance 11, 13, 23, 39, 143
Corr, Barry John 277
Coventry City 174, 186, 211, 212
Cove Rangers 371, 374
Cowdenbeath 53, 56, 61, 86, 87, 101, 147, 148, 150, 151, 153, 154, 169, 179, 180, 181, 182, 184, 270, 272, 273, 277, 296, 318, 319, 323, 325, 326, 327, 328
Cox, Jacky 29, 32
Coyle, Owen 166, 199, 230, 247
Crabbe, Scott 244, 246
Craig, Billy 14
Craig, David 235, 251
Craigie Park 101
Craigmark Burntonians 54
Cramond, Gordon 112, 113
Crampsey, Bob 38
Crampsey, Frank 38
Crawford, Ian 70, 71, 297
Creamery Park 1, 13, 14, 17, 22, 26, 27, 34, 53
Crilly, Mark 246, 270

Cringan, Robert 22
Cringan, Willie 22
Croatia 106
Cropley, Alex 95
Crossgates Primrose 36
Crosshill Thistle 40
Cruickshank, Jim 76
Cumbernauld 212
Cumnock 378
Cumnock Juniors 275
Curlett, Dave 34
Cuthbert, Kevin 307
Cuthill, Bob 113

D

Daily Express 62
Daily Record 67
Dalglish, Kenny 99
Dallas, Hugh 215
Dalton, John 256
Dalziel, Gordon 198, 202, 204, 205, 208, 211, 212, 214, 231, 234, 237, 238, 242, 247, 248, 270
Dam Park 93
Darlington 186, 240
Darvel Juniors 51
Dempsey, Ben 372
Dempsey, Harry 76,
Dens Park 122, 192, 193, 292, 302, 360
Derby County 106
Deuchar, Kenny 265
Deveronvale 243, 291
Dick, Jim 213, 215, 216
Dijkstra, Sieb 225
Dingwall 280, 291, 292
Dingwall, Mervyn 118,
D'jaffo, Laurent 213, 219
Dobbie, Stephen 275, 345, 358
Docherty, Ross 328, 335, 338

402

Dodds, Billy 170
Dodds, Davy 137
Dodds, John 234
Doodson Sport Cup 314
Doohan, Ross 344, 345, 346, 353
Dougal, Stuart 239
Douglas, Bryan 256
Douglas Park 173, 182
Douglas Water Thistle 22
Dowds, Anton 384, 387
Downie, Andrew 294
Doyle, Jamie 261
Doyle, John 20, 81, 82, 92, 95, 97, 99, 105, 107, 108, 113, 114
Drinan, Aaron 355, 356
Drogba, Didier 351
Drongan United 40, 41
Drybrough Cup 126
Drysdale, John, 7
Duffy, Jim 121, 364, 365
Duffy, Neil 235, 246
Dumbarton 20, 46, 50, 54, 56, 70, 96, 99, 102, 123, 137, 138, 145, 150, 169, 179, 180, 205, 207, 208, 226, 235, 241, 246, 247, 252, 260, 261, 262, 265, 266, 267, 268, 269, 295, 296, 297, 332, 333, 335, 336, 338
Dumfries 71, 108, 158, 247, 345, 352, 353, 357
Duncan, Cammy 182, 193, 197, 198
Duncan, Russell 248
Dundee 46, 56, 70, 108, 109, 121, 122, 123, 128, 140, 154, 170, 174, 175, 192, 193, 197, 198, 218, 233, 235, 264, 274, 292, 302, 303, 307, 344, 356, 358, 360, 362, 364, 371, 373, 375, 377
Dundee NCR 39
Dundee United 49, 50, 64, 65, 70, 93, 95, 96, 103, 108, 109, 113, 130, 137, 147, 186, 225, 244, 293, 330, 332, 345, 346, 347, 349, 350, 351, 352, 354, 356, 363, 379, 383, 385, 386
Dundonald 101
Dundonald Bluebell 36, 279
Dunfermline Athletic 39, 54, 56, 64, 82, 84, 135, 136, 153, 157, 158, 159, 178, 181, 182, 184, 188, 195, 200, 211, 230, 231, 233, 243, 244, 247, 266, 270, 276, 288, 290, 291, 314, 315, 317, 319, 320, 325, 326, 328, 332, 333, 338, 339, 345, 348, 353, 354, 364, 365, 368, 369, 379, 384, 385, 387, 388, 389, 390
Dunlop, Alastair 118
Dunlop, Archie 118
Dunlop, Michael 254, 263, 264, 296

E

East, Euan 369
East End Park 39, 153, 188, 195, 230
East of Scotland Amateur Cup 40
Easter Road 14, 74, 77, 95, 117, 124, 144, 146, 163, 177, 222, 297, 331, 335, 336, 338
East Fife 49, 62, 71, 90, 91, 200, 202, 203, 283, 296, 298, 299, 310, 312, 314, 318, 341
Easthouses Lily 36
East Kilbride 235, 388, 389
Easton William 294
East Park Road 25
East Stirling 4, 33, 34, 68, 70, 129, 132, 190, 192, 203, 204, 237, 282, 302, 308, 319, 339
Ecrepont , Finn 346
Edinburgh 11, 12, 36, 39, 40, 42, 74, 90, 111, 124, 144, 148, 177, 217
Edinburgh City 288, 329, 363
Edinburgh Evening Dispatch 48

Edinburgh Royal Infirmary 10
Eintracht 51
El Alagui, Farid 336
Elgin City 65, 66, 243, 294, 359, 361, 369, 370, 374, 379
Elliot, Billy 28
Employee Benefit Trusts 244
England team 18, 20, 54, 55, 97, 99
European Cup 14, 29, 93, 106, 111, 137
European Cup Winners' Cup 29, 93
Evans, Gareth 219
Evans, Stevie 139
Evening Citizen 48, 67
Evening Times 1, 30, 38, 48, 78, 94
Everton 10, 47, 51

F

Falkirk 4, 5, 6, 24, 25, 54, 56, 89, 96, 134, 143, 145, 161, 166, 188, 192, 211, 218, 221, 222, 226, 229, 236, 238, 239, 241, 243, 246, 247, 251, 253, 254, 255, 257, 259, 262, 302, 305, 307, 314, 325, 330, 332, 333, 348, 350, 351, 363, 375, 377, 379, 386, 387, 388, 389, 390, 391
Falside 23
Falside Terrace 17
FC Copenhagen 231
Ferguson, Alex 99, 256
Ferguson, Andrew 249, 254, 255, 264
Ferguson, Barry 319
Ferguson, Ian 213, 215, 219
Ferguson, Jacky 69, 72, 76
Ferguson, Stephen 252
Fernie, Willie 112
Festival of Britain 169
Festival St.Mungo Quaich 169

Field Mill 106
Filippi, Joe 92, 113
Finnbogason, Kristjan 218
Firhill 59, 91, 96, 111, 130, 138, 158, 160, 169, 178, 197, 215, 218, 225, 344, 355, 375, 384, 390, 391
Fir Park 170, 175, 208
Firs Park 192
First Division 47, 60, 62, 63, 64, 65, 66, 70, 72, 77, 82, 96, 101, 103, 115, 119, 121, 122, 125, 126, 128, 130, 136, 140, 141, 145, 157, 174, 178, 184, 190, 191, 211, 212, 216, 218, 220, 222, 224, 228, 229, 239, 241, 242, 243, 245, 246, 251, 253, 276, 287, 289, 290, 300, 301, 303
Fish 3, 367
Fisherton 24
Fitzpatrick, Tony 162
Fjortoft, Markus 368
Flavell, Bobby 121, 366
Fleeting, Jim 123
Fleming, Greg 326, 328, 332, 333, 334, 370
Fleming, Rikki 70, 72, 78, 92
Fleming's of Crosshouse 88
Florence, Jim 46
Flynn, Jim 92
Foinavon 65
Football Monthly 63
Forfar Athletic 49, 50, 52, 68, 70, 71, 96, 114, 140, 141, 143, 144, 162, 171, 177, 201, 203, 261, 264, 265, 272, 276, 296, 297, 299, 303, 307, 309, 310, 312, 313, 314, 316, 317, 318, 320, 322, 323, 328, 339, 340, 341
Forrest, Alan 314, 318, 336, 338, 341, 354
Forrest, Eddie 280
Forsyth, Tom 98

Fortes, Jose 193
Fort George 376
Forthbank Stadium 184, 380
France 10, 29, 101, 109
France (National Team) 77, 106, 213, 301
Fraser, Ally 173
Frye, Derek 126, 129, 130, 136, 137, 140
Fulham 293
Fullarton, Adam 164, 166
Fullarton, Ned 165, 166
Fulton, Billy 28, 34

G

Gallacher, John 34, 50
Gallagher, Willie 71
Geggan, Andy 338
Gemmell, John 373
Geoghegan, Andy 107
George, Duncan 176, 180, 193, 198
Gibson, Billy 296,
Gibson, Chris 367
Gigg Lane 367
Gill, Thomas 230, 234
Gillespie, Alan 169
Gilmour, Brian 315, 331
Glasgow 16, 67, 78, 85, 90, 96, 105, 106, 126, 127, 219, 222, 230, 267, 274, 284, 286, 294, 303, 309, 346, 351, 357
Glasgow Herald 78, 114, 127
Glasgow Road 13, 17
Glebe Park 189, 300, 322
Glenavon 38
Goldson, Connor 384
Goram, Andy 233
Gorgues, Regis 193
Gormley, David 286, 296
Gothia Cup 185, 186

Grady, James 235, 236, 243, 248, 250
Graham, Ally 177, 180, 314
Graham, Brian 304, 384
Graham, Brian (Wallacefield) 118
Graham, David 260
Graham, Jim 250
Graham, Johnny 90, 92, 93, 94, 106, 111
Graham, Luke 388
Grand National 43, 65
Grant, Johnny 60, 61
Grant, Lewis 344
Grant, Lex 195
Grant, Willie 243
Gray, Jim 59
Greaves Sports 67
Greenock 51, 53
Greenock Telegraph 389
Greig, John 98, 99
Gretna 265, 266, 267, 268
Grier, Jim 92
Grindlay, Stephen 284, 292
Gwardia 105

H

Hagen, David 236
Halbeath Road 39, 181
Halifax Building Society 66, 132, 143
Halifax Town 72
Hall, John 230
Hamilton Accies 56, 119, 133, 138, 140, 141, 160, 162, 169, 171, 173, 175, 182, 197, 198, 205, 207, 208, 209, 212, 214, 215, 218, 222, 225, 229, 260, 276, 301, 304, 307, 311, 329, 358, 363, 364, 371, 372, 390
Hamilton, David 274
Hamilton, Ian 28

Hampden 18, 20, 37, 38, 39, 40, 42, 74, 77, 91, 95, 96, 107, 126, 137, 138, 234, 243, 244, 253, 277, 305, 313, 329, 337, 344, 370, 379, 383, 390
Hannah, Bill 33, 46
Hansen, Jens 232
Hardy, Lee 256
Harthill 14
Hartlepool United 252
Harvie, Daniel 344
Hawkhill Bridge 255, 341
Hawkshaw, Ian 60
Hearts 12, 13, 14, 22, 29, 30, 32, 39, 40, 42, 59, 60, 76, 77, 78, 101, 103, 108, 112, 113, 123, 124, 127, 130, 133, 136, 140, 151, 158, 217, 257, 266, 288, 302, 303, 320, 359, 360, 378
Heathfield 117, 224, 229, 241
Heathfield Primary 25
Heathside 117
Henderson, Darren 205, 263, 386
Henderson, Jay 386
Henderson, Murray 274, 280
Hendrie, Ian 118
Hendrie, Sam 118
Hendry, Billy 129
Hendry, John 118
Hepburn, Bob 20, 21
Herald, Jim 233
Heriot-Watt University 74
Herron, Des 46
Heysel Stadium 141
Hibernian (Hibs) 12, 13, 14, 18, 23, 24, 29, 39, 74, 75, 77, 86, 95, 101, 117, 124, 127, 128, 174, 177, 222, 223, 224, 225, 235, 239, 243, 244, 264, 265, 297, 302, 305, 306, 329, 331, 332, 335, 336, 337, 338, 346, 389
Hibernians (Malta) 370
Higginbotham, Kallum 302
Higgins, Craig 274

Hillcoat, John 261
Hillman Minx 38, 39
Hing Sing Chinese Supermarket 329
Hogarth, Myles 239
Hogg, Keith 231
Holland 10, 105
Hood, Gregg 177, 193, 198, 211
Hood, Harry 69
Hood, Neil 77
Hope, Kenny 132
Hopetoun Arms 36
Hopkin, David 360, 361, 364
Horace, Alain 206, 207
Howard, Nigel 195
Howe, Charlie 339
Hubbard, Johnny 46, 47, 50
Hughes, Jim 155, 162, 195
Hughes, John 235, 236, 237, 246, 254
Hull City 105
Hume, Ian 87
Hunt, Roger 55
Hunter's Avenue 25, 26
Hurlford 101
Hurst, Geoff 55
Hurst, Glynn 220, 222, 225, 230, 231, 232, 235, 236, 237, 312
Hutton, David 317
Hutton, Joe 44

I

Ibbotson, Derek 55
Ibrox 20, 40, 42, 71, 77, 78, 84, 93, 98, 99, 109, 113, 115, 127, 237, 315, 316, 318, 345, 383
Ingram, Alex 64, 69, 72, 77, 82, 84, 92, 96, 99, 106, 107, 113, 273, 295
Innes, Chris 242
Institute Place 12

Inter-Cities Fairs Cup 29, 30
Inverness Caledonian Thistle
  64, 95, 237, 238, 239, 241, 243,
  247, 248, 249, 268, 290, 292,
  293, 302, 344, 348, 353, 355, 356,
  359, 360, 361, 362, 367, 369, 372,
  373, 376, 377, 379, 381, 385
Inverness Courier 355
Inverness Thistle 53
Ipswich Town 355
Ireland (All) 20
Irish Republic 191
Irn Bru Cup 332, 339, 344
Irvine, Brian 235
Irvine Meadow 54

J

Jack, Ross 141
Jackson, Jim 92
Jackson, Justin 193
Jamieson, Ian 118
Jamieson, Willie 209, 211
Japp, Willie 350
Jardine, Sandy 151
JC Roda 105
Jefferies, Jim 285
Jellema, Raymond 276
Jemson, Nigel 230
Johnstone, Brian 103, 208
Johnstone Burgh 53
Jones, Sandy 50

K

Kean, Stewart 245, 249, 250,
  254, 259, 261, 262, 263, 292
Keenan, Dean 284, 294
Keith, Marino 237
Kello Rovers 72
Kelty Hearts 382

Kendal Town 314, 315
Kennedy, David 169, 178, 182, 183
Kennedy, John F. 52
Kerr (Bearsden) 37
Kerr, Billy 59
Kerr, Mark 352, 360
Kerrigan, Stevie 206
Kilbirnie 101
Kilbowie Park 122, 130, 161, 199
Kilgannon, Johnny 46, 50
Kilmacolm 39
Kilmarnock 87, 99, 143, 219
Kilmarnock FC 21, 30, 40, 51, 52,
  54, 56, 57, 59, 60, 66, 77, 82, 83,
  84, 86, 90, 94, 96, 97, 98, 105,
  107, 111, 112, 113, 121, 122, 130, 132,
  133, 136, 137, 138, 140, 142, 143,
  144, 147, 149, 155, 156, 157, 158,
  159, 160, 166, 168, 171, 173, 174, 175,
  178, 180, 181, 184, 187, 189, 194,
  195, 204, 215, 217, 224, 225, 232,
  241, 242, 243, 254, 259, 265, 284,
  285, 304, 305, 319, 338, 362, 363,
  364, 365, 367, 368, 370, 386, 387
Kilsyth Rangers 66, 261
Kilwinning 101, 184
Kilwinning Rangers 260
Kimmetton Park 20
Kinnaird, Paul 204, 219
Kinning Park 234
Kirkcaldy 79, 90, 133, 153, 177,
  181, 290, 337, 342, 343, 381
Kirkintilloch 137
Kirk o' Shotts 164
Knudsen, Jens 234

L

La Liga 337
Lambert, Paul 180
Lamie, Ricki 308

Lamont, Billy 179
Lanarkshire 22
Lannon, Brian 92
Lavety, Barry 180
Law, Bobby 204
Law, Denis 18
Lawson, Kirkie 91
League Challenge Cup 200, 204, 211, 229, 236, 242, 246, 247, 252, 259, 265, 270, 276, 282
League Cup 24, 46, 51, 54, 57, 60, 67, 69, 70, 71, 72, 74, 77, 82, 90, 91, 93, 95, 98, 103, 106, 107, 109, 114, 121, 123, 127, 130, 133, 136, 140, 143, 147, 150, 157, 161, 164, 174, 177, 178, 186, 191, 195, 200, 202, 204, 205, 211, 221, 229, 231, 235, 241, 242, 243, 244, 246, 247, 252, 254, 260, 265, 270, 275, 283, 290, 294, 302, 303, 304, 305, 308, 309, 314, 319, 324, 329, 330, 338, 344, 345, 346, 349, 357, 358, 362, 363, 369, 378, 379, 386
League One 313, 315, 319, 320, 321, 324, 326, 329, 338, 340, 344, 348, 357, 375
Leckie (Pencaitland Amateurs) 37
Lee, Gordon 110
Leeds United 94, 98
Leicester City 99
Leishman, Jim 153, 239
Leith Walk 329
Lesser Hampden 370
Leyton Orient 252
Lifeboys 51
Lilley, Derek 267
Limekiln Road 242
Lincoln Cathedral 374
Lincoln City 141
Lindau, Peter 235
Linn, Bobby 317

Liverpool 4, 18, 24, 47, 84, 103, 129, 130
Livingston 13, 204, 205, 206, 207, 209, 228, 236, 237, 238, 239, 264, 270, 275, 287, 297, 298, 299, 305, 307, 325, 328, 349, 350, 358, 378, 379, 387, 388, 389, 390
Livingstone, Archie 10
Loanhead Mayflower 36
Lochee United 284
Lochside 117
Logan Cup 7, 12
Logan, Raymond 266
Longridge, Jackson 307, 308, 316
Lorde's Fish and Chips 367
Lorwood 39
Loudon, Sandy 171
Lovering, Paul 235, 247, 249, 250
Love Street 229
Lowing, David 269, 277, 280
Lowland League 43, 389
Luton Town 141, 204, 293
Lyle, Willie 249, 250, 261, 264, 270
Lyon King of Arms Act 334
Lyons, Andy 224

Mac/Mc

McAdams, Aidan 365
McAllister, Ian 136, 140, 148, 149, 155, 159, 167, 170, 171, 174, 186
McAllister, Kevin 236
McAlpine, Kenny 99
McAnespie, Alex 54, 92, 119, 195, 202, 293, 386
McBain, Neil 46, 47, 48, 50
McCall, Ian 321, 322, 324, 329, 331, 336, 338, 340, 344, 351, 352, 355, 366
McCall, Walker 111, 114, 121
McCall's Avenue 358

McCann, Jim 156, 162, 166, 195
McCloy, Peter 40, 96
McColl, Mark 249
McColl, Ronnie 77
McCowan, Luke 348, 353, 358
McCracken, Craig 347
McCracken, Dougie 153
McCreath, Tom 60, 62
McCulloch, Davy 69, 72, 92, 109
McCulloch, Scott 264
McCulloch, Willie 92
McDaid, Declan 344
McDiarmid Park 162, 273, 380
MacDonald, Alex 98, 151
MacDonald, Malcolm 94
McEwan, Craig 246
McFadzean, Jim 92, 94
McGee, Lawrie 138
McGeown, Mark 268, 273, 277
McGhee, Jim 28, 34
McGhee (Pencaitland Amateurs) 38
McGibbons, Terry 134
McGinlay, Pat 235, 238, 243, 246
McGinn, John 336
McGinty, Sean 362, 370, 379, 381
McGlashan, Colin 160, 187
McGovern, Jock 7
McGovern, Phil 84, 92
McGowan, Chris 275
McGowan, Neil 275, 287
McGregor, Alex 92
McGuffie, Craig 336, 341
McHardy, Darryl 370
McHugh, Harry 384
McInally, Alan 136, 138, 140, 186
McInnes, Andy 373
McIntosh, Leighton 317
McIntosh, Stuart 197
McIntyre, Alastair 34
McIntyre, George 34
McIntyre, Stevie 146
McIntyre, Willie 28, 34
Mckay, Billy 385
McKenna, Michael 353
McKenna, Mike 2, 3
McKenna, Scott 336
McKenzie, Alistair 109
McKenzie, Bob 115
McKenzie, Mark 360, 368, 377
McKeown, John 246
McKinstry, James 270
McLaren, Andy 241, 242
McLaughlin, Barry 260
McLaughlin, Brian 114, 123
McLaughlin, Scott 295
McLean, Ally 92
McLean, George 92, 93
McLean, Jim 28, 34
McLean, Jim (Dundee United) 130, 172
McLean, Tommy 172
McLean, Willie 121, 123, 130, 132, 136, 190
MacLeod , Ally 57, 60, 61, 62, 64, 66, 68, 79, 82, 88, 92, 94, 95, 105, 107, 109, 119, 120, 121, 122, 123, 127, 144, 145, 147, 148, 150, 153, 157, 161, 169, 171, 172, 175, 224, 256, 258, 264, 303, 357, 368
McManus, Allan 247, 250
McManus, Tam 292
McMillan, Andy 231, 232
McMillan, Sam 28, 31, 34, 61, 92, 277
McNab, Neil 186
McNeil, Norrie 127
McNeill, Billy 157
McNiven, John 140
McPhee, Ian 159
MacPherson, Gus 243
McRoberts, Lewis 349, 350

McRoberts, Shirley 349, 350
McSherry, Jim 109, 115
McWilliam, Bill 136

M

Maguire, Chris 283, 356, 375
Mainge, Willie 213
Mair, Gordon 179, 180, 181
Malone, Dick 57, 61, 69, 72, 76, 77, 89, 307, 356
Malta 370
Manchester City 186, 340, 343
Manchester United 46, 106, 256, 267, 272, 301, 315
Mann, Bobby 280
Mansfield Town 99, 106
Marillion 3
Marshall, Davy 61
Marshall, Gordon 225
Martin, Nancy 87
Mason, Billy 64
Masonic Hall 294
Masterton, Danny 111
Mathie, Ross 82, 83, 85
Maxwell, James 358, 367
Maxwell, Paul 295, 296
Mays, Gerry 46
Meadowbank Thistle 138, 140, 141, 148, 149, 159, 172, 174, 177, 178, 180, 184, 214
Methil 314
Middlesbrough 191
Milla, Roger 173
Millar, Blair 143
Millar, John 143
Millen, Andy 218, 222, 225, 250
Miller, Michael 358
Mill Park 13
Millwall 141, 204
Mitchell, Dougie 72, 92, 119

Mitchell-Lawson, Jayden 356
Moffat, Michael 298, 300, 312, 316, 319, 338, 344, 346
Moller, Rene 78
Monaco 213
Monan, Eddie 54, 61, 64, 65
Money, Campbell 248, 254, 260
Montford, Arthur 54
Montgomerie, Ray 179, 225
Montrose 51, 52, 61, 107, 121, 122, 150, 151, 153, 169, 202, 203, 288, 304, 339, 388
Monty Python 324
Moore, Allan 173
Moore, Bobby 55
Moore, Craig 335, 338, 342, 344, 354
Moore, Eddie 54, 57, 58, 59, 64
Moore, Michael 274
Moore, Sandra 137
Moore, Vinnie 198
Moore's Chippy 330
Morris, Eric 126, 127, 128, 136
Morrison, Steve 226
Morton 51, 53, 56, 84, 90, 91, 99, 127, 138, 157, 158, 159, 179, 188, 190, 211, 218, 222, 227, 230, 237, 261, 263, 265, 267, 268, 271, 288, 290, 293, 301, 302, 304, 312, 320, 322, 323, 331, 332, 335, 337, 339, 344, 345, 346, 348, 352, 356, 360, 361, 362, 364, 365, 366, 371, 375, 381, 388, 389
Motherwell 5, 26, 29, 40, 69, 70, 71, 91, 103, 106, 107, 109, 113, 121, 122, 123, 127, 130, 132, 133, 140, 170, 171, 175, 176, 186, 187, 208, 209, 221, 233, 234, 252, 253, 288, 308, 338, 357
Muirhead, Aaron 355, 356
Muirhead, Robbie 390

Muirkirk 22
Muirton Park 24, 159
Mullin, Josh 377
Munro, Iain 172
Murphy, John 51, 61, 62, 72, 92, 99, 107, 119, 277, 303
Murray, Bruce 193
Murray, David 154
Murray, Neil 247, 250, 251
Murray, Simon 370
Murrayfield 39
Mutch, Robbie 384

N

Naismith, Jason 363
Nanninga, Dick 105
Nardini's 154
National Hunt 53
Nelson, Craig 234, 251, 280, 300
Nelson, Drew 57
Nelson, Helen 70, 71, 89, 126, 147, 160
Nelson, Hugh 70, 71, 88, 126
Newcastle 220
Newcastle United 10, 82, 94, 99, 109, 110, 315
New Farm Loch 143
Newton Park 26, 53, 117
Newton Park School 26
Nicol, Stevie 129, 130, 186
Nicolson, Iain 246, 250
Nigeria 109
Nile Court 294
Northern Ireland 93
Northfield 117
Northfield Avenue 26
Norway 101, 220
Norwood, Oliver 301
Nottingham Forest 77, 99, 110, 111
Nylen, Niclas 193

O

Oakley, George 387, 389
O'Brien, Simon 242
O'Brien, Thomas 353
Ochil Hills 342
Ochilview Park 254, 282, 370, 374
O'Halloran, Charles 62
Oldham Athletic 262, 367, 384
Old Racecourse 47
Old Trafford 46
Oliphant, Charlie 53, 57
Oliver, Peter 76
O'Neil, Jim 373
Ormiston Primrose 36
Oxford United 228

P

Paisley 66, 126, 133, 184, 263, 298, 309
Paisley 2021 Stadium 337
Palmerston Park 68, 108, 160, 202, 237, 247, 249, 254, 292, 306, 330, 345, 357, 366, 369
Parc des Princes 14
Paris 14, 127, 134
Parker, Keigan 307
Parkhead Juniors 22
Parlane, Derek 93
Partick Thistle 31, 56, 58, 59, 79, 91, 93, 96, 130, 133, 158, 159, 177, 178, 187, 211, 214, 216, 217, 218, 219, 233, 234, 241, 242, 245, 252, 264, 267, 276, 277, 290, 296, 302, 304, 306, 314, 325, 326, 344, 351, 352, 355, 364, 365, 369, 371, 372, 373, 378, 379, 384, 385, 387, 388, 391
Pascali, Manuel 284
Paterson, Arthur 54, 61

Paterson, Garry 193
Paterson, John 28
Paton, Willie 28, 31
Patrick, Millar 256
Pencaitland Amateurs 7, 11, 12, 13, 23, 36, 38, 39, 40, 41, 117
Pereira, Ramon 256, 257
Perth 23, 24, 66, 77, 91, 134, 136, 154, 163, 247, 273, 378, 380
Peterhead 56, 249, 265, 269, 273, 274, 277, 279, 280, 283, 286, 296, 320, 321, 322, 323, 325, 326, 327, 328, 379, 388
Petershill 42
Petrofac Training Cup 319, 324
Pettigrew, Craig 271
Phillips, Eric 268
Phillips, Gerry 105, 109, 121
Pittodrie 85, 91, 93, 95, 113
Pogba, Paul 106, 301
Pollok 374
Ponfeigh 22
Pope, Gordon 316
PO Phones 39
Port Vale 350
Powderhall 39
Pownall, Ed 299
Premier League 103, 105, 106, 111, 113, 114, 115, 116, 122, 123, 125, 126, 127, 130, 133, 138, 141, 147, 153, 156, 163, 164, 169, 178, 191, 195, 200, 211, 217, 218, 224, 226, 228, 233, 243, 244, 253, 266, 268, 270, 290, 302, 303, 308, 324, 329, 337, 344, 348, 355, 357, 362, 378, 388, 389, 390
Price, Gavin 214
Price, Peter 25, 26, 27, 28, 29, 32, 33, 237, 271, 325
Programme Monthly 103
Prunty, Bryan 282, 296
Pryde, Eckie 7, 12
Purves, Wullie 7, 12

Q

Queen of the South 56, 61, 68, 108, 119, 127, 133, 159, 160, 167, 169, 174, 202, 247, 249, 250, 254, 270, 275, 292, 302, 303, 304, 306, 307, 309, 311, 330, 331, 332, 333, 337, 345, 353, 354, 356, 358, 359, 361, 365, 368, 369
Queen's Park 20, 39, 56, 64, 82, 105, 127, 136, 150, 221, 264, 275, 277, 281, 286, 288 314, 333, 335, 339, 341, 344, 370, 372, 373, 374, 379, 383, 388, 390
Queen's Park Rangers 200
Queen's Park Strollers 20
Quinn, Stan 72, 78, 82, 83, 92, 94, 293, 303

R

Radio Clyde 137, 259
Railway End 52, 68, 82, 245
Raisbeck, Alex 4
Raith Rovers 4, 20, 32, 56, 61, 79, 107, 121, 128, 138, 147, 149, 153, 171, 173, 177, 181, 184, 195, 197, 198, 211, 218, 229, 230, 233, 238, 255, 256, 257, 264, 266, 271, 273, 274, 277, 280, 282, 283, 284, 285, 286, 290, 292, 301, 302, 304, 307, 330, 332, 336, 337, 338, 339, 340, 341, 342, 360, 364, 366, 368, 371, 376, 381, 385, 387, 388, 389
Ramsay, Dougie 255, 266, 270
Ramsdens Challenge Cup 301, 314
Ramsey, Alf 54, 55
Rangers 18, 20, 26, 29, 30, 33, 40, 46, 62, 64, 71, 74, 76, 83, 84, 90,

93, 94, 96, 98, 99, 101, 103, 106, 108, 113, 115, 126, 137, 138, 140, 141, 153, 157, 182, 192, 205, 214, 219, 221, 234, 244, 245, 249, 267, 288, 294, 313, 314, 315, 316, 317, 318, 324, 327, 329, 331, 337, 341, 345, 363, 383, 384
Rattray, Alan 261
Raydale Park 265
Reading 293
Reading, Paddy 367
Real Madrid 14, 51, 106, 138
Recreation Park 214
Redding Athletic 4, 5
Redding Colliery 3, 5, 6, 9
Red Lion Caravan Park 24
Reid, Brian 270, 273, 277, 278, 282, 291, 296, 302, 304, 305, 306, 308
Reilly, Robert 195, 263, 273
Reims 13, 14
Rennie, Stuart 123
Renwick, Michael 235
Reserve League 46, 87, 93
Reynolds, Mickey 229, 233, 236
Reynolds, Tommy 85, 86, 92
Ritchie, Iain 69
Robb, Jim 134
Roberts, Dale 188
Roberts, Mark 287, 290, 296, 298, 300, 301, 303, 306, 308, 310, 311, 312, 316, 318, 319, 321
Robertson, Chris 269
Robertson, Davy 92
Robertson, John 218, 233, 234, 246,
Robertson, John (Hearts) 257
Robertson, Malky 107, 109, 111, 113
Robertson, Ross 302, 307
Robison, Rob 7
Robson, Bobby 172
Robson, Bryan 191

Rodgers, Andy 301
Rodie, Hugh 45, 46
Rogerson, Drew 94
Rolling, Franck 193, 198
Roma 137
Romania 20, 107
Ross County 56, 203, 204, 235, 241, 251, 255, 265, 275, 276, 280, 303, 306, 307, 324, 345, 354, 355
Rough, Alan 130
Rough, Bobby 69, 72, 77, 92
Rovde, Marius 234, 238
Roxburgh, Andy 40, 172
Roy, Ludovic 254, 261, 264
Royal College of Science and Technology 36
Rugby Park 51, 52, 57, 87, 93, 94, 107, 112, 140, 166, 285, 305, 363, 367

S

Samson, Craig 292
Sanders, Jack 384
Sargent, David 362
Scarlett (Bearsden) 38
Scotland team 4, 17, 20, 22, 24, 40, 47, 54, 77, 97, 98, 107, 108, 119, 130, 272, 337, 350, 364, 387
Scotsport 38
Scott, Archie 96
Scott, Robert 207, 209
Scottish Amateur Cup 36, 40
Scottish Cup 14, 18, 22, 32, 38, 49, 53, 54, 58, 62, 65, 70, 71, 84, 91, 95, 96, 99, 101, 105, 106, 108, 109, 110, 112, 115, 122, 123, 127, 130, 132, 134, 137, 138, 141, 144, 148, 158, 162, 173, 175, 181, 182, 189, 197, 203, 204, 206, 211, 214, 215, 217, 224, 233, 234, 237, 238,

239, 243, 244, 245, 249, 255, 263, 266, 267, 268, 273, 277, 284, 288, 291, 292, 297, 298, 304, 305, 310, 315, 320, 325, 326, 329, 333, 335, 336, 337, 340, 346, 347, 354, 355, 359, 361, 365, 366, 374, 375, 377, 379, 382, 383, 389
Scottish Football Association 101, 160, 197, 294, 357, 365
Scottish Junior Cup 20, 42, 53, 66
Scottish League 57, 77, 112, 169
Seafield Drive 23
Seaside League 259, 260, 269, 282, 287, 300, 328
Second Division 4, 13, 18, 20, 26, 27, 31, 34, 39, 48, 50, 52, 53, 60, 63, 64, 66, 69, 111, 126, 148, 150, 200, 208, 219, 233, 252, 264, 285, 294, 307, 313, 343
Sedan 30
Self Preservation League 224
Shankland, Lawrence 333, 339, 340, 341, 343, 344, 345, 346, 349, 351
Shankland, Mark 316
Shanks, Mark 260, 261, 263
Sharples, John 194, 198
Shaw, Nathan 373
Shawfield 52, 77, 115, 119, 122, 136
Sheerin, Paul 241, 242, 244, 247, 250
Sherry, Jim 197
Shields, Bobby 111
Shields, Jim 118
Shilton, Peter 99
Shotton, Malky 187, 228
Shrewsbury 376
Silva, Fabio 384
Sinisalo, Viljami 358
Sloan, Tommy 195
Sludden, John 144, 147, 148, 149, 151, 153, 158

Smith, Chris 303, 304
Smith, David 354, 359, 386
Smith, Graeme 313
Smith, Henry 204, 207
Smith, Jimmy 220
Smith, Tom 213
Smyth, David 169, 170
Smyth, Marc 247, 249, 250, 252, 261, 264
Snedden, Iain 385
Solway Star 20
Somerset Park 1, 4, 20, 24, 26, 27, 30, 33, 35, 46, 47, 49, 50, 52, 54, 57, 60, 65, 68, 74, 76, 79, 88, 93, 94, 101, 106, 127, 128, 134, 137, 138, 147, 149, 157, 158, 163, 164, 166, 171, 174, 176, 178, 182, 191, 192, 206, 211, 215, 221, 226, 228, 232, 233, 241, 243, 245, 248, 251, 254, 255, 256, 262, 263, 264, 275, 281, 286, 289, 290, 291, 296, 298, 309, 310, 314, 315, 321, 323, 327, 328, 329, 342, 343, 346, 347, 348, 350, 354, 360, 361, 368, 378, 382, 383, 386, 387
Somerset Road 26, 31, 114, 224, 225
Somerset Road End 50, 52, 74, 82, 88, 89, 107, 134, 174, 179, 224, 225, 242, 243, 262, 277, 293, 313, 331, 392
Sonor, Luc 213, 214
Souness, Graeme 157
Southampton 186
South Ayrshire Council 371
Spain Park 340
SPFL 319, 336, 357, 371, 379, 388, 389
SPFL Trust Trophy 371, 379, 388, 389
SPL 224, 253, 357
Sproat, Hugh 123, 127, 143
Stadium of Light 356

Stainrod, Simon 188, 189, 190, 191, 192, 193, 195, 197, 200, 201
Stair Park 48, 195, 206, 309, 316
Stanger, George 384
Stark, Billy 321, 366
Stark's Park 181, 368
St.Columba's Church 256
Stein, Colin 76, 78, 93
Stenhousemuir 3, 44, 49, 50, 56, 62, 69, 148, 150, 154, 174, 202, 206, 207, 208, 282, 299, 307, 308, 312, 313, 315, 318, 320, 321, 322, 323, 325, 326, 328, 344, 370, 378, 386
Stevenage 93
Stevenson, Ryan 272, 273, 276, 277, 280, 282, 287, 326, 333, 336
Stewart, David 246
Stewart, Davy 66, 67, 72, 91, 92, 93, 303
Stewart, Rab 47
Stewart, Sandy 352
St.George's Road 26
Stillie, Derek 360
Stirling 123, 128, 230, 267, 268, 342, 378
Stirling Albion 46, 56, 70, 71, 121, 128, 133, 148, 149, 150, 152, 153, 156, 166, 169, 184, 187, 189, 190, 201, 202, 203, 204, 208, 213, 214, 216, 217, 218, 252, 261, 263, 264, 265, 267, 269, 270, 271, 272, 283, 286, 320, 322, 323, 378, 380
Stirlingshire 3, 6, 11
Stirlingshire Cup 4
St.John, Ian 26
St.Johnstone 24, 46, 50, 62, 65, 91, 108, 123, 136, 151, 153, 154, 159, 160, 162, 163, 173, 174, 204, 205, 246, 247, 250, 254, 255, 256, 272, 273, 355, 369, 378, 387

St.Mirren 56, 64, 66, 67, 68, 93, 114, 126, 133, 141, 162, 163, 164, 179, 180, 184, 187, 193, 197, 218, 221, 222, 229, 230, 232, 243, 251, 256, 262, 263, 288, 290, 298, 302, 309, 329, 331, 332, 333, 336, 337, 339, 366
St.Mirren Park 229, 303
Stockport County 237
Strain, Chris 272
Strang, James 7
Stranraer 21, 33, 47, 48, 49, 56, 59, 68, 101, 148, 149, 174, 191, 192, 195, 197, 202, 206, 215, 219, 221, 242, 260, 262, 263, 270, 272, 273, 274, 284, 286, 309, 312, 313, 314, 315, 316, 317, 318, 320, 321, 326, 327, 328, 329, 339, 340, 341, 342, 350, 358
Stuart, Alex 107, 109, 115, 119, 123
STV 164
Sunderland 22, 89, 178, 356
Sunnybank 288, 297
Supporters' Association 68, 79, 80, 87, 88, 96, 160
Sweden 24, 219, 220, 235
Swift, Stephen 274
Swindon Town 186
Swinton, Jimmy 12
Sykes, John 118
Syla, Roy 384
Symington, Douglas 63, 71, 74, 79, 80, 85, 89

T

Tait, Bobby 92
Tambling, Bobby 55
Tannadice Park 49, 70, 103, 113, 137, 219, 244, 330, 346
Tarrant, Neil 232, 233

Tartan Army 97, 98, 99
Taylor, Jacky 7
Taylor, Jock 7
Taylor, John 98
Teale, Gary 225, 226, 231, 233, 236, 240
Telfer, John 24
Telfer, Johnny 118
Templeton, Henry 144, 150, 151, 153, 158, 159, 162, 169, 170, 277, 303, 305
Tesco Bank 97, 351
Teviot Street 25
Texaco Cup 93, 94, 99, 103
The Hub 386
The Proclaimers 23
The Smiddy Inn 12, 13
The United Men of Ayr 64
The Wee Mair 25
Thomas, Dom 370
Thompson Hugh 92
Thomson, Adam 57
Thomson, John 20
Thomson Park 284
Thow, Louis 99
Tiehi, Jean-Pierre 372
Tiffoney, Jonathan 294, 308
Timmins, Joe 180, 184
Titanic Museum 313
Todd, Josh 362
Tokely, Ross 243
Toner, Kevin 237
Toner, Willie 237
Torfason, Gudmunder 162
Torino 18
Tottenham Hotspur 25, 200, 186, 303
Townhead Park 378
Tranent Juniors 41, 42, 43
Traynor, John 213
Troon 144, 388

Trouten, Alan 275, 301
Truesdale, Tommy 64
Tryfield Place 25, 47, 54, 136, 201, 368
Tuffey, Jonny 290
Tunnock's Caramel Wafer Challenge Cup 350
Turnbull, Eddie 40
Tuttie's Neuk 317
Tweed Street 25, 26, 35, 53
Tynecastle Park 36, 37, 42, 59, 78, 101, 112, 123, 124, 133, 158, 177

U

Unirea Urziceni 289
University of Strathclyde 36

V

Vale of Leven 234
Valetta, Claudio 193
Valletta 370
Vareille, Jerome 269, 272
Viewpark Boys' Guild 82
Voluntary Park 53
Volunteer Park 18, 20

W

Walker, Andy 220, 225
Walker, Ethan 390
Walker, Jason 267
Walker, Scott 283, 296
Walker, Tommy 151, 159, 160, 168, 169, 180, 181, 195,
Wallace, Jock 12
Wallace, Willie 92
Wallacefield Amateurs 117, 118
Wallacestone 4
Wallacetown 117

Wanyama, Victor 390
Wardlaw, Gareth 268, 269, 270, 272, 277
Watson, George 199
Watson, Paul 219
Watt, Neil 74, 274, 277, 321
Weaver, Paul 267, 268
Weir, Jim 310
Weir, Peter 164, 171, 172, 173
Wells, Davy 92, 96, 122, 171
Wembley Central 87, 97
West, Colin 170
West Ham United 127
West Sanquhar Road 26
West Sound Radio 41, 160, 259, 265
Western League Cup 54
Whalen, Stephen 250, 251
Whelan, Dave 256
Whitburn 42
White, David 308, 360, 366, 382
White, John 25
White, Sprigger 345
Whitehead, Ian 82
Whitletts 77, 361
Whitletts Community Centre 197
Whitletts Victoria 20, 21, 53
Whitley Bay 240
Whittaker, Stevem 382, 387
Wigan Athletic 240, 384
Williams, Alex 276, 280, 284, 285
Willoughby, Kurt 384
Wilson, Johnny 118,
Wilson, Kenny 149
Wilson, Marvyn 232, 235, 239, 246
Wilson, Mike 175, 232, 303
Winnie, David 246
Wishaw 18
Wishaw Thistle 22
Wolverhampton Wanderers 293
Wrexham 228, 350
Wyness, Dennis 268

X

X74 357
X77 346, 357

Y

Yoker Athletic 42
Young, Cutty 72, 74, 76, 82, 303
Young, Jason 208
Younger, Tommy 24

Z

Z training 12

www.ingramcontent.com/pod-product-compliance
Lightning Source LLC
Chambersburg PA
CBHW061248230426
43663CB00022B/2946